CAMBRIDGE LIBRARY COLLECTION
Books of enduring scholarly value

Maritime Exploration

This series includes accounts, by eye-witnesses and contemporaries, of voyages by Europeans to the Americas, Asia, Australasia and the Pacific during the colonial period. Driven by the military and commercial interests of powers including Britain, France and the Netherlands, particularly the East India Companies, these expeditions brought back a wealth of information on climate, natural resources, topography, and distant civilisations. Their detailed observations provide fascinating historical data for climatologists, ecologists and anthropologists, and the accounts of the mariners' experiences on their long and dangerous voyages are full of human interest.

A Voyage to the South-Sea and along the Coasts of Chili and Peru, in the Years 1712, 1713, and 1714

The first reliable maps of the Chilean and Peruvian coasts were drawn by the French explorer Amédée-François Frézier (1682–1773). In 1712, he was sent on a spying mission to the Spanish ports and fortifications of South America, travelling along the Pacific coastline as far as Callao, the port of Lima. His maps were later used by two of France's most famous explorers, Bougainville and Lapérouse. Frézier also took a keen interest in botany, mineralogy, economics and anthropology. His most celebrated achievement is the introduction to Europe of the Chilean strawberry, which was used to create the hybrid species known today as the garden strawberry. Frézier's observations and illustrations of the people, plants and animals he encountered on his South American travels are given in this popular account, published in Paris in 1716 and reissued here in the English translation of 1717.

Cambridge University Press has long been a pioneer in the reissuing of out-of-print titles from its own backlist, producing digital reprints of books that are still sought after by scholars and students but could not be reprinted economically using traditional technology. The Cambridge Library Collection extends this activity to a wider range of books which are still of importance to researchers and professionals, either for the source material they contain, or as landmarks in the history of their academic discipline.

Drawing from the world-renowned collections in the Cambridge University Library and other partner libraries, and guided by the advice of experts in each subject area, Cambridge University Press is using state-of-the-art scanning machines in its own Printing House to capture the content of each book selected for inclusion. The files are processed to give a consistently clear, crisp image, and the books finished to the high quality standard for which the Press is recognised around the world. The latest print-on-demand technology ensures that the books will remain available indefinitely, and that orders for single or multiple copies can quickly be supplied.

The Cambridge Library Collection brings back to life books of enduring scholarly value (including out-of-copyright works originally issued by other publishers) across a wide range of disciplines in the humanities and social sciences and in science and technology.

A Voyage to the South-Sea and along the Coasts of Chili and Peru, in the Years 1712, 1713, and 1714

With a Postscript by Dr. Edmund Halley and an Account of the Settlement, Commerce, and Riches of the Jesuites in Paraguay

AMÉDÉE FRANÇOIS FRÉZIER

CAMBRIDGE
UNIVERSITY PRESS

University Printing House, Cambridge, CB2 8BS, United Kingdom

Cambridge University Press is part of the University of Cambridge.
It furthers the University's mission by disseminating knowledge in the pursuit of
education, learning and research at the highest international levels of excellence.

www.cambridge.org
Information on this title: www.cambridge.org/9781108077002

© in this compilation Cambridge University Press 2014

This edition first published 1717
This digitally printed version 2014

ISBN 978-1-108-07700-2 Paperback

This book reproduces the text of the original edition. The content and language reflect
the beliefs, practices and terminology of their time, and have not been updated.

Cambridge University Press wishes to make clear that the book, unless originally published
by Cambridge, is not being republished by, in association or collaboration with,
or with the endorsement or approval of, the original publisher or its successors in title.

A VOYAGE TO THE SOUTH-SEA,

And along the

COAST OF CHILI and PERU,

In the Years 1712, 1713, and 1714.

PARTICULARLY DESCRIBING

The Genius and Constitution of the Inhabitants, as well *Indians* as *Spaniards*: Their Customs and Manners; their Natural History, Mines, Commodities, Traffick with *EUROPE*, &c.

By Monsieur FREZIER, Engineer in Ordinary to the *French* King.

Illustrated with 37 COPPER-CUTTS of the Coasts, Harbours, Cities, Plants, and other Curiosities: Printed from the Author's Original Plates inserted in the *Paris* EDITION.

With a POSTSCRIPT by Dr. *Edmund Halley*, *Savilian* Professor of Geometry in the University of *Oxford*. And an Account of the Settlement, Commerce, and Riches of the Jesuites in *Paraguay*.

LONDON:
Printed for JONAH BOWYER, at the *Rose* in *Ludgate-street*.
MDCCXVII

TO

His Royal Highness

GEORGE

PRINCE of *WALES*,

GOVERNOR

OF THE

SOUTH-SEA Company:

THIS

Translation of Monsieur F<small>REZIER</small>'S
Voyage to the SOUTH-SEA

IS

With all Respect and Humility,

DEDICATED.

THE PREFACE TO THE READER.

S the Accounts of Voyages and Travels are univerſally well received and eſteem'd, if drawn up with a due Regard to Truth ; it is no wonder that of Monſieur *Frezier* to the *South Sea,* and along the Coaſts of *Chili* and *Peru,* ſo little known to all the *Europeans* except the *Spaniards,* ſhould be well approved of in *France* and *Holland,* in the *French* Tongue : Eſpecially, if it be conſider'd, who the Author of it is, and what his Performance.

As for the firſt of theſe, the late *French* King, *Lewis* XIV. who owed the Brighteſt Part of his Glory, and his Grandeur, to his Encouragement of the Arts and Sciences, and to his ſingular Judgment in the Choice of fit Perſons to improve them,

A   having

To the Reader.

having been at a vaſt Expence to ſupport his Grandſon upon the Throne of *Spain*, thought this a proper Opportunity of getting a full Information of the leaſt known Parts of the *Spaniſh Weſt-Indies*, before the *French*, as well as all other Nations, ſhould be excluded thoſe Seas by a Peace. For this end, he pitch'd upon our Author, an experienced Engineer and Mathematician in his Service, whom he knew to be every way qualify'd to make Hydrographical Obſervations for the Uſe of Mariners, and for the Correction of the Charts; and alſo to take exact Plans of the moſt conſiderable Forts and Fortreſſes along the Coaſts whither he was going; to direct to their beſt Anchorages, and to point out their reſpective Dangers; (things which might hereafter be of great Uſe to the *French*, if a War ſhould happen to break out again between the two Nations) And this Gentleman he ſent at his own Charge on board a Merchant-Ship, in the Year 1712, to paſs as a Trader only, the better to inſinuate himſelf with the *Spaniſh* Governors, and to have all Opportunities of learning their Strength, and whatever elſe he went to be inform'd of. And we find in his *Dedication* of this Work to the Regent of *France*, that he had ſo well executed the late King's Deſign, that upon his Return that Great Prince made Monſieur *Frezier* explain to him the Plans he had drawn, and ſignify'd his Approbation of them both by gracious Expreſſions, and by a generous Reward. But

his

To the Reader.

his Moſt Chriſtian Majeſty dying before the Book was ready to appear in the World, the Duke of *Orleans*, who now governs the Kingdom, was pleas'd to permit our Author to addreſs it to him: And the Account he gives him of it, is, that ' it is a Collection of the Obſervations which he ' made in Navigation, on the Errors of the Maps, ' and the Situation of the Harbours and Roads he ' had been in; together with a Deſcription of the ' Animals, Plants, Fruits, Metals, and whatſo- ' ever the Earth produces of Curious, in the richeſt ' Colonies in the World; and laſtly, a moſt exact ' Account of the Commerce, Forces, Government, ' and Manners, as well of the *Creolian Spaniards*, ' as of the Natives of the Country, whom he ' treats with all the Reſpect which is due to ' Truth.'

Neither muſt we omit any thing that is of Uſe in the Author's *Preface*, where he is more particular; and eſpecially as to the Difference between this Work and Father *Feüillée's* Journal. He tells us, that that Learned Monk apply'd himſelf chiefly to Aſtronomy, Botany, and other Parts of Natural Philoſophy; whereas Monſieur *Frezier*'s Buſineſs hath been to take Plans, and to bring the Navigators acquainted with the Seaſons, general Winds, Currents, Rocks, Shelves, Anchorages, and Landing Places, where-ever he came. It muſt not therefore ſeem ſtrange, that the Plans of thoſe two

To the Reader.

Authors do no better agree: But Monſieur *Frezier* produces ſeveral Inſtances of the Father's Miſtakes:
'The Mouth of the Bay of *La Conception* (ſays he)
'is made too wide in *Feüillée*'s Plan by almoſt the
'Half; the Streets of *Callao* are all confounded;
'and the Baſtion of S. *Lewis* hath a defenceleſs
'Face, tho' there is a Line of Defence *fichante* up-
'on the Spot. Theſe laſt Faults are not, how-
'ever, to be imputed to him: The Addition of
'ſeveral Works, which were never inſerted in
'any other Deſign than that of the late Monſieur
'*Roſſemin*, Engineer of the Place, ſhews, that they
'are not his, but the Copyer's, from whom I had
'alſo the ſame Plan and the Deſigns. In that of
'the Road of *Callao*, he makes the Town, which
'doth not really exceed 600 Toiſes, as big as the
'Iſle of S. *Laurence*, which is almoſt 4000 Toiſes.
'Laſtly, he himſelf owns, that in his Plan of
'*Lima*, the Quarter call'd *Malambo* falls ſhort of
'a ſixth Part, whereas that Quarter makes at leaſt
'a ſixth Part of the Town; that of *Cercado* is
'placed without the Incloſure, tho' it is really
'within it; and he reckons the Baſtions but 25,
'when there are 34. Not to mention other Plans,
'whoſe Imperfections are of leſs Conſequence.
'Moreover, that Father places *Arica* and *Ylo* under
'the ſame Meridian, within eight Seconds of Time,
'or two Minutes of a Degree; whereas I know by
'my own Obſervation, that thoſe Ports, which are

about

To the Reader.

'about 28 or 30 Leagues diſtant one from the
'other, lie S. E. and N. W. on the Globe, which
'cauſes a Difference of at leaſt a Degree.

For the reſt, our Author acquaints us, that his Plans (except three, *viz.* of *Callao, Valparaiſo,* and *Copiapo*) are drawn by the ſame Scale, that ſo their Proportion may be ſeen at once; and that he hath been more particular in his Relation of the Cuſtoms and Manners of the *Indians,* and of their Mines, and Methods of working them; ſo that his Book and Father *Feuillée*'s have very little in common.

To ſpeak Truth, this laſt-mention'd Part of Monſieur *Frezier*'s Hiſtory is ſo very New and Curious, that it might alone be thought a ſufficient Motive to the Tranſlation, and Publiſhing of it in *Engliſh*, had it wanted the Recommendation of the Judicious, which it doth not: For, after the Privileges granted by the *Spaniards* to our *South-Sea* Company, of trading in thoſe diſtant Countries, and the Settlement of *Engliſh* Factories by their Conſent at *Vera Cruz, Cartagena, Panama, Portobelo,* and *Buenos Ayres,* (to bring home Gold and Silver, no doubt) What could be of ſo great Advantage to the *Engliſh,* as an Account of the Manner of diſcovering, opening, and working their Mines?

Before we entirely bid Adieu to Monſieur *Frezier*'s own Abſtract of his Work, we cannot but take Notice how unaccountable it ſeems, that a-
mong

To the Reader.

mong the *Indians* of *Chili*, there should be no Track, or Sign, or Foot step, either of the Worship of a Deity, or of the Cohabitation of Men, as in all other known Parts of the World; but that they should content themselves with living separately under a sort of Hutts made of the Branches of Trees.

Upon the whole matter, we have taken due Care to have a just Translation of this Useful Work: And lest any Blunder might be made in copying Monsieur *Frezier*'s Plans, &c. (which too commonly happens in Affairs of this nature) we have at a considerable Expence procured a Number of Cutts printed from the Original Plates at *Paris*, by that Author's Permission; the *French* Explanations whereof being render'd into *English*, and inserted at the Foot of their proper Pages, the Reader will at the same time understand them with Ease, and have the Satisfaction that the Plates are true and genuine.

One Objection doth indeed lie against Monsieur *Frezier*, arising perhaps from his Ambition to be thought to correct the General Sea Chart of our Country-man Dr. *Halley*, *Savilian* Professor of Geometry in the University of *Oxford*; but besides that the Reputation of this Chart is establish'd by the Experience of our Navigators in most Voyages, beyond the Power of Monsieur *Frezier* to hurt it; we must remember that our Author is a *French-man*:

To the Reader.

man: And therefore we need give no farther Account of their Difference, than is contain'd in the *Letter* subjoin'd, which Dr. *Halley* was pleas'd on that Occasion to write to us; and in the *Postscript* at the End of M. *Frezier*'s Book.

What follows that, being a Relation of the Jesuites Settlement and Commerce in *Paraguay*, which are sometimes mention'd in the Course of Monsieur *Frezier*'s Voyage, we judg'd it not improper to give it a Translation from the Edition printed in *Holland*, and to annex it to ours in *English*.

Mr.

April 6. 1717.

Mr. Bowyer,

I Am glad to hear you have undertaken to print, in English, *the Voyage of Mr.* Frezier *to and from the Coasts of* Peru *and* Chili. Our People are very much unacquainted with those Seas; and those that are, commonly want either Will or Language to inform the World properly of what they find worth Notice, and of what may be of Use to those that shall hereafter make the like Voyages: *The* French *have the Faculty of setting off their Relations to the best Advantage*; and particularly your Author has informed us, in a very instructive manner, of several things that are not only very entertaining, but also what may be of eminent Service to us, either in case of Trade or War in the Seas he describes. On this account I cannot doubt but your Design must answer your Expectation, especially since you bestow on the Book so elegant an Edition. But however it may have pleased me in other Respects, I find myself obliged to desire of you the Liberty to subjoin a small Postscript in Defence of my Chart of the Variation of the Compass, (whereby I hoped I had done Service to the Sailors of all Nations) against the groundless Exceptions of your Author, who seems to seek all Occasions to find Fault, and is otherwise unjust to me. If you please to grant me this Favour, you will, without any Prejudice to yourself, very much oblige

Your very humble Servant,

To Mr. Jonah Bowyer Edm. Halley.
  These.

A

A VOYAGE TO THE SOUTH-SEA.

HE Structure of the Universe, which is naturally the Object of our Admiration, has ever also been the Subject of my Curiosity: From my very Infancy I took the greatest Pleasure in all such Things as could advance me in the Knowledge of it: Globes, Charts, and Books of Travels were my singular Delight: I was scarce capable of observing Things by myself, when I undertook a Journey into *Italy:* The Pretence of studying afterwards serv'd me to travel through some Part of *France*; but being at length fix'd, by the Employment I have had the Honour to obtain in the King's Service, I thought there was no more Expectation of indulging my Inclination to travel, when his Majesty was pleas'd to permit me to lay hold of the Opportunity that then offer'd, of seeing *Chili* and *Peru*.

I embark'd at S. *Malo*, in the Quality of an Officer, aboard a Ship of 36 Guns, 350 Tons Burden, and 135

Men, call'd the S. *Joseph*, commanded by the Sieur *Duchêne Battas*, a Man commendable for his Experience and Knowledge in Marine Affairs, and for much Understanding and Activity in Trade, which was very suitable to our Design.

On *Monday, November* 23, 1711, we set sail from the Port of S. *Malo*, in Company with the *Mary*, a small Vessel, of 120 Tons Burden, commanded by the Sieur *du Jardais Daniel*, who was to serve for our Storeship. We went to lie for a fair Wind near Cape *Frehel*, under the Cannon of the Castle *de la Latte*, in the Bay *de la Frenaye*, where we anchor'd the same Day; but we waited in vain for near two Months.

The Tediousness of so long a Stay, the Sharpness of the Winter, then well advanc'd, the Wind, the Cold, and the Rain, which I must be expos'd to every other four Hours, during the Watches we kept alternatively Day and Night without Interruption, according to the Custom of the Sea; and the Inconveniency of a Merchant-ship, in which a Man scarce knew where to bestow himself, began to make me sensible of the Hardships of a Sailor's Life, and how opposite it was to that Quiet and Retiredness which are requisite for Study and Meditation, my greatest Delights ashore*. In short, I soon saw the utmost of Misfortunes in a Shipwreck which happen'd before our Eyes. Here follows an Account of it.

It is first to be observ'd, That most of the Ships that sail from the Port of S. *Malo*, come to an Anchor in the Road of *Frenaye*, which is but four Leagues from it to the Westward, either to wait for a fair Wind, or to gather their Crews, which do not go aboard till the last Minute. On the 9th of *December* there were five Ships, the *Count de Girardin*, the *Michael-Andrew*, the *Hunter*, the *Mary*, and we, when the Chevalier *de la V———*, who commanded the *Great-Britain*, a Privateer of 36 Guns, came at Six in the Evening, and dropp'd his Anchor near us; but the Buoy-rope, which thro' Neglect

*—*jam inde ab adolescentia, Ego hanc clementem vitam urbanam & otium Secutus sum, &, quod fortunatum isti putant, Uxorem nunquam habui. Ter. Adel. 1, 1.

was still fast aboard, having hinder'd it from taking hold, *Shipwreck.*
the Ebb carry'd the Ship near to a Shoal that is at the Foot
of the Fort *de la Latte*, before they could drop another:
That same held them during the Ebb, within a Pistol
Shot from the Rock; but upon the Return of the Flood,
the Violence of the Current soon cast them upon that
Shoal. The Captain perceiving himself in that inevitable Danger, fir'd several Guns to desire Assistance of the
other Ships in the Road. Every one sent Men to his
Assistance with all possible Expedition, to bring him off;
but it prov'd in vain, the S. E. Wind rising, and driving
out so violently to Sea with the Tide, that no Boat could
come up to the Ship; and the Boat belonging to the
Count *de Girardin* was drove so far out of the Bay, that
it could not return aboard its own Ship that Night; that
of the *Hunter* was cast away, and had it not been for
ours, the Men had been lost. At length, about Midnight, the Ship struck, and was stav'd in so short a time,
that the Crew was sav'd with much Difficulty, at the
Foot of the Castle; only three Men being drown'd,
among whom was an Officer.

The next Morning we still saw the dismal Hull of the
Ship lying on its Side, beaten by the Waves, which in
twenty four Hours drove it all away in Shivers. It is
easy to imagine, what dismal Reflexions all Men made
upon that fatal Spectacle; especially myself, who was
making my first Essay of Navigation in a Voyage of two
Years at the least.

We had lain there twenty seven Days in almost continual foul Weather, the Wind not permitting us to put *Return to S. Malo.*
out to Sea, when Orders were brought us from our
Owners * to return to S. *Malo*, for fear of being surpriz'd * *The Brothers* Vincent
by some *English* Vessels, which were to attack us there, *and* M. Du-
of which they had receiv'd Advice. Accordingly we *hamel.*
return'd thither on *Sunday* the 20th of *December*, and
continu'd there till the 6th of *January* of the ensuing
Year 1712.

B 2 That

Second Sailing from S. Malo.

That Day, the Wind coming about to the East, we fail'd the second time from the Road of *Rance*; but no sooner were we out of the Mouth of the Road, than we were oblig'd to come to an Anchor, for fear of running, during the Night, upon the Rocks, near which Ships must pass to go into the Channel. The Wind was at N.N.E. and a rolling Sea made us pitch so violently, that the Cable snap'd as soon as the Anchor had taken hold. Thus were we oblig'd to go and anchor again at the Mouth of the Bay *de la Frenaye*, where we had an ill Night.

The next Morning we fail'd, to look for our Anchor, with the *Mary*, to which the like Accident had befallen; and she found hers, but ours was lost, because the Buoy was slipp'd away. Whilst we were looking for it, a Calm came upon us, and then we anchor'd a third time, a League and half from the Castle *de la Latte*, to wait till the Wind, which shifted every Moment, would fix at some Point.

At Break of Day we would have fail'd out to Sea, but our Cable appearing to have been gnaw'd within thirty Foot of the Anchor, it was thought fit to cut it, and fetch another at the Town, and make good the Anchor we had lost; and therefore we drew near, making a Waft with our Colours. We made a Signal, by firing a Gun, that we wanted Assistance; and then return'd to anchor a fourth time since this second Coming out, under the Castle *de la Latte*. Immediately two Officers were sent away to fetch what we wanted; which they did the next Morning.

We lay there eight Days longer, waiting for an East Wind, nothing worth noting befalling us. That time we spent in stowing the Ship, which being too heavy upwards, could not carry much Sail, as we had found by Experience the Day we came out the second time.

PART

PART I.

Containing the Passage from France *to* Chili.

T length, after having suffer'd much by the Weather, which was foul and contrary, the Wind came to E. by S. We immediately sail'd to pass thro' the great Channel between *Rochedouvre* and *Guernsey*, and by that Means to get into the Middle of the *English* Channel, to avoid the Enemy's Privateers, who us'd to infest the Coast of *Bretagne*. We pass'd thro' successfully during the Night, having, about Ten, had a Sight of *Rochedouvre* about a League to the S. W. of us.

Some Hours after, we discover'd, by the Moon Light, a Ship which observ'd us narrowly. We immediately put up our Fights, and made ready to engage, being persuaded that it was a *Jersey* Privateer; but he durst not attack us, and fell astern, so that before Day we had lost Sight of him.

The three Days following we saw several others, of whom we got clear without fighting, by our good working.

The East Wind, which blew very fresh, at length carry'd us out of the most dangerous Parts, and set us out of the Channel. In the Latitude of 40 Degrees we had a Gust of Wind astern, from the North and N. N. E. which would scarce permit us to carry our Mizzen reef'd. The *Mary* not being able to keep up with us, we were oblig'd to drive without any Sail; and in that Posture we ran near three Leagues an Hour.

During

During that Time, we difcover'd a fmall Ship, which we judg'd to be a *Portugueze* from the Ifland of *Madera*; but the Sea ran too high, and we had too much Bufinefs of our own, to go about to take Prizes. However, that Wind did us no other Harm, than breaking down our Lar-board Gallery; but on the contrary, caus'd us to make much Way. No fooner were we come into the Latitude of 32 Degrees, than we found a delightful Sea, and Trade-winds from the N. and N. E. which, without difturbing the Sea, drove us along with their agreeable Frefhnefs, and caus'd us to rid much Way with great Eafe.

After a ftormy difmal Seafon, we enjoy'd the Pleafure of a fine Climate, and of fair ferene Days, when we difcover'd Land, towards the Evening, bearing S. E. and by E. about 15 Leagues diftant. It was a frefh Satisfaction to us, to know we were near the Ifland of *Palma*; and more particularly to me, who, by my Reckoning, found myfelf at that Diftance exactly; not that I ought to afcribe that Exactnefs to my own Skill, it being the Effect of Chance and of the Calculation of the two firft Lieutenants, who took Care to keep the Account by the Log; but becaufe the reft, who knew I had never learnt Navigation, nor been at Sea, could not be perfuaded, that, with a little Help of the Mathematicks, a Man can do the fame that thofe of the Profeffion do Mechanically, without being able to give any Geometrical Reafon for the meaneft of their Performances.

Palma Ifland.

It is true, that four or five Obfervations of the Sun's Meridian Altitude, fet us very right; ever fince our coming out, we found our felves, for the moft part, lefs advanc'd than our Reckoning. I was of Opinion, that the faid Error was occafion'd by the Divifion of the Log line, to which our Navigators ufe to allow only 41 Foot and 8 Inches from Knot to Knot, for the third Part of a League, making the Sea League to contain

Remarks on the Log-line.

15000

15000 *French* Foot; wherein they are grosly miſtaken, if a Degree contains 57060 Toiſes, or Fathoms, and the Sea League 2853 of thoſe of the *Chatelet* at *Paris*, as the Gentlemen of the Academy meaſur'd it, by the King's Order, in the Year 1672; for, according to that Calculation, the League containing 17118 Foot, the Log-line ought to have, between every Knot, to anſwer the Half-minute Glaſs, 47 Foot, 6 Inches, and 7 Tenths. According to this Principle, the Knots being too ſhort, I did not wonder that we made leſs Way than appear'd by our Reckoning; we could not but make one Ninth and $\frac{11}{750}$ Parts, that is, about one Tenth leſs.

I was confirm'd in this Opinion on the 31ſt of *January*, when, having run about 100 Leagues ſince the laſt Obſervation, I found eight Leagues and one Third too much in the Reckoning, and others found more; but in the Proceſs of the Voyage, I was ſenſible of the Uncertainty of the Log, which Experience and good Senſe are to correct, according to the Manner of Caſting it, and the Inequality of the Wind, which rarely continues in the ſame Degree of Force during the Interval of two Hours that the Log is not caſt. The Setting of Currents unknown, is ſtill another Cauſe of Uncertainty; ſo that it often happen'd, that the Log-table anſwer'd exactly with the Latitude obſerv'd; and at other times it fell out, that inſtead of retrenching, they were fain to add to it.

There were ſome alſo, who relying on their Reckoning, queſtion'd whether it was really Land that had been ſeen on the *Wedneſday* Evening; when on *Thurſday*, the 4th of *February*, we again diſcover'd Land at E. and by S. which was not queſtion'd to be the Iſland *Hierro*, or *Ferro*, by the Latitude obſerv'd, and our Run from the Iſland of *Palma*, which was very exact with the Diſtance between thoſe two Iſlands.

_{Hierro*Iſland*.}

Being ſure of the Place we were in, we ſtood for the Iſlands of Cape *Verde*, with a gentle Gale at N. E. and N. N. E. which in three Days carry'd us to the Tropick, where

where the Calms began to make us sensible of extreme Heats. They lasted but three Days, being now and then mitigated by a little Freshness from the West to the South.

Flying Fishes. In those fine Climates we began to see Flying Fishes, which are as big as large Pilchards, or Herrings; their Wings are nothing but long Fins; they serve them to fly no longer than they are wet. We often took some of them that fell into the Ship, or on the Chains; they are delicious and well tasted.

Dorado's. The Enemies of these Fishes are the *Dorado's*, or Gilt-heads, who continually pursue them, and with such a Bait they are easily taken. They are so very greedy, that if a counterfeit Flying Fish be made with Linnen, or any such Thing, they suffer themselves to be deceiv'd, tho' they bite at no other Bait. By that Means we took the first I ever saw, and I could never have done admiring their Beauty. On their Scales appears the brightest Lustre of Gold intermix'd with Shadowings of Azure, Green and Purple, than which nothing more beautiful can be imagin'd. The Taste of their Flesh is not answerable to that Beauty, tho' it is good enough, but somewhat dry.

Green Clouds. My Inclination to Painting caus'd me to take Notice, under the Tropick, of some Clouds beautifully green at Sun-setting: I had never seen any thing like it in *Europe*, nor have I since seen any of so sprightly a delicate Colour.

In 21 Degrees, 21 Minutes Latitude, and 21 Degrees, 39 Minutes Longitude, West from the Meridian of *Paris*, we found the Sea very white, for the Space of five or six Leagues; and casting the Lead, found no Bottom at 40 Fathoms; after which, the Sea recovering its usual Colour, we suppos'd we had pass'd over some shallow Place, which is not set down in the Charts.

For some Days we had a little fresh Air at N. W. which is not usual in those Parts; after which, the North and N. N. E. Gales brought us into the Latitude of 17 Degrees,

Degrees, 40 Minutes, where we lay by a Night, knowing we were near the Iſlands of Cape *Verde*.

Accordingly, the next Day, being the 15th of *February*, we diſcover'd a very high Land cover'd with a Fog, and the next Day diſtinctly perceiv'd that it was the Iſland of S. *Nicolas*, and afterwards the Iſland of S. *Lucy*, which bore S. S. W. from us. *Cape Verde Iſlands.*

We ſtood about to have Sea-room at Night, and having run eight Leagues N. E. and by E. we thought we ſaw Rocks by the Brightneſs of the Sea, which in thoſe Parts glitters very much; that is, it is, during the Night, very light and ſparkling, in caſe the Surface be never ſo little agitated by Fiſhes, or by Ships; ſo that the Ship's Way looks like Fire. I could ſcarce have believ'd this Effect of the Motion of the Sea-water, if I had not ſeen it, tho' I had before read the Accounts given of it by Phyſicians, particularly *Rohault*, who alſo adds Reaſons why it glitters more in hot Countries than elſewhere. However that is, we ſtood about, if I miſtake not, on account of a Shoal of Fiſh, and ran 14 Leagues W. and by N. and about Three in the Afternoon, we perceiv'd, thro' the Miſt, the Iſland of S. *Lucy*, to the Southward, about a League and half diſtant. *A light Sea.*

An Hour after, we diſcover'd that of S. *Vincent*, which we only knew by Gueſs, as well as the other Iſlands before-mention'd, becauſe none of our Men had ſeen them on the North-ſide. Then it was that I became ſenſible of the Uſefulneſs of the Draughts of Lands in the Latitudes where they are generally look'd for; however, this may be known by a low Land ſtretching out at the Foot of the high Mountains towards the N. W. next the Iſland of S. *Anthony*, and by a little Sugar-loaf Rock, which appears at the Mouth of the Bay, Weſt of the Iſland, about two Cables Length from the Shore. *Marks to know the Land by.*

C

Anchoring

Anchoring at the Island of S. Vincent, one of those of Cape Verde.

UPON the Certainty of these Marks, we, at Six of the Clock, enter'd the Channel between the two Islands of S. *Vincent* and S. *Anthony*, with a fresh Gale at N.N.W. and N. and ran along within Musket-shot of the little Rock to gain upon the Wind; it is very clean. At that Distance we found 27 Fathom Water: They say there is a Passage next the Land, and that it has 17 or 20 Fathom Water. In turning that little Island, Ships are expos'd to great Squawls or Gusts of Wind, which come down from the Mountain at N.E. Some Ships of Monsieur *du Guay*'s Squadron lost their Round-tops there, and among them the *Magnanimous*, which was oblig'd to put in.

See Plate I. At length we anchor'd in the Creek, in ten Fathom Water, the Bottom a fine Sand and Gravel, S. and by E. somewhat Easterly of the little Island, and East of the Star-board Point going in. At the same time the *Mary*
came

Plate II. Page 10. *explain'd in* English.

The Plan of the Bay of the Island of S. *Vincent*, near the Coast of *Africa*, West of Cape *Verde*, in 16 Degrees 50 Minutes of Northern Latitude, facing the Island of S. *Anthony*.

Partie de l'Isle de S. Vincent, *Part of the Island of S. Vincent.*
Marais, *A Marsh.*
Bois, *A Wood.*
Aigade, *The Watering-place.*
Anse où l'on va seiner, *A Creek for fishing.*
Ruisseau qui tarit, *A Rivulet that is sometimes dry.*
Terre basse, *Low Land.*
Echelle d'une lieüe marine, *A Scale of a Sea League.*
Partie de l'Isle de S. Antoine, *Part of the Island of S. Anthony.*
Vue de l'Isle de S. Vincent, à O.S.O. *A Prospect of the Island of S. Vincent, at W.S.W.*

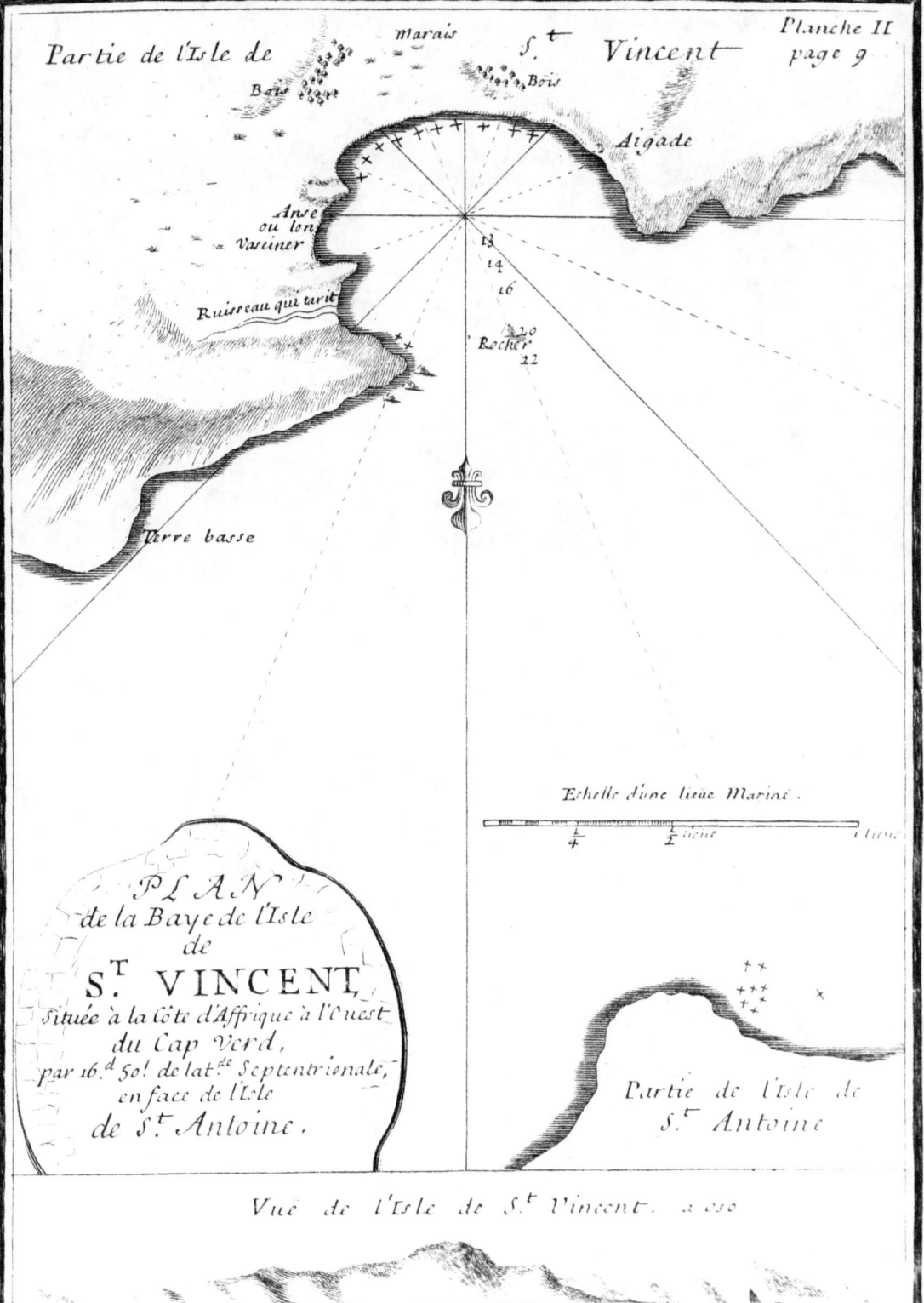

came to an Anchor S. E. from us, in eight Fathom Water, the Bottom an owzy Sand.

We reach'd the Island of S. *Vincent* very exactly with our Account, because in those fine Climates, where the Weather is always serene, we had an Observation almost every Day, which differ'd from our Reckoning five or six Minutes South every Day, even when there was a Calm; whence I conjectur'd, that the Currents carry'd us so far: On the contrary, from 19 Degrees Latitude, the Computation was before us. This Error might also proceed from the Log-line, as has been said before, because in a Day of 45 Leagues Run, abating four, I still found above one for the common Current, which drove us somewhat to the South. *Remarks on the Reckoning.*

The next Day, being the 16th of *February*, we thought to go and water in a Rivulet, which runs a great Part of the Year into a little Creek, the farthest Northward in the Bay; but we found only a dry Channel. Being surpriz'd at the Disappointment of so necessary a Recruit, a Detachment of Men and Officers was sent to seek some in the Island, and whether there was any Dwelling, whence some Cattle and Fruit might be had. They only found some salt Marshes, and no other Habitation but a few Cottages made of the Boughs of Trees, fitter for Beasts than Men, the Doors being so low, that there is no going into them but upon all four: All the Houshold-goods were some Leather Budgets and Tortois Shells, which serv'd for Seats, and for Vessels to hold Water. The Blacks, who are the Inhabitants, had abandon'd them, for fear of being carry'd away and sold, tho' by our Colours they should have taken us for *English*. Two or three of them were seen stark-naked, and they hid themselves in the Woods as soon as they saw our Men, who could never come near, tho' they call'd to them in a friendly manner.

At length, after long Search, at the South Point of the Bay, they found a little Gut of Water, which ran down *Watering.*

down from the Crags to the Sea They dug to make it run the better, and gather enough Water to lade it up. Thus we made our Provision in two Days, tho' with Trouble enough to get it aboard, becaufe the Sea is very rough there. This perfectly frefh Water was none of the beft ; but in feven or eight Days ftunk fo much, that it was a great Punifhment to be obliged to drink it.

Wood.   Whilft fome water'd, others wooded, 200 Paces from the Watering-place. It was a fort of Tamarind, which was eafy enough to fell, and near the Shore.

S. Anthony Ifland.   We had put up *Englifh* Colours, with the Pendant at the Main-maft, and had fir'd a Gun by way of Signal of Friendfhip, to induce the Inhabitants of the Ifland of S. *Anthony*, which is but two Leagues from thence, to come to us; but whether they miftrufted the Contrivance, or that the Fog obftructed their perceiving of us diftinctly, they came not. We only faw a Fire, which feem'd to anfwer that made by our Waterers, in the Night, on the Shore. However, the S. *Clement* of S. *Malo*, with its Pink, having anchor'd at the fame Place, was vifited by the Inhabitants of S. *Anthony*, who for their Money brought them Beeves, Goats, Figs, Bananas, Lemons, and very fweet Wine. They fay there may be about 2000 Perfons of both Sexes, and of all Colours and Conditions, in the Ifland; and that, above the Anchoring-place, there is a little Fort, with four Pieces of Cannon, in which there is a *Portugueze* Governor.

Fifh.   As for us, we had no other Refrefhment than what we got by Fifhing; whereof there is great Plenty in the Bay of S. *Vincent*, tho' there is only one Creek lying between two little Points towards the E. S. E. where the Sean can be us'd, becaufe in other Places the Shore is rocky; but Amends may be made with the Hook, for there is an infinite Number of Fifh, as Mullets, Rock-fifh, Manchorans, Pilchards, Grunters, white-tooth Longbeaks, and a fort which have a Rat's Tail and round

Plate XI.   Spots all over them. Here is the Figure of one of thofe

we

we took, which was six Foot long, and is very like the *Petimbuaba* of *Brasil*, mention'd in *Margrave*, p. 148. There are also sometimes taken Bourses, or Purses, a most beautiful sort of Fish, described in the Voyage of Monsieur *de Gennes*, by the Sieur *Froger*. In the Tortois Season, there are prodigious Numbers of them, as appears by the infinite Quantity of their Shells and Skeletons that lie along the Shore. The Inhabitants of the Island of S. *Anthony* come every Year to take and dry them, trading with, and feeding on them. In short, there are even great Numbers of Whales.

We could have wish'd to have found some Game to refresh us after our hard Fare at Sea, but there is scarce any in that Island; nor so much as a Beast, except wild Asses, and Goats on the Tops of the Mountains, hard to be come at; some few Pintados, and no other Birds.

Nor had we better Fortune as for Fruit, the Soil being so barren that it produces none; only in the Valleys there are little Tufts of Tamarind Trees, a few Cotton and Lemon Trees: However, I there saw some curious Plants, as the *Tithymalus arborescens*, or branch'd Spurge; the *Abrotanum mas*, or the Male Southernwood, of a most sweet Scent, and a beautiful Green; a yellow Flower, the Stem whereof has no Leaves; the *Palma Christi*, or *Ricinus Americanus*, by the *Spaniards* in *Peru* call'd *Pillerilla*; and they affirm, that the Leaf of it, apply'd to the Breasts of Nurses, brings Milk into them, and, apply'd to their Loins, draws it away; the Seed of it is exactly like the *Indian* Pine-apple Kernel; in *Paraguay* they make Oil of it; abundance of Housleek of several sorts, some of which have thick round Leaves like an Hazel-nut; *Coloquintida-apples*; *Limonium maritimum*, very thick; Lavender without any Scent; Doggrass, &c.

Plants.

Near

Ambergreafe. Near the little Island very good Ambergreafe is found, and the *Portugueze* have fold it to fome *French* Ships, and among the reft to the S. *Clement.*

As no Refreshment was to be found in that Island, we fet fail to get fome in that of S. *Anthony*; but the Wind blew too fresh at N. E. and the Sea ran too high to fend Boats; fo that we fet our Courfe to get out of the Channel that is form'd by thofe two Iflands. In paffing along, we perceiv'd the Anchoring-place towards the S. W.

Soon after we difcover'd, farther on, Land at a great Diftance, which we took for the Ifland *Fuego,* or *Fogo*; but the next Morning, after having run about 45 Leagues S. and by E. in the Night, we fpy'd a Fire, and when it was full Day a very high Land, which bore from us N. E. and by E. about five Leagues diftant, on the Top whereof there appear'd fome Smoak.

The Situation of that Land made us take it for the Ifland *Brava,* but the Smoak inclin'd us to fancy it was that of *Fuego,* or *Fogo.* If fo, the Iflands of Cape *Verde* muft be wrong laid down in *Vankeulen*'s *Sea-Atlas,* which we follow'd.

However, we still made the Beft of a good fresh Gale at N. E. which carry'd us within two Degrees of the Equinoctial, where we had two calm Days, with fome little Air from W. S. W. to South; after which, a little Gale at S. S. E. having carry'd us on into 40 Minutes Latitude, and 23 Degrees 50 Minutes Longitude, from the Meridian of *Paris,* we tack'd, for fear of falling in too near the Coaft of *Brafil,* where the Currents fet to the N. W. We ftood S. E. and by E. and the next Day, being the 5th of *March,* fteering S. and by E. cut the *Pafs the Line.* Line with a fmall Gale at W. S. W. at 355 Degrees from *Teneriff.*

The next Day, when it was no longer doubted that we were to the Southward of the Line, the foolifh Ceremony

mony of Ducking at the Line, practis'd by all Nations, was not omitted.

The Persons to be so serv'd, are seas'd by the Wrists to Ropes stretch'd fore and aft on the Quarter-deck for the Officers, and before the Mast for the Sailors; and after much Mummery and Monkey Tricks, they are let loose to be led one after another to the Main-mast, where they are made to swear on a Sea-chart, that they will do by others as is done by them, according to the Laws and Statutes of Navigation; then they pay to save being wetted, but always in vain, for the Captains themselves are not quite spar'd. *Ducking*

The dead Calm, which afforded the Men Leisure to duck one another, expos'd us for four Days successively to excessive Heats, without advancing, during that time, above 20 Leagues in our Course, by the Help of some little shifting Air; but a little Gale at S.E. and E.S.E. by Degrees carry'd us from that scorching Climate, and into 16 Degrees of South Latitude, without any Squawls or Rain, the Weather holding clear and serene. The Wind coming to N.E. and then to N.W. brought us some Showers of Rain, cloudy Weather, and some Hours Calm, for three Days, till we came into 23 Degrees and a half Latitude, and 36 of Longitude.

When we were between 21 and 22 Degrees of South Latitude, and 34 or 35 of Longitude, we saw abundance of Fowl, and believ'd we were not far from the Island of the *Ascension*. We cast the Lead without finding Ground, and had no Sight of it, nor of that of the *Trinity*, which, according to some Charts drawn by Hand, we should be near, in 25 Degrees and a half of South Latitude, where the Wind vary'd to the Southward with Intervals of Calm; but at length, being forwarded by a small Gale at S.S.E. N.E. and E. we in three Days arriv'd at the Island of S. *Katharine*, on the Coast of *Brasil*, exactly according to our Account, whereof these are the Particulars.

Remarks on the Calculation.

The next Day after our Departure from *S. Vincent*, our Account was somewhat before us; the next Day, on the contrary, we outstripp'd it; but the 26th of *February*, after having taken an Observation in 5 Degrees 54 Minutes, we found ourselves 8 Leagues farther to the Southward than we imagin'd, tho' two Days before we had found 9 Degrees 45 Minutes by Observation. The Mistake still continu'd on the same side, with those Marks of Currents which are call'd Channels of Tides, till towards 9 Degrees South of 5 or 6 Minutes, according to the Extent of the Day's Run, without reckoning the Correction of the Log-line. From 9 to 13 Degrees there was less than from 13 to 17; and the Difference was the more considerable, because we drew near Land, so that we found one Day we had sail'd 25 Leagues, when the Computation made but 16.

Of Currents.

It is plain, that these Errors were occasion'd by the Currents which set us to the Southward: Whether it be directly to the South, to the S. E. or to the S. W. cannot be positively known; but the most reasonable Conjecture, in my Opinion, is, that they must set to the S. W. or S. S. W. because they are so determin'd by the Position of the Coast of *Brasil*. This Experience reduces to a small Extent the Remark made by *Voogt*, who in his *Waggoner*, printed in *Vankeulen*, says, The Current on the Coast of *Brasil*, from *March* till *July*, sets violently along the Shore to the Northward; and from *December* till *March*, the South-current ceases; where if it be true as to the North-part of that Coast, it is not regular for the South-part from 10 Degrees of South Latitude, a little out at Sea.

It may nevertheless be objected against my Conjecture, that if the Currents did set S. W. they would carry the Ships that come from the *South-Sea* nearer to the Coast of *Brasil*; but Experience shews, that from *Sibald*'s Islands, there is found an Error of 2 or 300 Leagues contrary to the Draught to that Coast, or the Island of
Fernando

Fernando de Noronha; therefore the Currents cannot set to the S. W.

To this I answer, 1. That the Currents which set along the Coast of *Brasil*, coming to meet the new Lands of *Sibald*'s Islands and *Staten* Land, turn off to the Eastward, as several Ships have found by Experience; after which, they sometimes fall into another Channel of Currents, which sets to the Coast of *Guinea*. There needs no more than casting an Eye on the Charts of the Coasts of *Africa* and of *South America*, to be sensible of the Likelihood of this Conjecture.

2. These Errors proceed from the Charts, as shall be said in its Place, and particularly those of *Pieter Goos*, which our Navigators make most use of. This Error of Position is not always perceiv'd upon making the Coasts of *Brasil* coming from *Europe*, because Ships are often carry'd thither by the Currents, as I have just now observ'd; and that not knowing whether their Bent is to the East or to the West, they often do not correct the Leagues, as we almost all of us did in our Voyage, following therein the Example of most of the *Dutch*; so that it is not to be wonder'd that we found those Charts good which they have made by their Journals.

Be that as it will, it is certain, that from the Island of S. *Vincent* to that of S. *Katharine*, we ran above 60 Leagues to the Southward, beyond our Computation, tho' we had an Observation almost every Day, and took our Precautions upon our Error; and yet notwithstanding all that, we arriv'd at the Island of S. *Katharine* the 31st of *March*, exactly with our Points on *Pieter Goos*'s Chart, about ten Leagues more or less, one from another: Where it may be inferr'd, that if we had given way to the Westward, we had ran far in upon the Land, as has happen'd to most *French* Ships bound for the *South-Sea*.

Tuesday, March the 30th, believing ourselves to be near Land, we sounded about Six in the Evening, and found 90 Fathom Water, the Bottom Sand, Owze, and Shells;

two Leagues and half more to the Westward we had ten Fathom less, and pass'd the Night, heaving the Lead every two Hours, the same Depth and Bottom.

Island of S. Katharine. At Break of Day we saw Land, being six Leagues West of our second Sounding: We soon knew the Island of *Gal*, by its Shape and some little white Spots which are taken for Ships at a Distance, and by little Rocks or Islands that are near it; and it then bore W. and by S. from us, about eight or nine Leagues distant. We heav'd the Lead, and found 55 Fathom Water, the Bottom fine Sand, and owzy. At length we had an Observation, a League and half from that Island to S. and by E. and about three Leagues East from the North-point of S. *Katharine*'s Island; the Latitude 27 Degrees, 22 Minutes South. Thus it appear'd to us.

See Plate III.

A League and half farther West, we found 20 Fathom Water, the Bottom owzy Sand, more gray than before: We continu'd heaving the Lead at equal Distances, the Depth of Water decreasing regularly, to six Fathom, the Bottom gray Owze, where we came to an Anchor, between the Island of S. *Katharine* and the Continent, the Island of *Gal* bearing N. E. and by E. about three Leagues distant, in a Line with the two most Northerly Points of S. *Katharine*, and the N. and by E. Point of the Continent.

Touching at the Island of S. Katharine, *on the Coast of* Brasil.

THE next Day, being the first of *April*, the Captain sent our Boat and that of the *Mary*, with arm'd Crews, to find out a proper Place to water at, and the Dwellings of the *Portugueze*, to get some Refreshments. The Sieur *Lestobec*, second Captain, went at the same time in the Yawl, with three Officers, of which Number I was one, to discover whether there were no Ships of the Enemy at anchor in the Creek of *Arazatiba*, which is on the Continent, West of the South Point of the Island.

At

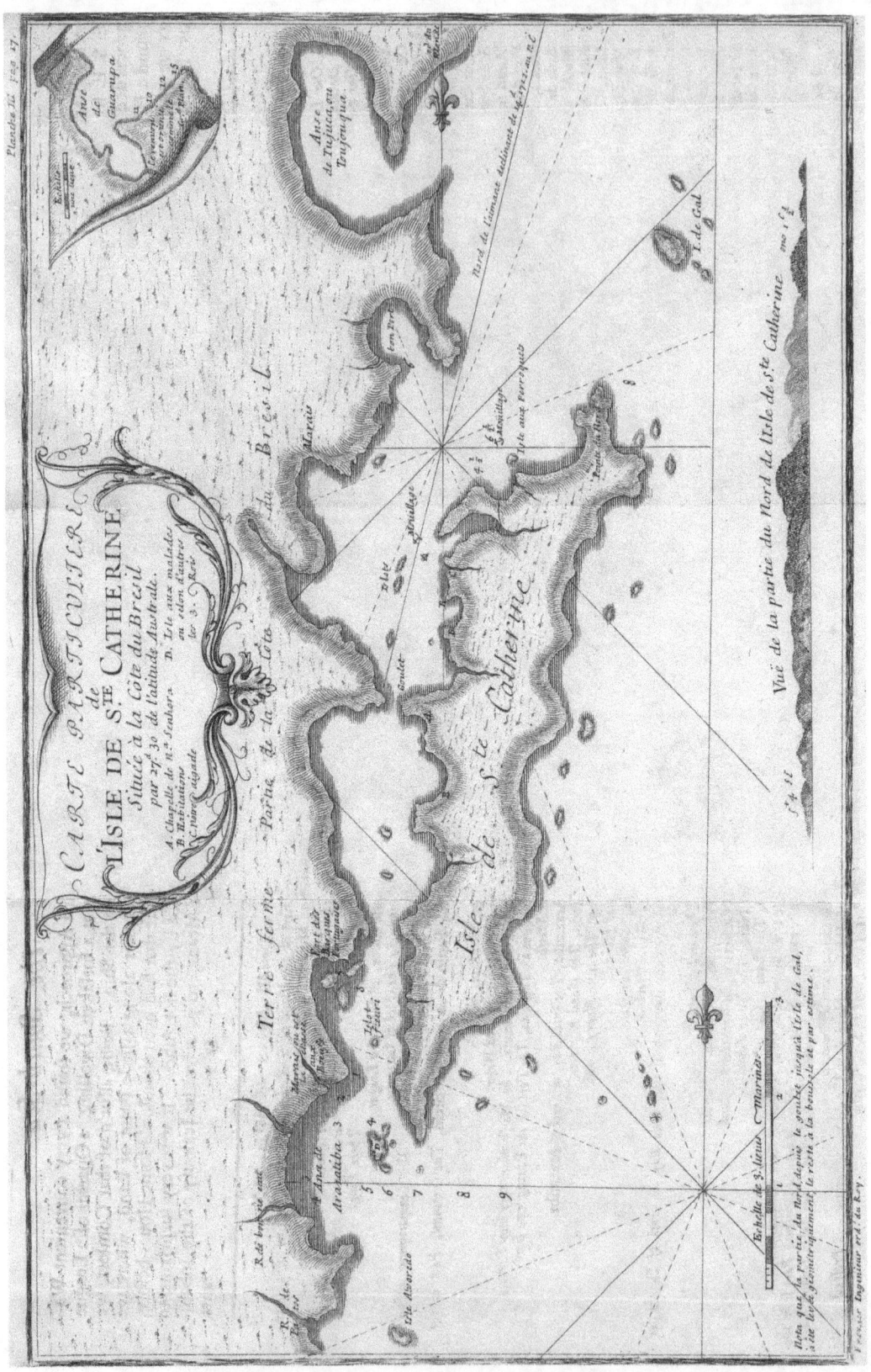

The material originally positioned here is too large for reproduction in this reissue. A PDF can be downloaded from the web address given on page iv of this book, by clicking on 'Resources Available'.

the South-Sea.

At our first Approach, we found a very convenient Watering-place at a forsaken Dwelling, a Quarter of a League E. S. E. from the Ship. Being assur'd of that Comfort, we proceeded farther along a little Point of Land, where we found a House that had been abandon'd some Hours before, as we guess'd by the hot Ashes. It was very surprizing to us, by that Means, to perceive the Jealousy of the Inhabitants,

---

Plate III. Page 18. *described in* English.

An exact Chart of the Island of S. *Katharine*, on the Coast of *Brasil*, in 27 Degrees, 30 Minutes, South Latitude.

A. *Our Lady's Chappel.*
B. *Dwellings.*
C. *Our watering Place.*
D. *The Island of the Sick, or according to others, the Three Kings.*

Echelle d'une Lieüe, *A Scale of a League.*
Anse de Guarupa, *The Creek of* Guarupa.
Ce renvoi est orienté comme le grand Plan, *This Compartiment answers the Position of the great Plan.*
Terre ferme, Partie de la Côte du Bresil, *The Continent, Part of the Coast of* Brasil.
R. de Patos, *The River of Geese.*
R. de bonne Eau, *River of good Water.*
Marais où est la chasse aux Bœufs, *The Marsh where they hunt Beeves.*
Port des Barques Portugaises, *The Port for the Portugueze Barks.*
Marais, *A Marsh.*
Anse de Arazatiba, *The small Bay, or Creek of* Arazatiba.
Isle Alvoredo, *The Island* Alvoredo.
Islot Fleury, *The little Flowry Island.*
Islots, *Small Islands.*
Mouillage, *Anchoring-place.*
Bon Port, *A good Harbour.*
Anse de Tujuca, ou Toujouqua, *The little Bay, or Creek of* Tujuca, *or* Toujouqua.
Goulet, *The narrow Channel, or Passage.*
Isle aux Perroquets, *The Island of Parrots.*
Isle de S. Catherine, *S. Katharine's Island.*
Point du Nord, *The North Point.*
I. de Gal, *The Island of Gal.*
Echelle de trois Lieües Marines, *A Scale of three Sea-Leagues.*
Nota que le partie du Nord, &c. *Note, That the Northern Part from the narrow Channel, or Passage to the Island of Gal, was taken Geometrically, the rest by the Compass and Estimation.*
Vue de la Partie du Nord de L'Isle de S. Catherine, *A Prospect of the Northern Part of the Island of S. Katharine.*

tants, because we had made a Signal as Friends, which Captain Sa*l*vador had agreed on a Year before, with the Sieurs *Roche* and *Besard*, Captains of the *Joyeux* and the *Lysidore*, who had anchor'd at *Arazatiba*, being a white Pendant under an *English* one, at the Main-maſt; but we had err'd in firing but one Gun inſtead of two. Beſides, they were otherwiſe frighted by the News of the Taking of *Rio de Janeiro*, which Monſieur *du Guay Trouin* had lately poſſeſs'd himſelf of, and ranſom'd, to revenge the Inſolence of the *Portugueze* towards the *French* Priſoners of War, and their Commander Monſieur *le Clerc*. In ſhort, as we were going to ſeek other Dwellings that had People in them, we ſaw three Men coming towards us in a *Piragua*, being ſent by the Governor or Captain of the Iſland, to deſire us not to land at the Dwellings; that, having been diſcover'd to be *French*, the Women, in a Fright, were already fled to the Mountains; that, if we would do them no Harm, they would let us partake of the Proviſions and Refreſhments they had, as they had done to other *French* Ships which put in there before. We receiv'd thoſe Meſſengers kindly, and ſent them aboard our Ship in the Boat belonging to the *Mary*, attended by ours, which we quitted to go and view the Anchoring at *Arazatiba*, as has been ſaid.

See the Chart of the Iſland, Plate III.

We firſt paſs'd thro' a little Streight, about 200 Fathom wide, form'd by the Iſland and the Continent, where there is but two Fathom and a half Water. Then we began to diſcover fine Dwellings on both Sides, to which we went not, becauſe we had promis'd the Meſſengers not to go. We ſounded all the Way we went, but never found Water enough for a Veſſel of ſix Guns. We coaſted along ſeveral fine Creeks of the Iſland, till Night coming upon us, we were oblig'd to put in to Land. Chance led us into a little Creek, where we had the good Fortune to find Water, and a little Fiſh we took very ſeaſonably, to which a ſharp Appetite was the beſt Sawce in the World. There we ſpent the Night upon our Guard againſt the Tigers, with

with which all those Woods swarm, and whose fresh Track we had newly seen on the Sand. At Break of Day, we still advanc'd half a League farther, to discover whether any Ship was at Anchor at *Arazatiba*, and saw none. One of our Officers, who had put in there two Years before, with Monsieur *de Chabert*, shew'd us a Point of low Land, where there are Herds of wild Bullocks; but we were not well provided to attempt that Sport, and yet we stood much in need of it, for there are none on the North-part of the Island; so that it would be much more advantageous to put into the South part, if Ships were safe there; but when it blows hard at East, E.S.E. and S.E. there is Danger of being cast away, as happen'd to the S. *Clement* and his Pink, in 1712: They there lost their Boat, with 14 Men, and were themselves at the very Point of perishing, tho' there was no Wind, being only beaten by the dreadful Surge of the Sea. This Road is in about 27 Degrees 50 Minutes Latitude, West of the South-point of the Island of S. *Katharine*. To the Eastward of the little Flowry Island, is a Creek, in which there is very good Water, and little green Oysters, of a delicious Taste. At our Return, we fell into that little Creek, and two others more Northward, and went into an abandon'd Dwelling, where we loaded our Yawl with sweet Oranges, Lemons, and large Limes. Opposite to this, near the Continent, is a little Island, behind which is a small Port, where the Governor of the Island generally keeps a Bark for the Use of the Inhabitants; but for the most part it only serves to carry on the Trade of Dry'd Fish, which they send to *Lagoa* and *Rio de Janeiro*.

The *Portugueze*, who had seen us pass by with *English* Colours at our Yawl, without landing at their Dwellings, at our Return came to meet us in their *Piragua*'s, to offer us Refreshments. We accepted of their Offers, and to oblige them, gave them Brandy, a Liquor they are very fond of, tho' they generally drink nothing but Water. At length, we got to our Ship about Midnight, where we
found

found the Governor *Emanuel Manſa*, with ſome *Portugueze*, who had brought Refreſhments. After having treated him handſomly aboard, he was ſaluted by way of Huzza.

His kind Reception ſo far reconcil'd the Inhabitants, that every Day they brought us *Piragua's* full of Fowl, Tobacco and Fruit. Whilſt we were making that little Excurſion in our Yawl, the Ship was waſh'd and tallow'd; 18 Pieces of Cannon were put into the Hold to make it lie more ſnug in the Water, conſidering the rough Parts we were to paſs beyond the Southern Lands. We alſo brought it nearer to the Iſland of S. *Katharine*, for the more eaſy watering; and becauſe the Tides are very ſenſible, tho' not very regular, or little known, and the Sea does not riſe or fall above five or ſix Foot, we moor'd E. N. E. and W. S. W. 200 Fathom from a little Iſland, which bore from us S. S. E. the Iſland of *Gal* bearing from us N. E. and by N. about four Leagues diſtant, half cover'd by the ſecond Point of the Iſland of S. *Katharine*, which is the moſt Northerly. After we had very commodiouſly made good Wood and excellent Water, we waited ſome Days for the Beeves, which the *Portugueze* had ſent for to *Lagoa*, 12 Leagues from the Iſland: But on the 9th of *April*, perceiving they ſtill demanded more Time to bring them, we thought it not convenient to loſe more Time, becauſe the Seaſon was already ſomewhat advanc'd, to turn Cape Horn, a Place to be dreaded, for the contrary Winds and foul Weather there met with in Winter; therefore, the next Day, being *Sunday*, we put out to Sea. Before we proceed on our Voyage, it will be proper, in this Place, to ſay ſomething of the Iſland of S. *Katharine*.

The Deſcription of the Iſland of S. Katharine.

THE Iſland of S. *Katharine* ſtretches North and South, from 27 Degrees, 22 Minutes, to 27 Degrees, 50 Minutes. It is a continu'd Grove of Trees, which are all the Year green: There are no Places in it paſſable, beſides
what

what have been clear'd about the Dwellings; that is, 12 or 15 Spots scatter'd about here and there along the Shore, in the little Creeks facing the Continent. The Inhabitants settled on them are *Portugueze*, some *European* Fugitives, and a few Blacks: There are also some *Indians*, who come voluntarily to serve them, or taken in War.

Tho they pay no Tribute to the King of *Portugal*, they are his Subjects, and obey the Governor or Captain he appoints to command them, if there be Occasion, against *European* Enemies, and the *Indians* of *Brasil*; with which last they are almost continually at War, so that they dare not go under 30 or 40 Men together, well arm'd, when they penetrate up the Continent, which is no less embarass'd with Forests than the Island. That Captain commonly commands but three Years, and is subordinate to the Governor of *Lagoa*, a small Town 12 Leagues distant from the Island to the S.S.W. He had at that Time 147 Whites within his District, some *Indians* and Free Blacks, Part whereof are dispers'd along the Shore of the Continent. Their usual Weapons are Hunting-hangers, Bows and Arrows, and Axes: They have but few Firelocks, and seldom any Powder; but they are sufficiently fortify'd by the Woods, which an infinite Quantity of Brambles of several Sorts render almost impenetrable; so that having always a sure Retreat, and but little Houshold-stuff to remove, they live easy, without any Fear of being robb'd of their Wealth.

In short, they are in such Want of all Conveniencies for Life, that none of those who brought us Provisions would be paid in Money, putting more Value upon a Bit of Linnen or Woollen-stuff to cover them, than on a Piece of Metal, which can neither maintain nor defend them against the Weather, being satisfy'd with a Shirt and Breeches for all Cloathing, the greatest Beaux adding a colour'd Vest and a Hat. Scarce any Man has Shooes or Stockings, yet they must cover their Legs when they go into the Woods; then the Skin of a *Tiger's Leg* is a Stocking ready made.

Neither

Neither are they more dainty in their Food, than in their Apparel; a little *Maize*, or *Indian* Corn, some Potatoes, Fruit, Fish, and Game, being mostly Monkeys, satisfies them. Those People, at first Sight, appear wretched; but they are, in Reality, happier than the *Europeans*; being unacquainted with the Curiosities and superfluous Conveniencies so much sought after in *Europe*, they are satisfy'd without thinking of them. They live in a Tranquillity which is not disturb'd by Taxes, or the Inequality of Conditions: The Earth, of its own Accord, furnishes them with all Things necessary for Life; Wood and Leaves, Cotton and the Skins of Beasts, to cover themselves and lie on: They covet not that Magnificence of Lodgings, Houshold-stuff, and Equipage, which only stir up Ambition, and for some Time cherish Vanity, without making a Man ever the more happy. What is still more remarkable, is, that they are sensible of their Happiness, when they see us seek for Plate with so much Fatigue. The only Thing they are to be pity'd for, is, their living in Ignorance: They are Christians it is true, but how are they instructed in their Religion, having only a Chaplain of *Lagoa*, who comes to say Mass to them on the principal Festivals of the Year? However, they pay Tythe to the Church, which is the only Thing exacted from them.

In other respects, they enjoy a good Climate, and a very wholsome Air: They seldom have any other Distemper besides that they call *Mal de Biche*, which is a Pain in the Head, attended with a *Tenesmus*, or continual Desire of going to Stool without doing any thing; and they have a very simple Medicine for it, which they look upon as a Specifick, which is, to apply to the Fundament a little Lemon, or else a Plaister of Gun-powder dissolv'd in Water.

They have also many Medicines of the Simples of the Country, to cure other Distempers that may seize them. *Sassafras*, the Wood so well known for its good Scent, and for its Vertue against Venereal Distempers, is so common

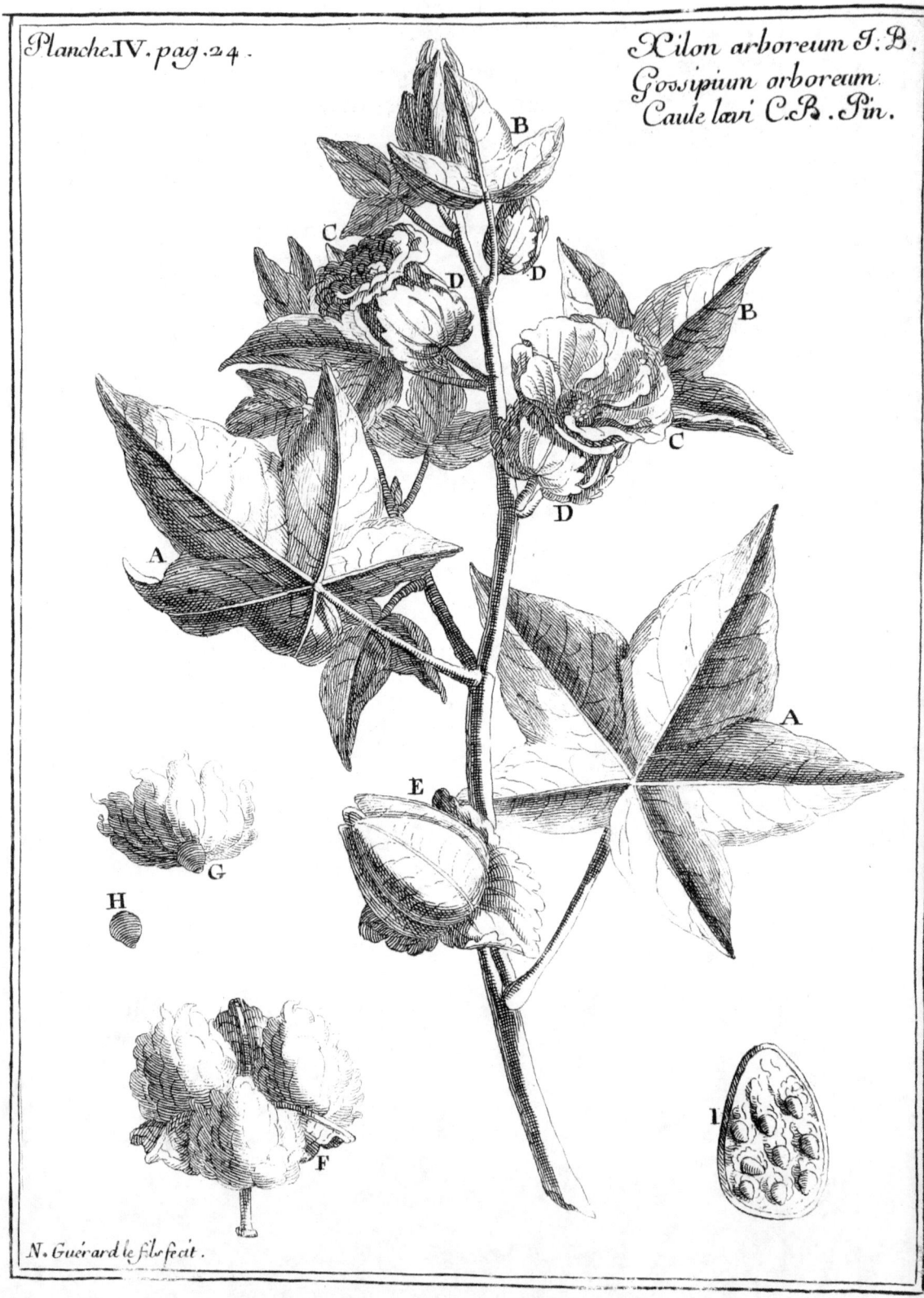

the South-Sea.

mon there, that we us'd to cut it to burn. The *Guayacum*, which is also us'd for the same Purposes, is not any scarcer. There is very fine Maiden-hair, and many Aromatick Plants, known by the Inhabitants for their Uses. The Fruit-trees there are excellent in their several Kinds: The Orange-trees are at least as good as in *China*: There are abundance of Lemon, Citron, *Guayava*, Cabbage, and *Banana* Trees; Sugar-canes, Melons, Water melons, Turnsoils, and the best Potatoes in the World.

There I first saw the Shrub that bears the Cotton; and, having been long desirous to see it, I drew one Branch, to preserve the Idea of it.

Of the Cotton.

THE Cotton-tree, or Shrub, which *Botanists* call *Gos-* See Plate IV. *sipium*, or *Xilon arboreum*, is a Shrub which seldom rises above ten or twelve Foot: Its large Leaves have five Points, and are pretty like those of the great Maple, or the Sycomore; but the little ones, that is, those which are nearest the Fruit, have only three Points. Both of them are somewhat thick, and of a deep Green.

The Flowers would be like those of the Mallow call'd *Paste-rose*, if they were somewhat more open, and of the same Colour. They are supported by a green Cup, compos'd of three triangular jagg'd Leaves, which enclose them but

---

Plate IV. *Pag.* 25. *explain'd in* English.
A. *The great Leaf with five Points.*
B. *The little Leaf with three Points.*
C. *Flowers or Blossoms differently shewn.*
D. *The Cup of triangular Leaves.*
E. *The Bud parting into four Cells.*
F. *Ripe Cotton.*
G. *A Seed cover'd with Cotton.*
H. *A Seed stripp'd of the Cotton.*
I. *The Cell of one of the Tufts before it is ripe.*
Note, *That this Draught represents half the Bigness of the natural Size.*

but very imperfectly: They are yellow at the top, and streak'd with red below.

The Flower or Blossom is succeeded by a green Fruit like a Rose-bud, which, when full ripe, grows as big as a little Egg, and divides into three or four Cells, each of them fill'd up with between eight and twelve Seeds, almost as big as Pease, which are wrapp'd up in a filaminous or thready Substance, known by the Name of Cotton, which proceeds from all their Surface, grows white, and causes those Cells to open as it ripens, so that at last the Tufts of it break loose, and drop of themselves. The Seeds are then quite black, and full of an oily Substance of an indifferent good Taste, said to be very good against the Bloody-flux.

This Cotton-tree differs very much from that which they cultivate at *Malta*, and throughout the *Levant*, and which is only a little annual Plant; that is, it must be sown and renew'd every Year, for which Reason it is call'd *Xilon herbaceum*: Besides, its Leaves are roundish, and notch'd, and much about the Bigness of those of Mallows.

To part the Seeds from the Cotton, they have a little Instrument consisting of two Rowlers, as thick as a Finger, which turning contrary Ways, pinch the Cotton and draw it away by Degrees. The Seed, which is round and thick, cannot pass between the Rowlers, so that it is stripp'd, and drops down as soon as the Cotton is pass'd thro'.

They say, those Cotton-trees are of the lesser Sort, because on the Continent there are some taller and thicker than our Oaks, which bear a Leaf like the former. They bear the Silk Cotton, which is very short; but it is a Sort they call *Houatte*.

Dampier has drawn another Sort there is in *Brasil*, call'd *Momou*. This is what he says of it: " The Flower or " Blossom is compos'd of little Filaments, almost as fine as " Hairs, three or four Inches long, and of a dark Red; " but the Tops of them are of an Ash Colour: At the
" Bottom

" Bottom of the Stem there are five Leaves narrow and
" stiff, six Inches long.

In the Woods there are also *Mahault*, or Mangrove- *Plants.*
trees, the Bark whereof consisting of very long Fibres,
serves to make Ropes of. There is a Tree very singular
for its Figure, which has given it the Name of the Flambeau, or Prickly-candle: Its Leaves are actually made like
a Branch of four Candles; that is, the Bottom of it is a
Cross rounded at the Angles: They grow like those of
the *Raquette*, one out of another: They are from eight to
fifteen Foot long, and produce a Fruit which much resembles a Fig, or green Walnut. There are abundance of
them in *Peru*, being six-sided, as Father *du Tertre* has represented them in his History of the *Caribbee* Islands. The
Manzanilla Tree is somewhat more rare there: It is one
of the most venomous Trees that are known, producing
an Apple beautiful to the Eye, which is Poison. From its
Bark proceeds a sort of Milk, whose Venom Seamen have
often Experience of: If in cutting of Wood to burn, they
happen to light upon this, and that the said Milk flies on
their Faces, or that they handle the Wood, immediately the
Part swells, and pains them for several Days. When the
Manzanilla's drop into the Sea, and the Fishes eat them,
their Teeth turn yellow and they become poisonous.

The Fishery is plentiful in many little Creeks of the *Fishery.*
Island, and of the Continent, where there is Conveniency
for casting a Net. We there took Fishes from four to five
Foot long, very delicious, somewhat shaped like Carps,
whose Scales were larger than a Crown Piece. Some
have them round, and they are call'd *Mero's*; others have
them square, and are call'd *Salemera's* in *Portugueze*, and
Piraguera's by the *Indians*. There is a smaller Sort call'd
Quiareo, which have a Bone in the Head exactly like a
great Bean; not to mention an infinite Number of Mullets,
Carangue's, *Machorans*, Rock-fish, Grunters, Gurnets,
Pilchards, &c.

Sword fish, Plate XVII.   We one Day took there a Sword-fish, which is a very singular Sort, having on its Head a flat Bone full of Points on both Sides, which serves to defend it against the Whales, as we once saw on the Coast of *Chili*; and it has another thing peculiar, which is, a Humane Mouth and another Humane Opening.

Sea-horse, Plate XVII.   Tho' the Sea-horse be sufficiently known in *Europe*, I here insert the Figure of one I took with a Hook, drawn from its natural Bulk.

Game.   Game is no less plentiful than the Fishery; but the Woods are of such difficult Access, that it is almost impossible to pursue it into them, and to find it when kill'd. The most common Birds are the Parrots, very good to eat: They always fly by two and two, very near one another. A Sort of Pheasants, call'd *Giacotins*, but not so delicious to the Taste. *Onara's*, a Sort of Fishers, all red, of a beautiful Colour: Others smaller, of a most agreeable Mixture of the liveliest Colours, call'd *Saiquida's*. There is also a very peculiar Bird, that has a large Beak, more beautiful than Tortois-shell, and a Feather instead of a Tongue: It is the *Toucan*, describ'd by *Froger*, and by Father *Feüillee*, p. 428. The common Game of the Inhabitants, is the Monkey, on which they feed for the most part: But the best of all for Ships that put in, is the Hunting of Beeves, whereof there are great Numbers on the Continent, near *Arazatiba*, as has been said before.

Seven Leagues to the Northward of the Island of S. *Katharine*, there is a Creek, where the *Portugueze* generally keep them, and whither the Boat of the S. *Clement* went *See Plate* III. for them. Near to it, is the Port of *Guarupa*, which the *at the little* same Boat discover'd, shelter'd from all Winds, as may be *Reference.* seen by the Plan which was given me. It is hard to be known, because without, it only looks like a great Creek, at the End whereof, is the little Mouth of the Harbour. We not knowing where to find Beeves, and the *Portugueze*, who, as they said, had sent for them to *Lagoa*, staying too long, we sail'd, as has been said, on *Sunday* the

the 10th of *April*; but the Wind would not permit us to get out, so that we were oblig'd to come to an Anchor again, almost in the same Place where we were at first.

We succeeded no better the next Day, making several Trips between the Island and the Continent, still sounding, and found much the same Water. We view'd very near a little Creek on the Starboard-side coming in, where there is good Anchorage in five or six Fathom Water, under Shelter from all Winds, and a little River of good Water, commodious for Ships that anchor near the first little Island, which is on the Larboard coming in, in a sandy Creek of the Island of *S. Katharine*, call'd, on the Plan, *Islot aux Perroquets*, or, *The little Island of Parrots*. In tacking, we discover'd the great Creek of *Toujouqua*, into which a great River falls: The Mouth of the Creek seems narrow, and, on the South-side of it, there are flat Rocks. Not being able to get out of the Channel, we were oblig'd to come to an Anchor S. W. and by S. of the Island of *Gal*, about a League and half distant, and W. N. W. of the first Point of the Island of *S. Katharine*, at half a League Distance.

At length, on *Tuesday* the 12th, we got out, with a fresh Gale at North, and N. N. E. which came about to S. W. and grew calm. The Winds vary'd almost continually, till the Latitude of 40 Degrees, where the fresh North and N. E. brought on such a thick Fog, that we were oblig'd, even in the Day-time, to fire Guns every now and then, to keep the *Mary* near us. A Calm, interrupted by a small Gale at N. N. E. and S. E. succeeded, and the Fog fell again in 43 Degrees and a half. *Departure from the Island of S. Katharine.*

In this Latitude, and that of Cape *Blanc*, being 46 Degrees, we saw abundance of Whales, and of new Birds like Pigeons, their Plumage mix'd white and black, very regularly; for which Reason our Sailors call them *Damiers*, that is, Chequers, or Draught boards; and the *Spaniards, Pardela's*. They have long Beaks somewhat hook'd, and in the Middle of them two Holes for Nostrils; their Tails spread, look like Furbelo-Scarves of Second-mourning. *Damiers.*

Being

A Voyage to

Error in the Charts.

Being always upon our Guard againſt the Currents, and the Errors in the *Dutch* Charts, which place Cape *Blanc* four Degrees more to the Weſtward than it really is, as has been obſerv'd by all the Ships that have put into S. *Katharine*, whence they have taken their Point, we began to ſound at 43 Degrees, 30 Minutes Latitude, and, according to my Computation, 52 Degrees, 33 Minutes Longitude, finding no Bottom; but in 46 Degrees, 50 Minutes Latitude, and 58 Degrees, 8 Minutes Longitude, we found 85 Fathom Water, the Bottom gray Sand mix'd with reddiſh. I reckon'd we were then 50 Leagues from Cape *Blanc*, by a Manuſcript Chart of *Grifon*, Maſter of Navigation of S. *Malo*; that is, 321 Degrees, 52 Minutes Longitude, from the Meridian of the Iſland *Ferro* or *Hierro*; or 323 Degrees, 32 Minutes, from that of *Teneriff*; which agreed well enough with the Soundings of ſome Ships which had ſeen that Cape. Whence it may be concluded, that, without regard to its exact Longitude, it is wrong laid down with reſpect to that of S. *Katharine*. It has been effectually obſerv'd, that the Deſart Coaſt, or of the *Patagons*, does not lie S. W. and S. W. and by W. as we ſee it in the Charts, but S. W. and by S. and S. S. W. which has brought many Ships into Danger. About 13 Leagues to the S. W. beyond our firſt Sounding, we found 75 Fathom Water; four Leagues farther on, ſtill holding the ſame Courſe, we had 70, then 66, the Bottom ſtill the ſame, as far as 49 Degrees and a half Latitude, where, in 75 Fathom, it was mix'd with Gravel, Owze, broken Shells, and little black and yellow Stones. In 50 Degrees, 20 Minutes, the Sand grows a little blackiſh, 60 and 65 Fathom Water. Still ſtanding S. W. within ſome ſmall Difference to the South, or Weſt, in order inſenſibly to draw near the Coaſt at 52 Degrees, 30 Minutes Latitude, and 65 Degrees, 45 Minutes Longitude, the Sand was gray, mix'd with little black and reddiſh Stones, in 55 Fathom Water. The Night between the 5th and 6th of *May*, we lay by, for Fear of ranging too near the Land,

and

and with good Reason; for the next Morning we found the Sea much chang'd, and about the Evening we discover'd a Low-land very plain, and five or six Hillocks like Islands, which bore W.S.W. nine or ten Leagues distant. Some took it for Cape *Virgins*, on the Credit of Journals, which place it in 52 Degrees, 30 Minutes, tho' it be more to the Northward in the Charts; but that Opinion did not answer our last Observation of Latitude. It is much more likely that it was the Cape of the *Holy Ghost*, in *Tierra del Fuego*. We heav'd the Lead, and found 36 Fathom Water, the Bottom a black Sand, mix'd with little Stones of the same Colour. *[Arrival at the Island of Tierra del Fuego.]*

The next Day, being the 7th, we distinctly saw *Tierra del Fuego*, which we coasted along, at four or five Leagues Distance. It is indifferent high, craggy in Precipices along the Shore, and appears wooded in Tufts: Over that first Coast appear high Mountains, almost ever cover'd with Snow. The Bearing of that Coast of the Island *Fuego*, may be ascertain'd to N.W. and by N. and S.E. and by S. in respect of the World, from the Streight of *Magellan* to that of *le Maire*, correcting a Half Rumb, or 23 Degrees of Variation N.E.

Having traced *Tierra del Fuego* till within five or six Leagues of Streight *le Maire*, we lay by, about four Leagues out at Sea, during the Night, in order to pass it the next Day. We had there 40 Fathom Water, the Bottom large clean Sand, as in Roads. That Night we felt heavy Blasts at S.W. by Squawls, or Gusts, which brought us Snow and Sleet from the Mountains up the Country: However, we fell off but little, a certain Sign that the Current was not violent, or that it set towards the Wind, which is not very likely, by Reason of the opposite Bearing of the Coast. *[Arrival at the Island of]*

Sunday the 8th of *May*, we sail'd for the Streight of *le Maire*, and easily knew it by three uniform Hills, call'd the *Three Brothers*, contiguous to one another, in *Tierra del Fuego*, over which, there appears an high Sugar-loaf Mountain *[Streight le Maire discover'd.]*

A Voyage to

Mountain cover'd with Snow, lying farther up the Country.

Plate V. About a League to the East of those Hills appears Cape S. *Vincent*, being a very low Land; then a second little Cape call'd Cape S. *James*; tho' I have Reason to believe, that Cape S. *Vincent* is much more to the North; and that the Cape to which they have given that Name, is Cape S. *James*, grounding this my Opinion on very ancient *Spanish* Manuscript Charts, perhaps taken from the Discovery of the *Nodales*.

When bearing N. N. W. and North from those little low Capes, as we drew near, we discover'd Streight *le Maire* (which they cover'd with *Staten-land*) opening by little and little, till at length, being three Quarters of a League East from the first of them, all the Opening appears. This Remark is necessary, to make sure of the Streight; because many Ships, and lastly, the *Incarnation* and the *Concord*, thought to have gone thro' there, tho' they were to the Eastward of *Staten-land*, and they only saw it on the West-side, being deceiv'd by the three Hills like the *Three Brothers*, and some Creeks like those of *Tierra del Fuego*.

The Tide of the Streight. No sooner were we got to the Eastward of Cape S. *Vincent*, than we found a strong and rapid Tide, as it were in a Torrent, which made us pitch so violently, that the Boltsprit-Topsail dipp'd in the Water; but having been inform'd of the Course of the Tide, which is six Hours, or six and a half, we had taken the Time that it might favour us, and ranged along the Coast of *Tierra del Fuego*, within a League and a Quarter of it at farthest. We enter'd successfully with the Flood, which runs rapidly to the Southward, and divides itself into two Currents; one of which takes along the Streight, which is but six or seven Leagues wide; and the other sets along *Staten-land* to the Eastward.

About the Middle of the Streight is Port *Maurice*, a little Creek, about half a League wide, at the Bottom whereof,

on

on the North-side, is a little River, where very good Water may be had, and easy Wooding.

Next to this, a Quarter of a League more to the Southward, is a Bay about a Quarter of a League wide, and much deeper, which some take for Port *Good Success*, and others for *Valentine*'s Bay, where there is Conveniency of Wood and Water, and even of a white and light Wood, whereof Top-masts might be made.

It is likely, that the Port of *Good-Success* ought to be the first Creek going out, after having turn'd Cape *Gonzales*, or of *Good-Success*. The Name itself seems to decide the Question that might be made, about the Situation of *Valentine*'s Bay and this; because it was really good Success for the *Nodales*, who made the Discovery, that they had pass'd Streight *le Maire*, and found beyond it a good Bay, where they might anchor in Safety. Be it as it will with the Name, several Ships, and lastly, the *Queen of Spain*, commanded by *Brunet*, put in there on the 6th of *November*, 1712, and anchor'd at the Mouth, in ten Fathom Water, an owzy Bottom: He water'd there in a little River

---

Plate V. p. 33. *explain'd in* English.

Streight le Maire, *At the Extremity of* South America, *between* Tierra del Fuego *and* Staten-Land, *in* 55 *Degrees,* 45 *Minutes of South-Latitude.*

Echelle de cinque Lieües Marines, *A Scale of five Sea-Leagues.*

Route, *The Ship's Way.*

Cap Gonzales, ou de Bon succés, *Cape* Gonzales, *or of* Good-Success.

Baye Valentin, Valentine's Bay.

Partie de l'Isle ou Terre des Estats, *Part of the Island of* Staten-Land.

Partie de l'Isle ou Terre du Feu, *Part of the Island of* Tierra del Fuego.

Baye de Bon succés, *The Bay of Good Success.*

Nord de l'aimant declinant au N. E. de 24 deg. *The North-Point of the Compass inclining* 24 *Degrees Eastward.*

Autre vue plus prés, *Another nearer View.*

A, *A Sugar-Loaf Hill up the Country.*

1, 2, 3, *Three Hills call'd the* Three Brothers.

Vuë de reconnoissance du detroit de Maire, *The View or Prospect by which to know Streight* le Maire.

Levé à la Bussole & par estime, 8 May, 1712, Frezier; *Taken by the Compass and by Estimation,* May *the* 8*th,* 1712, Frezier.

on the Starboard-side within; it look d a little reddish, but became clear and good. They also wooded there, and saw some Trees fit to make Top-masts. The Savages who came to see, did them no Harm: They are quite naked, tho' in a very cold Country. Some of them cover their Privities with the Skin of a Bird, and others their Backs with that of some Beast, as *Froger* represents those of *Magellan*'s Streights: They are almost as white as the *Europeans*. The S. *John Baptist*, commanded by the Sieur *de Villemarin*, of S. *Malo*, reports the same of those they saw in Streight *le Maire*, in *May*, 1713. Being becalm'd in the Middle of the Streight, and the Tide having drove him very near the Land, two *Piragua*'s of Savages from *Tierra del Fuego*, came aboard: They shew'd a strange Affection for any red Thing, and at the same Time an extraordinary Boldness; for the first of them that came up, spying a red Cap on the Head of an Officer, who came to receive him, snatch'd it off daringly, and put it on his Arm; another seeing the red Comb of the Fowl, tore it off to carry away; they would have taken away an Officer's red Breeches in the Boat: In short, they appear'd robust, better shaped than the *Indians* of *Chili*: The Women they had with them, handsomer, and all of them great Thieves. Their *Piragua*'s were made of the Barks of Trees, sew'd together very artificially. They despis'd all that was offer'd them to eat, and shew'd great Dread of the Cannon, near which they made Grimaces like Men in a Fright; it is likely, because they had seen some Ships fire, that put in. In short, one of *Brunet*'s Officers told me, that he having shot a Sea-Gull with his Piece, the Savages all fell down in a Fright.

About Noon, being to the Eastward of *Valentine*'s Bay, the Tide turn'd against us, and we could not stem it with a good Gale at S. W. which afterwards grew boisterous, with such dreadful Squawls and Gusts, that they brought the Gunwale to, under two Courses reef'd, yet it was requisite to carry more Sail to turn Cape S. *Bartholomew*, which

which is the Southermoſt of *Staten-Land*. We ſtood S. S. E. by the Compaſs, and yet our Courſe was ſcarce E. and by S. the violent Stream of Ebb carrying us away, as it ſets along the South-Side of *Staten-Land*, and returns that Way into Streight *le Maire*. At length we turn'd that Cape, and at the Cloſe of the Night it bore N. W. from us, about two Leagues diſtant; but the Weather growing tempeſtuous, we were oblig'd to lie by, under a Main-ſail back'd and reef'd, in great Fear for our Lives, knowing we were ſo near Land, and to the Windward of it. Then the moſt Undaunted took up ſerious Thoughts; for it may be ſaid, we only expected the Moment we ſhould be drove on the Coaſt, in a dark Night, and dreadful Weather, without any Hope of being able to help ourſelves. The Charts threatned inevitable Shipwreck; but, to our Happineſs, *Staten-Land* on the South-Side, does not bear E. S. E. and W. N. W. as laid down in the Charts, but lies E. and W. in reſpect to the Globe, and inclines a little to the North, near Cape S. *Bartholomew*, as we had obſerv'd before Night. In ſhort, lying by, we muſt have fallen off E. and by S. in reſpect of the Globe, and accordingly ſhould have inevitably periſh'd.

To this might be anſwer'd, that the ſame Current which carry'd us along the Coaſt of *Staten-Land*, might hinder our driving ſo much to N. E. as we ſhould otherwiſe have done, becauſe it muſt run as the Coaſt does, near the Land, and keep us at the ſame Diſtance. This Opinion would be probable, if other Ships had not better than we, obſerv'd the Poſition we ſpeak of. Beſides, it is evident that we drove very much to the Eaſt; for about Nine in the Morning, the Weather clearing up a little, we ſaw no more Land, tho' we could not be above two Leagues South, or S. E. from it at moſt, if it extends 13 or 14 Leagues from the Streight, as thoſe who have coaſted it, aſſure us.

Whilſt we were beginning to chear up and rejoyce for having eſcap'd being wreck'd, we were under much Uneaſineſs

easiness for the *Mary*, which we had left, at the Close of the Night, to the Leeward of us, and fallen off within about a League of the Coast; but our Joy was complete, when we espy'd her again the next Morning. She had suffer'd by the foul Weather; her Whipstaff had been broke, and her Beak-head shatter'd. A Calm succeeding, after that horrid Tempest, we had the Opportunity of sending Carpenters aboard her, to put her into a Condition to endure the Beating of the Sea, of which she had, till then, felt but a small Trial.

Accident befallen the Mary.

The Wind afterwards coming from N.N.W. to N.N.E. North about, a fresh Gale, we, in 24 Hours, recover'd Part of the Way we had lost lying by. From 43 Degrees and a half, to 57, we had had no Easterly Winds, and scarce any fair Days, but changeable and foggy Days, the Winds still ranging from North to South, West about, blowing fresh, excepting from 46 Degrees to 50, where we had two Days of gentle Wind. This Blast at N.N.E. was the more agreeable to us, because we did not expect any from thence; and it carry'd us from a Place where we had been in great Danger.

That good Wind started to S.E. in a violent manner, and obliged us to lie by some Hours; but it fell a little, and we took the Advantage of it for 24 Hours, well enough satisfy'd to endure the vehement Cold it brought, and the Tossing of a dreadful Sea, which still carry'd us on in our Course. It soon came back to South, and S.S.W. so violent, that we could scarce carry our two Courses reef'd.

May the 14th, being in 58 Degrees, 5 Minutes Latitude, and 64, or 61 of Longitude, we lost Sight of the *Mary*. We fancy'd she had tack'd to stand Westward; we tack'd an Hour after, in Quest of her, but in vain: We saw her no more till we came to *La Conception*.

The 17th, the Wind being at S.W. we stood, during the Night, S.E. and by S. for fear of falling in upon *Barnevelt*'s Islands, which some Manuscript Charts place in 57 Degrees Latitude, becauſe the Fog, the high Wind, and the rolling Sea, would not have permitted us to recover it, if we had fallen to the Leeward: 24 Hours after, the Wind came more to the Southward, and we bore away N. W.

We reckon'd ourſelves in 57 Degrees and a half Latitude, and 69, or 66 of Longitude, when the Wind blowing hard, and the Weather being foggy, about half an Hour after One in the Morning, the Starboard Watch ſaw a Meteor unknown to the oldeſt Sailors aboard; being a Light differing from that of the Ancients, call'd *Caſtor* and *Pollux*, and from Lightning; which laſted about half a Minute, and gave ſome little Heat. That unuſual Appearance in the cold Weather, and a high Wind, ſcared moſt of the Men, who ſhut their Eyes; and they ſpeak of it only as a Flaſh of Lightning, the Brightneſs whereof appear'd even thro' the Eye-lids; the others, who were more bold, affirm'd they had ſeen a Ball or Globe of a bluiſh Light, and very bright, about three Foot Diameter, which vaniſh'd among the Main-Top-Maſt Stays. *A new Meteor.*

All the Men look'd upon it to preſage a Storm: I did not like that Prophecy, the Weather was bad enough to fear worſe; for, beſides that, it was cold, and the Sea ran Mountain-high.: We had Wind a-head, which obliged us to tack every Moment, without gaining any thing in Longitude. However, the three next Days did not prove worſe: The 4th, we lay by ſome Hours reef'd; but the Wind, which had vary'd from Weſt to S. S. W. being come about to N. W. the Weather grew mild and clear'd up a little. The 23d and 24th, we got out of 59 Degrees, 58 Minutes Latitude, where we had ſtuck a long Time. The 25th, we were oblig'd to lie by ſome Hours, and the 26th were becalm'd.

I began then to flatter myſelf with the Hopes, that we ſhould ſoon be out of thoſe dreadful Parts, becauſe we reckon'd we were paſs'd the Longitude of Cape *Horn* nine or ten Degrees, that is, near 200 Leagues, when there came up such a violent Wind at N. W. and W. N. W. and such a dreadful Sea, that we were obliged to strike our Mizzen-Yard and Top-Mast to the very utmost. Being disgusted and tired with such a long Voyage, it griev'd me to the Heart that I had expos'd myself to such Hardships, being not only sensible of the present Evils, but in Fear for what was to come, if, as had hapned to several other Ships, we should be obliged to return and winter in the *River of Plate*, dreadful for its bad Anchorage, the Gusts of Wind, the Sand-Banks, and the Shipwrecks some of our Officers had been in. I compared the easy Life of the most wretched Persons ashore, with that of a Man of some Consideration aboard a Ship in a Storm; the fine Weather we had in *Europe* about the 27th of *May*, with those dark Days, which were not above six Hours long, and afforded us no more Light than a fine Moonshine-Night; the Beauty of the Fields adorn'd with Flowers, with the Horror of the Waves that swell'd up like Mountains; the sweet Repose a Man enjoys on a green Turf, with the Agitation and perpetual Shocks of so violent a Rolling, that unless a Man grasped something that was well made fast, there was no standing, sitting or lying; which had held us for near a Month, without Intermission: All this, added to the Remembrance of the terrible Night at **Streight** *le Maire*, did so dispirit me, that I was overcome with Grief, and then bethought myself of the Complaints of *Europa*, *Horace*, L. 3. Ode 27. & Sat. 6. L. 2.

―――― *Meliúsne fluctus*
Ire per longos fuit, an recentes
  Carpere flores?
O Rus! quando ego te aspiciam? quandoque licebit
Nunc veterum libris, nunc somno, & inertibus horis
Ducere sollicitæ jucunda oblivia vitæ?

It was our good Fortune that the Storm lasted but 24 Hours; after which, a N. W. Wind coming up by the West,

the South Sea.

West, and then a South to E. S. E. a fresh Gale, which is rare in those Parts, we got into 51 Degrees Latitude, and 84, or 82 of Longitude, according to our Computation; so that we could make Use of the S. W. and S. S. W. Winds, which are there most frequent. Three fair Days gave us Leisure to breathe after so much Trouble. The last of them, being the 2d of *June*, we saw, at our Larboard Watch, at Two of the Clock in the Morning, a Light run from our Mizzen-Pendant to the Main-Stay, where it vanish'd in a Moment. *A Meteor.*

The next Day, the Wind, which had shifted about from S. E. to N. E. by the South and West, after having blown violently at E. N. E. quite flatted there to a Calm, the Sea running very high, and then for three Days more took a different Turn, from North to South by the East, sometimes a fresh Gale, and sometimes a gentle Blast, and ceas'd at S. and by W. in about 45 Degrees Latitude, in a Calm, the Sea very rough. In fine, after having for two Days bore up against a strong Surge of the Sea coming from the North, by the Help of the East and South Winds, we came into 40 Degrees, 40 Minutes Latitude, where we were much surpriz'd to see Land 50 Leagues sooner than we expected, according to the Manuscript Chart of *S. Malo*, which we had found better than the *Dutch*, as far as Streight *le Maire*. In short, having found that *Pieter Goos* thrust back the Coast of the *Patagons* 60 Leagues too far Westward, in respect to *Brasil*, we had laid it aside; yet, according to his Longitude, we here came upon the Land very exactly with our Ship. *Land unexpectedly discover'd.*

The Manuscript Charts I have here spoken of, have been corrected on the Side of Cape *Blanc*, and of Streight *le Maire*, by the Journals of the S. *Malo* Ships, that have sail'd into the *South-Sea*; all which agree well enough about the Longitude of them both. I know not whether this general Agreement may form a certain Opinion, for there are visible Currents all along the Coast. From 32 to 35 Degrees Latitude, we advanc'd a little less than our *Remarks on the Computation.*

Com-

Computation: That might be occasion'd by an Error in the Log; but, on the other hand, from 37 to 41, we advanced more to the Southward by six or seven Leagues in 50; and three Days after, 16 Leagues and a half in a Computation of 70, that is, about a Quarter, afterwards diminishing; so that in about 49 Degrees, 50 Minutes, the Observations agreed very well with the Computation to Streight *le Maire*, which I found in the Longitude of 61 Degrees, 35 Minutes, answering to the 318 Degrees, 25 Minutes from the Island of *Hierro*, or *Ferro*, or 316 Degrees, 40 Minutes from the Meridian of *Teneriff*. From thence, I question whether the Charts could be corrected with good Reason, as to the Longitude of Cape *Horn* and the Coast of *Chili*; for the Ships that have ranged the same, assure us, they found Currents that drove them to the Eastward, at the same Time that they reckoned they had gain'd Ground to the Westward. Hence proceeds that Difference among the Sea-Charts, which allow 100 Leagues from the Streight to Cape *Horn*; whereas those that are Manuscript, allow only 40 or 50. This is very certain, that it is but in 55 Degrees, 50 Minutes Latitude, or 56 Degrees at the utmost; tho' in all the printed Sea-Charts it is laid down in 57 and a half, or 58 Degrees. As to the Distance between that Cape and the Coast of *Chili*, it is still less known, because few Ships have ranged the Coast of *Tierra del Fuego* on that Side. Prudence will not permit any to expose themselves to it, because the Winds generally come up from S.S.W. to West, so strong, that they might force them on the Coast. However, there is a Channel by which they might escape into the Streight of *Magellan*. That Channel was accidentally discover'd on the 25th of *May*, 1713, by the Tartane S. *Barbe*, as shall be said in another Place.

According to the Astronomical Observation of Father *Feüillée*, who places *La Conception* in 75 Degrees, 32 Minutes, 30 Seconds Longitude, that is, 25 Leagues more Westerly than the Manuscript corrected Charts, supposing that of

Streight

Streight *le Maire*, as I have mention'd it before, and 35 Leagues farther East than those of *Pieter Goos*, our Error was but of about 30 Leagues. It is certain, as has been said, that the Night we came out of that Streight, we fell off considerably to the Eastward, not only because the next Day we had no Sight of Land, but also because we found ourselves eight Minutes more to the North, upon a Computation of ten or twelve Leagues. Two Days after, in about 57 Degrees, 26 Minutes Latitude, we, on the other hand, found ourselves 22 Minutes more South, upon a Run of 70 Leagues. Afterwards, we were not sensible of the Currents for a long Time; for, after having been seven Days without an Observation, almost continually in foul Weather, tacking, lying-by, and running 80 greater Leagues in Longitude, we in 59 Degrees, 20 Minutes, found no Difference; and scarce any, three Days after, in 55 Degrees, 40 Minutes: But not having seen the Sun in eight Days, we found ourselves 27 Minutes more to the Southward than our Computation. This was in 53 Degrees, 6 Minutes Latitude, and perhaps 84, or 82 of Longitude.

According to this Error and the former, there seems to be Reason to conjecture, that there are two formal Currents, the one along the South-Sea, and the other along the North-Sea. This last must set from S. *Katharine* to *Tierra del Fuego*, S. S. W. and from the Streight S. E. and E. S. E. being determin'd to that Coast by the Coast of the *Patagons*, afterwards by the new Land of *Sibald*'s Islands, and that of *Tierra del Fuego* and *Staten-Land*. That in the South-Sea must pretty near follow the Bearing of the Land, from Cape *Pillars* to Cape *Horn*, and from thence turn off East and E. N. E. along *Barnevelt*'s Islands and *Staten-Land*, as Experience has shew'd us. It also follows, that there must be some little Current drawn by that of the Land's End, in the South Part of *Chili*, which likewise is agreeable to Experience; for when we made Land, we were still 20 Minutes South of our Computation.

Conjecture about Currents.

In fine, I do not pretend to determine the particular Setting of the Currents: They are not always of an equal Force, and near Land; some particular Cause may alter them, as is easy to comprehend. What I can affirm, is, that near Cape *Horn* they must set towards the N. E. for our *Mary* found herself upon the Island of *Diego Ramirez*, not only when she reckoned herself 40 Leagues from it, according to *Pieter Goos*, where it is thrust back 30 Leagues to the Westward farther than where the Manuscript Charts place it; but even when she reckoned herself two Degrees more to the South, tho' perhaps she was mistaken, and took the *Barnevelt*'s for *Diego Ramirez*.

Advice for turning of Cape Horn.

Thus every Ship which, coming from the East, designs to turn Cape *Horn*, is always to take one Half more than he thinks he has occasion for, of the South and West, either in regard that the Winds are always Westerly, or to be provided against the Currents that may set it back, as has actually happen'd to several Ships, which have found themselves upon the Land, when they thought they had weather'd the Cape, and were 40 or 50 Leagues out at Sea; whence, doubtless, has proceeded the Error in the *Dutch* Charts, which lay down too much Distance by the one Half between Streight *le Maire* and Cape *Horn*.

Be that as it will, we were very fortunate in that the Land was not cover'd with a Fog, and the West Wind strong; for at Break of Day, as we were standing North by the Compass, that is, N. and by E. according to the Globe, we were going to run upon a Point, which bore from us N. and by E. three or four Leagues distant, which we took for that of *Vallena*, because we had another to the East, which might be that of S. *Marcellus*. At length, we observ'd three or four little Islands a-stern of us, bearing S. S. E. which in all Probability were those of the Entrance of *Chili*, which the *Spaniards* call *Farellones de Carelmapo*, by which we had pass'd within half Cannon-Shot in the Night, and it was very dark. Being surprized to find ourselves so near Land, we immediately stood about with a

fresh

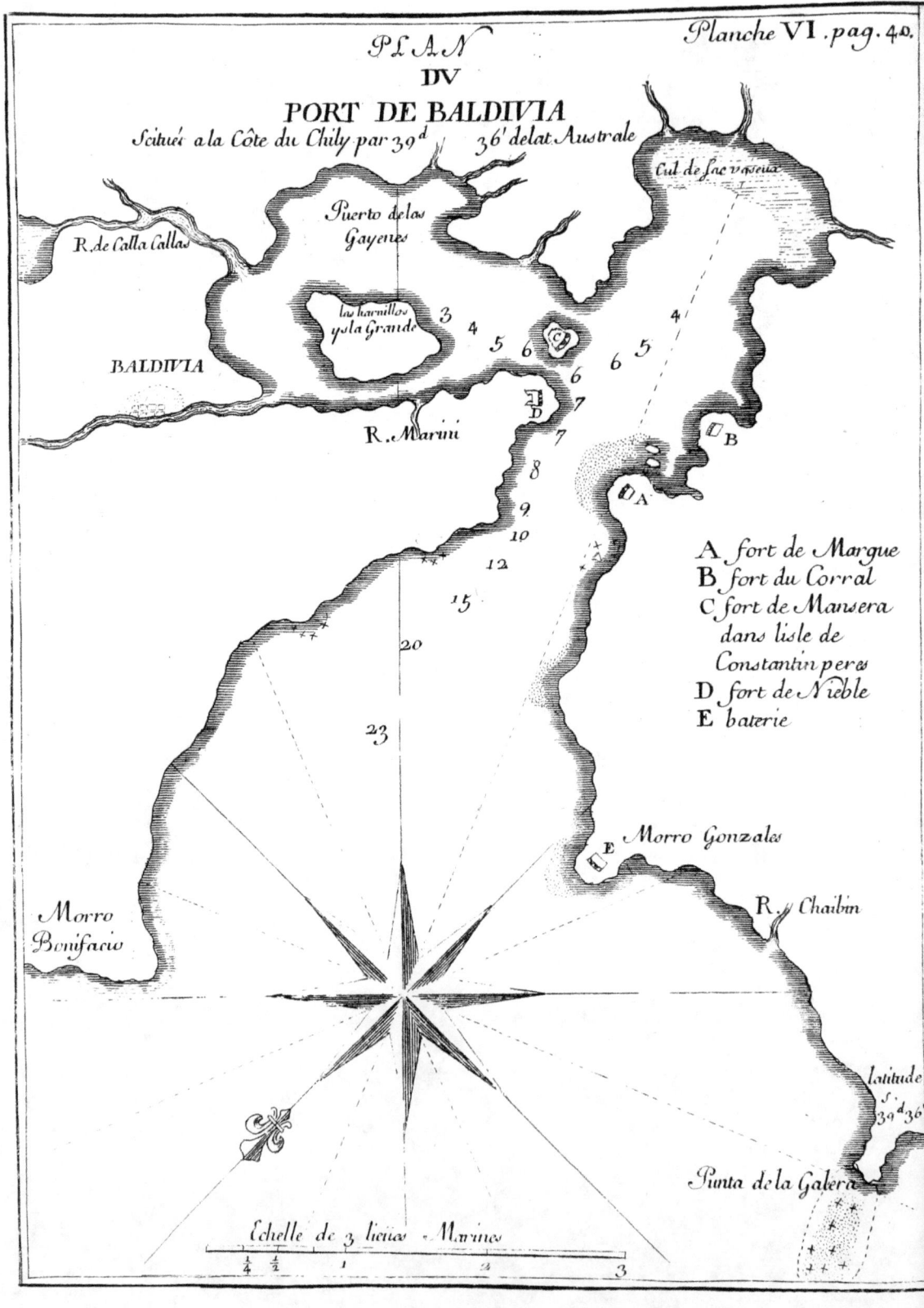

fresh Gale at W.S.W. with some sudden Showers of Rain and Hail: Thus we by Degrees stood out, because the Coast runs N. N. E. In the Evening we discover'd another Point at S. E. and by E. nine or ten Leagues distant, and one at N. E. and by N. by the Compass, about eight Leagues off, which it is likely was that of *La Galera*, where the Mouth of the River of *Baldivia* begins to form itself. I could have wish'd to have seen that Port, which, by the Help of Nature, and the Fortifications made there, is the best and strongest in all the Coast of the *South-Sea*: But that being no commodious Place for Ships that want to supply themselves with Provisions, because there is no Wine, and but little Corn, we only thought of holding on our Course for *La Conception*.

However, to satisfy my Curiosity, I procur'd a Plan of that Port, which I here add to the Account of it given me, by the Officers of our *Mary*, which put in there two Days after, as I shall mention in its Place.

The Description of the Port of Baldivia.

THREE Leagues to the Eastward of the Point *de la* Plate VI. *Galera* above-mention'd, is a Head-land call'd *Morro Gonzales*, on which is a Battery: To the N. E. by and E. of this, is that call'd *Morro Bonifacio*. At those two Heads

begins

Plate VI. Page 43. *explain'd in* English.

The Plan of the Port of *BALDIVIA*, on the Coast of *Chili*, in 39 Degrees, 36 Minutes of South Latitude.

A. *Fort* Margue.
B. *Fort* del Corral.
C. *Fort* Mansera, *in the Island of* Constantine Perez.
D. *Fort* Niebla.
E. *A Battery.*
Morro, *A Head land.*
Puerto de las Gayenes, *Port* Gayenes.
Isla Grande, *The Great Island.*
R. *A River.*
Punta, *A Point or Cape.*
Echelle de trois Lieües Marines, *A Scale of three Sea Leagues.*

begins the Mouth of the River of *Baldrvia*, which may be about four Leagues wide in that Place; but the two Coasts drawing together towards the S. S. E. form only a Gullet about half a League wide, the Entrance whereof is defended by four Forts, two on each Side; and more particularly by the first on the Larboard-Side, call'd *Fuerte de Niebla*, close under which, Ships must pass, to avoid the Sand-Banks, which reach out to the third Part of the Channel from the Foot of Fort *Marga*, being that on the Starboard-Side. If it be design'd then to come to an Anchor in the Port of *Corral*, they must come rounding towards the Starboard up to the Fort of the same Name, to anchor in four Fathom Water. If they will go up to the Town, that is, to the nearest Part of it, they must also pass by Fort *Niebla*, and that of *Manfera*, which is on the Island of *Constantine Perez*, ranging along the South-Side of a great Island, behind which, within the Continent, is a Port so commodious, that they there land Goods on a Bridge, or Key, without the Help of Boats.

From the Port of *Corral*, Boats have a shorter Way by half, along the Channel form'd by that great Island and the Land on the Starboard-Side. Ships do not pass that Way, for Fear of the Sands there in the Middle of it. Wheresoever a Ship anchors, it is safe against all Winds, because the Anchorage is good, the Bottom being a hard Owze, and there is no Sea, unless near the Port of *Corral* when the North-Wind blows. There is commodious Watering every where, and abundance of Wood, not only for Fewel, but also Timber to build Ships. The Soil there, when till'd, is extraordinary fertile for Grain and Pulse: Grapes indeed do not ripen, but the Want of Wine may be supply'd with Cyder, as in some Provinces of *France*; for there is such a Multitude of Apple-Trees, that there are little Woods of them.

The Advantageousness of that Port, has prevail'd with the *Spaniards* to erect several Forts to defend the Entrance against Strangers, because they look upon it as the Key of
the

the *South-Sea*. In short, the *Dutch* would have settled there, to secure a Resting-Place, in order to facilitate their entring the *South-Sea*. In 1643, they made themselves Masters of it; but Want, Diseases, and more particularly the Death of their General, having weaken'd them, they were oblig'd to withdraw themselves, and abandon their Baggage and 30 Pieces of Cannon, upon Advice of the Succours sent against them by the Marquis *de Mansera*, Viceroy of *Peru*.

At this Time there are above 100 Pieces of Cannon, *Artillery.* crossing one another, at the Entrance: Fort *Mansera* has 40, that of *Niebla* 30, that of *Marga* 20, and that of *Corral* 18, most of them Brass.

That this Port may not want Men, the Whites of *Peru Garrison.* and *Chili*, condemn'd to Banishment for any Crime, are sent thither; so that it is in the Nature of a Galley. There they are employ'd about the Fortifications, and other Uses of the Garrison, which is composed of none but such People, who are made Soldiers and Officers even during the Time of their Punishment. The Viceroy is to send 300000 Crowns a Year, to keep up the Fortifications and maintain the Garrison. That Supply is call'd *Real Situado*, in which are included the Provisions, and Stuffs to cloathe them. Tho' that Sum be not exactly furnish'd, the President of *Chili* never fails to send a good Supply every Year; of which the Governors make so considerable an Advantage, that this Post is the most sought after of any, on Account of the Revenue; tho' it ought to be disagreeable, by reason of the ill Company there is in it, and very tiresome during six Months of continual Rain every Winter.

The Town has also been re-peopled by banish'd Persons, and bears the Name of its Founder *Peter Baldivia*, after the *Indians* had ruin'd the first, built there. It is at present reckoned to contain 2000 Souls; is enclos'd with Walls to the Land, and defended by 12 Pieces of Cannon, which are 16 Pounders. It has one Parish-Church, and a House

of

of the *Jesuites*. The first Foundation was in the Year 1552, in a Plain, about four or five Fathom above the Surface of the Sea. Hard by, was a Fort to keep the *Indians* in Awe; but those People, tired with the tyrannical Government of the *Spaniards*, who made them work in the Gold Mines, which are there very plentiful, exacting of them the Value of 25 or 30 Crowns a Day for every Man, at length shook off that heavy Yoke, kill'd *Baldivia*, according to *Ovalle*, with a Club; and, according to the Tradition of the Country, cast melted Gold into his Mouth, saying, *Gorge yourself with that GOLD you so much thirsted after*. After which, they razed the Fort, and plunder'd the Town.

It is now rebuilt a little higher up the Land, on the Bank of the River.

Seven Leagues from thence, to the N. N. E. a Fort has been erected on an Eminence, call'd *las Cruzes*, or, *The Crosses*, in which there are two Pieces of Cannon, carrying Six-Pound Ball, and a Garrison of 20 Men, to prevent Excursions from the remoter *Indians*, who are not subdued. But enough has been said of a Place which I know only by Information from others: Let us return to our Voyage.

Lest the Winds should drive us down upon the Coast of *Baldivia*, we always endeavour'd to stand out, and with good Reason; for the Wind did come to W. S. W. and N. N. W. blowing so hard, that we could carry none but Main-Sail and Fore-Sail. A calm Interval brought it on again with more Violence at N. W. so that we were oblig'd to lie by: Then it came about to W. N. W. a fresh Gale, with some Squawls, and Flashes of Lightning.

The 15th of *June*, the Wind vary'd from W. S. W. to South, a small Gale, and calm.

S. Mary Island.

The 16th, we discover'd Land at East, about 12 Leagues distant. Some Hours after, we knew the Island of S. *Mary*, which is low, and almost plain. It is about three Quarters of a League in Length, from North to South.

To

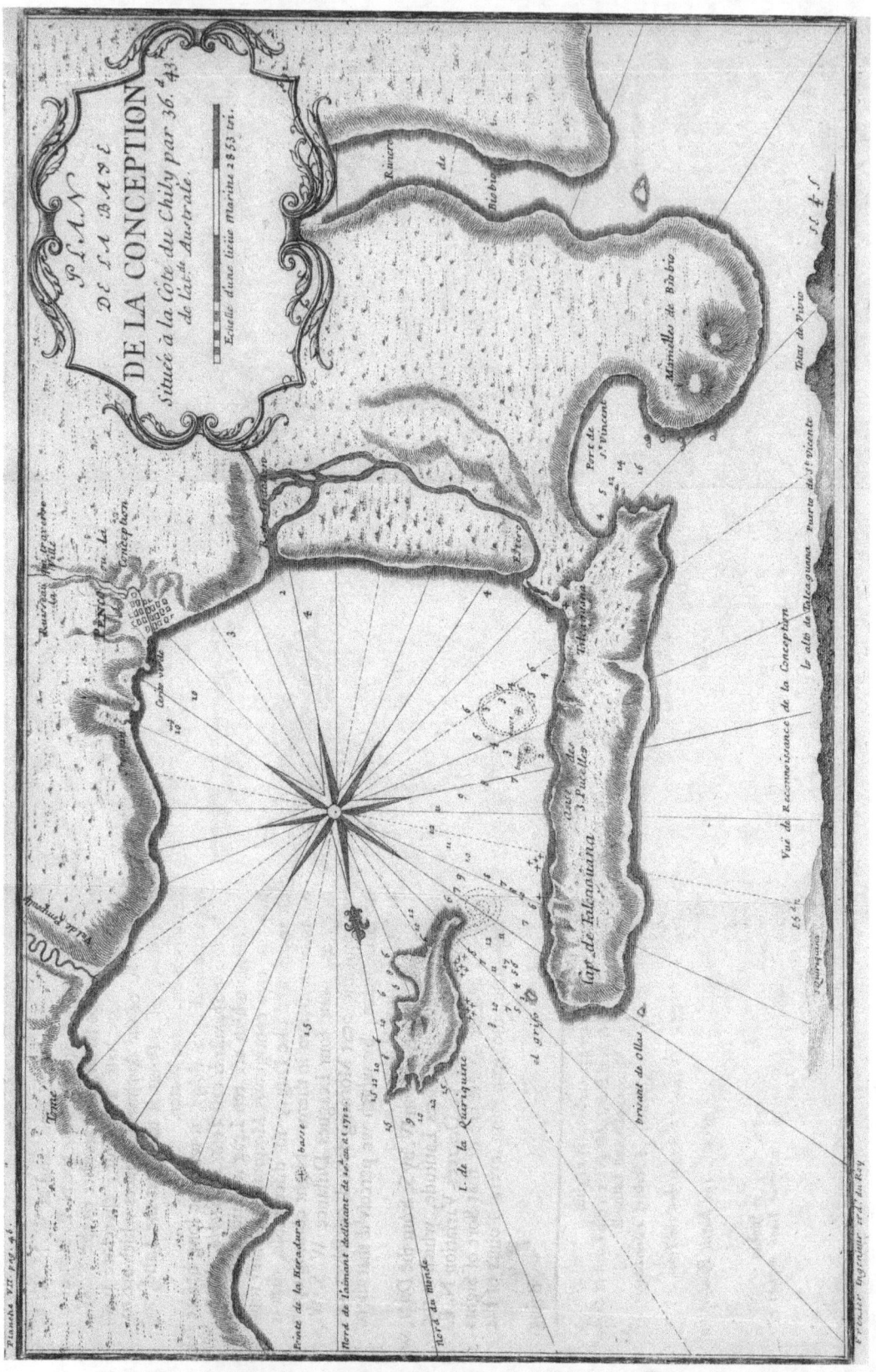

The material originally positioned here is too large for reproduction in this reissue. A PDF can be downloaded from the web address given on page iv of this book, by clicking on 'Resources Available'.

the South-Sea.   47

To the S. W. of it, is a little Island, and at W. N. W. a Rock, which is seen at a Distance. On the N. E. Side of it is said to be a dangerous Bank, and another to the N. W. which stretches out near half a League; therefore few think fit to make use of the Anchoring-Places which are to the North and South of a Point it has next the Land, as also because there is but little Water.

When we had pass'd by S. *Mary*, it was not long before we descry'd those the *Spaniards* call *Tetas de Biobio*, that is, *The Dugs of Biobio*, which are ten Leagues distant to the N. E. They are two contiguous Mountains, almost uniformly high and round like Dugs; so discernible, that it is impossible to be mistaken in them. Night coming upon us, we lay by at about four Leagues Distance W. S. W. from thence, and the next Morning found ourselves exactly in the same Place; by which we perceiv'd that there was neither Current nor Tide. *Tokens of La Conception*

At Noon we had an Observation W. by S. from the *Dugs*, and found 36 Degrees, 45 Minutes Latitude, which is the exact Position, with respect to 11 Degrees Variation N. E. Thus they appear at East; these are of that Sort of Sights of Land as vary little, tho' seen from several Points of the Compass. *See Plate VII.*

Being

Plate VII. Page 47. *explain'd in* English.

The Plan of the Bay of *La CONCEPTION*, on the Coast of *Chili*, in 36 Degrees, 43 Minutes of South Latitude.

Echelle d'une Lieüe Marine, 2853 Toises, *A Scale of a Sea-League, being* 2853 *Fathoms*.

Ruisseau qui traverse la Ville, *A Rivulet that runs thro' the Town.*

Basse, *A Shoal.*

Nord de l'aimant declinant de 10 D. au N. E. *The North Point of the Compass, inclining* 10 *Degrees to the N. E.*

Nord du monde, *The due North.*

Mamelles de Biobio, *Two Mountains call'd the Dugs of* Biobio.

Vue de reconnoissance de la Concepcion, *How the Land appears upon making* La Conception.

Alto de Talcaguana, *The High Land of* Talcaguana.

Puerto de S. Vicente, *Port S. Vincent.*

Tetas de Biobio, *The Dugs of* Biobio, *as above.*

Being assured of the Place where we were, by such certain Tokens, we made for the Port of *La Conception*, distinguishible by the Island of *Quiriquina*, two Leagues North of the *Dugs*. That Island is somewhat lower than the Continent, with which it forms two Passages: That to the W. S. W. is not very good for large Ships, tho' passable in Case of Necessity; but unless well known, it is dangerous venturing along a Ridge of Rocks, which advances far towards the Middle of it.

The N. E. Passage, being half a League wide, and clear of any Danger, we enter'd the Bay at Night, and very opportunely; for the N. W. Wind shifting to E. N. E. would have hinder'd us turning the Island half an Hour later. We anchor'd in 15 Fathom Water, the Bottom soft black Owze, South of the Point call'd *Herradura*, on the Continent, and S. E. and by S. of that of *Quiriquina*, which, with that above-named, forms the Entrance.

PART

PART II.

Containing the Voyage along the Coasts of Chili and Peru.

HE next Morning, being the 18th of *June*, after having sent the Yawl to see whether any Ships were at Anchor at *Talcaguana*, a thick Fog obstructing our Sight, we weigh'd, to go up thither; saluted the Town with seven Guns, and, according to Custom, it return'd us none. However, we proceeded, carrying little Sail, and sounding all the Way, towards our Yawl; which, after having view'd the Ships at Anchor, had posted herself with a Signal to shew she was a Friend, and brought us into bad Anchorage. It surpriz'd us very much to find only three Fathom Water, and then somewhat less; but at length, the Water deepening, we moor'd North and South, in four Fathom and a half Water, the Bottom owzy as before, two little Points of the Peninsula of *Talcaguana* bearing N. and by W. from us, upon a Line from each other, and the Creek of the *Three Maids* N. W.

To the Southward of us lay two *French* Ships, which had put in, in order to go and trade along the Coast: One of them was of *Marseilles*, call'd the *Mary-Anne*, commanded by the Sieur *Pisson*, of *Villafranca*, in the County of *Nice*; and the other call'd the *Concord*, commanded by the Sieur *Pradet Daniel*, of *S. Malo*, detach'd from Monsieur *du Guay*'s Squadron, who had sent him laden with Booty from *Rio de Janeiro*.

A Shoal in the Bay of La Conception.

Whilſt we were taken up enquiring for News, and all rejoicing to be in a Port, after ſo long a Voyage, the Sea, which the North Wind had ſwollen very high, fell off to ſuch a Degree, that our Keel touch'd a-ſtern: Then we perceiv'd that we were upon the Tail of a Shoal which appear'd to the N.N.E. about a Cable's Length diſtant. We immediately fell to-tow off to the Southward: The common Concern made all Men work with Vigour; and having at length found five Fathom Water under the Ship, we moor'd N.N.E. and S.S.W. with much Trouble; for, beſides the holding of the Anchors ſunk in the Owze, which could not be weighed without much Labour, we had the Inconveniency of a vaſt heavy Rain.

The Deſcription of the Bay of La Conception.

BY the Relation of this Accident it appears, that there are Marks to be obſerv'd for coming to an Anchor in the Bay of *La Conception*, tho' it be beautiful, and two Leagues wide from Eaſt to Weſt, by three from North to South. There are but two good Anchoring-Places in Winter, to be under Shelter from the North Winds, which are violent, and much to be apprehended during five Months in the Year. The one of them is at the South Point of *Quiriquina*, in ten or twelve Fathom Water, a Cable's Length from the Shore: This, tho' very good, and ſhelter'd from thoſe Winds, is not much frequented, becauſe too remote from the Town and from the Continent.

The other is at the Bottom of the Bay, near the Village of *Talcaguana*, in five or ſix Fathom Water, the Bottom ſoft black Owze. To come to this, Care muſt be taken to avoid the Tail of the Shoal I have juſt ſpoken of, which ſtretches out a Quarter of a League E.S.E. from what appears at Low-Water, where there are but three Fathom. To ſhun it, a Ship drawing near the Land on the Starboard-Side, is to keep a little low uneven Cape at the End of the

Marks to avoid the Shoal.

Bay, open with a little Hill of the same Height, lying somewhat higher up the Land, that is, the Cape of *Estero de Talcaguana*, with the Western Part of the little Hill of *Espinosa*: And if, at the same Time, the South Point of *Quiriquina* be kept in a Line with the West Part of the Island, you are exactly at the End of the Tail; then you draw near to the Houses of *Talcaguana*, till having closed *Quiriquina* by the Point *de la Herradura*, you may then come to an Anchor under Shelter from the North Wind. Care is also to be taken not to come too near *Talcaguana*, for Fear of a Shoal which is within a Cable's Length of the Shore. This is the only Place of Safety whilst the North Winds prevail; but in Summer you may anchor before the Town, N. W. from the Castle; or, which is the same Thing, S. E. from the South Point of *Quiriquina*, closing it with the outward Cape of *Talcaguana*; or before *Irequin*, a good Quarter of a League from the Shore, for Fear of the Rocks. There is every where Conveniency for Wooding and Watering, and even for Building of Ships. In Summer Boats go easily a-shore; in Winter the Case is quite alter'd.

The next Day after our Arrival, the second Captain was sent to compliment the *Oidor*, or Judge, and ask Leave to buy such Provisions as we had Occasion for, which was immediately granted; so that two Days after we fix'd a Store-House in the Town, and put a-shore at *Talcaguana* five or six Sailors sick of the Scurvy, who recover'd in a few Days. Thus, in our Passage, which lasted five Months to a Day, we lost not one Man, and had but few sick. It is true, it was time to put in, for several Men declin'd, and we wanted Fewel; but we soon found wherewith to supply all our Wants. *La Conception* is most certainly the best Place of all the Coast to put in, for all that a Ship can want, and for the Quality of the Provisions to be had there: And tho' the Town be in Reality no other than a good Village, there is agreeable Company enough to divert

52 *A Voyage to*

vert the Irkſomneſs of a Ship, in being continually with the ſame Perſons.

The Deſcription of the Town of Penco, *or* La Conception.

Its Situation. THE City of *La Conception*, otherwiſe call'd *Penco*, from the *Indian* Name of the Place, (*Pen* ſignifying to find, and *co* Water) is ſeated on the Coaſt of *Chili*, on the Edge of the Sea, at the Bottom of a Road of the ſame Name. On the Eaſt Side of it, in 36 Degrees, 42 Minutes, 53 Seconds of South Latitude, and perhaps in 75 Degrees, 32 Minutes, 30 Seconds of Longitude Weſt, or diſtant from the Meridian of *Paris*, according to Father *Feuillee*'s Obſervation.

It

Plate VIII. Pag. 52. *explain'd in* Engliſh.

The Plan of the Town of *La* CONCEPTION, or *PENCO*, on the Coaſt of *Chili*, in 36 Deg. 45 Min. of South Latitude. *Frezier*, 1712.

Vue de Penco, *a Proſpect of the Town of* Penco.

      Churches.
1. *The Cathedral.*
2. *The Jeſuites.*
3. San Juan de Dios, *Or, S.* John of God.
4. *S.* Dominick.
5. *S.* Francis.
6. *S.* Auguſtin.
7. *The Mercenarians.*
8. *The Hermitage.*

      Places of Note.
A. *The Square, or Market-Place.*
B. *The Council-Houſe.*
C. *The Palace.*
D. *The* Corps du Garde.
E. *The Fort and Battery.*
Baſſe de Chaloupes, *The Shoal of Boats.*
Echelle de 500 Toiſes, *A Scale of 500 Fathom.*

It was founded in the Year 1550, by *Peter Baldivia*, **Founder.** the Conqueror of *Chili*, after he had subdued the neighbouring *Indians*. He there erected a Fort, to secure a Retreat against them; but that General being kill'd, as has been said above, *Lautaro*, Chief of the *Indians*, made himself Master of it, and afterwards *Caupolican* utterly destroy'd it. A Supply sent from *Santiago*, settled the *Spaniards* there again; but *Lautaro* expell'd them a second Time: At last, the Viceroy of *Peru* having appointed his Son *Don Garcia Hurtado de Mendoza*, Governor of *Chili*, in the room of *Baldivia*, sent him by Sea with Recruits of Men He, under Colour of coming to conclude a Peace, possess'd himself, without any Trouble, of the Island of *Quiriquina*, whence he sent Men to build a Fort, on the Top of the Hills of *La Conception*, into which he put eight Pieces of Cannon.

At this Time there are no Remains of any Fort: The Town is open on all Sides, and commanded by five Eminences, among which, that of the Hermitage advances almost to the Middle, and overlooks it all. There is no **Fortifications.** other Defence but one low Battery, on the Edge of the Sea, which only commands the Anchoring Place before the Town, which is a good Quarter of a League from it, to the N. W. But besides that, it is not large, being only 35 Fathom in Length, and five in Breadth. It is in a bad Condition, one Half of it without any Platform, and but indifferently built with Rubbish.

The Cannon are in no better Condition: There are **Artillery.** nine of Brass, of irregular Bore, from 17 to 23 Pound Ball, that is, from 18 to 24 *Spanish*, whereof there are four mounted on scurvy Carriages. The greatest Pieces are 13 Foot and a Half long, 7 Foot and a Half from the Muzzle to the Trunnions, and 5 Foot 9 Inches from the Trunnions to the Ball: All the Touch-holes of these Guns are so wide, that they have been fain to fill them up with Iron. They were cast at *Lima*, in the Years 1618 and 1621.

At the Entrance into the Court of the House or Palace of the *Oidor,* or Judge, who commonly supplies the Place of a Governor, they have mounted two Four-Pounders near the *Corps du Garde,* which makes the Left-Wing of the Court. This Want of Fortifications is not made good by Men and able Officers.

Military Government. The *Maestre de Campo,* or Colonel, is a general Officer for all Martial Affairs without the Town. He is commonly one of the Inhabitants, who has no Experience, whom the President of *Chili* appoints for three Years: Under him is a Lieutenant-General to the President, a Major, and Captains. The Troops he commands are not numerous; reckoning only the Whites, they cannot make a Body of above 2000 Men, ill arm'd, both of the Town and Country about it; whereof there are two Companies of Foot, the rest being all Horse. They were all in the King's Pay, who allow'd for maintaining of 3500 Men, as well for the Defence of the Town, as of the advanc'd Posts and Garrisons, which the *Spaniards* call *Presidios:* But that Pay has fail'd for 14 Years past, and all Things are there in Disorder, the Soldiers having been obliged to disperse themselves up and down to get their Living; so that if the *Indians* should have a Mind to revolt, they would find the *Spaniards* defenceless, and, as it were, a-sleep, because they are at Peace. However, they have several little *Advanced Posts.* Forts, or little Intrenchments, in which they have some Pieces of Cannon, and some of the Militia and *Indian* Friends, when they think fit.

The farthest advanced of all those Posts, is that of *Puren,* 15 Leagues beyond the River of *Biobio.* A little more inward is that of *Nascimento,* or the *Nativity,* and towards the Coast of *Arauco,* the Walls whereof are almost quite fallen. In this there are six Pieces of Cannon, twelve Pounders, and four Four-Pounders, all without Carriages. Then along the River, is that of S. *Peter,* on this Side the *Biobio,* three Leagues from *La Conception.* Higher up, are *Talquemahuida,* S. *Christopher,* S. *Joanna,* and *Yumbel.*
Those

the South-Sea.

Those of *Boroa*, *Coloe*, *Repocura*, *Imperial*, and *Tucapel*, are destroy'd and abandon'd, and have had no Being but in our Maps, for 100 Years past.

The *Spaniards* indiscreetly neglect the Defences they might have against the Revolts of the *Indians*, whose Power they have been sensible of, and who only want an Opportunity to destroy them, whatsoever Appearance of Peace there be among them.

The Incursions of those People have occasion'd the removing of the Royal Court of Chancery, which had been establish'd at *La Conception* in the Year 1567, to the City of *Santiago*. At present, since the Reign of King *Philip* V. there is only one *Oidor*, that is, a Judge of the Court, who performs the Functions of Governor, or *Corregidor*, and Chief in the Administration of Justice; the Court, that is, the Civil Government of the City by the *Spaniards*, call'd *Cabildo*, being composed of six *Regidores*, or Aldermen, two *Alcaldes*, in the Nature of Bailiffs, one Royal Ensign, an *Alguazil Mayor*, or Head Sergeant, and one Depositary-General: All these Places are elective, and last but a Year. Their Dress is black, with a *Golilla*, or little Band standing out-right forwards, a Cloak and a Sword, after the *Spanish* Fashion. *Civil Government.*

The same Insurrections of the *Indians*, which remov'd from *La Conception* the Court of Royal Chancery, brought thither the Episcopal See, which is there at present; since the *Indians* possess'd themselves of the City call'd *La Imperial*, where it was establish'd, the Bishop withdrew himself to *La Conception*. His Diocese extends from the River of *Maule*, being the Boundary of that of *Santiago*, to *Chiloe*, which is the most Southern Province inhabited by the *Spaniards* and Christian *Indians*. He is Suffragan to the Archbishop of *Lima*, and his Chapter consists but of two Canons and some Priests. *Church Government.*

Few Persons well qualify'd, presenting themselves to be made Priests, he is obliged to conferr Orders on such as have but a small Knowledge in Grammar, and so little, that some can scarce read the Mass. It is easy to judge whether such ignorant Shepherds are capable of instructing their Flocks, and consequently how the *Indians* are instructed, whom the *Spaniards* are obliged to teach their Religion, when they are in their Service.

The Religious Men, excepting the *Jesuites*, are still more unlearned than the Clergy, and much addicted to Libertinism, which the too great Veneration the People have for their Habit, very much facilitates: I can here insert a Fragment of the Sermon which was made at the *Dominican* Monastery, on the Festival of their Patriarch, whilst we lay at *Talcaguana*. The Fryar, who made the Panegyrick, enlarged very much upon the Friendship there was between S. *Dominick* and S. *Francis*; whom he compared to *Anteros* and *Cupid*: Then, contrary to his own Interest, he affirm'd, That S. *Francis* was the greatest Saint in Heaven: That when he came into that Heavenly Abode, the Blessed Virgin finding no Place worthy of him, withdrew a little from her own, to make room for him between herself and the Eternal Father: That S. *Dominick* coming to Heaven, S. *Francis*, his Friend and faithful Witness of his Sanctity upon Earth, would, out of Humility, have given him the one Half of his Place; but that the Blessed Virgin, by those Offers, guess'd he was a great Saint, and would not have him share in his Friend's Place; therefore she withdrew a little farther, to allow an entire Place for him; so that those two Saints now sit between her and the Eternal Father. Let no Man believe I have invented this Story for my Pastime; there are Witnesses of three Ships who can testify the Truth of it. What Impression must such a Discourse make on the Minds of the People, and more particularly of the *Indians*? No doubt but that they will look upon the Apostles as inconsiderable Persons in the Sight of God, when compared with those two Founders of Orders; for those People are of a dull Comprehension in Matters of Religion.

Of the Indians of Chili.

ABOUT *La Conception* there are few *Indians* true Christians, besides those who are subject to, and in the Service of the *Spaniards*: And it is to be doubted whether they are so, any farther than being baptized, and that they are instructed in the essential Points of Religion. This is true, that they carry the Worship of Images almost to Idolatry: They take so great an Affection to them, as often to carry them Meat and Drink, judging no otherwise of Things than by what affects the Senses; so hard is it for them to conceive that there is a Soul in Man, which can be separated from the Body. If Care is not taken to make them comprehend, that by enjoying the heavenly Bliss, the Saints behold in God what is doing here below, that by that Means hearing our Prayers they intercede for us, and that their Images are no other than Signs made use of to represent to us their Actions; it is not to be thought strange that they should carry them Meat and Drink, since, seeing them magnificently clad and incens'd by the *Spaniards*, they imagine they must also have Food to nourish them, and that the Smoak of the Frankincense is not sufficient to support them.

The *Indians* on the Frontiers, especially along the Coast, seem well enough inclined to embrace our Religion, if it did not prohibit Polygamy and Drunkenness; nay, some of them will be baptized, but they cannot overcome themselves as to those two Points. The Bishop of *La Conception*, Don *Juan Gonzales Montero*, going a Visitation in his Diocese, in 1712, was expected beyond the River *Biobio*, by above 400 *Indians*, who, fancying that he came to take away their Wives, were positively for murdering of him. It was absolutely necessary, in order to save himself, to undeceive and assure them that he would not offer any Violence to them. I enquired carefully after their Religion, and was inform'd that they have none. A *Jesuite fuite* of Sincerity, Procurator of the Miffions the King of *Spain* maintains in *Chili*, affured me, That they were perfect Atheifts: That they worfhip'd no fort of Thing, and made a Jeft of all that could be faid to them as to that Point: That in Reality their Fathers made no Progrefs therein, which does not agree with the *Lettres Edifiantes*, written by the Miffioners, Vol. 8. where it is faid, That they converted many at *Nahuelhuapi*, in 42 Degrees Latitude, and 50 Leagues from the Sea, among the *Puelches* and the *Poyas*, in the Year 1704. Neverthelefs, they penetrate very near to the Streights of *Magellan*, and live among thofe People without receiving any Harm from them: On the contrary, thofe *Indians* have a fort of Veneration for the Miffioners; but they may, in Procefs of Time, make fome Advance, becaufe they defire the prime Caciques to give them their eldeft Sons to be inftructed. They breed up a certain Number of them in their College of *Chillan*, whofe Penfions the King is to pay; and when grown up, they fend them back to their Parents, inftructed in the Chriftian Religion, and bred up to *Spanifh* Literature; fo that there are at prefent fome Chriftians among them, and who are fatisfy'd with one Wife.

One Sign that the *Indians* of *Chili* have no Religion, is, That never any fort of Temples nor Idols have been found among them for their Worfhip, as is ftill to be feen in feveral Parts of *Peru*, efpecially at *Cufco*, where the Temple of the Sun is ftill to be feen; and if there be fome Appearance of Divination among them, it is no other than the Ufe of the Fifh, that frequently ferves them. There are fome who believe there is another Life, for which they put into the Monuments of the Dead, Meat, Drink, and Cloathing. The *Spanifh* Curates have not abolifh'd that Cuftom among thofe who are Chriftians: As it turns to their Account, they fupply the Place of the Dead Perfon, as has been feen at *Talcaguana*.

The Wives of thofe who are not Chriftians, ftay feveral Days by their Husbands Graves to cook for them, to

pour

pour *Chicha* on their Bodies, that is, their Liquor, and to fit their Equipage as for undertaking a very long Journey. It is not hence to be concluded, that they have any Notion of the Spirituality of the Soul, or of its Immortality: They look upon it as something corporeal, which is, to go beyond the Sea to Places of Pleasure, where they shall abound in Meat and Drink: That they shall there have several Wives, who will bear no Children, but will be employ'd in making them good *Chicha*, in serving them, *&c.*

However, this they believe very confusedly, and many of them look upon it as a Conceit of their own framing. Some of the *Spaniards* imagine, that this Notion has been instill'd into them by a Corruption of the Doctrine which S. *Thomas* the Apostle taught, on the other Side of the *Cordillera*, or Ridge of Mountains which separates *Chili* from the Inland of *South America*; but the Reasons on which they ground their Belief, that the said Apostle and S. *Bartholomew* came into that Province, are so wretched, as not to deserve being mention'd.

The *Indians* of *Chili* have no Kings or Sovereigns among them to prescribe Laws to them: Every Head of a Family was Master in his own House; but those Families increasing, those Chiefs are become Lords of many Vassals, who obey, without paying them any Tribute: The *Spaniards* call them *Caciques*. All their Prerogative consists in commanding in Time of War, and in exercising Justice. They succeed in that Dignity by the Right of Eldership, and every one of them is independent of any other, and absolute Master in his own Dominions. I do not only speak of those who are Savage, or Unconquer'd, but even of those who are reckoned Subdued; for tho', by a Treaty of Peace, they have consented to own the King of *Spain* for their Prince, they are not obliged to pay him any other Acknowledgment, but a Supply of Men to repair the Fortifications, and defend themselves against the other *Indians*. The Number of these is reckon'd to be 14 or 1500. *Their Government.*

Servitude of those who are subdu'd. It is not so with those who are subdu'd, and call'd *Yanaconas*; these being Tributaries to the King of *Spain*, to whom they pay the Value of ten Pieces of Eight yearly, either in Silver or Commodities: And they are also employ'd in the Service of the *Spanish* Families, to whom his Catholick Majesty, either as a Reward for their brave Actions, or Service, or for Money, grants a Number of *Indians*, who are obliged to attend them as Servants, and not as Slaves; for, besides their Diet, they are to pay them 30 Crowns a Year; and if they will not serve, they are free from it upon paying their Master ten Crowns, which is call'd *Encomienda*. Their Age to serve is from 16 to 50; above and under they are exempt from it: Besides, the *Indians* thus given *in commendam*, the *Spaniards* in *Chili* only have some in their Service who are Slaves, bought of the free *Indians*, who freely sell them their Children for Wine, Arms, Utensils, &c. This being an Abuse connived at, contrary to the King's Ordinances, they are not Slaves like the Blacks; those who buy, cannot sell them again, unless it be privately, and with the Slave's Consent, who, by means of a Letter, call'd *De Amparo*, that is, of Protection, may demand his Liberty. To this end, there is in every Town, and in the Court at *Santiago*, a Protector of the *Indians*, to whom they make Application.

By reason also of the Toleration or Connivance, the Sons of Slaves do not follow the Fate of the Mother, as is ordain'd in *Justinian*'s Institutes, when the Father is a Servant *in Commendam*; because the latter being permitted, the Advantage is to accrue to him preferable to the other. The Mixture of *Spanish* Blood makes those free whom the Father will own; and entitles the *Mestices*, that is, the Sons of a *Spaniard* and an *Indian* Woman, to wear Linnen.

To know the Original of this sort of Slavery, we must look back to the Conquest of *Peru*. The private Persons who are the first Authors, ought, by their Contract with the King of *Spain*, to have the *Indians* as Slaves during their

their whole Life; after which, they were to fall to the eldest of the Family, or to their Wives, in case they died without Issue. There was some Shew of Justice in that, not only to reward them for their Sufferings and Bravery, but also because they had undertaken and carry'd on that War at their own Charge. However, because they treated their Slaves inhumanly, some good People taking Compassion on those Wretches, earnestly represented to the Court of *Spain*, that they abused them, not only by excessive Exactions, but also that they exercised the utmost Cruelties on their Persons, even to the killing of them.

This Excess was taken into Consideration; and, to redress it, the Emperor *Charles* V. King of *Spain*, in the Year 1542, sent *Blasco Nunnez Vela* unto *Peru*, as Viceroy, with Orders to cause the *Indians* to be discharged of the Impositions laid on them, and restored to their Liberty. But the principal Wealth of the Colonies consisting in the great Number of Slaves, especially among the *Spaniards*, who scorn to labour, most of them refused to obey those Orders, which they thought too severe; and the Execution whereof would, in some Measure, have reduced them to Beggary: They would not, therefore, acknowledge the new Viceroy, which occasion'd those bloody Civil Wars, which we have at Length in *Zarate*.

At last, to make the Servitude of the *Indians* the more easy, and not ruin the *Spaniards*, the King seiz'd on those whose Masters died, and afterwards gave them to his Officers, and to several others, upon the Conditions abovemention'd.

That Servitude of *Encomienda* has been the Occasion of the bloody Wars the *Spaniards* have had with the *Indians*: They were willing to acknowledge the King of *Spain* for their Sovereign; but, as Men of Sense, they would preserve their Liberty. And upon these Conditions the last Peace was concluded, about 25 or 30 Years ago; for tho' those People seem Savages to us, they know very well how to agree about their common Interest: They assemble with

the

the Elders, and those who have most Experience; and if they consult about any Martial Affair, they, without Partiality, make choice of a General of known Merit and Valour, and punctually obey him: By their Conduct and Bravery, they formerly hinder'd the *Ingas* of *Peru* from coming among them, and put a Stop to the Conquest of the *Spaniards*, whom they have confined to the River *Biobio*, and to the Ridge of Mountains, call'd *La Cordillera*.

Assemblies of Indians.
The Manner of their Assemblies consists in carrying into a good Plain, chosen for that Purpose, a great Quantity of Liquor; and when they have begun to drink, the Eldest, or he who on some other Account is to make a Speech to the rest, undertakes to lay before them the Matter in hand, and delivers his Opinion with much Solidity; for they are said to be naturally eloquent: After which, the Resolution is taken by the Plurality of Votes, and publish'd by Beat of Drum; three Days are allow'd to consider on it, and if in that Time no Inconveniency be found, the Project is infallibly put in Execution, after confirming the Resolution, and settling the Means to bring it to Effect.

Those Means are within a very small Compass; for the *Caciques* furnish their Subjects with nothing to make War: They only give them Notice, and every Man brings with him a Bag of Meal, either of Barley or *Indian* Corn, which they put into Water, and live upon it many Days. Each of them has also his Horse and Arms always in a Readiness;

Plate IX. p. 62. *explain'd in* English.

A. *An* Indian *of* Chili, *in the Posture of Playing at* La Sueca, *a Sort of Bandy.*
B. *An* Indian *Woman holding the Liquor for her Husband.*
C. Cahouin touhan, *or an* Indian *Festival or Rejoycing.*
D. Spanish *Guards appointed to prevent Disorders.*
E. Pivellea, *A Whistle, or Pipe.*
F. Paquecha, *A Drinking-Dish with a long Beak.*
G. Coulthun, *A Drum.*
H. Thouthouca, *A Trumpet.*

A. Indien du Chili en Macuñ jouant a la Sueca, jeu de croce
B. Indienne en Choñi. C. Cahouin touhan ou fête des Indiens
D. Gardes Espagnoles pour empecher le desordre. E. Pivellca ou Sifflet
F. Paquecha ou tasse a bec. G. Coulthun ou tambour. H. Thouthouca ou trompette

ness; so that they form an Army in a Moment, without any Expence; and, to prevent any Surprize, there is always, in every *Caziqueship,* on the highest Eminence, a Trump, or Instrument made of a Bull's Horn, which can be heard two Leagues about. As soon as any Accident happens, the *Cacique* sends to sound that Horn, and every Man knows what is in Agitation, to repair to his Post.

" Our Poverty, said the *Scythians* to *Alexander* the Great,
" will always be more active than your Army laden with
" the Spoils of so many Nations; and when you will
" think us very remote, you will find us at your Heels;
" for with the same Celerity we pursue and fly from our
" Enemies.

Their Arms.
Their usual Weapons are Pikes and Lances, which they dart with extraordinary Dexterity. Many of them have Halberts, which they have taken from the *Spaniards*; they have also Axes and Broad-Swords, which they buy of them, wherein the latter fail in Point of Policy; for it is to be fear'd lest they be some day scourged with their own Rods: They also, but seldom, make use of Darts, Arrows, Clubs, Slings, and Leather Nooses, which they manage so dextrously, that they take hold of a Horse, *Noosing of Horses.* where-ever they please, in his Career. Those who want Iron for their Arrows, make use of a Sort of Wood, which being harden'd at the Fire, is not much inferiour to Steel. By long waging War with the *Spaniards*, they have got Coats of Mail, and all Sorts of Armour; and those who have none, make it of raw Hides, which is Proof against a Sword, and has this Advantage over the other, that it is light, and less cumbersome in Fight; in short, they have no Uniformity in their Weapons, but every Man makes use of those he is most expert at.

Their Manner of Fighting is, to form Squadrons in Files of 80, or 100 Men, some arm'd with Pikes, and others with Arrows intermix'd; when the foremost are broken, they succeed one another so quick, that it does not appear that ever they gave Way They always take

care

care to secure a Retreat into the Bogs, or Morasses, where they are safer than in the best Fortress. They march to Battle in a very fierce Manner, by Beat of Drum, with their Weapons painted, their Heads adorn'd with Plumes of Feathers; and before they engage, the General commonly makes a Speech; after which they all beat with their Feet, and give hideous Shouts, to encourage one another to fight.

When they are obliged to fortify themselves, they make Palisadoes, or else only entrench themselves behind great Trees: Before them, at certain Distances, they dig Pits, the Bottoms whereof they set full of Stakes upright, with Briars, and cover them with Turf, to impose upon their Enemies. Unhappy those who fall into their Power! for they tear them, draw out their Hearts, which they cut in Pieces, and wallow in their Blood like wild Beasts. If it happens to be a Man of any Note, they put his Head upon the Point of a Pike, afterwards drink out of the Skull, and at last make a Dish of it, which they keep as a Trophy; and of the Leg Bones they make Flutes for their Rejoycings, which are only dismal Drunken Bouts, and last as long as the Drink they have brought. This Debauch is so pleasing to them, that those who are Christians, celebrate, or rather prophane, the Festivals of their Religion in that Manner.

Festivals. I was Witness of a Festival the Slaves of an *Encomienda*, belonging to two *Spaniards* of the Name of *Peter*, kept on the Day of the Name of their Masters, in the Village of *Talcaguana*, near which we lay at Anchor. After hearing Mass, they mounted on Horseback to ride at a Fowl, as they ride at a Goose in *France*, with this Difference, that they all fall upon him who bears away the Head, to take it from him, and carry it to him in Honour of whom the Festival is kept. Running at full Speed, they jostled to get it from him, and gather'd up, as they ran, all that they threw down. After that Course, they alighted to dine; the Entertainment consisting of a great Number of Dishes, made of Calabashes, or Gourds, which they call *Mate*, placed in a Ring on the Grass, full of Bread steep'd in a Liquor made of Wine, and *Maiz*, or *Indian* Wheat. Then the *Indians*, who treated, brought each of the Guests a Bomboo Cane, about 18 or 20 Foot long, garnish'd with Bread, Flesh and Apples, made fast about it: Then having mov'd with a Cadency about the Meat, a little red Standard, with a white Cross in the Middle, was given to him that was appointed to make the Compliment to the *Indians*; they, on their part, deputed one to answer him, who made such a long Discourse of Compliments, that it lasted above an Hour: I ask'd the Reason, and was told, it was the Effect of their Style, which is so diffuse, that to talk of the most inconsiderable Thing, they go back to its very Original, and make a thousand needless Digressions.

When they had eaten, they mounted on a Sort of Scaffold made like an Amphitheatre, the Standard being in the Middle, and the others with their long Canes by it. There, being adorn'd with Feathers of Ostriches, Flamenco's, and other Birds of sprightly Colours, stuck round their Caps, they fell to singing to the Sound of two Instruments, made of a Piece of Wood, with only one Hole bored through it; blowing in which, either stronger or more gently, they form'd a Sound more or less sharp, or flat. They kept Measure alternatively with a Trumpet made of a Bull's Horn, fastned to the End of a long Cane, the Mouth of which had a Pipe, that sounds like a Trumpet. They fill'd up this Symphony with some Strokes of a Drum, whose heavy and doleful Sound was answerable enough to their Mien; which, in the Height of their Exclamations, had nothing in it that was gay. I observ'd them attentively on the Stage, and did not, during the whole Festival, see one smiling Countenance among them.

The Women gave them *Chicha* to drink, being a Sort of Beer, of which more hereafter, with a Wooden Instrument about two Foot and a half long, consisting of a Handle-

Cup at one End, and a long Beak at the other, with a winding Channel cut along it, to the end the Liquor may run out gently into the Mouth through a little Hole bored in the Bottom of the Cup or Dish at the Head of the Channel. With this Instrument they make themselves as drunk as Beasts, singing without Intermission, and all of them together; but in so unartificial a Tone, that three Notes would suffice to express the Whole.

The Words they sing have also neither Rhyme nor Cadency, nor any other Subject than whatsoever occurrs to their Fancy: Sometimes they recount the History of their Ancestors; sometimes they speak of their Family, and sometimes say what they think fit of the Festival, and of the Occasion of celebrating it, &c.

This same Track holds on Day and Night, as long as they have any thing to drink, which does not fail till after some Days; for besides that he, in Honour of whom the Festival is kept, is obliged to provide much Liquor; every one of those who celebrate it, whether invited or not invited, brings some. They sometimes drink and sing ten or fifteen Days successively, without ceasing: Those who are overcome with Drunkenness, do not therefore give out; when they have slept in the Dirt, and even in Ordure, they remount their Theatre to fill up the vacant Places, and begin a-fresh. We saw them relieve one another after this Manner Day and Night, a heavy Rain and stormy Wind no way making them desist, for the Space of thrice 24 Hours; those who have not Room on the Theatre, sing below, and dance about it with the Women, if it may be call'd Dancing, to walk two and two, bowing and standing upright again somewhat hastily, as it were to leap, without ever taking their Feet off the Ground; they also

also dance in a Ring almost like us. This Sort of Diversion, which they call *Cabouin Touhan*, and the *Spaniards Borrachera*, that is, Drunkenness, is so pleasing to them, that they do nothing of Moment without it; but they take care to appoint Part of their Men to guard them, whilst the rest get drunk and divert themselves. Those who are Christians cannot prevail upon themselves to quit that Sport, tho' the Sins it occasions are represented to them daily: In short, then it is that Quarrels are revived; and it is affirm'd, that they referr it to those Meetings to take Revenge of their Enemies, to the end that, being drunk, they may appear the more excusable for the Murders they commit. Others make themselves so extremely drunk, and for so many Days successively, that they burst, as happened at the Festival I speak of; because, besides the *Chicha*, they had much Wine.

Notwithstanding these frequent Debauches, they live whole Ages without any Distempers; so strong are they, and used to the Inclemencies of the Air: They endure Hunger and Thirst a long Time in War and Traveling. *Their Constitution and Food.*

Their common Food at their own Homes is a Sort of Earth-Nuts, or Roots, or *Taupinambours*, which they call *Papas*, of a very insipid Taste, *Maiz*, or *Indian* Corn in the Ear, only boil'd or roasted, Horses and Mules Flesh, and scarce ever Beef, which they say gives them the Gripes. They eat the *Maiz* several Ways, or, only boil'd in Water, or parch'd among Sand in an Earthen-Pot, and afterwards ground into Meal mix'd with Water. This they call *Oullpo*, when it is potable; and *Rubull*, when made into thick Hasty-pudding with Pepper and Salt. For grinding of the *Maiz*, after it is parch'd, instead of a Mill, they have oval Stones about two Foot long, on which, with another Stone eight or ten Inches long, they crush it on their Knees by Strength of Arm: This is the common Employment of the Women. Of this Meal they make Provision to go to the Wars, as has been said; and this is all their Provision. When they come to a Place where there

there is Water, they mix it in a Horn call'd *Guampo*, which always hangs at the Pommel of their Saddles, and thus eat and drink without stopping.

Their Drink. Their common Drink is the *Chicha* we have spoken of; they make several Sorts of it: The most common is that of *Maiz*, or *Indian* Corn, which they steep till the Grain bursts, as if it were to make Beer; the Best is made with *Maiz* chew'd by old Women, whose Spittle causes a Fermentation like that of Leaven in Dough. In *Chili*, much is made of Apples, like Cyder: The strongest, and most valued, is that which is made of the Berries, or Seeds of a Tree call'd *Ovinian*; it is much like that of the Juniper in Bigness and Taste; it gives the Water a Tincture like *Burgundy* Wine, and a strong Taste, which makes them drunk for a long Time. Their Manner of Eating among themselves, is to lie along on their Bellies, supporting themselves with their Elbows in a Ring, and to make their Wives serve them. The *Caciques* begin to make use of Tables and Benches, in Imitation of the *Spaniards*.

Their Colour. Their natural Colour is dark, inclining to Copper-Colour, wherein they differ from the *Mulatto's*, which proceeds from a Mixture of Whiteness and Blackness: This Colour is general throughout all *America*, as well North as South; whence it is to be observ'd, that it is not the Nature of the Air they breathe there, or of the Food the Inhabitants use, but a particular Affection of the Blood; for the Descendents of the *Spaniards*, who are settled there, and marry'd to *Europeans*, and have continued unmix'd with the *Chilinians*, are of a finer and fresher White and Red, than those in *Europe*, tho' born in *Chili*, fed almost after the same Manner, and commonly suckled by the Natives of the Country.

The Blacks they carry thither from *Guinea*, or *Angola*, do also retain their natural Colour from Father to Son, when they keep to their own Kind.

It

It is not so with the Air of *Brasil* and the *French* Islands: The *Creolians*, tho' born without any Mixture of Blood, lose there that ruddy Whiteness of the *Europeans*, and take a Sort of Lead-Colour. Here no other Alteration is perceiv'd, but that which is occasion'd by the Mixture of the several Kinds, very common in the *Spanish* Colonies, much in *Chili*, but more particularly in *Peru*; where, among 30 Faces, scarce two can be found of the same Colour; some come from Black to White, as the *Mulatto's*; others fall from White to Black, as the *Zambo's*, Sons of *Mulatto's*, and Blacks: Some come from the *Indian* Colour to White, as the *Mestizo's*; and others fall from the *Mestizo* to the *Indian*; and then each of these Mixtures causes others *ad infinitum.*

From what has been said, it seems lawful to believe, that, among the Children of our common Parent, God has formed three Sorts of Colours in the Flesh of Men; the one white, another black, and a third of a reddish Colour, which has something of the one and of the other.

The Scripture does not perhaps mention this last Kind; but there is no Doubt but that it speaks of the Second, in the Person of *Chus*, *Noah*'s Grandson, signifying Black, whence the *Abyssins* and the Inhabitants of *Chusistan*, or *Churistan*, are derived, because of the Resemblance of the Name. This Opinion appears to me more probable, than to ascribe the Colour of the *Indians* to some peculiar Diseases, as some Physicians have fancy'd.

Be that as it will, the *Indians* of *Chili* are well shaped: They have large Limbs; their Stomach and Face broad, without any Beard, not agreeable; their Hair as coarse as a Horse's, smooth or lank, wherein they also differ from the Blacks and from the *Mulatto's*; for the Blacks have no Beard or Hair, but a very short soft Wool, and the *Mulatto's* have always short Hair, and much curl'd. As for the Colour of the Hair, that of the *Indians* is generally black,

Shape and Hair.

black, and it is rare to find any inclining to fair, perhaps because they often wash their Heads with *Quillay*, of which I shall speak hereafter.

Puelches. The *Puelches* cut their Hair to their Ears, and have extraordinary small Eyes, which makes the Women hideous. All of them naturally have none or very little other Beard besides Whiskers, which they pull up with Pincers made of Shells.

There are some among those of the Plain, who have a white Complexion, with a little Red in the Face: These are descended from the Women taken in the *Spanish* Towns they destroy'd, as *Angol, Villarica, Imperial, Tucapel, Baldivia,* and *Osorno,* where they carry'd all away, Laity and Religious, by whom they had Children, who still retain some Affection for the Nation of their Mothers, which is the Reason that they are almost always at Peace; such as those toward *Arauco,* tho' their Country is the Theatre of War made by their Neighbours. Since that time, no Monasteries of Nuns have been permitted, except at *Santiago.* However, the Bishop of *La Conception* will build one there, without apprehending the like Prophanation.

Their Habits. The Habit of the *Indians* is so plain, that they are scarce cover'd: They wear a Wastecoat or Jerkin, which reaches to the Waste, so closed, that there is only the Hole for the Head, and one Arm to put it on, which they call *Macun*; a Pair of Breeches open down the Thighs, scarce cover their Nakedness. Over all, in rainy Weather, or for a more decent Garb, they have a sort of square long Cloak like a Carpet, without any Shaping, in the Midst of which is a Slit to put their Heads through: On the Body it looks almost

---

Plate X. Page 70. explain'd in English.

A. *A* Chilinian Indian *Woman grinding Maiz,* or Indian *Corn, to make Meal.*

B. *An* Indian *in his loose Garment, call'd* Poncho *and* Buskins.

C. *An* Indian *Woman in her* Chonni *and* Iquella, *the Names of her Cloak and Coat.*

D. *An* Indian *casting a Noose at a Bull, to stop him.*

A Indienne du Chily broyant du mays pour en faire de la farine
B Indien en Poncho et Polainas
C Indienne en Choñi et yquella
D Indien jettant le laps au taureau pour l'arreter

most like the *Dalmatica*, used on certain Occasions by Priests. Their Heads and Legs are generally bare; but when Necessity or Decency obliges them to be cover'd, they have a Cap, to which hangs a Flap to cover the Shoulders, and a sort of Buskins or Gamashes on their Legs. Very few cover their Feet, unless they happen to be among Stones, when they make themselves Sandals of Thongs, or of Rushes, which they call *Ojota*'s. The *Spaniards* have taken up the Use of the *Chony*, or *Poncho*, and of the Buskins, by them call'd *Polaina*'s, to ride in, because the *Poncho* keeps out the Rain, is not undone by the Wind, serves for a Blanket at Night, and for a Carpet in the Field.

All the Cloathing of the Women is a long Robe, without Sleeves, open from the Top to the Bottom on one side, where it is held together and girt with a Sash under the Breasts, and on the Shoulders by two Silver Hasps, with Plates of three or four Inches Diameter. This Garment is also call'd *Chony*, and is always blue, or else of a dark gray, inclining to black. In the Towns, they wear over it a Petticoat, and a Veil on their Heads; and in the Country, a little square Piece of Stuff call'd *Iquella*, the two Sides whereof are made fast on the Breast with a great Silver Pin, which has a flat Head four or five Inches diameter, by them call'd *Toupo*. They have long Hair, often in Tresses on their Backs, and cut short before; and at their Ears Silver Plates two Inches square, like Pendants, which they call *Oupelles*. The *Romans* wore such, hanging with a Hasp. See *Gaspar Bartolini* Thom. *de inauribus veterum syntagma.* Amstel.

Their Dwelling is never any other than a Cottage made of the Boughs of Trees, large enough to shelter a Family together, having nothing but a little Chest and Sheep-Skins to lie on: They do not stand in need of much Room. They do not use Keys to secure what they have, Honesty is religiously observ'd among them; but among the *Spaniards* they are not so nice, especially the *Puelches*, who are expert Thieves. All their Houses are scatter'd up and down:

Their Houses.

down: They never draw together to live sociably, wherein they differ from the *Peruvians*; so that, throughout all *Chili*, there is not a Town or Village of the Natives of the Country to be seen. Nay, they are so little fix'd to the Place they take up for their Habitation, that, whensoever they take a Fancy to remove, they either abandon, or carry their Houses elsewhere: Whence it is, that the Art of making War on them, does not consist in going out to find them, but in taking Post in the Midst of their Country, with a small Number of Troops, obstructing their Sowing, destroying their Corn, and driving away their Cattle. This way of living dispers'd up and down, makes the Country look like a Desart; but, in reality, it is very populous, and their Families are very numerous. As they have many Wives, so they have also many Children, wherein their Wealth consists, because they sell them, especially the Daughters, who are bought for Wives: Thus they become perfect Slaves, whom they sell again, when they do not like them, and put them to the hardest Labour. The Men only hough the Land once a Year to sow their *Indian* Corn, *French* Beans, Lentils, and other Grain they feed on; and when they have done, they meet their Friends, drink, get drunk, and rest. Then the Women sow, water, and gather in the Harvest. She who lies with the Master, dresses his Meat that Day, takes care to treat him well, and to saddle and bridle his Horse; for they are so little used to walk a-foot, that tho' they are to go but 200 Paces they will ride; and they are excellent Horsemen: They go up and down such steep Places, that our *European* Horses would not be able to stand on them without any Burden. When obliged, upon a Rout, to fly into the Woods, they place themselves under the Bellies of the Horses, to prevent being torne by the Boughs of the Trees. In short, they perform on Horseback, all that we are told extraordinary of the *Arabs*, and perhaps they out-do them. Their Saddle is a double Sheep's Skin, which serves them to lie on in the Field. Their Stirrups are square wooden Boxes or
Cases

Cafes for the Feet, such as the *Spaniards* use of Silver upon Solemnities, which are worth 4 or 500 Crowns.

It is true, that their Horses being come from *Europe*, they have imitated their Furniture, making that of Wood or Horn, which they saw made of Iron or Silver. Considering the prodigious Number there is at present throughout all that Continent, it is amazing that they should have multiply'd so much in less than 200 Years, that those which are not extraordinary beautiful, are not worth above two or three Crowns at *La Conception*; and yet, as has been said before, the *Indians* eat many; and when they ride, they take so little Care of them, that many of them burst.

The *Indians*, to keep the Account of their Flocks, and preserve the Memory of particular Affairs, make use of Knots in Wool, which by the Variety of Colours and Knitting, serve instead of Characters and Writing. The Knowledge of those Knots, which they call *Quipos*, is a Science and a Secret which Parents do not reveal to their Sons, till they think themselves near their End; and as it often happens, that for want of a ready Wit, they do not comprehend the Mystery, those Knots occasion them to mistake, and so become of no Use. To supply the Want of Writing, they employ those who have good Memories, to learn the History of their Country, and to recite it to others. Thus they preserve the Memory of the ill Usage of the *Spaniards* towards their Ancestors, when they subdued them, which perpetuates their Aversion for them: But when they are put in Mind of the Advantages they afterwards gain'd over those Strangers, whom they drove from five Towns they had built in their Country, their natural Fierceness revives, and they only wish for an Opportunity to drive them again from *La Conception*: But as long as they see *French* Ships coming and going, they dare not take off the Mask, being persuaded that they would afford the *Spaniards* considerable Assistance. Being themselves haughty, they unwillingly bear with the Vanity of those who would command them;

Knots instead of Writing.

yet they know how to diffemble, and trade with them for Beeves, Goats and Mules, receive them in their Houfes, and entertain them as Friends.

Their Trade. A *French* Man, who had gone with a *Spaniard* to trade among the *Puelches*, an *Indian* Nation hitherto not fubdued, and inhabiting the Ridge of Mountains, call'd *La Cordillera*, told me how they managed it. They go directly to the *Cacique*, or Lord of the Place, and appear before him without fpeaking a Word; then he breaking Silence, fays to the Merchant, *Are you come?* Then he anfwering, *I am come. What have you brought me?* replies the *Cacique*. *I bring you*, rejoins the *Spaniard*, *fome Wine*, (a neceffary Article) *and fuch a Thing*; whereupon the *Cacique* fails not to fay, *You are welcome*. He appoints him a Lodging, near his own Cottage, where his Wives and Children bidding him welcome, each of them alfo demand a Prefent, which he gives, tho' never fo fmall. At the fame time the *Cacique*, with the Horn-Trumpet, before fpoken of gives Notice to his fcatter'd Subjects of the Arrival of a Merchant, with whom they may trade: They come and fee the Commodities, which are Knives, Axes, Combs, Needles, Thread, Looking-glaffes, Ribbons, &c. The beft of all would be Wine, were it not dangerous to fupply them wherewith to make themfelves drunk; for then they are not fafe among them, becaufe they are apt to kill one another. When they have agreed upon the Barter, they carry the Things home without paying, fo that the Merchant delivers all without knowing to whom, or feeing any of his Debtors. In fhort, when he defigns to go away, the *Cacique* orders Payment, by founding the Horn again: Then every Man honeftly brings the Cattle he owes; and becaufe thofe are all wild Beafts, as Mules, Goats, and efpecially Oxen and Cows, he commands a fufficient Number of Men to conduct them to the *Spanifh* Frontiers. By what has been faid, may be obferv'd, that as much Civility and Honefty is to be found among thofe

People,

People, whom we call Savages, as among the most polite and well-govern'd Nations.

That great Number of Bullocks and Cows, which is consumed in *Chili*, where abundance are slaughter'd every Year, comes from the Plains of *Paraguay*, which are cover'd with them. The *Puelches* bring them through the Plain of *Tapatapa*, inhabited by the *Pehvingues*, or unconquer'd *Indians*, being the best Pass to cross the Mountains call'd *La Cordillera*, because divided into two Hills, of less difficult Access than the others, which are almost impassable for Mules. There is another 80 Leagues from *La Conception*, at the Burning-Mountain call'd *La Silla Velluda*, which now and then casts out Fire, and sometimes with so great a Noise, that it is heard in the City. That Way the Journey is very much shortned, and they go in six Weeks to *Buenos-Ayres*. *Trade of La Conception.*

By these Communications, they yearly make good all the Herds of Beeves and Goats, which they slaughter in *Chili* by thousands, for Tallow and Lard, made by trying up the Fat and the Marrow of the Bones; which, throughout all *South-America*, serves instead of Butter or Oil, not used by them in their Sauces.

The Flesh they either dry in the Sun, or in the Smoak, to preserve it, instead of salting, as is used in *France*. These Slaughters also afford the Hides, and especially the Goats Skins, which they dress like *Morocco* Leather, by them call'd *Cordovanes*, and sent to *Peru* to make Shooes, or for other Uses.

Besides the Trade of Hides, Tallow, and Salt Meat, the Inhabitants of *La Conception* deal in Corn, with which they every Year lade eight or ten Ships, of 4 or 500 Tuns Burden, for the Port of *Callao*, besides the Meal and Bisket they supply the *French* Ships with, which take in Provisions there, to proceed to *Peru*, and to return to *France*. All this would be inconsiderable for so fine a Country, if the Land were well improved: It is extraordinary fertile, and so easy to till, that they only scratch it with a Plough, for the most part made of one single crooked Branch of a Tree, drawn by two Oxen; and tho' the Grain is scarce cover'd, it seldom produces less than a hundred fold. Nor do they take any more Pains in Pruning their Vines to have good Wine; but, as they know not how to glaze the Jars they put it into, they are fain to pitch them, which, together with the Taste of the Goat Skins in which they carry it about, gives it a Bitterness like Treacle, and a Scent to which it is hard for Strangers to accustom themselves.

Fruit. Their Fruit grows after the same Manner, without any Industry on their part in Grafting. Apples and Pears grow naturally in the Woods; and, considering the Quantity there is of them, it is hard to comprehend how those Trees, since the Conquest, could multiply, and be diffused into so many Parts, if it is true that there were none before, as they affirm.

See Plate XI. *Chili Strawberries.* They there plant whole Fields with a Sort of Strawberry Rushes, differing from ours, in that the Leaves are rounder, thicker, and more downy. The Fruit is generally as big as a Walnut, and sometimes as a Hen's Egg, of a whitish Red, and somewhat less delicious of Taste than our Wood Strawberries. I have given some Plants of them to *Monsieur de Jussieu*, for the King's Garden, where Care will be taken to bring them to bear.

Besides these, there is Plenty in the Woods of our *European* Kind. And in short, all manner of Garden-Product among us, grow there plentifully, and almost without any Trouble; and some are also to be found in the Fields, without cultivating, as Turneps, *Taupinambours* Endive of two Sorts, &c.

Aromatick.

Plate XI. Page 76. *explain'd in* English.
Frutilla, *Being the large Strawberry of* Chili, *drawn after its natural Bigness.*
Nancolahui, *Or the Mountain-Flax.*

Fraise du Chili dessinée de grandeur naturelle

Dwarf Cypress, bearing a yellow and red Flower, as here represented. The other small Medicinal Herbs, which we have in *France*, are also very common there; as Maiden-Hair; and especially some like that of *Canada*; Mallows, Marshmallows, Mercury, Foxglove, Polypody, Mullen, Milfoil, Crane's-Bill, both ordinary and scented, Silver-week, and many more unknown to me, and peculiar to the Country.

Herbs for Dying.

Besides the Medicinal Herbs, they have others for Dying, in such Manner that the Colour will not come out with often washing in Soap. Such is the Root of the *Reilbon*, a Sort of Madder, the Leaf whereof is smaller than ours; they, like us, boil the Root in Water to dye Red. The *Poquell* is a Sort of Gold Button, or *Abrotanum fœmina folio virente vermiculato*, Female Southernwood with green checquer'd Leaves, which dyes Yellow, and holds as well; the Stem of it dyes Green. The *Annil* is a Sort of *Indigo*, which dyes blue: Black is dy'd with the Stem and the Root of the *Panque*, the Leaf whereof is round and plaited, like that of the Thorn-tree; it is two or three Foot Diameter, tho' Father *Feüillee*, who calls it *Panke Anapodophili folio*, confines it to ten Inches. When the Stem is Reddish, it is eaten raw, to cool the Body, and it is very astringent; they boil it with the *Maki* and the *Gouthiou*, Shrubs of that Country, to use it for dying Black, which is beautiful, and does not rot Stuffs, as the *European* Black does. This Plant is only found in Marshy Places.

Aromatick Trees.

The Woods are full of Aromatick Trees, as several Sorts of Myrtle; a Sort of Laurel-tree, the Bark whereof smells like Sassaphras, and sweeter; *Boldu*, the Leaf whereof smells like Frankincense, and the Bark has a biting Taste, with somewhat of the Flavour of Cinnamon: But there is another Tree which bears that very Name, tho' differing from the *East-India* Cinnamon, and has the same Quality; the Leaf of it is like that of the great Laurel-tree, only a little longer. *Virgil* seems to have described it in his *Georgicks*, Lib.

Ipsa

Ipfa ingens arbos, faciemque simillima lauro,
Et, si non alium late jactaret odorem,
Laurus.erat. folia haud ullis labentia ventis;
Flos apprima tenax; animas, & olentia Medi
Ora fovent illa, & senibus medicantur anhelis.

Thus English'd by Mr. *Dryden.*

Large is the Plant, and like a Laurel grows,
And did it not a different Scent disclose,
A Laurel were; the fragrant Flowers contemn
The stormy Winds, tenacious of their Stem.
With this the *Medes* to lab'ring Age bequeath
New Lungs, and cure the Sowrness of the Breath

This Tree among the *Indians* is dedicated to the Ceremonies of Peace. When they concluded the Peace with the *Spaniards*, in the Year 1643, they kill'd many of the Country Sheep, of which we shall speak hereafter; they dipp'd into their Blood a Branch of this Cinnamon, which the Deputy of the *Caciques* deliver'd into the *Spanish* General the Marquis *de Baydes*'s Hand, in Token of Peace. This Ceremony, tho' practis'd by Savages, is not without an Example in Holy Writ, *Exod.* Chap. xii. and S. *Paul* to the *Hebrews*, Chap. ix. says, *When* Moses *had spoken every Precept to all the People according to the Law, he took the Blood of Calves and of Goats, with Water, and Scarlet Wool, and Hyssop, and sprinkled both the Book and all the People, saying; This is the Blood of the Testament which God hath enjoined unto you.* *Ceremony at making Peace.*

There is a very common Tree, called *Licti*, the Shade whereof causes the Bodies of those who sleep under it to swell, as happen'd to a Sea Officer, who had slept some Hours in the Shade of the said Tree; his Face swell'd so high, that he could not see. To cure this Distemper, they take an Herb call'd *Pellboqui*, being a Sort of Rindweed, or Ground-Ivy, or Winter-Cherry, which they pound *Licti venomous Tree.*
with

with Salt, rub the Person with it, and the Swelling goes off in two or three Days, so that nothing of it remains. There is also a Tree call'd *Peumo*, a Decoction of whose Bark is very good against the Dropsy; it bears a Fruit of a red Colour, and like an Olive; the Timber of it may be used for building of Ships; but the best for that Use is the *Roble*, being a Sort of Oak, the Bark whereof is like Cork; the Wood is hard, and lasts long in the Water. Along the River *Biobio* there are abundance of Cedars, not only fit for Building, but to make excellent Masts. The Difficulty of conveying them along the River, which has not Water enough for a Ship at the Mouth, is the Reason why no Use can be made of them. Bamboo Canes are very common every where.

Peumo Tree, good for the Dropsy.

The Plains swarm with an infinite Number of Birds, especially Ring-doves, abundance of Turtles, Partridges, but not so good as in *France*; Snipes, Ducks of all Sorts; one of which they call *Patos reales*, which have a Comb on the Beak, Curlews, Teals, *Pipelienes*, somewhat resembling those Water-Fowls we call Sea-Gulls, having a red, strait, long Bill, narrow as to Breadth, and flat as to Thickness, with a Streak of the same Colour over the Eyes, and their Feet like the Ostriches, they are well tasted; Parrots, *Pechicolorado's*, or Robin-Red-Breasts, which sing finely; some Swans, and those they call *Flamenco's*, whose Feathers the *Indians* value very much, to adorn their Caps on Festivals, because they are a beautiful white and red, a Colour they are very fond of. The Diversion of Shooting is there interrupted by certain Birds, which our People call *Criards*, that is, Shriekers, because, when they see a Man, they set up a Cry, and flutter about him, making a Noise, as it were to give Notice to the other Birds, who fly away as soon as they hear it: They have above the Joint of each Wing, a red Point standing up an Inch long, which is hard, and as sharp as a Cock's-Spur, which serves them to fight with other Birds.

Wild Fowl.

We

We one Day, in a Marsh, took one of that Sort of Am- *Penguins.*
phibious Creatures call'd *Penguins*, larger than a Goose;
instead of Feathers, it was cover'd with a Sort of gray
Hair, like that of the Seals, or Sea-Wolves; their Wings
are also very like the Fins of those Creatures. Several
Travelers have spoken of them, because they are very
common about the Streights of *Magellan*. See it drawn
from the Life, Plate XVI.

There are such Multitudes of Seals, or Sea-Wolves, *Seals.*
above-mention'd, that all the Rocks about the Island of
Quiriquina are often cover'd with them. They differ from
the Northern Sea-Wolves, in that the others have Paws,
whereas these have two Fins, stretching out almost like
Wings towards their Shoulders, and two other little ones
which close up the Tail. Nature has, however, at the Ends
of the two great Fins, preserv'd something like Paws; for
there are four Talons that terminate the Extremities; perhaps they use them to go ashore, where they are much delighted, and whither they carry their Young, whom they
feed with Fish, and cherish very tenderly, as is reported.
There they make a Noise like Calves, for which Reason,
in several Relations of Voyages, they are call'd Sea-Calves;
but their Head is more like a Dog's than any other Beast's,
and therefore with good Reason the *Dutch* call them Sea-Dogs. Their Skin is cover'd with very smooth thick Hair,
and their Flesh is very oily, and ill-tasted, so that none but the
Livor is usually eaten: However, the *Indians* of *Chiloe* dry,
and lay up Provision of it for their Sustenance: The *French*
Ships draw the Oil from it for their Use. They are very
easily taken, there being no Difficulty in coming near to
them both on the Land and in the Water; and they are
kill'd with one Blow on the Nose. There are several Sizes
of them: In the South they are as big as large Mastive
Dogs; but in *Peru* there are some 12 Foot long. Their
Skins serve to make Floats, being blown full of Air, instead of Boats; but at *La Conception*, the Fisher-Men only
bind together three Faggots of light Wood, with Leather
Thongs,

Thongs, in such manner that the Middlemost may be a little lower than the other two, and go out to Sea on them. The properest Wood for that Purpose, is the Stem of a sort of Aloes, six or seven Foot long.

Fish. When Ships put in at *Talcaguana*, they go a fishing in the *Estero*, which is a little River at the Bottom of the Bay on the same Side. There they take abundance of Mullets, large Soles, *Rovalo's* a delicate Sort of Fish like a Pike, having a black Streak on the Back; a Sort of Gurnards, call'd all along that Coast *Peze Rey*, that is, King Fish, because of its Delicacy.

Gold Mines. *La Conception* is seated in a Country abounding in all Things, not only to supply the Necessities of Life, but also containing infinite Wealth: All about the City there is Gold found, especially 12 Leagues to the Eastward, at a Place call'd *Estancia del Rey*, the King's Station; where, by washing, they get those Bits of Gold, which the *Spaniards* call *Pepitas*, that is, Grains; there have been some found weighing eight or ten Marks, (note a Mark is eight Ounces) and extraordinary fine. Formerly much was got about *Angol*, which is 24 Leagues off; and if the Country were inhabited by laborious People, it might be had in a thousand Parts, where they are satisfy'd there are good Washing Places; that is, Lands, whence it is taken by only washing, as shall be observ'd hereafter.

If they penetrate as far as the long Ridge of Mountains, call'd *La Cordillera*, there is an infinite Number of Mines of all Sorts of Metals and Minerals; and, among the rest, on two Mountains, which are only 12 Leagues from the *Pampas de Paraguay*, and 100 Leagues from *La Conception*. *Copper Mines.* In one of them they have discover'd Mines of pure Copper, so singular, that there have been found in them Grains, or Lumps of above a hundred Quintals Weight, (note that a Quintal is a hundred Weight.) The *Indians* call one of those Mountains *Payen*, that is, Copper; and *Don John Melendes*, who made the Discovery, call'd it S. *Joseph*. He drew thence one Piece of 40 Quintals Weight,

of

of which he was, during my Stay at *La Conception*, making six Field-Pieces, all Six Pounders.

There are Stones, which are partly Copper quite form'd, and partly imperfect Copper; for which Reason they say of that Place, that the Earth there breeds, that is, that Copper is there daily form'd. * In that Mountain there is also Lapis Lazuli.

<small>* Job xxviii. 2. *Brass is molten out of the Stone.*</small>

The other Mountain adjoining, by the *Spaniards* call'd *Cerro de Santa Ines*, or S. *Agnes*'s Hill, is remarkable for its great Plenty of Load-stone, which composes almost the whole Body of it. <small>*Loa*</small>

In the next Neighbouring Mountains, inhabited by the *Puelches*, there are Mines of Sulphur and Salt. At *Talcaguana*, at *Irequin*, and in the very City, there are excellent Coal Pits, without digging above a Foot or two: The Inhabitants do not know how to make their Advantage of it; they were much surprized to see us dig up Earth to make Fire, when we laid in Provision for our Forge. <small>*Sulphur and Salt.*</small>

Whilst we lay there, News was brought by Land from *Chiloe*, that the *Indians* there had revolted, and had kill'd 60 *Spaniards* of both Sexes. In short, those poor Slaves being made desperate by the Cruelty of the *Spaniards*, and particularly of the Governor, who exacted of each of them a certain Quantity of Cedar Planks, which is the Wood they trade with to *Peru* and *Chili*, and other Tyrannies, mutiny'd and kill'd thirteen or fourteen *Spaniards*, and a Woman: But the *Spaniards* took a cruel Revenge; for, drawing together, they slew all they met, and went into the very Islands to seek out and destroy them. It was said they kill'd above 200, to regain their Reputation and the Authority of the Whites, who are but a small Number in Comparison of the *Indians*; for they do not reckon that there are in that Province above 1000, or 1200 Men, able to bear Arms; and there are, at least, ten Times as many *Indians*, but they are naturally fearful and tractable, and know not how to make their Advantage of the Supineness of the *Spaniards*, who are ill arm'd, and have on- <small>*Revolt at Chiloe.*</small>

ly one little Fort, call'd *Chacao*, which is always ill provided with Warlike Stores; for as to the Town of *Castro*, the Strength of it is compared to that of *La Conception*: However, it would import them to have some Force in those Islands, because, if the *European* Nations would make any Enterprize in the *South Sea*, it would be easy to possess themselves of them; bating Wine, they would there find all necessary Refreshments and Provisions; and there is also much Ambergrise found.

The *Indians* of the Country about *Chiloe* are call'd *Chono's*. They go stark-naked, tho' in a very cold Climate, and among Mountains; they only cover themselves with a Skin cut square, without any other fitting, two Corners whereof they cross over their Stomach; one of the other two comes upon their Head, and the other hangs down in a Point on their Back.

Giants, if it be true that there are any. Farther up the Country is another Nation of *Indian* Giants, whom they call *Caucahues*: They being Friends to the *Chono's*, some of them now and then come with them to the Dwellings of the *Spaniards* of *Chiloe*. Don *Pedro Molina*, who had been Governor of that Island, and some other Eye-Witnesses of the Country, told me, they were near four *Vara's* high, that is, about nine or ten Foot. These are the same they call *Patagons*, who inhabit the East Coast of the Desart Country ancient Travels have taken Notice of, which has afterwards been represented as a Fable, because *Indians* have been seen in the Streights of *Magellan*, who did not exceed the Size of other Men: And this is what deceiv'd *Froger*, in his Relation of the Voyage of Monsieur *de Gennes*; for some Ships have at the same time seen both Sorts. In *July*, 1704, the Men belonging to the *James* of *S. Malo*, commanded by Captain *Harrington*, saw seven of those Giants in *Gregory* Bay: Those of the *S. Peter* of *Marseilles*, commanded by *Carman* of *S. Malo*, saw six, among whom there was one who bore some Mark of Distinction above the rest. His Hair was platted in a Net Cap made of the Guts of Birds, with Feathers

quite

quite round his Head: Their Garment was a Bag of Skins, with the Hair inwards: Along their Arms, in the Sleeves, lay their Quivers full of Arrows, some of which they gave them, and help'd them to bring their Boat ashore. The Sailors offer'd them Bread, Wine and Brandy, but they would not taste any: The next Day they saw from aboard the Ship, 200 of them in a Body. Those Men, tho' larger, are more sensible of the Cold than the others; for the smaller Size have no other Cloaths but a single Skin on their Backs.

What I have here deliver'd upon the Testimony of Persons of Credit, is so agreeable to what we read in the Relations of the most famous Travelers, that I am of Opinion, it may be believ'd, without the Guilt of an Over-Credulity, that there is in that Part of *America*, a Nation of Men much exceeding us in Stature. The Particulars of Time and Place, and all the Circumstances attending what is said about it, seem to carry a sufficient Character of Truth to overcome the natural Prejudice we have on the other Side. The Extraordinariness of the Sight may perhaps have occasion'd some Exaggeration in the Measure of the Height; but if we ought to regard it as guess'd at, and not taken exactly, we shall find that they differ very little from one another. The Reader will give me leave, in order to justify what I have here advanced, to collect in this Place, what is to be found dispers'd in several Books relating to this Subject.

Anthony Pigafeta, to whom we are indebted for the Journal of *Ferdinand Magalhanes*, or, as we call him, *Magellan*, tells us, That in the Bay of S. *Julian*, in the Latitude of about 49 Degrees and a half, the *Spaniards* saw several Giants, so tall, that they did not reach up to their Wastes. He speaks, among others, of one, who had the Figure of a Heart painted on each Cheek: Their Weapons were Bows and Arrows, and they were clad in Skins. _{Ozorius de rebus Emanuelis regis Lusitaniæ, Lib. 2.}

Bartolome Leonardo de Argensola, in the first Book of his History of the Conquest of the *Molucco* Islands, says, That the _{Ciertos Gigantes de mas de quinze Palmos.}

the same *Magellan*, in the Streight that bears his Name, took some Giants who were above 15 Spans high, that is, 11 Foot, 3 Inches of our Measure; but they soon died, for want of their usual Sustenance.

<small>Consta por otras que tiene cada uno destos mas de tres varas de alto.</small>
The same Historian, in his third Book, says, That the Men of *Sarmiento*'s Ships, fought with Men that were above three Yards high, that is, about eight Foot of our Measure: The first time they repuls'd the *Spaniards*; but the second, the latter put them to Flight, with such Precipitation, that, to make use of the *Spanish* Expression, *A Musket Ball would not have overtaken them. According to this Instance,* says he, *the Books of Knight-Errantry have good Reason to represent Giants as Cowards.* However, I have heard the Inhabitants of *Chiloe* say, that the *Caucahues* were as brave as they were tall.

<small>Die 7 Maii, 1599. Quorum ut conjectura dabat longit. 10 aut 11 pedum erat. Hist. Antip. Pars 9. Vasto ac procero corpore sunt pedes 10 vel 11 equante. Hist. Ant. p. 9.</small>
We find a Circumstance much to the same Purpose, but perhaps more magnify'd in *Sibald de Wert*'s Voyage, who being at Anchor with five Ships in the *Green-Bay*, 21 Leagues within the Streight of *Magellan*, saw seven *Piragua's*, or large *Indian* Boats, full of Giants, who might be about ten or eleven Foot high, whom the *Dutch* fought, and who were so frighted at the Fire-Arms, that they were seen to tear up Trees to shelter themselves against the Musket-Balls.

Oliver de Noort, who enter'd the Streight some Months after *Sibald*, saw Men ten or eleven Foot high, tho' he had also seen others of our Size.

<small>* Conspexerunt autem ibi ad terram de Fogue immanis admodum & horrendæ longitudinis hominem. Journal of Schouten's Voyage, Amst. 1619.</small>
George Spilbergen entring the Streight of *Magellan*, the 2d of *April*, 1715, saw, on *Tierra del Fuego*, a * Man of a prodigious Height, who was got upon a Hill, to see the Ships pass by.

William Schouten, on the 11th of *December* of the same Year, being in Port *Desire*, in about 47 Degrees and a half Latitude, his Men found on the Mountain, Heaps of Stones placed in such Manner, as gave them a Curiosity to see what they cover'd, and found *Humane Bones between ten*

and

and eleven Foot *long*, that is, nine or ten *French* Measure, to which all the former are to be reduced.

I have thought fit to make this little Digression, to justify a Matter of Fact which is suspected of Falshood, tho' the reading of Holy Writ and Historians, and the Examples of Giants we often enough see born and living among us, ought to dispose us to believe something extraordinary. I return to the Account of my Voyage.

They added to the News of the Revolt of the *Indians* of *Chiloe*, that a *French* Vessel, which put into that Island, had supply'd the *Spaniards* with Powder against the *Indians*. That Circumstance made us believe it was the *Mary*, which we lost about Cape *Horn*; but we understood soon after, that she was put into *Baldivia*. At last, on the 8th of *August*, she came and join'd us at *La Conception*.   *The* Mary *joins them.*

They inform'd us, that, after having run thro' much foul Weather, they had found themselves on the Island of *Diego Ramirez*, at the Time when they reckon'd themselves 80 Leagues to the Westward of it, by the Manuscript Charts, and 60 Leagues by the Printed, and two Degrees more to the Northward than they really were: But having corrected their Errors upon that View of Land, they had arrived very exactly at *Baldivia*, by *Pieter Goos*'s Charts; which confirms the Conjectures I made before, in relation to the Currents.

Notwithstanding the continual Rains, we had already laid in our Provisions when the *Mary* arriv'd; it only remain'd to do the same for her; when, the *Oidor* or Judge of *La Conception* receiv'd Orders from the President of *Chili* to oblige all the *French* Ships that were in the Road, upon what Pretence soever, to depart, and that within four Days at the farthest; but those Orders were not much regarded, being given on Occasion of a notable Piece of Gallantry. The *Concord* did not sail till the 19th of *July* for *Valparaiso*, and the *Mary Anne* the 20th for *Hilo*; and we staid there some Days longer to make an End of our Business.

In

In the mean time, the fair Weather began to succeed the Winter Rains and Winds, and the Hope of Trade could not detain us at *La Conception*, because, besides that the two Ships above-nam'd, had furnished the City with what little Goods it had Occasion for, *Champloret le Brun*, Captain of the *Assumption*, had been there ever since the 24th of *June*, endeavouring to sell as much as would pay for his Provisions; so that we thought of sailing, to go and trade in *Peru*.

Departure from La Conception.

WE sail'd out of the Bay of *La Conception*, on the 30th of *August*, uncertain what Place to resort to; nothing but the Desire of receiving some Information made us put into *Valparaiso*, where, nevertheless, we stay'd above eight Months. By the Way, we had continually the Winds contrary, weak or variable: We also observ'd, contrary to what is usual, that there are in these Parts fair and serene Days at the Time when the North-Wind prevails. Six Days after our Departure, we discover'd the Head call'd *Morro del Obispo*, or, *The Bishops Head-land*, two Leagues to the Southward of Cape *Curaoma*, which is generally made in order to get to the Windward of *Valparaiso*, to the end that the strong Breezes at S. and S. W. may not drive Ships from that Port, which it would be hard to recover, without running far out to Sea. At five in the Evening, it appear'd to us thus:

Land discover'd to the Windward of Valparaiso.

Plate XII

It being then late, we would not venture to go into *Valparaiso* by Night, tho' the Opening of the Road is very wide; we took a Trip out to Sea, and the next Morning making Land again, saw the same Head-Land, which alters but little, because it is high and round like a Bell.

After turning Cape *Curaoma*, two Leagues to the N. E. and by E. appears the Point of *Valparaiso*, which with that Cape forms the Creek of *Lagunilla*, where no Ships anchor, because the Bottom is naught.

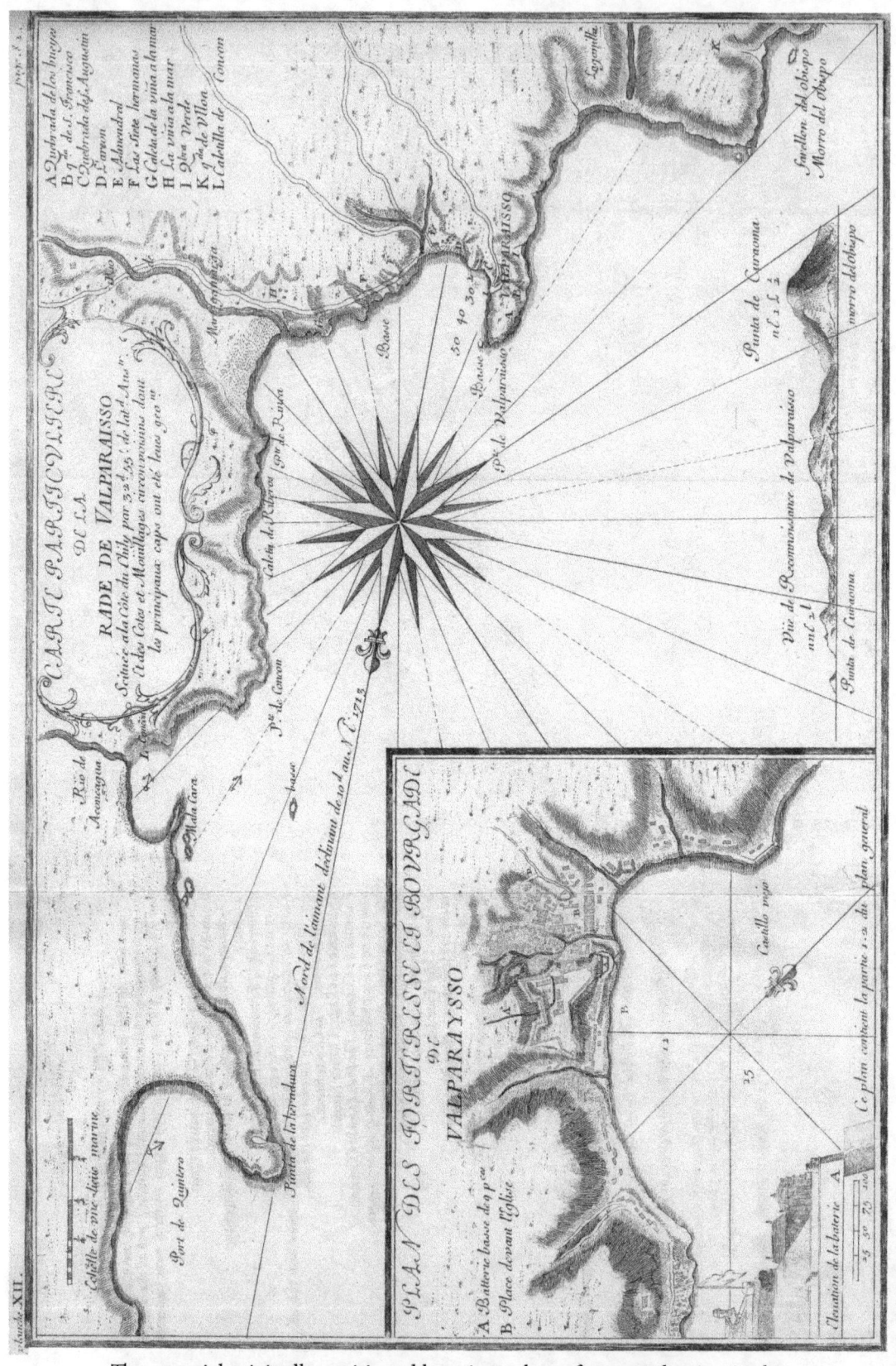

the South-Sea.

Plate XII. *Page* 89. *explain'd in* English.

An exact Chart of the Road of *VALPARAISO*, on the Coast of *Chili*, in 32 Degrees, 55 Minutes of South Latitude; and of the adjacent Coast and Anchoring Places, the principal Capes whereof were Geometrically taken.

A. Quebrada de los Bueyes, The Break of Oxen.
B. Punta de S. Francisco, *Point* S. Francis.
C. Quebrada de San Augustin, *The Break of* S. Augustin.
D. Larion.
E. Almendral, *The Almond Grove.*
F. Las siete hermanas, *The* Seven Sisters.
G. Galeta de la vinna à la Mar, *The Creek of the Vineyard next the Sea.*
H. La vinna à la Mar, *The Vineyard next the Sea*
I. Quebrada verde, *The* Green Break.
K. Quebrada de Ulloa, Ulloa's Break.
L. Caletilla de Concon, *The little Creek of* Concon.
Echelle d'une Lieüe Marine, *A Scale of a Sea-League.*
Rio de Aconcagua, Aconcagua *River.*
Rio de Margamarga, Margamarga *River.*
Port de Quintero, Quintero *Port.*
Mala Cara, Ugly-Face Island.
Punta de la Herradura, *Horseshooe Point.*
Basse, *A Shoal.*
Punta de Concon, Concon *Point.*
Caleta de Riberos, Riberos *Creek.*
Punta de Rinca, Rinca *Point.*
Punta de Valparaiso, Valparaiso *Point.*
Lagunilla, *The little Lake.*
Punta de Curaoma, Curaoma *Point.*
Vue de la Reconnoissance de Valparaiso, *Thus* Valparaiso *appears, and is to be known from the Sea.*
Morro del Obispo, *The Bishop's Head-Land.*
Farellon del Obispo, *The Bishop's Great Rock.*

Plan des Forteresse & Bourgade de Valparaiso, *A Plan of the Fort and Town of* Valparaiso.
A. Batterie basse de neuf Pieces, *A low Battery of nine Guns.*
B. Place devant l'Eglise, *The Square before the Church.*
Elevation de la Batterie *A*, *The Elevation of the Battery* A.
Castillo viejo, *The Old Castle.*
Ce Plan contient la partie 1-2 du Plain General, *This Plan contains Part* 1-2 *of the general Plan.*

Description of the Bay of Valparaiso.

IN order to enter the Port of *Valparaiso*, upon turning the Point, Ships muſt range cloſe along the Shoal, which ſhews itſelf within about half a Cable's Length from the Shore, for getting to the Windward. That Rock is very ſafe, for we have ſeen a *Spaniſh* Ship in a Calm, within a Boat's Length of it, without touching. When Ships keep too far from it, they are obliged to make many Trips to recover the Anchoring-Place, as happened to us. We came to an Anchor on the 5th of *September*, in 27 Fathom Water, the Bottom gray Owze, inclining to an Olive Colour, the Point of *Valparaiſo*, bearing N. E., and by N. the white Battery W. S. W. and Cape *Concon* N. and by E. As ſoon as our Anchor was down, we ſaluted the Fort with ſeven Guns, and it anſwer'd with one. We found in the Road the *Concord*, and ſeven *Spaniſh* Ships lading Corn for *Callao*.

Anchoring at Valparaiſo.

Thoſe Ships generally run in ſo cloſe to the Shore, that they have three Anchors on the Land, made faſt to Stones, or Piles, and at that diſtance they ſtill have eight or ten Fathom Water; that Way of making faſt is very good, becauſe in the Summer, every Day regularly about Noon, the Breezes come up at S. W. and S. ſo ſtrong, that they make the beſt Anchors give way. However, Care muſt be taken of a Shoal, that is within a Cable's Length of the Shore, near the Battery call'd *Caſtillo Blanco*, or, *The White Caſtle*, on which there is not above thirteen or fourteen Foot Water at the Ebb. The *Aſſumption* commanded by *Champloret* touch'd there lightly one Day, becauſe the Sea riſes and falls ſix or ſeven Foot. In other reſpects, the Bay is very ſafe, and Ships may turn and anchor every where from fifty to eight Fathom Water; only Care muſt be taken when they take a Trip towards the *Siete Hermanas*, or *Seven Siſters*, that is, to the Eaſtward, not to draw nearer the Shore than two Cables Length and a half, oppoſite to

a

a little running Water, cross'd by a great reddish Road; in that Place there is a Shoal, on which there is no more than two Fathom and a half Water.

Ships generally anchor only in that Nook of the Road which is before the Fort, for the Conveniency of Trade, and the more Safety; yet after all, that Road is quite naught in Winter, because the North Winds which blow in at the Mouth, without any Opposition, make the Sea there so boisterous, that Ships have been sometimes forced ashore. The South Winds are no less Violent there in Summer; but as they come over the Land, they make no Sea, and in case they should force Ships from their Anchors, they can only be drove out to Sea.

The next Day after our Arrival, the Captain went to pay his Respects to the Commander in Chief, call'd *Governador de las Armas*, Governor of Arms, for so he is distinguish'd from the President of *Chili*, who is call'd Plain Governor. It was then Don *John Covarrubias*, a Man of Birth, who having serv'd in *Flanders*, had much Kindness for the *French*; tho' he is subordinate to the President, he owns him not by that Name, but by that of Captain General of *Chili*.

The Fort where he commands, is of little Moment, as well because it is ill built, as because the Road it defends is near other Creeks, which afford the same Conveniencies as that. Such an one is that of *Quintero*, which is defenceless, and but five Leagues from it. True it is, that the Bay of *Valparaiso*, as nearest to the Capital, is the most frequented in all *Chili*; for which Reason, it has been thought fit to secure it against any Insults of the *English* and *Dutch*, who have often ranged along those Coasts. Formerly, there was only a little Battery level with the Water, but within these last thirty Years they have built the great Fortress, at the Foot of the Mountain: It stands on an Eminence of an indifferent Height, cross'd towards the S. E. and N. W. by two Streams, which form two natural Ditches between twenty and twenty-five Fathom deep,

Description of the Fort.

A Voyage to

Plate XIII. Page 92. *explain'd in* English.

The Profile of the Fort of *VALPARAISO*, by the Line A. B.

1. *The Key before the Battery.*
2. *The low Battery, call'd* Castillo Blanco, *or the* White Castle.
3. *The Stairs and Ascent to go up to the Fort under Cover of the Epaulment.*
4. *The Corps du Garde.*
5. *The Place for setting up the Colour.*
6. *The Port.*
7. *The Chappel.*
8. *The Corps du Garde.*
9. *The Magazine.*
10. *The Rampart.*
11. *The Fort next the Mountain.*
12. *The Half-Bastion over the Town.*
13. *The Rivulet that supplies the Place with Water.*

The Profile by the Line C. D.

A. *The Break of S. Augustin.*
B. *The Berm, or Foreland about the Fort.*
C. *The Flank of the Bastion of S. Augustin.*
D. *The Faces of the Demi-Bastions.*
E. *The Flank of the Demi-Bastions.*
F. *The Gate in the Middle of the Curtin next the Mountain.*
G. *The Corps du Garde.*
H. *Magazines and Lodgings.*
I. *The Brook.*
K. *The Cleft.*
L. *The Curate's House.*
M. *The Houses of the Town.*

Echelle des Profils double du celle du Plan, *The Scale of the Profiles, being double that of the Plan.*

The Prospect next the Anchoring-Place.

a. *The Gate of the Fort, on the Land-Side.*
b. *The Gate to go down to the Low Battery and to the Town.*
c. *The Gate to the Low Battery, at the Foot of the Stairs of the Upper Fort.*
d. *The Parish-Church.*
e. *The Governor's House.*
f. *The Church and Monastery of S. Augustin.*
g. *The Redans, or indented Work of S. Augustin.*
h. Spanish *Ships lading Corn.*

funk

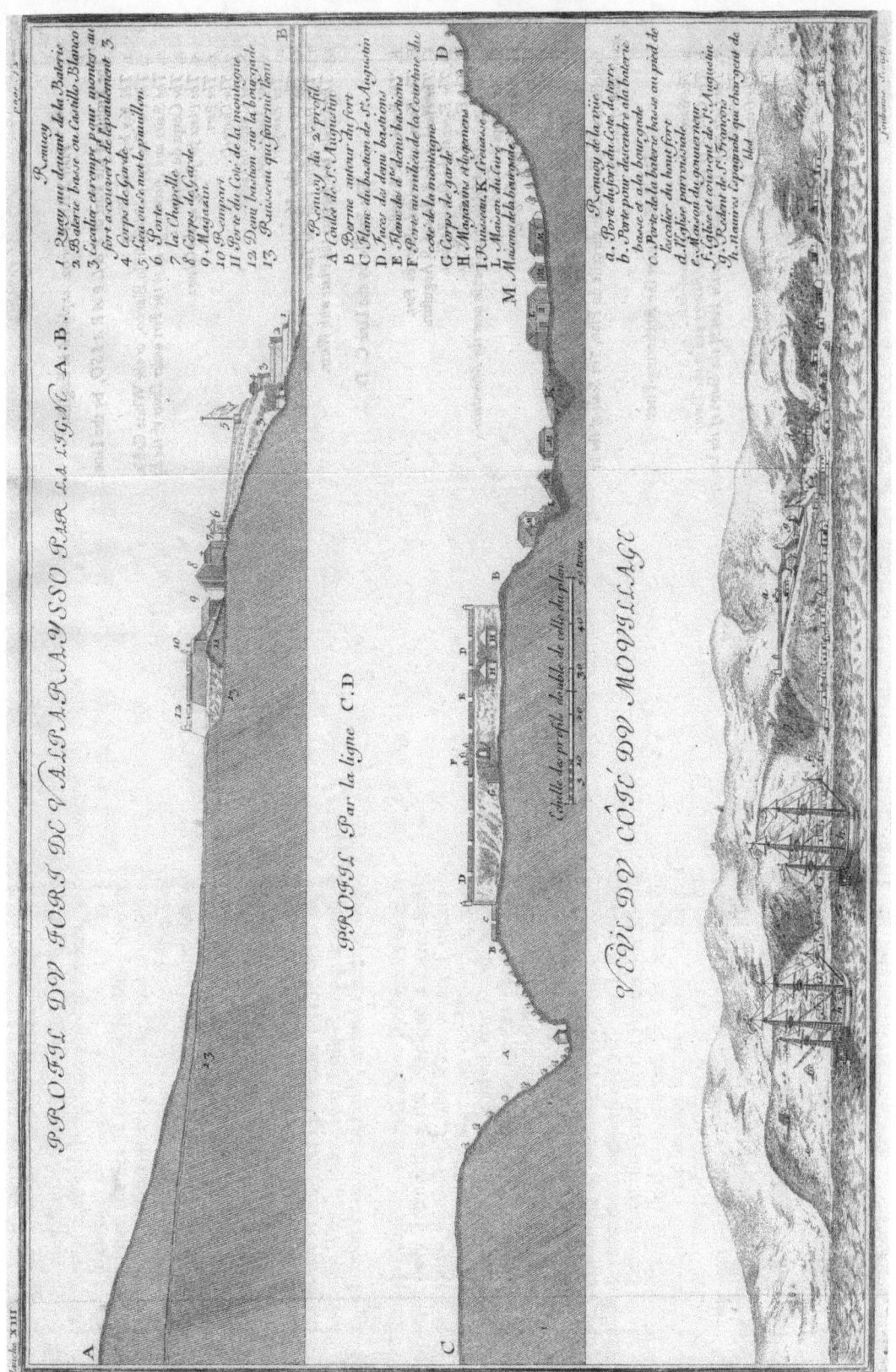

sunk down almost to the Level of the Sea. Thus it is absolutely parted from the Neighbouring Eminences, which are a little higher.

The Side next the Sea is naturally so steep, that there is no going up without much Difficulty, and on the Land Side, or next the high Mountain, it is defended by a Ditch, which crosses from one Stream to the other, and thus cuts off the Enclosure of the Fortress something near to a Square. The Situation of the Place would not permit the making of a regular Fortification; it cannot properly be call'd any other than Walls of Intrenchment, following the Compass of the Height, which flank one another but very little, and sometimes not at all. At the Middle of the Wall, which is above the Town, there is a little *Redan*, or indented Work, of seven Fathoms in Front, with a *Guerite*, or Sentinel's Box.

The opposite Side, which is above the Stream of S. *Augustin*, is only defended by the Flank of a Demi-Bastion, which forms a dead Angle, the Face whereof makes too oblique a Defence. The Side next the Mountain, consists of a Courtin of 26 Fathoms, and of two Demi-Bastions of 20 Fathoms Face and 11 Flank, so that the Line of Defence is but of 45 Fathoms. All this Part is built with Brick, rais'd 25 Foot in height on a Berm, or Foreland, being a small space of Ground between the Wall and the Moat. The Depth of the Ditch is about ten Foot, and its Breadth three Fathoms towards the Salliant-Angles, whence it has its Defence to the Angle of the Epaule, or Shoulder of the Bastion. It is dug, or cut, in a soft Rock, which has been made a little steep at the two Ends, to render it inaccessible by way of the Streams. The Parapets are but two Foot and a Half thick, and the rest of the Enclosure of the Place is only a Piece of Masonry made up of Rubbish, weak enough. There is no Rampart but on the Land-Side, to cover the Fortress, and hinder its being overlook'd by the Mountain, which rises gently: But the Misfortune is, that the Flanks can be batter'd in Reverse, that is, on the

Backs

Backs, and the Curtins and Faces enfiladed, or fcour'd along their whole Length by neighbouring Eminences within Musket-Shot, so that it is very easy to render them useless. At the Foot of the high Fort, adjoining to the Town, is a Battery of nine Pieces of Cannon, rais'd thirteen Foot high, on a Key of the same Height, whence they can fire upon the Anchoring-Place level with the Water: But besides that it has no Defence from its Position, it is commanded by all the Parts about. It is call'd *Castillo Blanco*, or *White-Castle*, because it has been whitened, that it may be seen at a Distance. Behind that Battery, are the Gate, the Stairs, and the Ascent, which lead from the Town to the Fortress along a Way cover'd with a Piece of Wall; and higher up, a *Boyau*, or Branch of a Trench, the Epaulment whereof does not cover the Gate of the Body of the Place, which is all open to the Road.

In the Middle of the Curtin, on the Side next the Mountain, is another Gate, to which they climb up out of the Ditch for want of a Drawbridge. That Way passes the Conduit of Water drawn from the Stream of S. *Augustin* for the upper Fort, which might be easily cut off, and the Garrison could have no other but that of the Rivulet, which runs from the Bottom of the Stream of S. *Francis* through the Middle of the Town. Thus we see how little the Fortress of *Valparaiso* is to be fear'd, if Men were landed, as may be done in fair Weather, at that open Shore, which is at the Bottom of the Road, at the Place call'd *Almendral*, where the Cannon can scarce do any Harm.

Cannon. In the low Battery there are 9 Brass Guns, from 12 to 18 Pound Ball, *Spanish* Weight, whereof no two can fire upon that Landing-Place; and the rather, for that it is almost half a League distant. In the Upper-Fort there are five, from six to twelve Pound Ball, and two little Drakes, making in all 16 Brass Guns. I must here take Notice by the By, that this Artillery was put into a Condition to be of Use by the Carpenters of *Boisloret*, Captain of the Ship *le Clerc*, in the Year 1712: But had not the Governor been

more

more grateful than the President of *Santiago*, for the Service he did the *Spaniards*, he had been the first at feeling the Exactness of the Work on Account of a little Difference in trading.

At the Foot of the Fortress, in a little Gut, or narrow Space, is the Borough or Town of *Valparaiso*, consisting of about a hundred poor Houses, without any Order, and of several Heights; it also stretches out along the Sea, where the Stores of Corn or Granaries are. As little as the Place is, there are besides the Parish, two Monasteries; the one of *Francicans*, and the other of *Augustins*. Of 150 Families there may be in the Place, there are scarce 30 of them Whites; the rest are Blacks, Mulatto's, and Mestizo's. The Number of Men able to bear Arms there is very inconsiderable; but the Neighbouring Dwellings, or Farms, upon the first Signal from the Fortress, furnish six Troops of Horse, mounted at their own Expence; most of whom have no other Arms but Swords, which the Whites always wear at the vilest Employments. Upon Notice given by the Sentinels kept along the Coast, they are very regular in drawing together, at least, some Part of those Troops, when a Ship appears which is not thought to be *Spanish* built. We have often heard a Shot in the Night by way of Alarm, upon the least Suspicion, and without any Ground. *Valparaiso Town.*

Some Days after our Arrival, the second Merchant of our Ship obtain'd Leave of the President to go to *Santiago*, on the Business of Trade.

During that Interval, the *S. Charles*, a *French* Ship, bought by the *Spaniards*, was cast away on the most Easterly Island of *John Fernandes*, 80 Leagues West from *Valparaiso*, as it was coming to lade *Bacallao*, or Salt Cod, of which some *French* Men had a Fishery there, under the Direction of one *Apremont*, formerly one of the King's Guards. Sailing along the Coast, the Ship struck on a Shoal, so near the Land, that all the Men were saved. Some of them ventur'd to come in their Boat to *Valparaiso*, to *Ship cast away.*

desire

desire of the Governor to send a Ship to fetch off the Fishermen left on the Island, and lade what dry Fish they had. Upon our Offers of Service before made to the President, he desired our Ship *Mary* for that effect; but she being incumber'd with Goods, we could not grant it; so that he was obliged to send the *S. Dominick*, a *Spanish* Ship newly come from *Callao* to lade Corn, which sail'd the 1st, and return'd the 14th of *October*.

John Fernandes Island.

That most Easterly Island of *John Fernandes* would be very fruitful, if cultivated: There is no Want of Wood and Water; there are wild Swine and Goats, and a prodigious Quantity of Fish: The Road where Ships anchor has a good Bottom, but there is much Water close under the Shore. There the *English* and *French* Buccaniers often had their Retreat, when they were ranging the Coast about the Year 1682.

The great Plenty of Commodities the Country was furnish'd with at the Time of our Arrival, and the low Price they bore made us resolve not to sell, till the Trade was somewhat more advantageous; which reduced us to a tiresome Idleness, and made us seek out for some Diversion. The Festival of the Rosary came on the 2d of *October*, which entertain'd us eight Days successively.

Festival of the Rosary.

This Festival among the *Spaniards* is one of the first Class; they kept it with as much, nay, I dare say, more Veneration, than those of the most sacred Mysteries of our Religion: For solemnizing of it, there were Illuminations on the Eve, and Fireworks, consisting of some Sky-Rockets, made in Canes instead of Cartridges, and several Volleys of Chambers. The three next Days a private Person entertain'd the Publick with a Bull Feast, which I thought did not much satisfy my Curiosity. We saw nothing there that was worth looking at, but only a Man astride on one of those mettled Animals, with Spurs, the Rowels whereof were four Inches Diameter, after the Country Fashion. That Engagement was perform'd in a Place hemm'd in with Scaffolds, fill'd with as many People

ple as there were Inhabitants, who are much delighted with that Sport. The three next Days they acted Plays in the same Place, before the Gate of S. *Francis*'s Church, by Candle-light, in the open Air. It would be hard to relate the Subjects, so much they vary'd and changed; to speak properly, they were no other than Interludes of Farces, mixed with Dancing of several Sorts, well enough perform'd, and even fine, after the Manner of the Country, bating the Symphony, which consisted in only one Harp, and some Guitars; but that which made their Recitative ridiculous, and no way edifying, was an impertinent Mixture they made of the Praises of *our Lady of the Rosary*, with downright Buffoonry, and Obscenities not clean couch'd.

After this Festival, being tired with seeing nothing continually but a Village, I bethought me of seeing the Capital of the Country, of which the Inhabitants gave me great Accounts; but it being requisite for that Purpose to have the President's Leave, which I would not ask, for fear, lest, being acquainted with my Profession, he should refuse it me, I pretended to go away to embarque at *La Conception*, with a *French* Captain, who was returning to *France*. The great Credit he had given the President, had purchased him his Friendship; so I went with him under that Pretence to *Santiago*, as it were only taking it in my Way, without fearing to be stopp'd, and sent back with Fetters at my Heels, as had happen'd to some *French* Men, who went thither without Leave. A Privateer Captain, who having lost his Ship at *Buenos Ayres*, was passing through *Santiago* towards the *South Sea*, to endeavour to embarque on some *French* Ship, was imprison'd upon no other Account. *Dangerous going to Santiago.*

It might be here ask'd, why the *French*, who go to *Santiago*, are so ill used. There are two Reasons for it: The first, because, by the Laws of *Spain*, Strangers are forbid entring the Colonies of the *South Sea*; the second and chiefest is, because the Merchants of the City, among *Reasons why.*

O whom

whom the President must be reckoned, complain, that the *French* carry Goods thither, which they sell cheaper than the Shops, and by that means ruin their Trade; so that I was to take double Precautions.

Road from Valparaiso to Santiago.

We set out from *Valparaiso* on the Eve of *All Saints*, and pass'd the great Road of *Zapata*. I was much amazed the first Day's Journey, to see not only that it must be perform'd without drawing Bit, but that at Night we must lie in the open Field, for want of a House, tho' I had been promis'd a good Lodging; but I was inform'd, that what they call *Alojamiento*, or Lodging in *Chili*, only signifies a Place where there is Water and Pasture for the Mules. However, we had pass'd within half a Quarter of a League of *Zapata*, which is a Hamlet, and the only one there is in 30 Leagues traveling; but it is not the Custom of the Country to lie in Houses.

Zapata Mountain.

Poangue Vale.

Cuesta de Prado Mountain.

Podaguel River.

The next Morning we pass'd over the Mountain of *Zapata*, which is very high; and after crossing the Vale of *Poangue*, where a little River runs, which is dangerous in Winter rainy Weather, we pass'd another Mountain more difficult than the former, call'd *La Cuesta de Prado*, and went to lie at the Descent on the other side, on the Bank of the little River of *Podaguel*. During those two Days, we scarce saw any Lands till'd; all the Plains are desart; they are only full of a Sort of Thorny Trees, which make the Roads very incommodious.

At length, on the 20th of *October* in the Morning, we arrived at *Santiago*, which was but four Leagues from our Lodging beyond *Podaguel*. Thus I reckon'd that it is eight and twenty Leagues from *Valparaiso*, tho' *Herrera* reckons but fourteen.

The Description of the City of Santiago, Capital of Chili.

Situation.

THE City of *Santiago*, or S. *James* the Apostle, is seated in 33 Degrees 40 Minutes of South Latitude, at the West Foot of the Chain of Mountains call'd *La Cordillera*,

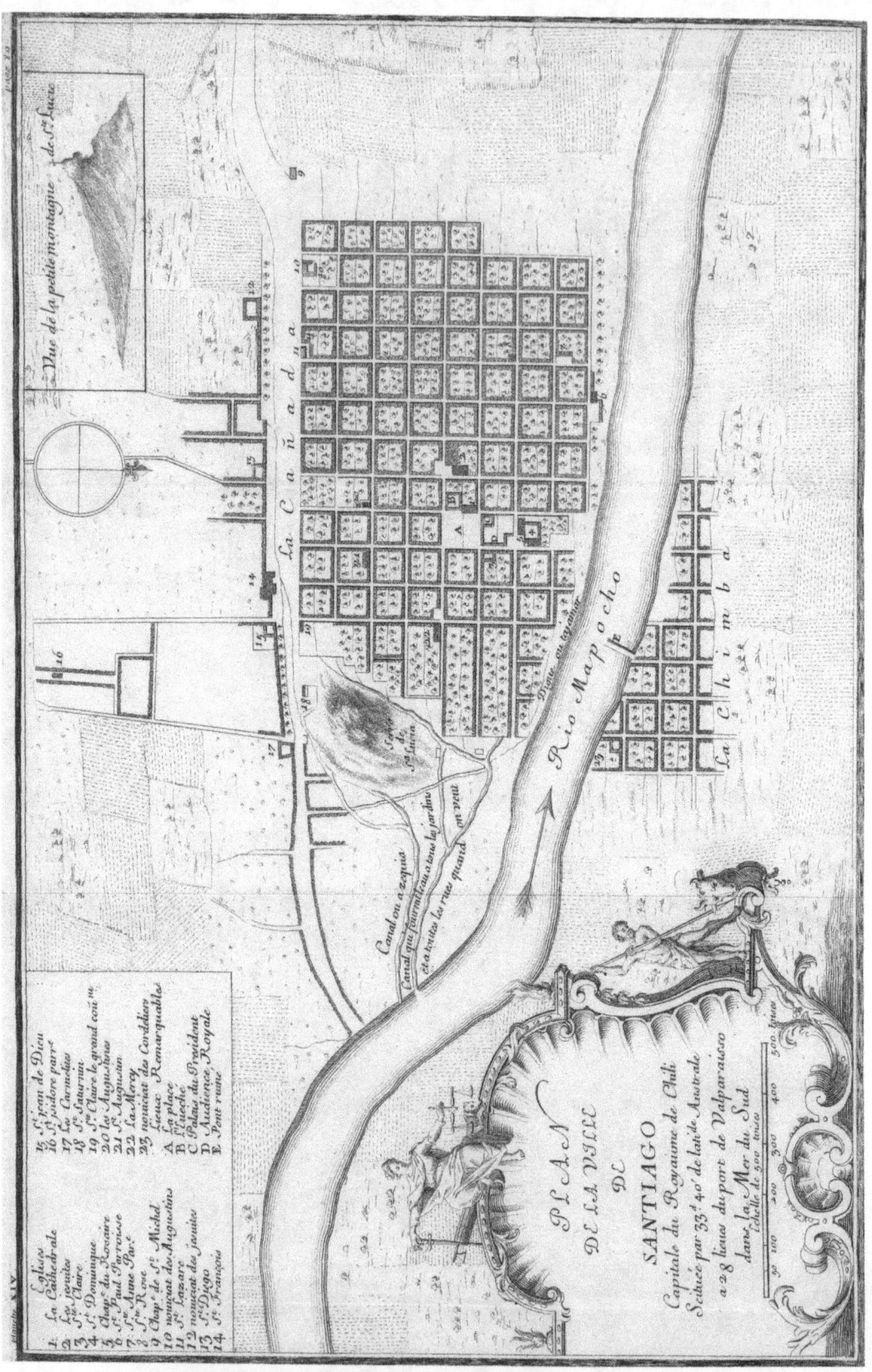

The material originally positioned here is too large for reproduction in this reissue. A PDF can be downloaded from the web address given on page iv of this book, by clicking on 'Resources Available'.

dillera, which runs quite through *South America* from North to South: It stands in a beautiful Plain of above 25 Leagues Surface, closed to the East by the Foot of the *Cordillera* Mountain, on the West by the Mountains of *Prado* and *Poangue*, on the North by the River of *Colina*, and on the South by that of *Maypo*.

It was founded by *Peter de Baldivia*, in the Year 1541. *Foundation.* That Conqueror of *Chili* having found a great Number of *Indian* Dwellings in the Vale of *Mapocho*, by it made a Judgment of the Fertility of the Soil; and the delightful

Situation

Plate XIV. *Page* 99. *explain'd in* English.

The Plan of the City of *SANTIAGO*, Capital of the Kingdom of *Chili*, in 33 Degrees, 40 Minutes of South Latitude, 28 Leagues from the Port of *Valparaiso*, in the *South-Sea*.

Churches.
1. *The Cathedral.*
2. *The* Jesuites.
3. *S. Clare.*
4. *S. Dominick.*
5. *The Chappel of the* Rosary.
6. *S. Paul, a Parish.*
7. *S. Anne, a Parish.*
8. *S. Rose.*
9. *S. Michael's Chappel.*
10. *The Noviciate of the* Augustins.
11. *S. Lazarus.*
12. *The Noviciate of the* Jesuites.
13. *S. James.*
14. *S. Francis.*
15. *S. John of God.*
16. *S. Isidore, a Parish.*
17. *The Carmelites.*
18. *S. Saturninus.*
19. *S. Clare, the Great Monastery.*
20. *The Augustins.*
21. *S. Augustin.*
22. *The Mercenarians.*
23. *The Noviciate of the* Franciscans.

Places of Note.
A. *The Square.*
B. *The Bishop's Palace.*
C. *The President's Palace.*
D. *The Royal Court.*
E. *A ruin'd Bridge.*

Vue de la petite Montagne de S. Lucie, *A Prospect of the little Hill of S. Lucy.*
La Cannada, *The Reed Ground.*
Canal, ou Azequia, *A Canal, or Trench.*
Canal qui fournit l'eau à tous les Jardins, & à tous les Rues quand on veut, *The Canal or Trench which supplies all the Gardens with Water, and the Streets, when thought fit.*
Cerro de Santa Lucia, *S. Lucy's Hill.*
Digue, ou Tajamar, *A Dike, or Fence, against the Water.*
Rio Mapocho, Mapocho *River.*
La Chimba, *A Place so call'd.*

The Plan.

Situation of the Place seeming to him proper to execute the Design he had of building a Town, he caus'd the Plan of it to be mark'd out in Squares, like a Draught-Board, by the same Measures as those of *Lima*, that is, 150 *Varas*, or *Spanish* Yards, or 64 Fathoms on each Side; whence came that Measure call'd *Quadra*, which they use in that Country to divide the Till'd Land, as it were into Acres. Each of those Squares of Houses was divided into four Parts, call'd by them *Solares*, for every Person to have a commodious Apartment. In short, tho' in Process of Time, that Space has been divided into several Parts: They have still so much Room, that there is scarce a House in the Town without a Court before it, and a Garden behind.

Waters.

The Town is water'd on the East Side by the little River of *Mapocho*, which is swell'd in Summer by the melting of the Snow on the Mountain call'd *La Cordillera*, and by the Rains in Winter: However, it is, for the most part, fordable. Being very rapid, its Water is almost always foul; but the Inhabitants, who have no other, take care to filtrate, or strain it through a Sort of Stones fit for that Purpose, especially at the Time when the Snows thaw, because it is then unwholsome, if not cleans'd: They might, nevertheless, without any great Trouble, bring Water from the Neighbouring Springs, which are not above half a League from the City.

Dyke and Trenches.

To prevent Inundations when the River overflows, they have built a Wall and a Dyke, by means whereof they at all Times convey Rivulets or Trenches to water their Gardens, and to cool the Streets when they think fit; an inestimable Conveniency to be found so naturally in few Cities in *Europe*. Besides these small Trenches, they draw larger Streams to drive the Mills there are in several Parts of the City, for the Conveniency of each Quarter.

Streets.

The Streets are laid with the four Cardinal Points of the Horizon, North, South, East and West. They are five Fathoms wide, exactly in a Line, and neatly paved with small Stones, divided in the Nature of Furrows, by others larger,

larger, crossing both Ways at equal Distances, and leaving in the Middle about two Foot and a half of running Water, to wash or cool them when they please. Those which run East and West, receive their Waters from the first Canals of the River; and those which cross from North to South from those which run in the Middle of the Squares of Houses a-cross the Gardens and the Streets, under little Bridges, whence it is caus'd to flow out. Were it not for that Relief, the Gardens would produce Nothing, for Want of Rain, during eight Months in the Year; whereas, by this Means, the City affords all the Delights of the Country, in relation to Fruit and Herbs; in the Day the cool Shade, and at Night the sweet Scents of Orange-Flowers and *Floripondio's*, which perfume the Houses.

The Earthquakes, which are there frequent, have much *Earthquakes.* endamaged the City; and among them, those of 1647 and 1657 The first of them was so violent, that it almost o-verturn'd the whole, and left such unwholsome Vapours in the Air, that all the Inhabitants died, except about 3 or 400. Since that Time there has been some little Alteration in the Plan, by the enlarging of the Monasteries; some of which have extended themselves beyond the strait Lines: However, it is still so open, and well distributed for the Conveniency of the publick and private Persons, that if the Houses were raised above the Edge of the Street, and of a better Structure, it would be a very agreeable City.

Much about the Middle of it is the great Square, call'd *Royal Square Plaça Real*, or the Royal Square, made by the Suppression of one Quarter, the Surface whereof contains 4096 Fathoms, besides the Breadth of four Streets; so that there are eight Avenues leading into it. The West Side contains the Cathedral and the Bishop's Palace; the North Side, the President's new Palace, the Royal Court, the Council House, and the Prison The South Side is a continued Row of Portico's, or uniform Arches, for the Conveniency of Merchants, with a Gallery over it to see the

Bull

Bull Feasts: The East Side has nothing peculiar. In the midst of the Square is a Fountain, with a Brass Bason.

Houses and Churches.

The Structure of the Houses is the same as is used throughout all *Chili*; they have only a Ground Floor, built with unburnt Bricks, excepting that here they are handsomer than elsewhere, and the Churches richer in gilding; but all the Architecture is of an ill Taste, excepting that of the *Jesuites*, which is a *Latin* Cross, arch'd, on a *Dorick* Order; they have all a small open Place before them for the Conveniency of Calashes and of Processions: Most of them are built with Brick; there are some of regular Stone, as also of small Stone, which they have from a small Rock that is at the East End of the City, call'd S. *Lucy*'s Hill, from the Top of which there is an entire View of all the City and Parts adjacent, which afford a very agreeable Landskip.

Towns in Chili.

This City is the Capital of *Chili*, a large Kingdom, but so ill peopled, that in 400 Leagues Extent from North to South, there are scarce five Towns better than our good Villages, not including that we are speaking of. Those Towns are *Castro* in the Island of *Chiloe*, *La Conception* or *Penco*, *Chillan*, *Coquimbo* or *La Serena*, and *Copiapo*. There is a 6th beyond the Mountain call'd *La Cordillera*, which is *Mendoza*. The best Boroughs are *Maule*, *Valparaiso*, *Quillota*, *Aconcagua*, and S. *John de la Cordillera*, where there are very rich Silver Mines; but which cannot be wrought above four Months in the Year, because of the Snows. Throughout all the rest, there are only Farms, which they call *Estancias*, so remote from one another, that the whole Country, as I have been inform'd from

Number of Inhabitants.

good Hands, cannot raise 20000 Whites fit to bear Arms, and particularly *Santiago* 2000; the rest are all *Mestizo's*, *Mulatto's*, and *Indians*, whose Number may be three Times as great, without including the Friendly *Indians* beyond the River *Biobio*, who are reckon'd to amount to 15000, whose Fidelity is not to be depended on.

What may be said in general of the Strength of the *Spa-* *Military*
niards in that Country is, that their Military Power is *Power.*
composed of Men who are much scatter'd about, not disciplin'd, and ill arm'd ; that the North Part of *Chili* is almost desart, and that the conquer'd *Indians* in the South
Part are not well affected towards that Nation, whom
they look upon as their Tyrants, whose Yoke they would
willingly shake off; and in Couclusion, that the *Spaniards*
have no Fortifications in their Lands, where they may secure themselves, unless they fly to the Mountains ; and a-
gainst a Maritime Force, they have none but those of *Baldivia* and *Valparaiso* ; the one full of Men, who are Prisoners, and the other ill built, and in a bad Condition.
I do not here reckon the Fort of *Chacao*, in the Island of
Chiloe, which does not deserve that Name, either on Account of its Structure, or its Stores.

 The Governor of the Kingdom has his usual Residence *The Governor.*
at *Santiago*. The Sieur *de Fer* rely'd too much on ancient
Relations, and was mistaken in the Discourse he inserts in
the last Chart of the *South-Sea*, where he says, The President resides at *La Conception*. Formerly, those who were
zealous for the King's Interest, liv'd at *La Conception*, or on
the Frontiers of *Arauco*, to carry on the Conquests over
the *Indians* ; and they are obliged to go thither every three
Years; but at present they save themselves the Trouble,
because they are at Peace with those *Indians*, and that the
Royal Allowance call'd *Situado* is not paid.

 The Governor also takes the Title of President and *The Royal*
Captain-General, on account of his two Employments of *Court.*
the Sword and Gown, and from the latter he derives his
Name, as presiding in the Royal-Court, composed of four
Oidores, or Judges, two *Fiscals*, or Attorneys General,
one of whom has the Charge of Protecting the *Indians*
and the Affairs of the *Croisade* ; also an *Alguazil Mayor de
Corte*, or Head Serjeant of the Court, the Chancery-Se-
cretary, Reporters, *&c.* There lies no Appeal from a
Judgment upon a Writ of Error, or Review upon a Royal
                 Decision,

Decision, which only takes Cognifance of Matters of Moment, or such as have been before decided in other Courts, unless it be to the Royal Council of the *Indies*.

The City Council.
Lesser Matters are decided in the Council-House, which like that of *La Conception* is composed of two *Alcaldes*, a Royal Ensign, an *Alguazil Mayor*, or Head Serjeant, one Depository-General, and six *Regidores* or Aldermen, the one half whereof are *Encomendaderos*, or such as have *Indians* committed to them, others only Inhabitants, and others call'd Proprietors, because they have bought their Employments, the Badge whereof is a Wand six or seven Foot long.

President.
Tho' the President is subordinate to the Viceroy of *Peru*, the Distance very much lessens the Subordination; so that he may be look'd upon in *Chili* as a Viceroy himself, for the seven Years his Government lasts. He that was then in the Post was call'd *Don John Andres Ustaris*, formerly a Merchant in *Sevil*, who, tho' he had changed his Condition, had not changed his Inclination or Occupation; for notwithstanding the Laws of the Kingdom, he traded publickly with the *French*, who have considerably rais'd his Fortune by the great Credit they have given him. It is true, he has fairly made Satisfaction, a Thing to be commended in a Country where a Man may abuse his Authority, where they borrow with more Ease than elsewhere, but do not pay so well.

Church Government.
The Ecclesiastical State, as well as the Secular, has a Dependence on *Lima*, the Metropolis of *Peru*; but the Bishop's Power is very much circumscribed; first by the Laws of the Country, which do not allow him the Disposal of any Cure; he has only a Right to present three Persons, of whom the President chooses one in the King's Name, whatsoever Month it is in; so that even the Pope has not his Turn, as in *Europe*: Secondly, the Religious Men pretend to encroach upon the Functions of Curates, which the *Jesuites* think they have a Right to perform wheresoever they please, not to mention an infinite Number

of other Privileges they have in the *Indies*, and whereof they were making a particular Theological Treatise at the Time when I was at *Santiago*; for which Reason the Parish Churches are little resorted to there: There are three besides the Cathedral, being S. *Paul*, S. *Anne*, and S. *Isidore*, whose Churches are the smallest, and the most neglected. There are eight Monasteries of Men, three of *Franciscans*, two of *Jesuites*, one of the *Mercenarians*, one of the Brethren of S. *John* of God, and one of *Dominicans*, which are the only Orders establish'd throughout all *Chili*. There are five of Nuns, one of *Carmelites*, one of *Augustins*, one of *Queazels*, a 'Confraternity of the Rule of S. *Augustin*, and two of *Poor Clares:* All these Communities are numerous, and in some of them there are above 200 Persons.

The Tribunal of the Inquisition of *Chili* is also settled there; the Commissary General resides at *Santiago*, and his Officers, as those call'd *Familiares*, and Commissaries are dispers'd through all the Towns and Villages subordinate to him. They employ themselves upon the Notions of Sorcerers true or false, and certain Crimes, the Cognizance whereof belongs to the Inquisition, as *Polygamy*, &c. For as for Hereticks, I am sure none fall into their Hands. They there study so little, that they are not subject to run astray through too much Curiosity; only the Desire to distinguish themselves from others by an honourable Title, makes some Church-men learn a little School Divinity and Morality, to bear the Name of Licentiate, or Doctor, which the *Dominicans* and the *Jesuites* can conferr by a Privilege obtain'd from the Popes, tho' there be no University establish'd at *Santiago*; but these Titles are to be had of them so easily, that there are some among the Licentiates who know little *Latin*, which they do not look upon as necessary for attaining the Sciences. *Inquisition.*

Whilst I was taken up in viewing and getting acquainted with the City of *Santiago*, an Affair happen'd, which obliged me to withdraw. The Boat belonging to the Ship, call'd *Unlucky Accident.*

call'd the *Virgin of Grace* of *S. Malo*, which had put into *La Conception*, in her Way back to *France* being laden with some Goods to be set ashore, occasion'd some Difference between the *French* and the *Corregidor*'s Guards, who opposed it. The said *Corregidor* resenting that Opposition, went away to the Ship's Store-house, follow'd by the Mob, and plunder'd it; but a *French* Man firing a Piece that was charged with small Shot, unfortunately kill'd a Soldier. All the *French* then in the Town were committed to Gaol, Search being made for them from House to House. The Captain immediately sent an Officer to the President, to complain of that Violence, and demand Justice. This Advice made some Noise at *Santiago*; and the *Spaniards* naturally hating our Nation, tho' we be never so little Blame-worthy, among them our Crimes are look'd upon as enormous: I therefore thought it convenient to withdraw myself, whilst the President and Council gave Judgment against the unfortunate Strangers, and condemn'd them to pay a Fine of 9000 Pieces of Eight.

The Gold Mines of Tiltil.

THE earnest Desire I had to see Gold Mines, and new Places, made me take the Way of *Tiltil*, which is only two Leagues round about, to return to *Valparaiso*. That Country is somewhat less desart than the other of *Zapata*: There are now and then some Till'd Lands to be seen; and tho' there is a very uncooth Mountain to pass, there are none of those troublesome Defiles among the Thorny Trees. where a Man is torne on every Side. I arrived at *Tiltil*, a small Village seated a little above half way up a high Mountain, all full of Gold Mines; but besides that they are not very rich, the Stone of the Mine, or Mineral, is very hard, and there are few Labourers, since others richer have been discover'd elsewhere; as also, because the Mills want Water four Months in the Year. When I pass'd that Way, there were five of those Mills, which

Tiltil village and Mines.

the *Spaniards* call *Trapiches*, being made much after the Manner of those used in *France* to grind Apples for Cyder: They consist of a Trough, or great round Stone, about five or six Foot Diameter, with a circular Channel cut in it 18 Inches deep. This Stone is bored in the Middle, to let through the long Axle-tree of an Horizontal Wheel plac'd on it, and set round with Half Pitchers, on which the Water falls to make it turn; by that Means there comes to roll along the Circular Channel a Milstone, placed upright, and answering to the Axle-tree of the great Wheel. That Mill-stone is call'd *Volteadora*, or, that turns about; its usual Diameter is three Foot four Inches, and its Thickness ten, or fifteen Inches: Through the Center of it runs an Axle-tree, fix'd into the Main-tree, which causing it to turn vertically, grinds the Stone taken from the Mine, which those Country People call the Metal, and we, according to Founders Terms, the Ore. Some of it is white, some reddish, and some blackish; but most of it shews little or no Gold to the Eye.

Mills.

When the Stones are a little broken, they put to them a certain Quantity of Mercury, or Quicksilver, which clings to the Gold the Mill has separated from the Stone it has ground: Then they let fall into the Circular Trough a Stream of Water, rapidly convey'd along a little Channel, to dissolve the Earth which it forces out at a Hole made for that Purpose. The Gold incorporated with the Mercury sinks to the Bottom, and is detain'd there by its own Weight: They grind in a Day half a *Caxon*, that is, 25 *Quintals*, or hundred Weight of the Ore; and when they have done grinding, they gather up that Paste of Gold and Quicksilver which lies at the Bottom of the deepest Part of the Trough; they put it into a Linnen Bag to squeeze out the Mercury, as near as they can; then they put it to the Fire for the rest to evaporate: And this is what they call *Oro en pinna*, or Gold clung together like a Pine-Apple.

How the Gold is extracted.

P 2 In

Refining.   In order to clear the Gold quite from the Quicksilver it is still impregnated with, the Lump must be run, and then they know the exact Weight, and the true Fineness. It is not done any otherwise there; the Weightiness of the Gold, and the Facility of its making an *Amalgama*, or Paste with the Mercury, makes the Dross immediately part from it. This is an Advantage the Gold Miners have over those of Silver; they every Day know what they get; whereas the others sometimes do not know it till two Months after, as shall be said in another Place.

Gold weight.   The Weight of Gold is regulated by *Castellano's*, and a *Castellano* is the hundredth Part of a *Spanish* Pound Weight: It is divided into eight *Tomines*; just six *Castellano's* and two *Tomines* make an Ounce. It is to be observ'd, that the *Spanish* Weight is 6 ⅓ per Cent. less than the *French* Standard.

Fineness.   The Fineness of the Gold is reckon'd by *Quilates*, or Carats limited to 24 for the highest; that of the Mines I speak of, is from 20 to 21.

Product of Gold.   According to the Nature of the Mines, and the Richness of the Veins, every *Caxon*, or 50 Quintals, that is, hundred Weight, yields four, five, or six Ounces; when it yields but two, the Miner does not make good his Charges, which often happens; but he has also sometimes good Amends made him, when he meets with good Veins; for the Gold Mines are, of all those which produce Metals, the most unequal; they follow a Vein, which grows wider, then narrower, and sometimes seems to be lost in a small Space of Ground. This Sport of Nature makes the Miners live in hopes of finding what they call the Purse, being the Ends of Veins, so rich, that they have sometimes made a Man wealthy at once; and this same Inequality sometimes ruins* them, which is the Reason, that it is more rare to see a Gold Miner rich than a Silver Miner, or of any other Metal, tho' there be less Expence in drawing it from the Mineral, as shall be said hereafter: For this Reason also the Miners have particular Privileges, for they

* *Gold hath been the Ruin of many, and their Destruction was present.* Eccl. xxxi. 6.

cannot

cannot be sued to Execution on Civil Accounts, and Gold pays only a 20th Part, to the King, which is call'd *Covo*, from the Name of a private Person, to whom the King made that Grant, because they used before to pay the Fifth, as they do of Silver.

The Gold Mines, like all others of what Metal soever, belong to him who first discovers them. There needs nothing but presenting a Petition to the Magistrates to have them adjudg'd to him. They measure on the Vein 80 *Vara's*, or *Spanish* Yards in length, that is, 246 Foot, and 40 in breadth, for him it is adjudg'd to, who chooses that Space as he thinks fit. Then they measure 80 more, which belong to the King; the rest goes to the first Claimer, according to the same Measure, who disposes of it as he pleases. That which belongs to the King, is sold to the highest Bidder, who is willing to purchase an unknown and uncertain Treasure. Farthermore, those who are willing to labour themselves, easily obtain of the Miner a Vein to work on: What they get out of it is their own, paying him the King's Duty, and the Hire of the Mill, which is so considerable, that some are satisfy'd with the Profit it yields, without employing any to work for them in the Mines.

To whom Mines belong

Formerly the Practice was otherwise, and there were more Formalities in adjudging the Mines in *Germany*, as may be seen in *Agricola*, L. 4. He who had made a Discovery, signify'd the same to the Intendant of the Mines, who repair'd to the Place with another Officer and two Witnesses, to examine the Claimer, where his Mine was, which he was obliged to point out, and, at the same time, to swear that it was his own: Then the Intendant assign'd him, for his Part, a certain Extent, containing two Acres and a half, according to the Custom of the Country. Then he measur'd one for the Prince, another for the Princess, a Third for the Master of the House, a Fourth for the Cup-Bearer, a Fifth for the Chamberlain, and lastly, he kept one for himself.

Ancient Practice, as to Mines.

Departing-

Rich Stream.   Departing from *Tiltil*, I continued my Journey for *Valparaiso*. On the Descent of the Mountain on the West Side, they shew'd me a Stream, where there is a rich *Lavadero*, or Place for washing of Gold. They there sometimes find Bits or Lumps of pure Gold, which weigh about an Ounce; but the Water failing in the Summer, they cannot work there above three or four Months in the Year.

Natural Crucifix.   The same Day I proceeded to *Limache*, a Village, where a Tree was found, the Figure whereof Father *Ovalle* gives, in his Relation of the Missions of *Chili*. There is such another at *Rincan*, two Leagues W. N. W. from *Santiago*. It is a Cross form'd by Nature, on which is a Crucifix of the same Wood, as it were in Bass Relief: The Carvers have spoil'd it, by having touch'd up several Parts; for there is now no seeing what it was when first found.

Another.   Don *Francisco Antonio de Montalvo*, mentions such a Tree found in the Year 1533, at *Callacate*, in the Territory of *Caxamalca*, in the Kingdom of *Peru*, on the Day of the Invention of the Holy Cross. Don *John Ruiz Bravo*, who discover'd it, having left it, it was again found in the same Place in 1677, on the Day of the Exaltation of the Cross: If these Circumstances are true, they have something miraculous. This Cross is 22 Foot long, and 15 in the Arms, whereof the Thickness of the Tree takes up a third Part. From its three Extremities, Branches sprout out, which form so many more little Crosses.

Bad Travelling.   At length I arrived at *Valparaiso*, displeas'd with travelling in that Country, where neither Houses nor Provisions, nor Places to lodge, are to be found; so that Travelers must carry so much as their very Beds, unless they will comply to lie like the Natives on the Ground, upon Sheeps Skins, with the Sky for their Canopy. It is true, that way of traveling has this Advantage, That *Rablais*'s Quarter of an Hour, that is, when the Reckoning is to be paid, does not disturb a Man *

* Note, That the Pasture along the Road is common by Order of the King.

To

the South-Sea.

To make amends for not having seen the Ore ground at *Tiltil*, I went, some Days after my Return, to see Gold taken by washing, near *Palma*, four Leagues E. and by S. from *Valparaiso*, where the *Jesuites* had Men at work for them.

They dig in the Bottom of Streams, in the inward Angles, which are form'd in Process of Time, where they judge by certain Tokens that there may be Gold; for it does not appear to the Eye where it is. To facilitate this Digging, they let a Rivulet into it, and whilst it runs, they turn up the Earth, to the end that the Current may dissolve and carry it away the better. At length, when they are come to the Floor of Earth where the Gold is, they turn off the Stream to dig by Strength of Arms: That Earth they carry on Mules to a little Bason, made in the Shape of a Smith's Bellows, into which they turn a little rapid Stream of Water to dissolve it; and to the end it may the better soak in and loosen the Gold that is mix'd with it, they continually stir it about with an Iron Hook, which also serves to gather the Stones, and these they throw out of the Bason with their Hands. This Precaution is necessary, to the end they may not stop the Water-Course, which is to carry all away, except the Gold, whose great Weight makes it sink to the Bottom of the Bason, among a sort of fine black Sand, where it is not much less hid than in the Earth, if there are no Grains at least as big as a Lentil. There are often larger found; and at the Washing-Place I speak of, they had found some of three Marks Weight, that is, twenty four Ounces. However, I do not question but that abundance of small Particles of Gold run out at that Channel from the Bason, which might be easily remedy'd. In *Turingia*, and on the *Rhine*, to save that Loss, they lay on the Channel some Linnen. Woollen, or Horses or Ox Hides, to the end that the small Grains of Gold may stick there; and afterwards they wash the Skins to recover it. Thus the People of *Colchis* gather'd it, having laid the Skins of Beasts in the hollow

Washing-place for Gold.

Parts

Parts of Springs, which gave occasion to the Poets to invent the Fable of the Golden-Fleece carry'd off by the *Argonauts*.

At last, after turning off the Water, they gather up that Sand which remains at the Bottom of the Bason, and put it into a great Wooden Platter, in the Middle whereof is a little Hollow or Depth of about a Quarter of an Inch: They stir and turn it with their Hands in Water, so that all the Earth and Sand there, runs over the Edges, only the Gold, which that little Motion of the Hand cannot sufficiently remove, remains at the Bottom in Grains bigger or smaller than Sand, of all sorts of Shapes, pure, clean, and of its natural Colour, without adding any other Help of Art.

This Way of getting Gold is much more beneficial, when the Earth is indifferently rich, than working at the Mines. The Expence is but small; there is no need of any Mill, nor of Quicksilver, nor of Crows, and other Instruments, to break the Veins with much Labour; a few Shovels sometimes made of the Blade Bones of Oxen are sufficient to dissolve the Earth that is wash'd.

Almost all the Streams in *Chili* have Earth, whence Gold may be drawn, only the greater or lesser Quantity makes the Difference. It is commonly reddish, and small on the Surface; at about the Depth of a Man, it is mix'd with Grains of coarse Sand, or Gravel, where the Bed of Gold begins; and, digging deeper, there are Layers of Stony Bottom, as it were a moulding Rock, bluish, mix'd with abundance of yellow Straws, which a Man would be apt to take for Gold, but which, in Reality, are no other than the *Marcassite*, or yellow Fire-stone, so small and light, that the Current of the Water carries them away. Below those Beds of Stone no more Gold is found; it seems to be detain'd above, as having fallen from a higher Place.

Opinion about Gold. The most learned Men in the Country ascribe this Mixture of Gold with the Earth to the universal Flood, which overturn'd the Mountains, and consequently broke up the

Mines,

Mines, and loofed the Gold, which the Waters drove into the lower Grounds, where it has continued to this Day.

This Opinion, which Mr. *Woodward* has very much en- *Difprov'd.* forc'd, is not well grounded on Scripture; which, instead of speaking of such Overturning, seems, on the contrary, to signify to us, that the Deluge made very little Alteration on the Surface of the Earth, since the second Time that *Noah* let go the Dove, she brought back an Olive Branch. It may perhaps be alledg'd, that it was a Piece that floated of a Tree torne up, or broken, since, according to the Report of Travelers, there are no Olive Trees about Mount *Ararat*, where the Ark rested, according to Tradition. Tho' that were so, it is at least likely, that the third Time she found something to subsist on, since she did not return, by which the Patriarch understood that the Waters were dry'd.

Without going back to such remote Times, I am of *Another Opi-* Opinion, that the Winter Rains alone may have caused the *nion.* same Effect; they are so heavy in *Chili* during the Months of *May, June, July* and *August*, and the Ground is so little supported by Rocks, that every Day there are new Breaks, or Channels, form'd and enlarged on the Declivity of the Mountains, which visibly sink in an Infinity of several Places.

The frequent Earthquakes have also, doubtless, occa- *Reinforc'd.* sion'd great Alterations in that Country. *Acosta* tells us of one, which in *Chili* overturn'd whole Mountains; the falling of which stopp'd the Course of Rivers, and turn'd them into Lakes, and made the Sea run several Leagues beyond its Bounds, leaving the Ships upon dry Ground.

This Reason will not fit other Countries, where Gold *More No-* Dust is found, as in the Rivers of *Guinea*, and Parts adja- *tions.* cent; it may be supposed, with the Author of the Book, entitul'd, *Curiositates Phiolosophicæ*, *Lond.* 1713, that the Mountains have been overturn'd by a Fermentation; and that the Mines, not yet rightly form'd, burst, and in Pro-

Q cess

cess of Time ran into the lower Parts, such as the Channels of Rivers.

Tho' we are not rightly inform'd of the Manner how great Movements or Alterations have been made in the Earth, yet there is no Reason to doubt of them, when we observe some Bodies that are found out of their natural Place, and particularly Shells. I have seen a Bank of them in the Island of *Quiriquina*, five or six Foot high, parallel with the Surface of the Sea, enclosed within an Eminence of Earth above 200 Foot high. Such Observations have been long since made in *Europe*, which have found the Learned much Employment, without being able to assign sufficient Reasons for it.

More probable Opinion.

It may also be supposed with many of the Natives of the Country, that the Gold is form'd in the Earth, even without any Mineral Vein; grounding their Opinion on this, that after many Years Gold has been found in the Earth that had been wash'd, as many Persons report it of the Washing-Places of *Andacol*, near *Coquimbo*. We shall examine this Opinion elsewhere.

Be it as it will, it is certain that those Washing-Places are very common in *Chili*; that the Negligence of the *Spaniards*, and the Want of Labourers, leave immense Treasures in the Earth, which they might easily enjoy; but as they do not confine themselves to small Advantages, they only apply themselves to the Mines, where a considerable Profit is to be found: If any such new Discovery is made, they all run thither. Thus have we seen *Copiapo* and *Lampanguy* peopled all on a sudden, and so many Workmen drawn thither, that in two Years they had erected six Mills at the latter of those Mines.

Lampanguy Mines.

The Mountain of S. *Christopher* of *Lampanguy* is near the *Cordillera* Ridge of Mountains, in about 31 Degrees of South Latitude, 80 Leagues from *Valparaiso*. In the Year 1710 many Mines were discover'd there of all Sorts of Metals, Gold, Silver, Iron, Lead, Copper and Tin, which overthrows the Arguments of the Author above-mention'd, who thinks that all the said Metals cannot be found in the same

same Place; but Experience proves the contrary, for Gold and Silver are often seen mix'd in the same Stone.

The Gold of *Lampanguy* is from 21 to 22 Carats fine, the Ore is there hard; but two Leagues from thence, on the Mountain of *Llaoin*, it is soft, and almost crumbling; and there the Gold is in such fine Dust, that no Sign of it appears to the Eye.

It may be said in general, that all the Country is very rich, and that the Inhabitants are nevertheless very poor in Cash, because, instead of working at the Mines, they are satisfy'd with the Trade they drive of Hides, Tallow, dry'd Flesh, Hemp and Corn. *Trade of Chili.*

The Hemp comes from the Vales of *Quillota, Aconcagua, La Ligua, Limache,* and other Places.

The Vale of *Quillota* is nine Leagues N. E. and by N. from *Valparaiso*; it is one of the first Places where the *Spaniards* began to make Settlements, and to meet *Indians*, who opposed the Progress of their Conquests: That Opposition made that Vale and the River of *Chili*, which crosses it, famous; and as the first Names of a new Country are those which happen to be most taken Notice of, this same was afterwards given to all that great Kingdom, which the *Spaniards* call *Chile*, and Foreigners, corruptly, *Chili*. This is, doubtless, the true Etymology of the Name, which some Historians derive from an *Indian* Word, signifying Cold, according to them; for, in short, that Name would be very improper for so agreeable and temperate a Country as that is. *Quillota Vale.*

Chili, why so call'd. Herrera, *Dec.* 7. *l.* 1.

Be that as it will the Vale of *Quillota* did so abound in Gold, that General *Baldivia* thought fit to erect a Fort there for the Security of the Settlement, and to curb the *Indians* he employ'd to get the Gold but they possess'd themselves of it by a very ingenious Stratagem. One of them, on an appointed Day, carry'd thither a Pot full of Gold Dust, to excite the Curiosity and Covetousness of the Garrison-Soldiers. In short, they all soon gather'd about that little Treasure; and whilst they were busy contending *Indian Stratagem.*

about their private Interest to divide the same, an Ambuscade of *Indians*, conceal'd and arm'd with Arrows, rush'd in upon them, and found them defenceless. The Victors then destroy'd the Fort, which has never been rebuilt since; and they have given over searching for Gold there. At present that Vale is only remarkable for the Fertility of the Soil: There is in it a Village of about 150 Whites, and perhaps 300 *Indians* and *Mestizo's*, who trade in Corn, Hemp, and Cordage, which are carry'd to *Valparaiso*, to rig and lade the *Spanish* Ships, which thence transport it to *Callao*, and other Parts of *Peru*. They make their Cordage white, and without Tar, because they have none but what is brought them from *Mexico* and *Guayaquil*, which burns the Hemp, and is only good for the Timber of Ships. For the rest, the Plain of *Quillota* is very agreeable in itself: I was there at the Carnaval Time, or Shrove-Tide, which, in that Country, falls about the Beginning of Autumn. I was charm'd to behold such great Plenty of all *European* choice Fruits, which have been transplanted thither, and answer to Admiration; especially Peaches, of which Trees there are little Groves, that are never pruned, nor have any other Care taken of them, than to cause Trenches, drawn from the River of *Chili*, to water their Roots, to supply the Want of Rain in the Summer.

Corn Country. The River of *Chili* is also call'd the River of *Aconcagua*, because it comes from a Vale of that Name, famous for the prodigious Quantity of Corn carry'd from it yearly. From thence, and from the Country about *Santiago*, towards the *Cordillera* Ridge of Mountains, comes all that is transported from *Valparaiso* to *Callao*, *Lima*, and other Parts of *Peru*. Unless a Man be acquainted with the Nature of the Soil, which generally yields 60 or 80 for one, he cannot comprehend how so desart a Country, where no till'd Lands are to be seen, but only in some Vales at ten Leagues Distance from each other, can furnish so much Corn, besides what is requisite for the Maintenance of the Inhabitants.

During

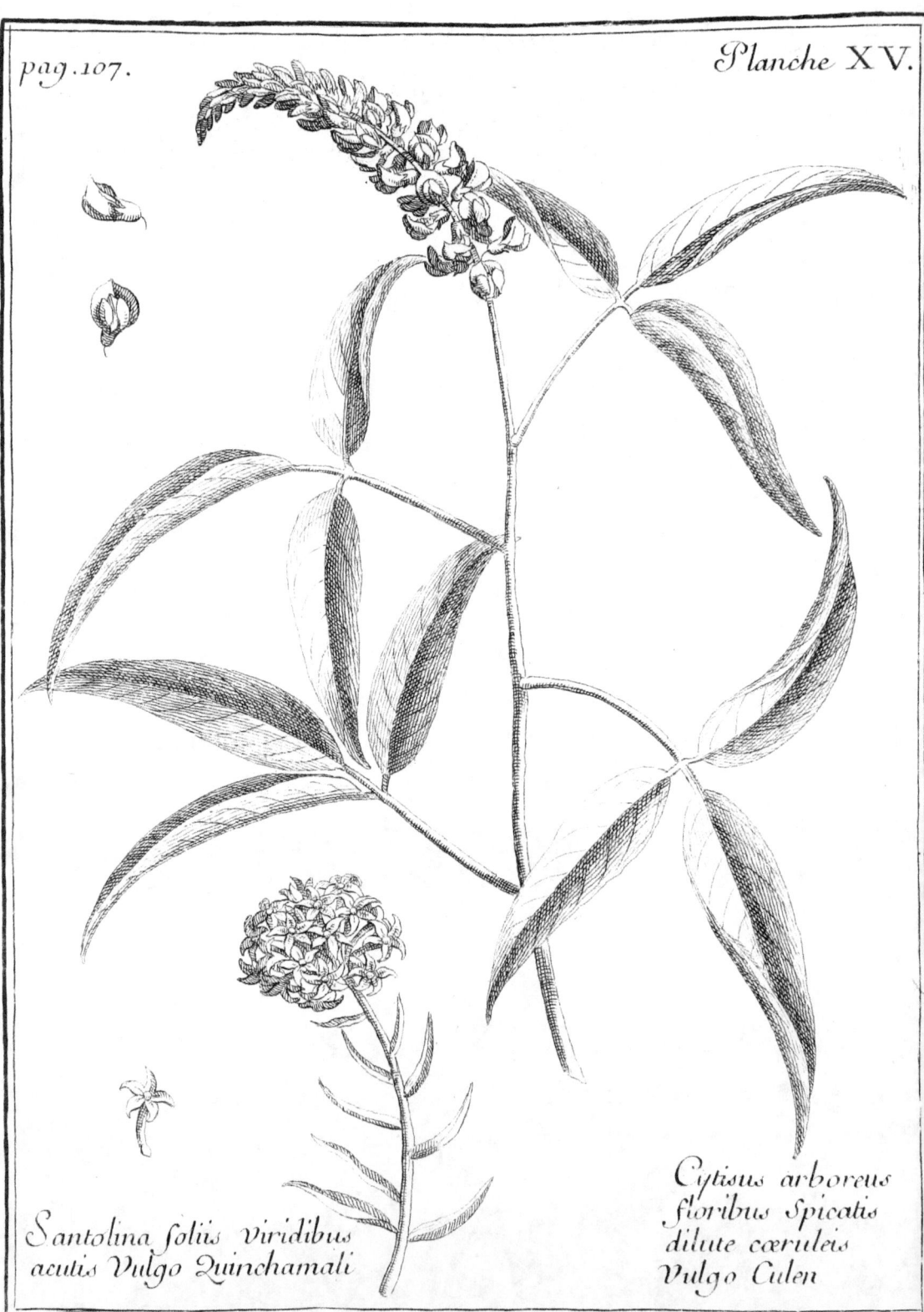

the South-Sea.   117

During the eight Months we stay'd at *Valparaiso*, thirty *Its Great Cheapness.* Ships sail'd from thence laden with Corn, the Burden of each of which may be reduc'd to 6000 *Hanegas*, or 3000 Mules Burden, which is enough to feed 60000 Men a Year. Notwithstanding that great Exportation, it is very cheap there, the *Hanega* weighing 150 Pounds, being sold from 18 to 22 Royals, which is about 9 or ten Livres *French*, a very inconsiderable Price for that Country, where the smallest Coin is a Silver Piece of four Sols and a Half *French*, which may be compared to two Liards, or an Half-Penny, with respect to the Division and Value. But as it does not rain there for eight or nine Months in the Year, the Land cannot in many Places be till'd, where there are no Brooks.

However, the Hills are cover'd with Herbs, among *Plants.* which there are many Aromatick, and Medicinal. Among the latter, the most famous with the Inhabitants of the Country is the *Cachinlagua*, a Sort of small Centaury, which seem'd to me more bitter than the *French*, and consequently more full of Salt, reckon'd an excellent Febrifuge. The *Viravida*, a Sort of Sempervive, the Infusion whereof was used with great Success by a *French* Surgeon for curing of a Tertian Ague. There is also a Sort of Senna, exactly like that which is brought us from *Seyde*, or *Sidon* in the *Levant*; for want of which, the Apothecaries at *Santiago* make use of this, which the *Indians* call *Unoperquen*; it is somewhat smaller than the *Mayten*, a Tree of that Country.

The *Alvahaquilla*, in the *Indian Culen*, is a Shrub which *Sweet Basil.* has the Scent of our Sweet Basil, and contains a Balm of great Use for Sores, whereof we saw a wonderful Effect at *Plate* XV. *Yrequin*, on an *Indian*, whose Neck was deeply ulcerated. I also had Experience of it on myself. The Flower of it

is

Plate XV. *Page* 117. *explain'd in* English.
The Quinchimali *Plant, a Sort of Dwarf Cypress, with sharp green Leaves.*
The *Plant* Culen, *being the Shrub call'd* Cytisus Arboreus, *or the large* Cytisus, *with Flowers like Ears of Corn, of a pale Blue.*

is long, growing up like an Ear of Corn, of Colour white inclining to Violet, and is of that Sort which is put into the Number of *Leguminous*.

Harillo. Another Shrub call'd *Harillo*, different from the *Harilla* of *Tucuman*, serves also for the same Use: It has a Flower like Broom, and the Leaf very small, of a strong Scent, somewhat inclining to that of Honey: It is so full of Balm, that it is all glutinous.

Payco. The *Payco*, is a Plant of an indifferent Size, the Leaf whereof is very much jagg'd; it smells strong of a rotten Lemon; its Decoction is a Sudorifick, very good against Pleurisies. They have also much Bastard Rosemary, which has the same Effect.

Palqui. The *Palqui* is a Sort of very stinking Walwort, having a yellow Flower, and serves to cure the Scurf, or Scald-Heads.

Thoupa. The *Thoupa* is a Shrub like Horse-Tongue, the Flower of it long, of an Aurora Colour, resembling that of Birthwort. Father *Feüillée*, who gives the Figure of it, calls it *Rapuntium spicatum foliis acutis*; from its Leaves and Rind proceeds a yellow Milk, wherewith they cure some Ulcers: In other respects they pretend it is a Poison, but not so sharp as he says, for I have handled and felt it without finding any Harm.

Bisnagas. The *Bisnagas* so well known in *Spain* for making of Pick-tooths, cover the Vales about *Valparaiso*; this Plant is very like Fennel.

Quillay. The *Quillay* is a Tree, the Leaf whereof somewhat resembles that of the green Oak; its Bark ferments in Water like Soap, and is better for washing of Woollen Cloaths, but not for Linnen, which it makes yellow. All the *Indians* make use of it for washing their Hair, and to cleanse their Heads instead of Combs; it is thought to be that which makes their Hair so black.

Coco Tree. The Coco Tree has Leaves much resembling those of the Date Palm Tree; it bears a Cluster of round Coco Nuts, as big as little Walnuts, and full of a white oily Substance, good to eat. The Country about *Quillota* furnishes *Lima* with them to preserve, and to entertain the

Children.

the South Sea.

Children. This Fruit is wrap'd up in several Coverings; that which is about the Shell, is a Rind like that of green Walnuts, by which they are knotted together like a Bunch of Grapes. Another Rind wraps up the whole, which opens when yellow and ripe, into two large Hemispheroides, three Foot long, and one in Breadth, according to the Quantity of Fruit it contains. Father *Ovalle* says, these Trees never produce Fruit single, but that there must be a Female by the Male, but the Inhabitants told me the contrary.

The Fruit Trees carried thither from *Europe*, answer in that Country to perfection; the Climate is so fertile when the Ground is water'd, that the Fruit is coming forward all the Year. I have often seen the same on one Apple-tree, which we here see in Orange-Trees, that is, Fruit of all different Ages or Growths, in Blossom, knotted, form'd Apples, half grown, and quite ripe, all together. *Great Fertility.*

A League and a Half N. E. from *Valparaiso*, is a little Vale called *La Vina à la Mar*, or the Vineyard next the Sea, where there are not only Trees fit for Fewel, whereof Ships lay in their Store, tho' somewhat remote, but also to make Planks and Ledges; and going up four or five Leagues farther, there is Timber fit to build Ships. We there cut Planks of a Sort of Bay-Tree, the Wood whereof is white and very light; of *Bellota*, another white Wood; of *Peumo*, which is very brittle; and of *Rauli*, which is the best and fastest. For Knee Timbers, there is the *Mayten*, the Wood of it is hard, reddish and fast. *Champloret le Brun*, Captain of the *Assumption*, whilst we were there, built a Bark of 36 Foot in the Keel, of the same sorts of Wood. *Wood.*

In the same Places is found the *Molle*, which the *Indians* call *Ovighan*, or *Huinan*, the Leaf of it is almost like that of the *Acacia*, its Fruit is a Cluster of little red Berries, like the *Dutch* Gooseberries, bating that these turn black as they ripen; it tastes of Pepper and Juniper. The *Indians* make *Chicha* or Drink of it, as good and as strong or *Molle.*

stronger

A *Voyage to*

stronger than Wine: The Gum of the Tree dissolv'd serves for a Purge. From this Tree they draw Honey, and they also make Vinegar. A little Incision being made in the Bark, there owzes from it a Milk which is said to cure the Web that grows on the Eyes; of the Heart of its Sprigs, they make a Water which clears and strengthens the Sight: Lastly, the Decoction of its Bark makes a Coffee Colour Tincture inclining to red, wherewith the Fishermen of *Valparaiso* and *Concon* dye their Nets, to the end the Fish may discern them the less.

Floats of blown Skins.

Plate XVI.

In order to cast their Nets in the Sea, those Fishermen make use of Floats instead of Boats, being great Bags made of Seal's Skins, fill'd with Wind; so well sew'd, that a very considerable Weight will not force any of it out, for there are some made in *Peru*, which will carry twelve Quintals and a Half, or fifty *Arrova's*, which is twelve Hundred Weight and a Half: The Manner of sewing them is peculiar, they pierce the two Skins put together with an Awl, or a Bone of the Fish call'd *Pezegallo*, and into every Hole they put a Wooden Pin, or Fish Bone, on both which they cross wet Guts over and under, to stop the Passage of the Air exactly. They tie two of those Blown Bags together, by means of certain Staves laid over them both, in such manner that the Fore-part be brought nearer than the Hind-part, and on that a Man ventures out, with a *Pagay*, or an Oar with two Paddles, or Blades, and if the Wind can help him, he puts up a little Cotton Sail:

Lastly,

Plate XVI. Page 120. *described in English.*
 A. *The Figure of a Float, made of the Skins of Sea-Wolves, or Seals, sew'd up, and blown full of Air, like Bladders.*
 B. *An* Indian *on a Float, seen Side-way.*
 C. *Another View fronting.*
 D. *Cross Pieces to unite the two Sides, or Halves of the Float.*
 E. *The Hole to blow it full of Air.*
 F. *The Manner of sewing the Skins.*
 G. *A Sea-Wolf, or Seal ashore.*
 H. *A Penguin.*

A. Plan d'une Balse faite de peaux de loups marins cousues et pleines d'air
B. Indien sur une Balse viie de Coté. C. autre viie de front
D. Trauerses pour rassembler les deux moitiez de la balse E trou pour
lenfler et la remplir d'air. F. maniere de Coudre les peaux
G. Loup marin a terre H Pingoüin.

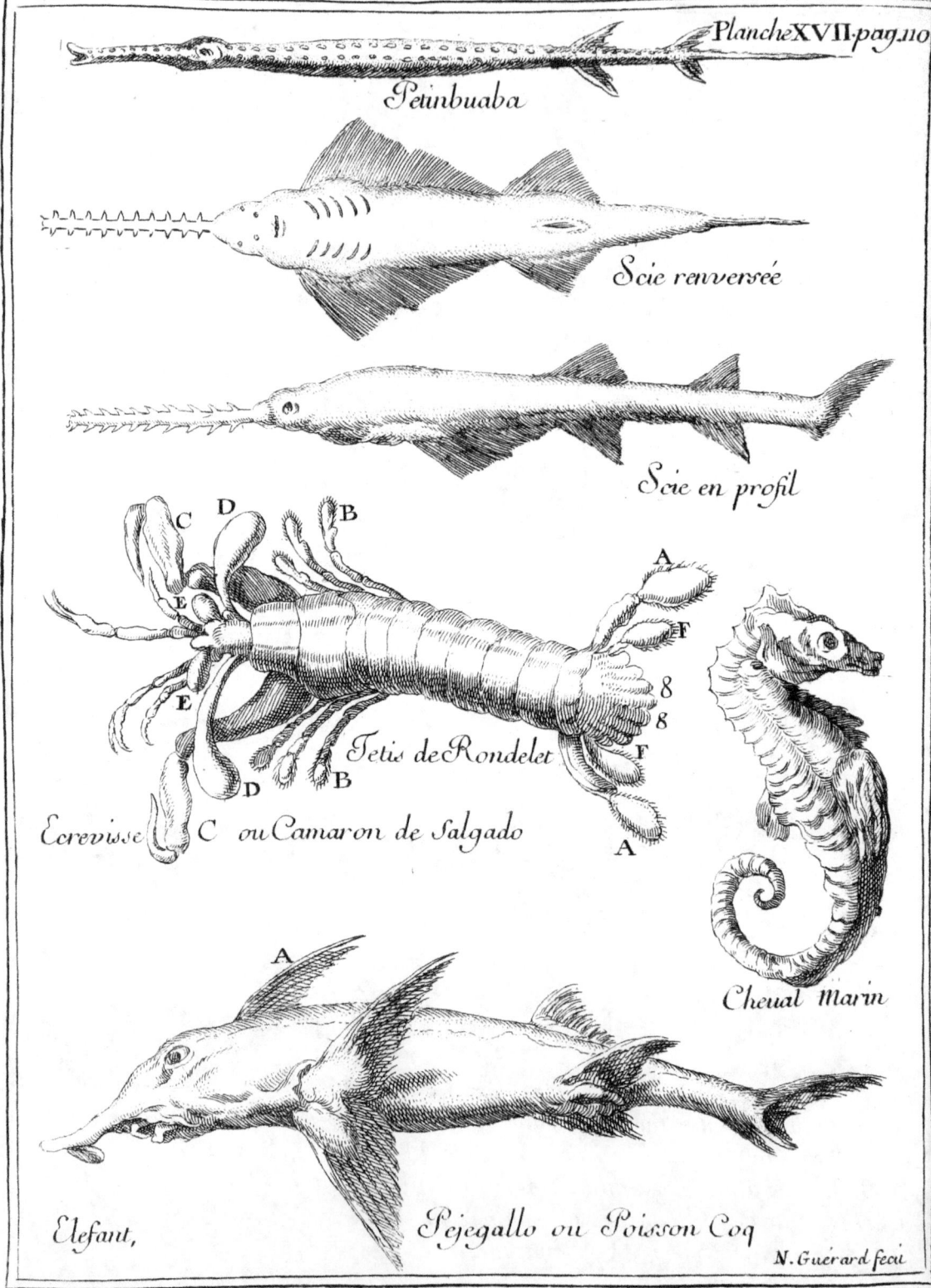

the South-Sea.

Lastly, to make good the Air that may get out, he has two Leather Pipes before him, through which he blows into the Bags when there is Occasion.

That Sort of Invention is not new in our Continent: When *Alexander* the Great pass'd the *Oxus* and the *Tanais*, Part of his Troops cross'd those Rivers on Hides fill'd with Straw; and S. *Jerome*, in his Epistles, tells us, that *Malchus* made his Escape on Goats Skins, with which he cross'd a River.

The great Fishery is carry'd on at *Concon*, a Hamlet two Leagues N. and by E. from *Valparaiso* by Sea, where there is a Creek into which the River of *Aconcagua*, or of *Chili*, which runs by *Quillota*, falls. There is Anchorage for Ships, but the Sea almost continually runs high: There they take *Corbinos*, a Sort of Fish known in *Spain*, *Tollos* and *Pezegallos*, which they dry to send to *Santiago*, which is also serv'd with fresh Fish from thence. *Fishery.*

The last of them takes its Name from its Shape, because it has a Sort of Comb, or rather a Trunk, which has given Occasion to the *Creolians* to call it *Pezegallo*, that is, Cock-Fish. The *French* call it *Demoiselle*, or *Elephant*, because of its Trunk, which is here to be seen, as I drew it by the Life; that mark'd A. is a Point so hard, that it may be made use of instead of an Awl to pierce the dryest Hides. *Pezegallo. Plate XVII.*

In the Bay of *Valparaiso*, there is a plentiful Fishery of all Sorts of good Fish, as *Pezereyes*, delicate Gurnards, Soles as above spoken of, Mullets,&c. not to mention an infinite Number of other Fishes that come in their proper Seasons, *Fishes.*

R   sons,

Plate XVII. *Page* 121. *explain'd in* English.

Petinbuaba, *A Fish so call'd.*
Scie renverse, *A Saw-Fish turn'd on its Back.*
Scie en Profil, *The Profile of the same Fish.*
Ecrevisse, &c. *A Sea-Crab, or Craw-Fish.*
Cheval Marin, *A Sea-Horse.*
Peze Gallo, ou Poisson Coq, *The Cock-Fish.*

sons, as Pilchards, and a Sort of Cod, which comes upon the Coasts about the Months of *October*, *November* and *December*; Shads, large Pikes, a Sort of Anchovies, whereof there is sometimes so great a Multitude, that they take whole Baskets full of them on the Surface of the Water.

I here represent a particular Sort of Crab, like that which *Rondelet* calls *Tetis* in *Greek*; and *Rumphius*, l. 1. c. 4. of his Natural History, *Squilla Lutaria*, the Colours whereof were extraordinary sprightly, and of singular Beauty; the two oval Fins A. were of the finest Blue that could be seen, edg'd with little Shaggs or Fringes of a Gold Colour; the Legs or Claws B. the like; the Defences C. were of the same Blue; D. represents two transparent Wings, or Fins; E. the Eyes; F. two Fins, inclining to Green, edg'd also with Jaggs, or Fringe; the Shell is of a Musk Colour, and the Extremities 8 are of a Flesh Colour, edg'd white; under the Head are 6 other Legs, or Claws doubled, which do not appear, the Extremities whereof are round, flat, blue and edg'd like the other Parts, with gilded Jaggs or Fringes.

Butchers Meat. Butchers Meat is not so good there, as at *La Conception*, especially in Summer. Most of the Sheep have four Horns, *Seven horned Sheep.* and sometimes five or six; I have seen some that had seven, four on the one Side, and three on the other; or three on each Side, and one in the Middle.

Wild Fowl. The like may be said of the Game, the wild Fowl is not well tasted there: However, about the farther Ends of Streams, there are abundance of Partridges, but they are dry, and almost insipid. The Wood Pigeons are there bitter, and the Turtle Doves are no Dainty. We one Day *Condor, Bird of Prey.* kill'd a Bird of Prey, call'd a *Condor*, that was nine Foot from the end of one Wing to the end of the other, and had a brown Comb, or Crest, but not jagg'd like a Cock's. The Fore-Part of its Throat is red, without Feathers like a *Turky*, and they are generally large and strong enough to take up a Lamb. In order to get them from the Flock, they draw themselves into a Circle, and advance towards

them

them with their Wings extended, to the end that being drove together, and too close, they may not be able to defend themselves; then they pick them out, and carry them off. *Garcilasso* says, there are some in *Peru* sixteen Foot, from the Point of one Wing to the other, and that a certain Nation of *Indians* adored them.

I must not here omit a Creature of so singular a Sort, that *Pulpo,* if seen without moving, it is taken for a Piece of a Branch *strange Creature.* of a Tree, cover'd with a Bark like that of a Chesnut Tree. It is as thick as a Man's little Finger, six or seven Inches long, and divided into four or five Knots or Joints, which grow smaller towards the Tail, which, as well as the Head, looks like no other than a broken Piece of a Bough of a Tree: When it stretches out its six Legs, and holds them close towards the Head, one would take them for so many Roots, and the Head for a broken Vine Branch. The *Chilinians* call it *Pulpo,* and say, that if it be handled with the naked Hand, it benums it for a Moment, without doing any farther Harm; which makes me believe, it is a Grashopper of the same Kind as that Father *Du Tertre* has drawn and described by the Name of *Coqsigrue,* in the History of the *Caribbee* Islands; with this Difference, that I did not observe it had a forked Tail, nor the two little Excrescences like Points of Pins, which he gives to his *Coqsigrue.* Besides, he does not mention a little Bladder the *Pulpo* has, full of a black Liquor, which makes very fine Ink to write with. Be that as it will, this is doubtless the *Arumazia Brasilia* of *Margrave,* l. 7. Pag. 251.

We also took at *Valparaiso* two monstrous and hairy *Monstrous* Spiders, like those which Father *Du Tertre* has drawn, which *Spiders.* he says are full of a dangerous Poison: However, these are not reckon'd so in *Chili.*

We continued eight Months at *Valparaiso,* during which *Earthquakes.* Time, there was nothing remarkable: There were several Earthquakes, especially in the Months of *October* and *November,* on which we shall make some Remarks elsewhere.

Frier complimented. The Commissary General of the *Franciscans* in the *West-Indies*, who came from *Europe* by the Way of *Buenos Ayres*, arrived there towards the latter End of the Year 1712; the Fortress upon his Arrival, saluted him with three Guns, and the same at his Departure on the 10th of *January*. When he embark'd in the Road for *Lima*, all the *French* Ships saluted him with seven Guns each, by the Governor's Order. By this may be judg'd, in what Esteem Religious Men are with the *Spaniards*, since even those in Command endeavour to cultivate their Friendship.

Reception of Nuns. Some time after, four *Capucin* Nuns also arriv'd from *Spain*, by the way of *Buenos Ayres*, and embark'd on the 13th of *January* for *Lima*, to settle and govern a Monastery of their Order that had been founded and built there. They were saluted by the Fort, and all the Ships that were in the Road, with seven Guns, a remarkable Epocha for the Annals of the Sisters of the Order of S. *Francis*. At their Arrival at *Lima*, they were received by the whole City in Procession, and with as much Solemnity as could have been done for the King.

The 22d of the same Month, the S. *Clement*, a Ship of fifty Guns, commanded by the Sieur *Jacinte Gardin* of S. *Malo*, arrived from *La Conception*, with its Pink of twenty Guns. It carry'd *Spanish* Colours and Pendants, as having the King of *Spain*'s Licence to trade along the Coast, for 50000 Crowns. It brought the *Oidor*, or Judge, Don *Juan Calvo de la Torre*, who was retiring to *Santiago*, being weary of struggling continually with the bad Inclination of the People of *La Conception*, where he had been Governor.

General of the South-Sea. On the 8th of *April*, the General of the *South-Sea*, Don *Pedro Miranda*, arrived from *Buenos Ayres*, to go and take Possession of his Post at *Lima*. The Fort saluted him with five Guns at his Arrival, and the same at his Departure: Then all our Ships saluted him with seven Guns, and the *Spanish* Ships with as many as they had.

For the reſt, all that was remarkable in relation to our Ship, was the Ducking of a Sailor, for having abſented himſelf from on board, for twelve Days, contrary to the Orders given. *Ducking.*

The 26th of *January*, the ſame Puniſhment was inflicted on another Sailor convicted of a Theft, which he confeſs'd; the next Day he was whipp'd at the Main-maſt, inſtead of being duck'd at the Yard-Arm, as is uſed at Sea.

The 6th of the ſame Month, the *Mary* being leaky, was carreen'd, and only tarr'd, for want of other Neceſſaries.

On *Maundy Thurſday*, the *Auguſtins* gave the Sieur *Ducheſne* the Key of the Tabernacle of their Church, in which the bleſſed Sacrament was kept: That is a Cuſtom cunningly invented by the Religious Men, to eaſe themſelves of the Expences they are obliged to be at on that Day. They do a Lay-man the Honour of giving him that Key to wear 24 Hours, hanging about his Neck with a broad Gold Ribbon, or Galoon; in Return for which, and in good Manners, the Keeper is obliged to preſent the Monaſtery with a Quantity of Wax; to treat the Monks, notwithſtanding the Penitential Time; and beſides, to perform ſome other Act of Generoſity towards them. The ſame Night, after a Sermon of the Sorrows of the Virgin *Mary*, they perform'd the Ceremony of taking our Saviour down from the Croſs, having a Crucifix purpoſely made, in the ſame Manner as might be done to a Man. As they drew the Nails, and took off the Crown of Thorns, and other Inſtruments of the Paſſion, the Deacon carry'd them to an Image of the bleſſed Virgin, clad in Black; ſo contrived, that ſhe took them in her Hands, and kiſs'd them one after another. At laſt, when he was taken down from the Croſs, he was laid with his Arms folded, and his Head ſtrait, into a ſtately Bed, between two white Sheets laced, and under a rich Damask Counterpoint; about the Bed, there is coſtly carv'd Work gilt, and ſet with abundance of Candles. In moſt of the Pariſh Churches throughout *Peru*, and thoſe of the *Mercenarians*, ſuch Beds *Maundy-Thurſday.*

are

are kept for this Solemnity, which is call'd *Entierro de Chrifto*, the Funeral of Chrift. In this Pofture he was carry'd through the Streets by Candle Light; feveral Penitents, who went in the Proceffion, were cover'd with a Linnen Frock, or Bag, open at the Back, who fcourged themfelves fo that the Blood trickled down the naked Part, which may be call'd an ill-contriv'd Devotion; for according to *Tertullian*'s Opinion, we are not to mortify our Flefh to the fhedding of Blood. *Gerfon* to that Purpofe quotes the Firft Verfe of the Fourteenth Chapter of *Deuteronomy*, *Ye are the Children of the Lord your God, ye fhall not cut yourfelves*; and according to the *Hebrew*, *ye fhall not tear yourfelves, for this the Idolaters did.*. That Cuftom had prevail'd in *France*, but the Parliament of *Paris* prohibited publick Whippings, by a Decree made in the Year 1601.

Hift. des Flagellans.

They fay, that at *Santiago* they hire Comforters to ftay the Zeal of that Sort of Whippers, who vye with one another in lafhing themfelves. Others who were not inclined to tear themfelves in that Manner, attended the Solemnity with a heavy Piece of Timber laid on their Necks, their Arms being extended on it in the Form of a Crofs, and faft bound to it; fo that not being able to fet right the unequal Weight, which fometimes fway'd them to the Right, and fometimes to the Left, others were fain now and then to fupport them, and to balance that unwieldy Weight; moft of thefe laft were Women, and the Proceffion lafting fomewhat too long, notwithftanding that Affiftance, they funk under the Burden, fo that they were forced to unbind them.

During the whole Night, the Ships in the Road fired a Gun every feven Minutes fucceffively, till the next Morning, when the Ceremony of the Monument ended.

After having careen'd the *Mary*, we made Show of fending her to *Peru*, to fee whether the *Spaniards* would not be brought to buy; but they fcarce offer'd the Price that was current at *Peru*, fo that we continued eight Months at *Valparaifo*, without felling any thing but a few Trifles to purchafe purchase the Provisions we wanted, relying on the Hopes that the Peace would be soon concluded, and that no more Ships coming from *France*, we could not fail of retrieving the Trade, and making our Advantage of the last Opportunity of coming into those Seas. On these vain Notions, the Captains, *Gardin*, *Battas*, and *le Brun*, agreed among themselves for three Months, engaging to one another, upon Forfeiture of 50000 Crowns, not to sell their Goods under a certain Price agreed on in their Contract; but all those Precautions did not prevail on the Merchants.

At length, Winter beginning to bring on the North Winds, we one Day found by Experience how high those Winds, tho' then weak, made the Sea run in the Road; by which we guess'd what would be in foul Weather, and did not think fit to stay any longer there, to avoid running any Hazards.

Departure from Valparaiso.

WE sail'd from *Valparaiso* on *Thursday* the 11th of *May* 1713, to go and winter at *Coquimbo*, where Ships are safe from all Winds. A fresh Gale at South, which had carry'd us out, held but 24 Hours; then the North Wind came upon us so violent, that one Day, in that which they call the Pacifick Sea, we were obliged to take in all our Sails during eight Hours, the Sea running high, the Weather dark, with Thunder and Lightning. A Remark against Father *Ovalle*, who says, there is never any in *Chili*; however, every Night regularly the Weather grew fairer, even to a Calm: Thus that Passage, which is usually perform'd in 24 Hours, held us nine Days. At length the Wind coming again to South, we made the Bay of *Tongoy*, remarkable for a little Hill, call'd *Cerro del Guanaquero*, and for a Point of Low-Land, call'd *Lengua de Vaca*, or Neats-Tongue, which closes that Bay to the Westward.

The Land of the Coast, tho indifferently high, looks at 25 or 30 Leagues Distance out at Sea, as if it was o-

Tongoy Bay.
Cerro del Guanaquero Hill.
Lengua de Vaca Point.

verflow'd,

verflow'd, the high Mountains over it appearing always cover'd with Snow; which is a sensible Effect of the Roundness of the Sea, which appears considerably in so small a Distance.

Coquimbo Bay how known.

When a Ship has Sight of the Bay of *Coquimbo*, it is eight Leagues to the Southward of *Coquimbo*, and must keep up with the Land to see the Mouth of the Bay, and get to the Windward, the South and S. W. always prevailing there, except two or three Months in Winter. Short of it, about three Quarters of a League to the Windward, is

Herradura Creek.

the Mouth of a little Creek, call'd *La Herradura*, or the Horse-shooe, about two Cables Length wide: Next to the Leeward appear three or four Rocks, the largest of

Paxaro Ninno Rock. Tortuga Point.

them, which is farthest out at Sea, call'd *Paxaro Ninno*, is the third Part of a League N.W. and by N. from Point *Tortuga*, being the Starboard Point of the Continent that closes the Port of *Coquimbo*. To the Southward of that first Rock, which lies in the Latitude of 29 Degres, 55 Minutes, is a little Island somewhat smaller, between which and the Continent is a Passage of 17 Fathom Water, but very narrow, through which some *French* Ships foolishly pass'd; for the Mouth of the Bay is about two Leagues and a half wide, and without any Danger.

Description of the Bay of Coquimbo.

IT is true, that by reason the Winds blow continually from S. to S. W. it is convenient to keep close to the Starboard Point, and run close under the aforesaid Rock, call'd *Paxaro Ninno*, which is clear within a Boat's Length, to gain, at the fewer Trips, the good Anchoring Ground, call'd the Port, which is within half a Cable's Length

Anchorage.

of the West Shore. There they anchor from six to ten Fathom Water, the Bottom black Sand, near a Rock ten or twelve Foot long, which rises five or six Foot above the Water, shaped like a Tortois, from which it takes its Name. Ships are shelter'd from all Winds,

by

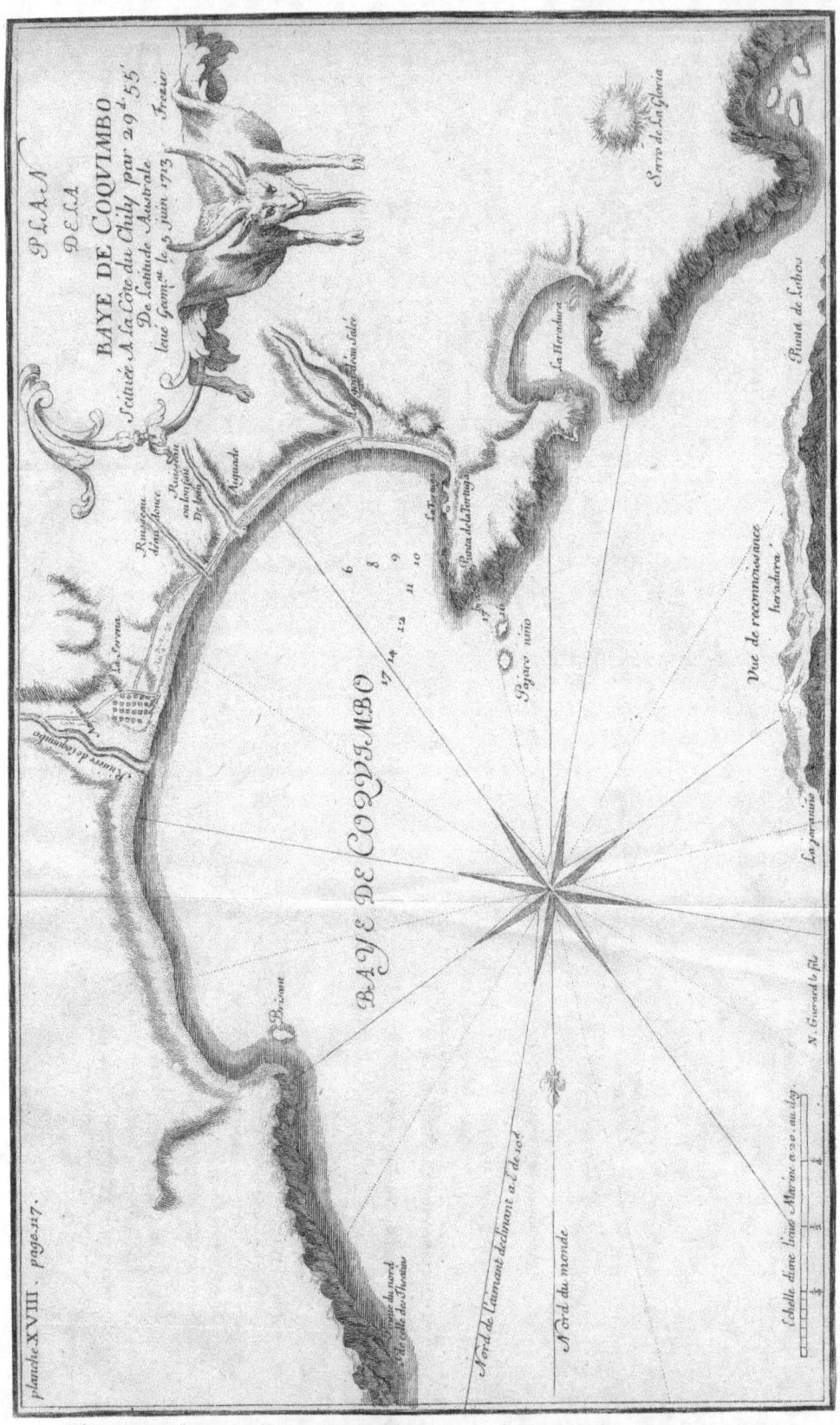

The material originally positioned here is too large for reproduction in this reissue. A PDF can be downloaded from the web address given on page iv of this book, by clicking on 'Resources Available'.

by closing the Starboard, or *Tortuga* Point, with the Larboard Point, so that the Land appears on all Sides, and there is no rolling Sea; only 25 or 30 Ships can enjoy that Benefit, and tho' the Bay is large, and the Bottom is every where good, Ships are no where so well and easy; for next the Town, there is less Water and less Shelter than in the Port.

If in entering or coming out, a Ship should happen to be becalm'd, Care must be taken not to come to an Anchor near the Rock *Paxaro Ninno*, in 40, or 45 Fathom Water, because the Bottom is full of Rocks, which cut the Cables, or else so engage the Anchors, that they cannot be weigh'd by the Buoy Rope. The *Solide*, a Ship of fifty Guns,

Caution about Anchoring.

Plate XVIII. Page 129. explain'd in English.

The Plan of the Bay of COQUIMBO, on the Coast of *Chili*, in 29 Degrees, 55 Minutes of South Latitude, taken Geometrically the 5th of *June* 1713, by Monsieur *Frezier*.

Riviere de Coquimbo, Coquimbo *River*.
Azequia, *A Trench*.
La Serena, *The Town so call'd*.
Ruisseau d' eau douce, *A Rivulet of fresh Water*.
Ruisseau où l'on fait de l'eau, *A Rivulet where Ships water*.
Aiguade, *The Watering-Place*.
Brisant, *A Rock*.
Point du Nord à 2 l. de celle des Theatins, *The North Point two Leagues from that of the* Theatins.
Baye de Coquimbo, Coquimbo *Bay*.
Lagon d' eau salée, *A Salt Water Lake*.
Nord de l' aimant declinant a E. de 20 D. *The North Point of the Compass inclining East 20 Degrees*.
Nord du Monde, *The due North*.
La Tortuga, *or the Tortois, A Place so call'd*.
Punta de la Tortuga, *Tortois Point*.
Paxaro Ninno, *An Island so call'd*.
La Herradura, *The Horse-shooe*.
Cerro de la Gloria, *The Hill of Glory*.
Echelle d' une lieüe Marine a 20 au deg. *A Scale of a Sea League, after the Rate of 20 to a Degree*.
Vue de reconnoissance, *So the Land shews by which the Port is known*.
Punta de Lobos, *The Point of Sea-Wolves, or Seals*.

Guns, commanded by Monsieur *de Ragueine*, lost two Anchors there in *April* 1712.

In the Port there is the Conveniency, not only of riding at Anchor very near the Shore, as still as in a Bason; but besides in Case of Need, a Ship of twenty four Guns may be careen'd on the *Tortuga* Rock above-mention'd, where there is twelve Foot Water at low Ebb quite close to it; some *French* Ships have made use of it to that Purpose.

Inconveniences in the Port.

But as it is rare to find all Conveniencies in one Port, this has its Defects: The most considerable of them is, that Ships anchor there a League from the Watering-place, which is to the E. N. E. in a Rivulet that runs into the Sea; and tho' it be taken at low Ebb, the Water is always somewhat brackish; however it does not appear to be unwholsome. The second is, that there is no Wood for Fewel, but that of some Bushes, which is only fit to heat an Oven, without going far into the Vale, which is three Leagues from the Port.

It may be reckon'd as a third, to be two Leagues from the Town by Land, and that there is no landing at it by Sea, the Sea is so rough there.

The Description of the Town of La Serena.

THe Town of *Coquimbo*, otherwise call'd *La Serena*, is seated at the lower Part of the Vale of *Coquimbo*, * a Quarter of a League from the Sea, on a little rising Ground, about four or five Fathoms high, which Nature has form'd like a regular Terrass, extending from North to South in a strait Line all along the Town, the Space of about a Quarter of a League: On it, the first Street forms a very pleasant Walk, whence is a Prospect of the whole Bay and the neighbouring Country; it goes on still in a Line, turning away from West to East, along a little Vale full of ever-green Trees, being most of them Myrtles, by the *Spaniards* call'd *Arrayanes*. In the midst of those pleasant Groves, the River of *Coquimbo* runs winding, almost

F. Feüillée places it in 29 Deg. 54 Min. 10 Sec. Lat. and 7 Deg. 35 Min. 45 Sec. Longitude.

Coquimbo River.

every

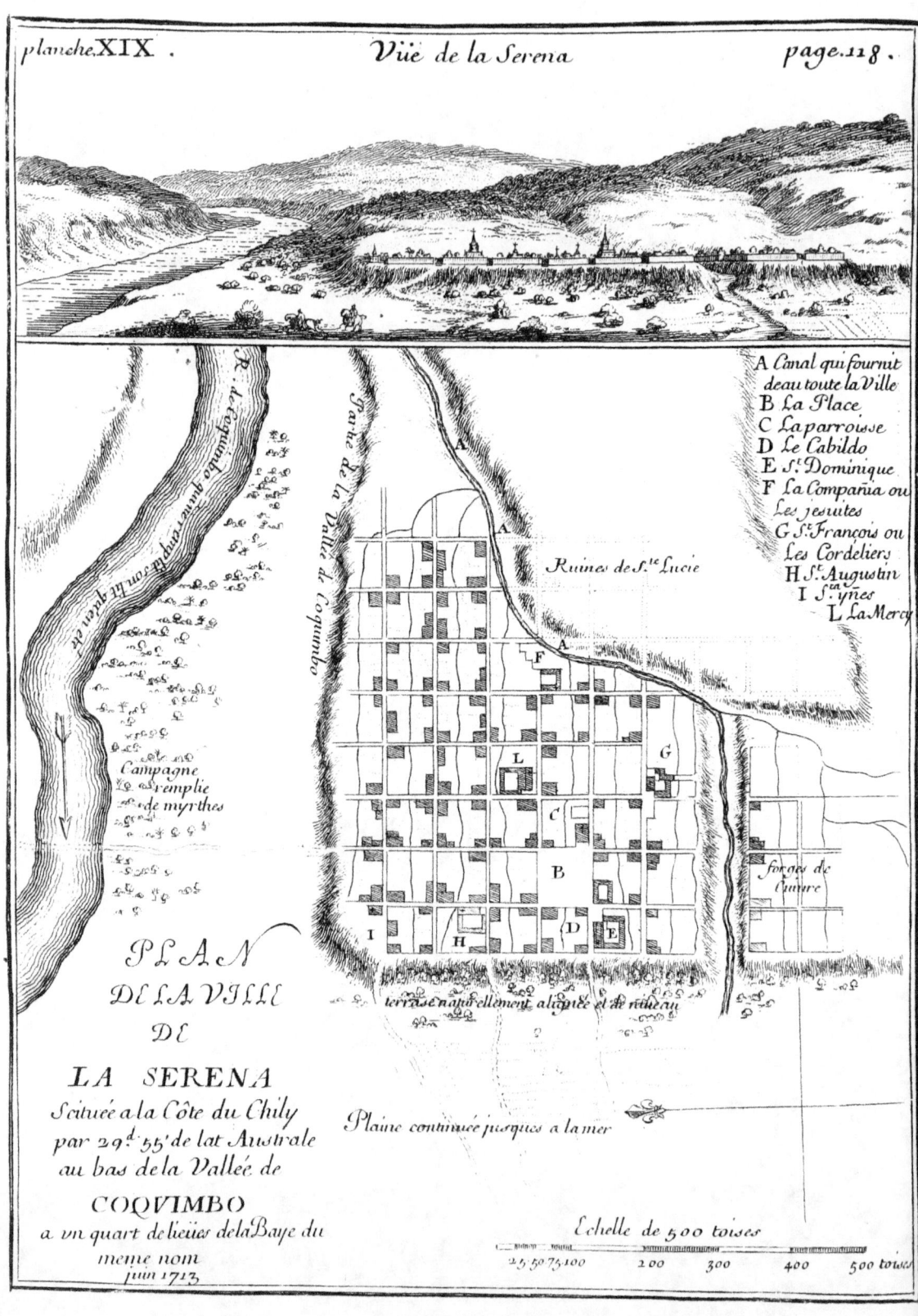

every where fordable, supplying the Town with Water, and freshning the adjacent Meadows, after having made its Escape from among the Mountains, where in its Passage it fertilizes several fine Vales, whose Soil refuses no Sort of Tillage.

Peter Baldivia, who made Choice of this curious Situation, in the Year 1544, to build a Town on, which might serve for a Retreat in the Passage from *Chili* to *Peru*, ravish'd with the Deliciousness of the Climate, call'd it *La Serena*, the Name of the Place of his Birth, to which it had more Right than any other Place in the World, the Name signifying *the Serene*; and, in short, there is continually a serene and pleasant Sky. That Country seems to have retain'd the Delights of the Golden Age: The Winters are there warm, and the sharp North Winds never blow there: The Heat of the Summer is always temper'd by refreshing Winds, which come to moderate the Heat about Noon; so that all the Year is no other than a happy Union of Spring and Autumn, which seem to join Hands

S 2   to

Plate XIX. *Page* 131. *described in* English.
Vuë de La Serena, *A Prospect of* LA SERENA.
The Plan of the Town of *LA SERENA*, on the Coast of *Chili*, in 29 Degrees, 55 Minutes of South Latitude, at the Bottom of the Vale of *Coquimbo*, a Quarter of a League from the Bay of the same Name, *June* 1713.

A. *A Trench which supplies all the Town with Water.*
B. *The Square.*
C. *The Parish Church.*
D. *The Council House.*
E. *S. Dominick.*
F. *The Jesuites.*
G. *The Franciscans.*
H. *S. Augustin.*
I. *S Agnes.*
L. *The Mercenarians.*

R. de Coquimbo qui ne remplit son lit qu en ete, *The River of* Coquimbo, *which is full of Water only in Summer.*
Partie de la Vallée de Coquimbo, *Part of the Vale of* Coquimbo.
Ruines de S_{te} Lucie, *The Ruins of S.* Lucy.
Forges de Cuivre, *Copper Works.*
Terrasse naturelment alignée & de niveau, *A Terrass naturally form'd in a Line, and level.*
Plaine continuée jusques à la mer, *A Plain extending to the Sea.*
Echelle de 500 Toises, *A Scale of* 500 *Fathoms.*

to reign there together, in order to produce at once both Flowers and Fruits; so that we may, with much more Truth, say of it what formerly *Virgil* said of a certain Province in *Italy*, Georg. l. 2.

Hic ver assiduum, atque alienis mensibus æstas,
Bis gravidæ pecudes, bis pomis utilis arbos:
At rapidæ Tigres absunt, & sæva Leonum
Semina.

Thus *English'd* by Mr. *Dryden.*

----- Perpetual Spring our Climate sees,
Twice breed the Cattle, and twice bear the Trees,
And Summer Suns recede by slow Degrees.
Our Land is from the Dread of Tygers freed,
Nor nourishes the Lyon's angry Seed.

No wild Beasts, nor venomous Creatures. This last Commendation of being free from wild Beasts and venomous Creatures, is due, as the Inhabitants say, to all the Kingdom of *Chili*, where they lie at all Seasons in the open Air, without fearing any Poison. Nevertheless, whatsoever Father *Ovalle* may say of it, I have seen Toads at *La Conception*, Snakes and monstrous Spiders at *Valparaiso*; and, lastly, white Scorpions at *Coquimbo*. It is likely, all those Creatures are of a different Nature from ours in *Europe*; for there is no Instance that ever any body was hurt by them.

Plan of the Town. The Plan of the Town is answerable enough to the Advantages of Nature; the Streets are all exactly strait in a Line from one End to the other, like *Santiago*, answering to the four Cardinal Points of the Horizon, from East to West, and from North to South. The Quarters or Squares they form, are also of the same Dimensions, with each a Rivulet running through it; but the small Number of Inhabitants, the Foulness of the Streets which are not pav'd, the Meanness of the Houses made of Mud Walls, and Thatch'd,

Thatch'd, make it look but like a Plain, and the Streets like the Walks in Gardens; and in short, they are set round with Fig, Orange, Olive, Palm-Trees, &c. which afford them an agreeable Shade.

The most considerable Part of it is taken up by two Squares and six Monasteries of *Dominicans*, *Augustins*, *Franciscans*, *Mercenarians* and *Jesuites*, without reckoning the Parish and the Chappel of S. *Agnes*. Formerly there was a Church of S. *Lucy*, on an Eminence of the same Name, which runs out in a Point to the Middle of the Town: It is of the same Height as the first Terrass, and commands all the Town by reason of the Lowness of the Houses, which have only a Ground Floor. From thence, as it were from an Amphitheatre, appears a curious Landskip, form'd by the Town, the Plain which reaches down to the Sea, the Bay and its Mouth. All the Quarter of S. *Lucy* was formerly inhabited; but since the *English* and other Pyrates plunder'd and burnt the Town, it has not been rebuilt, any more than the South Part: This has happened twice within forty Years. *Churches,&c.*

The Discovery of the Mines of *Copiapo*, and the Vexations of the *Corregidores*, or Chief Magistrates, daily contribute towards unpeopling of it; tho' those Mines are near a hundred Leagues from *Coquimbo* by Land, several Families are gone thither to settle; so that at present there are not above two hundred Families, and at most, three hundred Men fit to bear Arms, not including the Neighbourhood. In those few Houses, there are some of the Fair Sex of a pleasant and obliging Conversation, which adds very much to the other Delights of the agreeable Place and Climate. *Copiapo Mines.* *Inhabitants.*

The Fertility of the Soil keeps abundance of People in the Country, in the Vales of *Elques*, *Sotaquy*, *Salsipued*, *Andacol*, *Limari*, &c. whence they bring Corn to load four or five Ships, of about 400 Tuns Burden, to send to *Lima*. They also supply *Santiago* with much Wine and Oil, reckon'd the best along the Coast: These Provisions, together with some few Hides, Tallow, and dry'd Flesh, are all the *Product and Trade.*

the Trade of that Place, where the Inhabitants are poor, by reason of their Slothfulness, and the few *Indians* they have to serve them; for that Country is one of the richest in the Kingdom, in all Sorts of Metals.

> *Hæc eadem argenti rivos ærisque metalla*
> *Ostendit venis, atque auro plurima fluxit.* Virg. Geo. 2.

Thus *English'd* by Mr. *Dryden*.

> *Our Quarries deep in Earth, were fam'd of old*
> *For Veins of Silver and for Ore of Gold.*

Plenty of Gold.   In Winter, when the Rains are somewhat plentiful, Gold is found in almost all the Rivulets that run down from the Mountains, and it would be found all the Year if they had that Help. Nine or ten Leagues to the Eastward of the Town, are the washing Places of *Andacol*, the Gold whereof is 23 Carats fine; the Work there always turns to great Advantage when there is no want of Water. The Inhabitants affirm, that the Earth breeds; that is, that Gold is continually growing, because 60 or 80 Years after it has been wash'd, they find almost as much Gold as they did at first. In that same Vale, besides the Washing-Places, there are on the Mountains so very many Gold Mines, and some of Silver, that they would employ 40000 Men, as I have been inform'd by the Governor of *Coquimbo*: They propose to set up Mills there out of hand, but they want Labourers.

Copper Mines.   The Copper Mines are also very common, three Leagues N. E. from *Coquimbo*: They have wrought a long Time at a Mine, which supplies almost all the Coast of *Chili* and *Peru* with Utensils for the Kitchin; it is true, they use fewer of that, than of Earthen Ware or Silver. They there give eight Pieces of Eight *per* Quintal, or Hundred Weight for Copper in Ingots, which is an inconsiderable Price in respect of the Value of Silver in the Country. The *Jesuites* have another Mine five Leagues North from the City, on a

Mountain

Mountain call'd *Cerro Verde*, or Green Hill, which is high and shaped like a Sugar-loaf; so that it may serve for a Land-Mark to the Port. There is an infinite Number of others, which are neglected for want of Sale. It is affirm'd, that there are also Mines of Iron and of Quick-silver.

I must not here omit some Particulars of the Country, which I was told by the Guardian of the *Franciscans* at *Coquimbo*. The first of them, That ten Leagues to the Southward of that Town there is a blackish Stone, from which flows a Spring only once a Month, at an Opening like unto that humane Part, whose regular Flowing it imitates, and that Water leaves a white Track on the Stone. *Strange Spring.*

The second is near that they call *La Hazienda de la Marquesa*, or the Marchioness's Estate, six Leagues East from the Town: There is a gray Stone of the Colour of Lead Ore, as smooth as a Table, on which there is exactly drawn a Buckler and a Head-Piece, both red, the Colour sinking deep into the Stone, which has been purposely broken, in some Places, to see it. *Remarkable Stone.*

The third, that in a Vale there is a small Plain, on which if a Man falls asleep, when he awakes he finds himself swollen, which does not happen some few Paces from thence. *Singular Plain.*

The Port of *Coquimbo* being no Place of Trade for *European* Commodities, of which not above the Value of 12 or 15000 Pieces of Eight can be sold in a Year, the *French* Ships resort thither only for fresh Provisions, Wine and Brandy. The Beef is there somewhat better than at *Valparaiso*, and much about the same Value of eight or ten Pieces of Eight a Beast. There are Partridges, but they are insipid: On the other hand, the Turtle Doves are very delicious; there are abundance of Ducks in a little Pool near the Port. The Fishery is plentiful enough in the Bay, yielding abundance of Mullets, Pezereyes, Soles, and a Sort of Fish without Bones, very delicious, call'd *Tesson*, and peculiar to that Coast; but there is no good casting *Provisions.*

Plants.

of a Net, becaufe the Shore is full of Stones; the Sea is rough and breaking.

The Plants in thefe Parts are almoſt the fame as at *Valparaiſo.* The *Paico* is there fmaller, and more aromatick, and confequently a better Sudorifick. There is abundance of a Sort of Stone-Fern, which they call *Doradilla,* the Leaf whereof is all curl'd; they drink the Decoction of it to refreſh themfelves after the Fatigue of Traveling, and hold it in great Efteem for cleanfing the Blood. There is a Sort of Lemon Balm, which laſts all the Year, call'd *Lacayota*; they make it run up the Tops of Houfes, and it is an excellent Preferve. There is great Plenty of that they call *Algarroba,* being a Sort of Tamarind, bearing a very rofiny Bean; the Cod and Grain whereof dry'd, pounded, and in Infufion, ferve to make very good Writing-Ink, adding to them a little Copperas; it is alfo call'd *Tara,* from its Refemblance with the Cod of that Plant, tho', in Reality, it be fomewhat different.

Lucumo Tree.

In this Climate we begin to fee a Tree, which does not grow in any other Part of *Chili,* and is peculiar to *Peru*; it is call'd *Lucumo:* The Leaf of it fomewhat refembles that of the Orange-Tree and the *Floripondio*; the Fruit is alfo very like a Pear, which contains the Seed of the latter; when ripe, the Rind is a little yellowiſh, and the Fleſh of it very yellow, almoſt of the Taſte and Confiſtence of a new-made Cheeſe: In the midſt of it is a Kernel, exactly like a Chefnut in Colour, Hairinefs and Subſtance, but bitter, and good for nothing.

Poiſonous Plant.

In the Valley, near the Ridge of Mountains call'd *La Cordillera,* is a Herb, which, when young, may be eaten as Sallad; but when beginning to grow large, it becomes fo deadly a Poifon for Horfes, that as foon as they eat it they become blind, fwell, and burſt in a ſhort Time.

DEPAR-

DEPARTURE from COQUIMBO.
The Author goes a-board another Ship.

THE little Likelihood there was that the Sieur *Duchene* should sell his Goods at the Price he demanded, and the Resolution he had taken to wait till the Peace was proclaim'd, designing to stay the last on the Coast, flattering himself that no more Ships would come from *France*, prevail'd with me to take such Measures as might be agreeable to his Majesty's Orders, who limited the Leave he had been pleas'd to grant me, for performing this Voyage, to two Years; being persuaded that the *S. Joseph* would be still two Years longer on the Coast, and upon its Voyage.

I embarqued on board a *Spanish* Ship, call'd the *Jesus Mary Joseph*, laden with Corn for *Callao*, commanded by Don *Antonio Alarcon*, in order to come to some of the *French* Ships that had done trading, and would suddenly return to *France*. The Opportunity was favourable, because we were to touch at the Ports resorted to, call'd *Puertos Intermedios*, or Ports in the Way.

The 30th of *May* we set Sail to get out of the Bay of *Coquimbo*; but a Calm taking us without, the Current carry'd us in again, and we anchor'd in 17 Fathom Water E. S. E. of the Rock *Paxaro Ninno*. The next Day the same Thing befell us, and we came to an Anchor again.

It is no easy Matter to get out of that Bay, unless a Ship sets out with a good Land Breeze, which generally blows only from Midnight till Day. No Man must expose himself to be becalm'd a little without the Mouth of the Bay, because the Currents, which set to the Northward, drive Ships in between the Islands of *Pajaros*, or Birds, and the Continent that is beyond the Point of the *Theatins*. Those Islands are seven or eight Leagues to the N. W. of the Compass, or N. W. and by N. of the World, in respect to Point *Tortuga*. It is true, that with a fair Wind a Man might

Directions for getting out of the Bay of Coquimbo.

might get off, because there is a Passage; but besides that it is dangerous, and little frequented, the Tides set upon the Islands, where some *Spanish* Ships have perish'd: For which Reason, if the Land Breeze is not fix'd, a Ship must not go out but with the S. S. W. Breeze, and run some Leagues W. N. W. to get enough to Seaward of those Islands, which the *Spanish* Pilots shun as a Shoal in a Calm, and the more, for that the Tides are not known to be regular. However, I do not think the Case is the same for the inner Part of the Bay: I thought I observ'd that the Delay was not that of the Moon's passing to the Meridian, but perhaps of the Third Part, or of a Quarter of an Hour. I do not affirm any thing as to this Particular: Such an Observation would require several Months to be satisfy'd.

At length, on the 7th of *June* about Four in the Morning, we got out with the Wind at East. At Noon I took an Observation West of the Rock *Paxaro Ninno*, which I found to be in 29 Degrees, 55 Minutes of South Latitude, as has been said before. The Breeze coming up, we in the Night pass'd by the Island *Choros*, which is four Leagues North from those of *Paxaros*, and even thought in the Dark that we had some Sight of it.

Choros *Island*.

The next Morning we found ourselves four Leagues N. W. and by N. of the Island of *Channaral*, join'd to the Continent by a Bank of Sand, which the Sea covers with a North Wind: It is four Leagues from the Island of *Choros*, and 16 from Point *Tortuga*. This Island is almost plain, and very small.

Channaral *Island*.

Four or five Leagues farther Northward, they shew'd me a white Spot near a Break, call'd *Quebrada honda*, or the Deep Break, above which there are rich Copper Mines.

Quebrada honda *Break*.

Afterwards, towards the Evening, we descry'd the Bay of *Guasco*, where there is good Anchorage in 18 or 20 Fathom Water, very near the Land. That Port is not frequented, because there is no other Trade but that of a private Person, who takes Copper out of the Mines. It is

Guasco *Bay*.

open

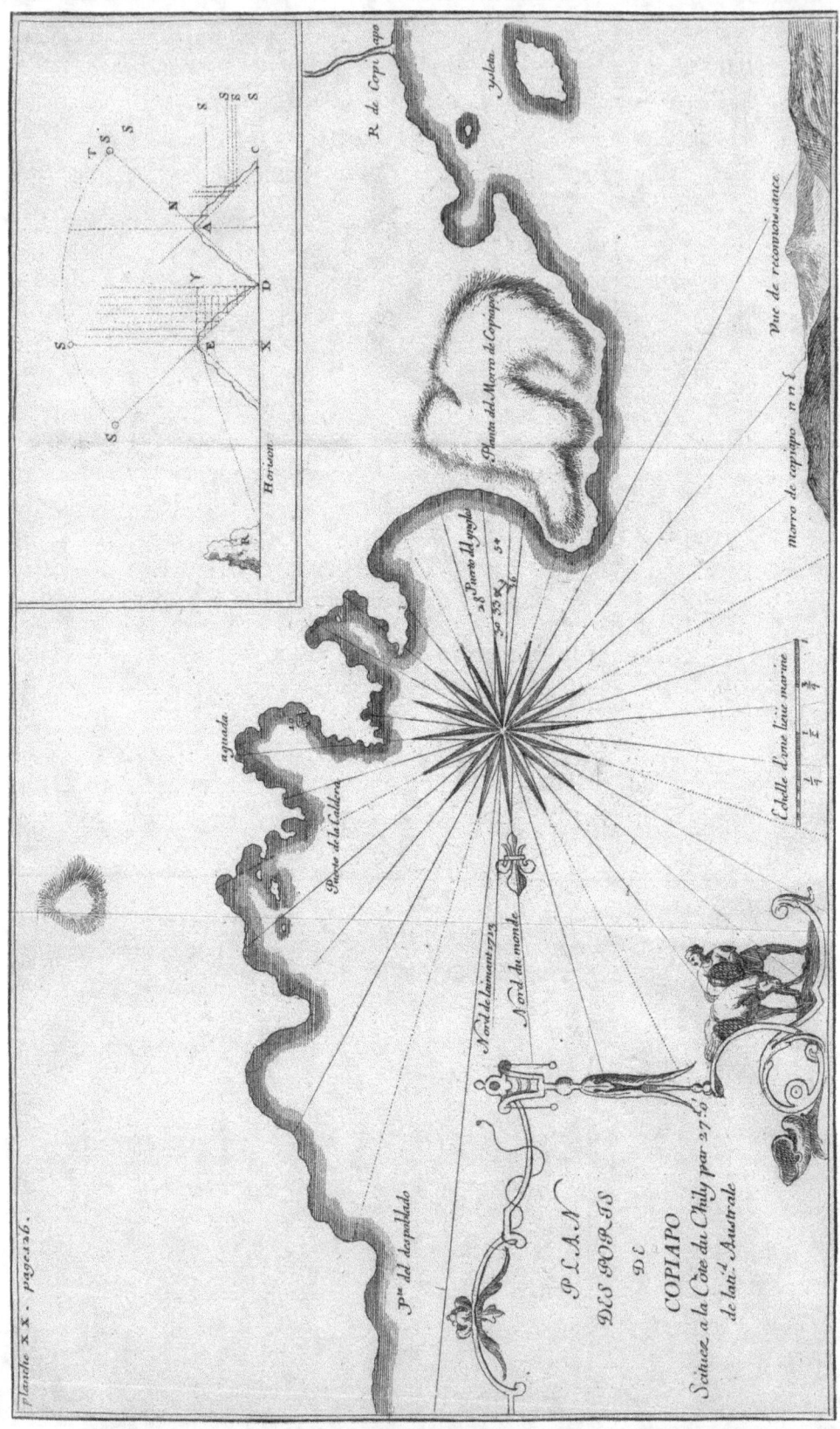

open to the North about a League wide, and there is good Water.

The next Day from four or five Leagues out at Sea we discover'd the Creek of *Totoral*, where there is Anchorage: It is not to be perceiv'd any otherwise, than that it lies about the Mid-way, between a Cape call'd *Cerro Prieto*, or Black Cape, and a low Point, which is the Southermost of the Salt Bay. Totoral Creek.

The 10th we had Sight of the Head call'd *Morro de Copiapo*, which appears at a Distance like an Island, because it joins to the Continent by a very low Neck, or Point, for which it is very remarkable. That Head is of a less than indifferent Height, in 27 Degrees Latitude; it is compared to S. *Helen*'s Point in *Peru*. It appears thus, seen from the Southward, and but little different from the Northward, or Leeward. Morro de Copiapo Head.

Plate XX

As you draw near it, there appears a little low Island of about a Quarter of a League Diameter, between which and the Continent they say there is Anchorage under Shelter from the North, towards the Bottom of the Creek into which the River of *Copiapo* falls.

Opposite to that Creek we were thwarted by the North Winds, and a Calm made me observe, that the Currents drove us Southward; which confirms what the *Spanish* Pilots Currents.

Plate XX. *Page* 139. *explain'd in* English.
The Plan of the Ports of *COPIAPO*, on the Coast of *Chili*, in 27 Degrees of South Latitude.

Punta del despoblado, *The Point of the Desart Country.*
Aguada, *The Watering-Place.*
Punta de la Caldera, *The Point of the Kettle.*
R. de Copiapo, *Copiapo River.*
Nord de l'aimant, *The North Point of the Compass.*
Nord du Monde, *The true North Point.*
Puerto del Yngles, *The* Englishman's *Port.*
Planta del Morro de Copiapo, *The Plan of the Headland of* Copiapo.
Yſleta, *A small Island.*
Echellé d'une lieuë marine, *A Scale of a Sea League.*
Morro de Copiapo N. N. E. *The Headland of* Copiapo N. N. E
Vuë de reconnoiſſance, *The View to know the Port by.*

Pilots say, that when the North Wind blows, they go like the Wind.

Puerto del Ingles Creek. At length the South Wind coming up again, we put in at Night, and anchor'd in a Creek, which they call *Puerto del Ingles*, the *English* Man's Port, because a Pyrate of that Nation was the first that anchor'd there. We rode in 36 Fathom Water the Bottom Sand and Shells, N. E and by N of the Head of *Copiapo*, and S. and by E. of the Starboard Point of *Caldera*, the nearest. I went the next Day to sound in that Creek, and found a Rocky Bottom towards the Head, and much Water; and, on the contrary, a Sandy Bottom, and less Water on the North-side.

Description of the Port de la Caldera.

TUESDAY the 13th we sail'd for the Port *de la Caldera*, which is parted from the former by a Point of Land, before which there is a Rock, which we coasted within Pistol-Shot, and so held on along the Starboard Shore, which is very clear, in order to gain upon the Wind, and get into the Anchoring Place, without being obliged to make several Trips. In Conclusion, we came to an Anchor without shifting our Sails, in 10 Fathom Water S. E. and by E. of the most advanced Land on the Starboard Side, the low North Point bearing N. and by E three Leagues distant. There we unladed a little Corn for the Town of *Copiapo*, and laded Sulphur, which we found upon the Shore, where it had been laid against our coming.

Anchoring.

This Port is secured against the South Wind; but in Winter, tho' the North Winds are no longer violent in that Latitude, the Sea runs high. It is the nearest to *Copiapo*, but little frequented, because it affords no Conveniency: Wood is very scarce there, and they must go five or six Leagues up the Vale, thro' which the River runs, to get it. The Watering-Place is bad; it is taken in a Hollow 50 Paces from the Edge of the Road, where a little brackish Water meets: There is no Dwelling about it, but only a Fisher-

Wooding, Watering, &c.

a Fisherman's Cottage, at the Bottom of the N. E. Creek. The Town is 14 Leagues distant Eastward, the shortest Way by the Mountains, and 20 Leagues the common Road, which keeps the Course of the River; the Mouth whereof is five Leagues to the Southward of *La Caldera*, as has been said.

All the Shore of *La Caldera* is cover'd with Shells, especially that Sort they call *Locos**; so that *Dampier* is in the wrong to say, that there is no Shell-Fish all along that Coast.

<small>* See Plate XX. Dampier wrong.</small>

Copiapo is an open Town, the Houses whereof do not stand in any Order, but scattering up and down. The Gold Mines that have been discover'd there within six Years past, have drawn some few People thither; so that at present there may be above 900 Souls. This Increase of the Number of *Spaniards* has occasion'd an Order for dividing the Lands, by which they take from the poor *Indians* not only their Lands, but their Horses also, which the *Corregidor* or chief Magistrate, sells to the new Comers for the King's, or rather for his Officers Advantage, under Colour of making more easy the Settlements of those who improve the Mines. There are Mines directly above the Town, and others at two or three Leagues Distance, whence they bring the Ore on Mules to the Mills, which are within the Town. In the Year 1713, there were six of those they call *Trapiches*, and they were making a seventh of that Sort which they call *Ingenio Real*, the Royal Engine, with Hammers, or Pounders, of which we shall speak elsewhere, which can bruise or grind 12 times as much as the *Trapiches*, that is, six *Caxones*, or Chests, a Day, each Chest there yielding 12 Ounces, more or less; it must yield two to pay the Cost; the Ounce of Gold is there sold for 12 or 13 Pieces of Eight cast.

<small>Account of the Borough of Copiapo</small>

<small>Gold Mines of Copiapo</small>

Besides the Gold Mines, there are about *Copiapo* many Mines of Iron, Brass, Tin, and Lead, which they do not think fit to work: There is also much Load-stone, and *Lapis Lazuli*, which the People of the Country do not know

<small>Mines of all Sorts.</small>

know to be of any Value; these are 14 or 15 Leagues from *Copiapo*, near a Place where there are many Lead Mines. In short, all the Country is there full of Mines of Sal Gemm, for which reason sweet Water is there very scarce: Saltpeter is no less plentiful, being found in the Vales an Inch thick on the Ground.

On the high Mountains of the Chain call'd *La Cordillera*, 40 Leagues E.S.E. from the Port, there are Mines of the finest Sulphur that can be seen: It is taken pure from a Vein two Foot wide, without needing to be cleans'd. It is worth three Pieces of Eight a Quintal, or hundred Weight, at the Port, whence it is carry'd to *Lima*.

Sulphur.

At *Copiapo* they have also a little Trade of Stuff for paying of Ships, being a Sort of Rosin coming from a Shrub, the Leaf whereof is like Rosemary; it proceeds from the Branches, and from the Berries, which they cast into large square Cakes two Foot long, and ten or twelve Inches thick: It is very dry, and only good to use instead of Glazing, for the Earthen Jars in which they keep Wine and Brandy; it costs five Pieces of Eight the Quintal, or hundred Weight, in the Port. In other respects the Country is barren, scarce yielding enough to subsist the Inhabitants, who have their Provisions from about *Coquimbo*.

Rosin.

In the Mountains of this Country there are abundance of *Guanaco's*, a Sort of Creature between a Camel and a wild Goat, in whose Bodies the *Bezoar* Stones are found; formerly of such Value in Physick, that they were worth their Weight in Silver; but now it has been found out that Crab's Eyes and other *Alkalis* can serve instead of them; they have lost much of their Value in *France*; however the *Spaniards* give great Rates for them still.

Guanacos Beasts. Bezoar Stones.

Between *Copiapo* and *Coquimbo*, which is 100 Leagues, there is no Town nor Village, but only three or four Farms; and between *Copiapo* and *Atacama* in *Peru*, the Country is so hideous and desart, that the Mules starve for want of Grass and Water. In eighty Leagues Length there is but one River, which runs from Sun-rising till it sets, perhaps because

Great Desart.

because that Planet melts the Snow, which freezes again at Nigh ; the *Indians* call it *Anchallulac*, that is, the Hypocrite. Those are the dreadful Mountains which divide *Chili* and *Peru*, where the Cold is sometimes so excessive, that Men are frozen up, their Faces looking as if they laugh'd, whence, according to some Historians, the Name of *Chili* is derived, signifying Cold ; tho' beyond those Mountains the Country is very temperate. We read in the History of the Conquest of *Chili*, that some of the first *Spaniards* who pass'd it died there, sitting upright on their Mules. A much better Way has been now found out along the Sea-Coast.

The Sulphur we were to lade being brought aboard, we set sail on *Sunday* the 18th of *June* for *Arica* ; but the Calms and North Winds kept us within Sight of Land for some Days. The Owner of the Ship and the *Spanish* Captain being concerned at that Delay, perform'd, with the Sailors, a nine Days Devotion to S. *Francis Xaverius*, from whom they expected a Miracle, which was not wrought at the appointed Time ; they were so enraged at it, that they loudly declared they would no more pray to the Saints, since they did not vouchsafe to hear them. The Captain then address'd himself to a little Image of the blessed Virgin, which he hung at the Mizzen-Mast, and often said to it, *My dear Friend, I will not take you down from hence, till you give us a fair Wind*; and if it happen'd that our Lady of *Bethlem* did not perform, he hung there our Lady of *Mount Carmel*, of the Rosary, or of the *Solitude*, or Affliction ; whence may be inferr'd after what Manner most *Spaniards* honour Images, and what Confidence they repose in them.

Departure from Copiapo.

At length a fresh Gale at S.S.E. carry'd us into the Latitude of 22 Degrees 25 Minutes, which is that of *Cobija*, the Port to the Town of *Atacama*, which is 40 Leagues up the Country. It is to be known by this Land-mark, that from *Morro Moreno*, or the Brown Head-land, which is ten Leagues to the Windward, the Mountain goes on rising till

Cobija Port.

it comes directly over the Creek where it is, and from thence it begins to lower a little; so that the same is the highest Part of the Coast, tho' but little: This Mark is more certain than that of the white Spots seen there, because there are many all along that Coast.

Not safe. Tho we did not put in there, I will not omit inserting what I have been told by the *French* who have anchor'd there: They say it is only a little Creek, a third Part of a League in Depth, where there is little Shelter against the South and S W Winds, which are the most usual on the Coast.

They who will go ashore, must do it among Rocks, which form a small Channel towards the South, being the only one where Boats can come in without Danger.

Cobija Village. The Village of *Cobija*, consists of about fifty Houses of *Indians*, made of Sea Wolves, or Seal's Skins. The Soil being barren, they generally live upon Fish, and some little *Indian* Wheat and *Topinambours*, or *Papas*, brought them from *Atacama* in Exchange for Fish. In the Village, there is only one little Rivulet of Water, somewhat brackish, and all the Trees are four Palm, and two Fig-trees, which may serve for a Land-mark to the Anchoring-place. There is no Grass at all for Cattle, but they are obliged to send their Sheep to a Break towards the Top of the Mountain, where they find some Sprigs to subsist on.

This Port being destitute of all Things, it has never been frequented by any but *French*; who to draw the Merchants to them have sought the nearest Places to the Mines, and the most remote from the King's Officers, to facilitate the Trade, and the Transporting of Plate and Commodities. This Port is the nearest to *Lipes*, and to *Potosi*, which is nevertheless above a hundred Leagues distant, through a Desart Country; the Road whereof is thus: From *Cobija* they *Road from Cobija to Potosi.* must travel the first Day 22 Leagues without Wood or Water, to come to the little River of *Chacanza*, the Water *Chacanza River.* whereof is very Salt.

Next, they must travel seven Leagues to find the like again: In short, it is the same River under a different Name.

Then

Then nine Leagues to *Calama*, a Village of ten or twelve *Calama Village.*
Indians; two Leagues short of it, they pass through a
Wood of *Algarrovos*, or Carobs, being a Kind of Tamarinds.

From *Calama* to *Chiouchiou*, or the Lower *Atacama*, six *Chiouchiou Village.*
Leagues; being a Village of eight or ten *Indians*, 17 Leagues
South from the *Upper Atacama*, where the *Corregidor*, or
chief Magistrate, of *Cobija* resides.

From *Chiouchiou* to *Lipes* is about sixty Leagues, which *Desart Road.*
are travel'd in seven or eight Days, without meeting any
Dwelling; and there is a Mountain of twelve Leagues,
without Wood or Water, to be pass'd.

Lipes is a Place of Mines, as the *Spaniards* call it *Assi-* *Lipes Mines.*
ento, that is Settlement, which have for many Years yielded
much Silver; without reckoning the Settlements of other
lesser Mines in the Neighbourhood, as *Escala*, *Aquegua*,
and *S Christopher*, where there are six. *Lipes* is divided into
two Parts, at least half a Quarter of a League distant from
each other; the one call'd *Lipes*, and the other *Guaico*. *Guaico Mines.*
In these two Places, including the People that work at the
Bottom of the Hill where the Mines are, there may be about 800 Persons of all Sorts. That Hill is in the midst
between *Guaico* and *Lipes*, all full of Mouths of Mines;
one of which is so deep, that they came to the Bottom of
the Rock, under which there was Sand and Water, which
they call'd the *Antipodes*.

From *Lipes* to *Potosi* is about seventy Leagues, which
they travel in six or seven Days, without meeting in all
that Way above two or three *Indian* Cottages.

Potosi is that Town, so famous throughout all the World *Potosi Town*
for the immense Wealth formerly drawn from thence, and *and Mines.*
still taken out of the Mountain, at the Bottom of which it
stands: There are reckon'd to be above 60000 *Indians*
and 10000 *Spaniards*, or Whites; the King obliges the
Neighbouring Parishes to send thither a certain Number
of *Indians* yearly, to work at the Mines, which is call'd
Mita. The *Corregidores*, or chief Magistrates, cause them

U to

to set out on the Feast of *Corpus Christi*. Most of them take their Wives and Children with them, who are seen to go to that Servitude with Tears in their Eyes, and with Repugnance; however, after the Year's Duty, there are many who forget their Habitations, and continue settled at *Potosi*, which is the Occasion of that Place's being so populous.

The Mines are much decreas'd of their Value, and the Mint does not coin one Quarter of what it did formerly: There were once 120 Mills, at this time there are only 40; and for the most part, there is not Employment for half of them.

Conceited Remark. That Place is said to be so cold, that formerly the *Spanish* Women could not lie-in there, but were obliged to go twenty or thirty Leagues from thence, to avoid being expos'd to the Danger of Dying with their Infants; but now some lie-in there. That Effect of their Tenderness was look'd upon as a Punishment from Heaven, because the *Indian* Women are not subject to that Inconveniency: The other Particulars of that Town are to be found in several Relations.

Pavellon Island. Having pass'd *Cobija*, we were becalm'd in 21 Degrees Latitude, near the little Island call'd *Pavellon*, because it looks like a Tent; the upper Half black, and the lower white. Behind that Island, on the Continent, is a little Creek for Boats: On that Coast there are Beasts, which the Inhabitants call Lions, tho' much differing from those of *Africa*. I have seen their Skins stuff'd full of Straw, the *Lions of Peru.* Head whereof somewhat resembles a Wolf and a Tiger, but the Tail is less than that of either of them. These Creatures are not to be fear'd, for they fly from Men, and do Harm only among the Cattle. We continued two Days becalm'd, near the Island *Pavellon*, without being sensible of any Current.

Carapucho Head-land. Iquique Island. Some small Gales set us forward to the Land's Head call'd *Carapucho*, at the Foot whereof is the Island of *Iquique*, in a Creek where there is Anchorage, but no Water; the

the *Indians* who live on the Continent are obliged to go and fetch it ten Leagues from thence, at the Break of *Piſſagua*, with a Boat they have for that Purpoſe; but as it ſometimes happens, that the contrary Winds keep them back, they are then obliged to fetch it five Leagues by Land, at the Rivulet of *Pica*.

The Iſland of *Iquique* is alſo inhabited by *Indians* and Blacks, who are there employ'd to gather *Guana*, being a yellowiſh Earth thought to be the Dung of Birds, becauſe beſides that it ſtinks like that of the Cormorants, there have been Feathers of Birds found very deep in it: However it is hard to conceive, how ſo great a Quantity of it could be gather'd there; for during the Space of a hundred Years paſt, they have laden ten or twelve Ships every Year with it, to manure the Land, as ſhall be obſerv'd lower; and it is ſcarce perceivable that the Height of the Iſland is abated, tho' it is not above three Quarters of a League in Compaſs; and that beſides what is carry'd away by Sea, they load abundance of Mules with it for the Vines and plow'd Lands of *Tarapaca*, *Pica*, and other Neighbouring Places; which makes ſome believe, that it is a peculiar Sort of Earth: For my part, I am not of that Opinion; for it is true, the Sea Fowls are there ſo very numerous, that it may be ſaid without romancing, that the Air is ſometimes darken'd with them. In the Bay of *Arica*, infinite Multitudes of them are ſeen, rendezvouſing every Morning about ten o' Clock, and every Evening about ſix, to take the Fiſh which at that time comes up to the Surface of the Water, where they make a Sort of regular Fiſhery. *Guana, what it is.*

In the Year 1713, Silver Mines were diſcover'd twelve Leagues from *Iquique*, which they deſign'd to work out of hand; it is hoped they will be rich, according to all Appearance. *New Mines.*

From *Iquique* to *Arica*, the Coaſt is all the Way very high and clear, Ships muſt run cloſe along it, for fear leſt the Currents, which in Summer ſet N. and N. W. ſhould drive them out to Sea. However, it is alſo true, *Coaſts and Currents.*

that in Winter they sometimes set to the Southward, as we and several others have found by Experience.

Camarones and Vitor Breaks. Next to the Break of *Pissagua* is that of *Camarones*, which is larger; and four Leagues to the Windward of *Arica*, is that of *Vitor*, where there is Wood and fresh Water: It is the only Place where the Ships anchoring at *Arica* can be supply'd with them.

Marks to know Arica. When come within about a League of the Break of *Camarones*, the Head-land of *Arica* begins to appear, which looks like an Island, because it is much lower than the Coast towards the Windward; but when come within three or four Leagues of it, then it is known by a little low Island that is before it like a Rock, and by its Steepness, wherein none can be mistaken, because beyond it is a low Coast. It is in 18 Degrees 20 Minutes of South Latude.

Arica Head-land. This Head-land on the West Side is all white with the Dung of the Sea Fowls call'd *Cormorants*, who there gather in such Numbers, that it is quite cover'd with them: This is the most remarkable Place of all the Coast. When the Weather is fair, there may be seen up the Land the Mountain of *Tacora*, which seems to rise up to the Clouds, forming two Heads at the Top, near which is the Way that leads to *La Paz*. The Air there is so different from what is breath'd before, that those who are not used to pass it, suffer the same Dizziness in their Heads, and Qualms in their Stomachs, that People do usually at Sea.

Description of the Road of Arica.

Plate XXI. ENtering the Road of *Arica*, Ships may coast the Island of *Guano*, which is at the Foot of the Head-land within a Cable's length, and go and anchor N. and by E. of that Island, and N.W. from the Steeple of *San Juan de Dios*, distinguishable by its Height, from all the Buildings in the Town: There is nine Fathom Water, the Bottom tough Owze, little out of Danger from the Rocks under Water, which

Anchorage.

in

m several Places of the Road cut the Cables: There is no Shelter from the South and S. W. But the Island *Guano* something breaks the Swelling of the Sea.

As it is advantageous on that Account, it is offensive for the Stench of Birds Dung that covers it, and the more, because it lies directly to the Windward of the Ships; it is even thought, that it makes the Port unwholsome in Summer; but it seems to be more likely, that the Distempers of that Season are the Effect of the great Heats which the Winds cannot temper; because the Course of the Air is stopp'd by the North Coast, which forms a Gut of Sand and Rocks continually burning.

However, the Water Ships take in is good enough, tho' it be had after an odd Manner. When the Tide ebbs, they dig about half a Foot deep in the Sand on the Shore, from whence it falls off, and from those so shallow Cavities they take good fresh Water, which keeps well at Sea. *Odd Watering.*

The Shore being full of great Stones, having little Water, and always rough, the Boats cannot come to set any thing ashore, but only in three little Creeks, or Guts, the best of which is that at the Foot of the Headland. To enter it, they must pass between two Rocks, and coast along that on the Starboard Side, among Stones: It is bare at low Water, and may be perceiv'd at high: When Boats have pass'd it, they turn short to the Larboard Side, steering directly to the first Houses; and thus they enter the great Creek, the Bottom whereof is almost upon a Level, and there is so little Water at low Ebb, that Canoes are not afloat, and Boats laden touch at high Water; so that, to prevent their being staved, they are obliged to strengthen the Keel with Iron Bars. *Landing Places.*

To obstruct the Landing of Enemies in that Place, the *Spaniards* had made Entrenchments of unburnt Bricks, and a Battery in the Form of a little Fort, which flanks the three Creeks; but it is built after a wretched Manner, and is now quite falling to Ruin: So that the said Village deserves nothing less than the Name of a strong Place given it *Fortifications.*

by

Dampier's false Account.

by *Dampier*, because he was repuls'd there in the Year 1680. The *English* being convinced of the Difficulty of landing before the Town, landed at the Creek of *Chacota*, which is to the Southward of the Head-land, whence they march'd over the Mountain to plunder *Arica*.

Arica Town.

Plate XXI.

Those Ravages, and the Earthquakes which are frequent there, have at last ruin'd that Town, which is at present no other than a Village of about 150 Families, most of them Blacks, Mulattoes and *Indians*, and but few Whites. On the 26th of *November* 1605, the Sea being agitated by an Earthquake, suddenly flooded and bore down the greatest Part of it; the Ruins of the Streets are to be seen to this Day, stretching out near a Quarter of a League from

---

Plate XXI. Page 150. explain'd in English.

The Plan of the Road of *ARICA*, on the Coast of *Peru*, in 18 Degrees, 29 Minutes of South Latitude.

Village de S. Michel de Sapa, *The Village of S. Michael de Sapa.*
Vallee d' Arica, *The Vale of Arica.*
Ruisseau, *A Rivulet.*
Morne, *The Head-land.*
Anse de Chacota, *Chacota Bay.*
Isla del Guano, *Guano Island.*
Rade de Arsea, *Arsea Road.*
Echelle d'une lieuë Marine, *A Scale of a Sea League.*
Vuë de Reconnoissance de Arica, *The Prospect to know Arica by.*

The Plan of the Town of *ARICA*, which contains great Part of 1-2 of the general Plan.

D. Juan de Mur, *Don John de Mur.*
S. Francois, *S. Francis.*
Marais, *The Marsh.*
Partie du Morne, *Part of the Head-land.*
Ruines du Corps de Garde, *Ruins of the Corps de Garda.*
Passage des Chaloupes, *The Way for the Boats.*
Isla de Guana, *Guana Island.*

A. *S. Mark's Parish.*
B. *The Square.*
C. *The Mercenarians.*
D. *S. John of God.*
E. *The Fort.*
F. *The Ruins of the Entrenchments.*
G. *The Magazines of* Guana.
H. Project de S. Francois, *The Plan of S. Francis.*
I. *Guts, or Channels.*
K. *Watering-Place on the Edge of the Sea, in the Sand.*

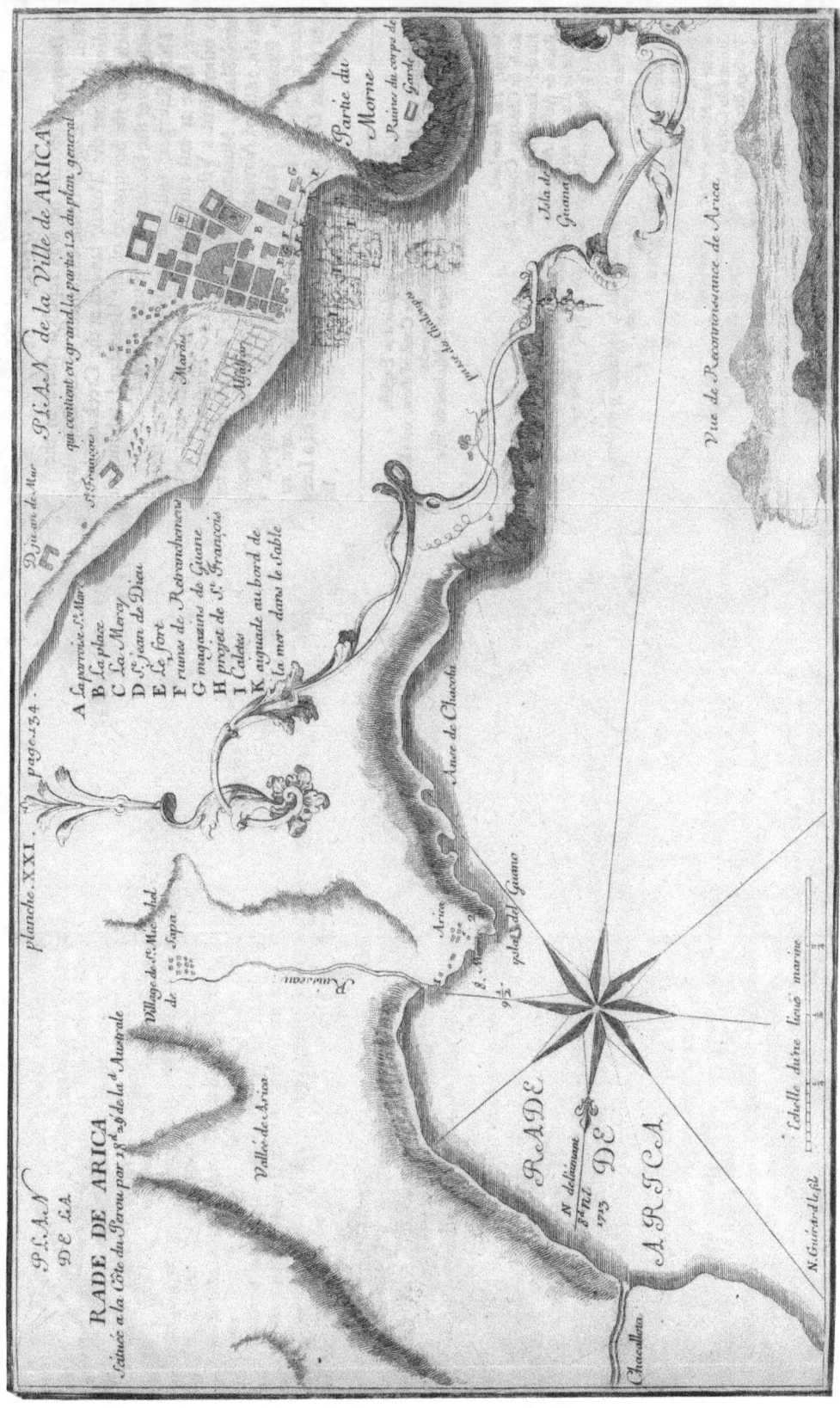

from the Place where it now stands. What remains of the Town is not subject to such Accidents, because it is seated on a little rising Ground, at the Foot of the Headland: Most of the Houses are built with nothing but Fascines, of a Sort of Flags or Sedge, call'd *Totora*, bound together, standing end-ways with Leather, Thongs and Canes crossing them; or else they are made of Canes set upright, and the Intervals fill'd up with Earth. The Use of unburnt Bricks is reserv'd for the stateliest Houses, and for Churches: No Rain ever falling there, they are cover'd with nothing but Mats, which makes the Houses look as if they were Ruins, when beheld from without.

The Parish Church is handsome enough, being of the Invocation of S. *Mark*: There is a Monastery of seven or eight *Mercenarians*, an Hospital of the Brothers of S. *John of God*, and a Monastery of *Franciscans*, who were coming to settle in the Town, after having destroy'd the House they had half a Quarter of a League from it, tho' in the pleasantest Part of the Vale, and near the Sea. *Churches.*

The Vale of *Arica* is about a League wide next the Sea; all a barren Country, except the Place where the old Town stood, which is divided into little Meadows of Clovergrass, some Spots of Sugar-canes, with Olive and Cottontrees intermix'd, and Marshes full of the Sedge, used as above to build Houses: It is thrust in to the Eastward, growing narrower that Way. A League up is the Village of S. *Michael de Sapa*, where they begin to cultivate the *Agi*, that is, *Guinea* Pepper, which is sown throughout all the rest of the Vale; and there are several scatter'd Farms, which have no other Product but that Pepper. In that little Space of the Vale, which is very narrow, and not above six Leagues long, they sell yearly of it to the Value of above 80000 Crowns. *Arica Vale.*

Agi Guinea Pepper.

The *Spaniards* of *Peru* are so generally addicted to that Sort of Spice, that they can dress no Meat without it, tho' so very hot and biting, that there is no enduring of it, unless well used to it; and as it cannot grow on the *Puna*, *Trade of Arica.*

that

that is, the Mountain Country, abundance of Merchants come down every Year, and carry away all the *Guinea* Pepper that grows in the Vales of *Arica, Sama, Taena, Locumba,* and others ten Leagues about; whence it is reckon'd there is exported to the Value of above 600000 Pieces of Eight, tho' sold cheap.

Considering the Smalness of the Place, it is hard to believe that such vast Quantities should go from them; for, excepting the Vales, the Country is every where so parch'd up, that there is no green to be seen. This Wonder is produced by means of that Bird's Dung, which, as was said before, is brought from *Iquique,* and fertilizes the Earth in such Manner, that it yields 4 or 500 for one, of all Sorts of Grain, Wheat, *Indian* Corn, &c. but particularly the *Agi,* or *Guinea* Pepper, when they know how to manage it right.

Great Fertility.

When the Seed is sprouted, and fit to be transplanted, the Plants are set winding, that is, not in a strait Line, but like an S, to the end that the Disposition of the Furrows, which convey the Water to them, may carry it gently to the Foot of the Plants; then they lay about each Plant of *Guinea* Pepper as much *Guana,* or Birds Dung, above-mention'd, as will lie in the Hollow of a Man's Hand. When it is in Blossom, they add a little more; and, lastly, when the Fruit is form'd, they add a good Handful, always taking care to water it, because it never rains in that Country; otherwise, the Salts it contains not being dissolv'd, would burn the Plants, as has been found by Experience. For this Reason it is laid down at several Times with a regular Management, the Necessity whereof has been found by Use, by the Difference of the Crops produced.

Cultivating of Guinea Pepper.

For carrying of the *Guana,* or Dung, to the Lands, they generally, at *Arica,* make use of that Sort of little Camels, by the *Indians* of *Peru* call'd *Llamas;* by those of *Chili, Chillehueque;* and, by the *Spaniards, Carneros de la Tierra,* or the Country Sheep. Their Heads are small in

Llamas, Sheep of Peru.

Propor-

Proportion to their Bodies, something resembling both a Horse's and Sheep's Head; the upper Lip, like a Hare's, is cleft in the middle, through which they spit ten Paces from them against any that offend them; and if that Spittle falls on their Faces, it makes a reddish Spot, which is often follow'd by an Itching. Their Necks are long, bowing downwards like the Camels, towards the fore Part of the Body, which would well enough resemble them, if they had a Bunch on the Back. The Figure I here insert may serve to explain what is wanting in this Description: Their Height is from four Foot to four and a half. *See Plate XXII.*

They generally carry only a hundred Weight, and walk holding their Heads up, with wonderful Gravity and Majesty, so regular a Pace, that no Beating will make them go out of it. At Night, it is impossible to make them move with their Burden; they lie down till it is taken off, to go and graze: Their common Food is a Sort of Grass, somewhat like the small Rush, bating that it is a little finer, and has a sharp Point at the end; it is call'd *Ycho*: All the Mountains are cover'd with nothing else; they eat little, and never drink, so that they are Creatures easily kept. Tho' they have Cloven Feet like Sheep, yet they make use of them in the Mines to carry the Ore to the Mill; as soon as loaded, they go without any Guide to the Place where they are used to be unloaded. Above the Foot they have a Spur, which makes them sure-footed among the Rocks, because they make use of it to hold, or hook by. Their Wool has a strong Scent, and even disagreeable; it is long, white, gray and russet in Spots, and very fine, tho' much inferiour to that of the *Vicunna's*. *Their Burden, Food, &c.*

The *Vicunna's* are shaped much like the *Llamas*, bating that they are smaller, and lighter: Their Wool being extraordinary fine and much valu'd; they are sometimes hunted after such a manner as deserves to be related. Many *Indians* get together to drive them into some narrow Pass, where they have made Cords fast across, three or four Foot from the Ground, with Bits of Wool and Cloth hanging at them. The *Vicunna's* coming to pass, are so frighted *Vicunna's how taken.*

at the Motion of those Bits of Wood and Cloth, that they dare not go any farther; so that they press together in a Throng, and then the *Indians* kill them with Stones made fast at the End of Leather-Thongs. If any *Guanaco's* happen to be with them, they leap over the Cords, and then all the *Vicunna's* follow them: The *Guanaco's* are larger and more corpulent; they are also call'd *Viscacha's*.

Guanaco's.

There is another Sort of Black Creatures like the *Llamas*, call'd *Alpaques*, whose Wool is extraordinary fine, but their Legs are shorter, and their Snout contracted, so that it has some Resemblance of a human Countenance. The *Indians* make several uses of those Creatures; they make them carry a Burden of about a hundred. Weight; their Wool serves to make Stuffs, Cords and Sacks; their Bones are used to make Weavers Utensils; and lastly, their Dung serves to make Fire to dress Meat, and to warm them.

Alpaques useful Creatures.

Before the last Wars, the *Armadilla*, or little Fleet, composed of some Ships of the King's and of private Persons, resorted every Year to *Arica*, to bring thither the *European* Commodities and Quick-silver for the Mines of *la Paz*, *Oruro*, *la Plata*, or *Chuquizaca*, *Potosi*, and *Lipes*; and then carry'd to *Lima* the King's Plate, being the Fifth of what Metal is drawn from the Mines; but since no more Galeons come to *Portobelo*, and the *French* have carry'd on the Trade, that Port has been the most considerable Mart of all the Coast, to which the Merchants of the five Towns above, being the richest in Mines, resort. It is true, that the Port of *Cobija* is nearer to *Lipes* and *Potosi*, than *Arica*; but being so desart and barren, that there is nothing to be had for Men or Mules to subsist, they choose rather to go some Leagues farther, and be sure to find what they want; besides that it is not a very difficult Matter for them to bring their Plate thither privately in the Mass, and to compound with the *Corregidores*, or chief Magistrates, to save paying the Fifth to the King.

Former Trade of Arica.

The

The Manner of taking the Silver out of the Mines:

OR,

The Management of the Ore to reduce it into Masses.

THOSE the *Spaniards* call *Pinnas*, are porous and light Masses of Silver, made of dry'd *Amalgama*, or Paste, before form'd by the Mixture of Quick-silver, and the Dust of Silver taken out of the Mines, as I am going to relate.

After having broken the Stone taken out of the Vein of Ore, they grind it in those Mills with Grind-stones above-mention'd, or in the *Ingenios Reales*, or Royal Engines, which consist of Hammers or Pounders, like the *French* Plaister-Mills. They have generally a Wheel of about 25 or 30 Foot Diameter, whose long Axle tree is set with smooth Triangles, which, as they turn, hook or lay hold of the Handles of the Iron Hammers, and lift them up to a certain Height, from whence they drop at once at every Turn, and they generally weighing about 200 Weight, fall so violently, that they crush and reduce the hardest Stone to Powder, by their Weight alone. They afterwards sift that Powder through Iron, or Copper Sieves, to take away the finest, and return the rest to the Mill. When the Ore happens to be mix'd with some Metals, which obstruct its falling to Powder, as Copper, they then calcine it in an Oven, and pound it over again. *Royal Engines.*

At the little Mines, where they use none but Mills with Grind-stones, they, for the most part, grind the Ore with Water, which makes a liquid Mud, that runs into a Receiver; whereas, when it is ground dry, it must be afterwards steep'd, and well moulded together with the Feet for a long Time. *Wetting the Ore.*

To this Purpose, they make a Court, or Floor where they dispose that Mud in square Parcels, about a Foot thick, each of them containing half a *Caxon*, or Chest, that is 25 Quintals, *Moulding and Mixtures.*

Quintals, or Hundred Weight of Ore; and these they call *Cuerpos*, that is, Bodies. On each of them they throw about two hundred Weight of Sea, or common Salt, more or less, according to the Nature of the Ore, which they mould and incorporate with the Earth for two or three Days. Then they add to it a certain Quantity of Quicksilver, squeezing a Purse made of a Skin into which they put it, to make it fall in Drops, with which they sprinkle the Body or Mass equally. According to the Nature and Quality of the Ore, they allow to each Mass ten, fifteen, or twenty Pounds; for the richer it is, the more Mercury it requires to draw to it the Silver it contains; so that they know not the Quantity but by long Experience. An *Indian* is employ'd to mould one of those square Parcels eight times a day, to the end that the Mercury may incorporate with the Silver; to that effect they often mix Lime with it, when the Ore happens to be greasy, where Caution is to be used; for they say it sometimes grows so hot, that they neither find Mercury nor Silver in it, which seems incredible. Sometimes they also strew among it some Lead, or Tin Ore, to facilitate the Operation of the Mercury, which is slower in very cold Weather than when it is temperate; for which Reason, at *Potosi* and *Lipes*, they are often obliged to mould the Ore during a whole Month, or a Month and half; but in more temperate Countries the *Amalgama* is made in eight or ten Days.

Fire used in some Places. To facilitate the Operation of the Mercury, they in some Places, as at *Puno* and elsewhere, make their *Buiterons*, or Floors on Arches, under which they keep Fires, to heat the Powder of the Ore for 24 Hours, on a Pavement of Bricks.

Essaying. When it is thought that the Mercury has attracted all the Silver, the Essayer takes a little Ore from each Parcel apart, which he washes in an Earthen Plate, or a Wooden Bowl, and by the Colour of the Mercury found at the Bottom of the Bowl, knows whether it has had its Effect; for when it is blackish, the Ore is too much heated, and then they add

more

more Salt, or some other Drug: They say that then the Mercury *dispara*, that is, shoots, or flies away; if the Mercury is white, they put a Drop under the Thumb, and pressing it hastily, the Silver there is among it, remains sticking to the Thumb, and the Mercury slips away in little Drops. In Conclusion, when they perceive that all the Silver is gather'd, they carry the Ore to a Bason into which a little Stream of Water runs, to wash it, much in the same *Washing of* nature as I have said they wash the Gold, excepting that *the Ore.* this being only a Mud, without Stones, instead of a Hook to stir it, an *Indian* stirs it with his Feet, to dissolve it. From the first Bason it falls into a second, where another *Indian* is, who stirs it again, to dissolve it thoroughly, and loosen the Silver: From the second it passes into a third, where the same is repeated, to the end that what has not sunk to the Bottom of the first and second may not escape the third.

When all has been wash'd, and the Water runs clear, *Separating of* they find at the Bottom of the Basons, which are lined with *the Mercury.* Leather, the Mercury incorporated with the Silver, which they call *La Pella*. It is put into a Woolen Bag, hanging up for some of the Quicksilver to drain through; they bind, beat, and press it as much as they can, laying a Weight upon it with flat Pieces of Wood; and when they have got out as much as they can, they put that Paste into a Mould of Wooden Planks; which, being bound together, generally form the Figure of an Octogen Pyramid cut short, the Bottom whereof is a Copper-plate, full of little Holes. There they stir, in order to fasten it; and when they design to make many *Pinna s*, as they call them, that is Lumps of various Weights, they divide them with little Beds, or Layers of Earth, which hinder their coming together. To that end the *Pella*, or Mass, must be weigh'd, deducting two Thirds for the Mercury that is in it, and they know within a small Matter what neat Silver there is.

They then take off the Mould, and place the *Pinna*, or *Separating of* Mass, with its Copper Base on a Trevet, or such-like In- *the Mercury.* strument,

strument, standing over a great Earthen Vessel full of Water, and cover it with an Earthen Cap, or Covering, which they again cover with lighted Coals; which Fire they feed for some Hours, that the Mass may grow violent hot, and the Mercury that is in it evaporate in Smoak; but that Smoak having no Passage out, it circulates in the Hollow that is between the Mass and the Cap, or Covering, till coming down to the Water that is underneath, it condenses and sinks to the Bottom, again converted into Quicksilver. Thus little of it is lost, and the same serves several Times; but the Quantity must be increas'd, because it grows weak: However, they formerly consumed at *Potosi* 6 or 7000 Quintals, or Hundred Weight, of Quicksilver, every Year, as *Acosta* writes, by which a Judgment may be made of the Silver they got.

Way of Heating. Plate XXII. There being neither Wood nor Coals throughout the greater Part of *Peru*, but only that Plant they call *Ycho*, before spoken of; they heat the Masses by Means of an Oven placed near the *Desazogadera*, that is the Machine for drying the Silver and separating the Mercury, and the Heat is convey'd through a Pipe, which violently draws it, as may be seen in this Figure.

Casting and Paying the Fifth. When the Mercury is evaporated, there remains nothing but a spungey Lump of contiguous Grains of Silver, very light, and almost mouldring, which the *Spaniards* call *La Pinna*, and is a Contraband Commodity from the Mines, because, by the Laws of the Kingdom, they are obliged to carry it to the King's Receipt, or to the Mint, to pay the Fifth to his Majesty. There those Masses are cast into Ingots,

---

Plate XXII. Page 158. explain'd in English.

A. Llamas, *or Sheep of Peru.*
B. Trapiche, *or a Mill to grind Ore.*
C. Buiteron, *or a Court to mould the Ore.*
D. Basons *to wash it.*
E. *The Plan of the Instrument to draw off the Quick-silver.*
F. *The Profile of the same.*
G. *The Mass of Silver*
H. *The Furnace to separate the Quicksilver.*

A Llamas ou moutons du Perou
B Trapiche ou moulin a minerai
C Buiteron ou cour ou l'on petri le minerai
D Bassins a laver
E Plan de la desazogadera
F Profil de la desazogadera
G La pigne
H Fourneau à tirer le vifargent

gots, on which the Arms of the Crown are ſtamp'd, as alſo thoſe of the Place where they were caſt, their Weight and Quality, with the Fineneſs of the Silver, to anſwer the Meaſure of all Things, according to an ancient Philoſopher.

It is always certain, that the *Ingots*, which have paid the Fifth, have no Fraud in them; but it is not ſo with the *Pinnas*, or Maſſes not caſt: Thoſe who make them, often convey into the Middle of them Iron, Sand, and other Things, to increaſe the Weight; ſo that in Prudence they ought to be open'd, and made red-hot at the Fire, for the more Certainty for if falſify'd, the Fire will either turn it black or yellow, or melt more eaſily. This Tryal is alſo uſeful to extract a Moiſture they contract in Places where they are laid on purpoſe to make them the heavier. In ſhort, their Weight may be increas'd one Third, by dipping them in Water when they are red-hot; as alſo to ſeparate the Mercury, with which the Bottom of the Maſs is always more impregnated than the Top: It alſo ſometimes happens that the ſame Maſs is of Silver of different Fineneſs.
 Frauds.

The Stones taken from the Mines, the Ore, or to ſpeak in the Language of *Peru*, the Metal from which the Silver is extracted, is not always of the ſame Nature, Conſiſtence, or Colour; there is ſome white and gray, mix'd with red or bluiſh Spots, which is call'd *Plata blanca*, white Silver; the Mines of *Lipes* are moſt of them of this ſort. For the moſt part there appear ſome little Grains of Silver, and even very often ſmall Branches extending along the Layers of the Stone.
 Ore.

There are ſome on the other hand, as black as the Droſs of Iron, in which the Silver does not appear, call'd *Negrillo*, that is blackiſh; ſometimes it is black with Lead, for which Reaſon it is call'd *Plomo Ronco*, that is, coarſe Lead, in which the Silver appears if ſcratch'd with ſomething that is harſh; and it is generally the richeſt, and got with leaſt Charge; becauſe inſtead of moulding it with Quickſilver, it is melted in Furnaces, where the
 Other Sorts.

Lead

Lead evaporates by dint of Fire, and leaves the Silver pure and clean. From that fort of Mines the *Indians* drew their Silver; becaufe having no ufe of Mercury, as the *Europeans* have, they only wrought thofe whofe Ore would melt, and having but little Wood, they heated their Furnaces with the *Ycho* above-mention'd, and the Dung of the *Llamas*, or Sheep, and other Beafts, expofing them on the Mountains, that the Wind might keep the Fire fierce. This is all the Secret the Hiftorians of *Peru* fpeak of, as of fomething wonderful. There is another fort of Ore like this, as black, and in which the Silver does not appear at all; on the contrary, if it be wetted and rubb'd againft Iron, it turns red, for which Reafon it is call'd *Roficler*, fignifying the Ruddinefs of the Dawn of Day; this is very Rich, and affords the fineft Silver. There is fome that glitters like Talk, or Ifinglafs; this is generally naught, and yields little Silver, the Name of it is *Zoroche*. The *Paco*, which is of a yellowifh Red, is very foft, and broken in Bits, but feldom rich; and the Mines of it are wrought only on account of the Eafinefs of getting the Ore. There is fome Green, not much harder than the laft, call'd *Cobriffo*, or Copperifh, it is very rare; however, tho the Silver generally appears in it, and it is almoft mouldring, it is the hardeft to be managed, that is, to have the Silver taken from it. Sometimes, after being ground, it muft be burnt in the Fire, and feveral other Methods ufed to feparate it, doubtlefs becaufe it is mix'd with Copper. Laftly, there is another fort of very rare Ore, which has been found at *Potofi*, only in the Mine of *Cotamifo*; being Threads of pure Silver, entangled or wound up together like burnt Lace, fo fine, that they call it *Aranna*, Spider, from its Refemblance to a Cobweb.

What Mines are richeft. The Veins of Mines, of what fort foever they be, are generally richer in the Middle than towards the Edges; and when two Veins happen to crofs one another, the Place where they meet is always very rich. It is alfo obferv'd, that thofe which lie North and South are richer than thofe which

which lie any other way. Those which are near Places where Mills can be erected, and that are more commodiously wrought, are often preferable to the richer that require more Expence; which is the Reason that at *Lipes* and *Potosi*, a Chest of Ore must yield 10 Marks, being 8 Ounces each Mark, of Silver, to pay the prime Charges; and at those of the Province of *Tarama* 5 pay them.

When they are rich, and sink downwards, they are subject to be flooded; and then they must have recourse to Pumps and Machines, or else drain them by those they call *Socabones*, being Passages made in the side of the Mountain for the Water to run out at, which often ruin the Owners by the excessive Expence they insensibly draw them into. *Mines flooded*

There are other ways of separating the Silver from the Stone that confines it, and from the other Metals that are mix'd with it, by Fire, or strong separating Waters, made use of at some Mines where I have not been and where they make a sort of Ingots, which they call *Bollos*; but the most general and usual Method being to make the *Pinnas*, or Masses above-mention'd, either for Easiness, or to save Fire and other Ingredients; the Curious may have Recourse to *Agricola*'s Treatise of Minerals, where what is practised at the Silver Mines in *Germany* is related See also *Cesalpin, Cesius, Kentmant, Etker, Eucelius, Van Helmont*, and *Quercetan*. *Other ways of separating.*

When we examine in what manner the Silver is mix'd with the Stone, in Grains or long Slips like Straws, separated by great Intervals of meer Stone, or else in fine Dust mix'd with the same Stone, it looks as if Nature had form'd them both at the same Time; and many are of that Opinion However, if we may believe the *Spaniards*, the Silver is daily form'd anew in certain Parts of the Mines, not only in the solid Stone, but even in external Bodies, which have been long since put into them. Experience has verify'd this Opinion in the Mountain of *Potosi*, where they have dug so much in several Places, that several Mines have *Silver how form'd.*

Y fallen

fallen in and bury'd the *Indians* that were working in them, with their Tools and Props to keep up the Earth. In process of time they have again dug the same Mines, and have found Threads of Silver in the Wood, the Skulls and Bones, running through them as they do in the Vein it self.

This matter of Fact is reported by so many several Persons, that it cannot be look'd upon as an Invention. Monsieur *Chambon*, in his Treatise of Metals, tells us something very like this, which may nevertheless be suspected *Strange Relation.* to be magnify'd. He tells us, That in a Mine of Gold and Silver, in *Hungary* it is likely, they assured him, that they had found three human Figures, of the same Matter of which the Veins of the Mine are composed; and that tho' the said Figures had been bruis'd and broken by the Hammers and Wedges, what was taken up had been so well put together, that there was no occasion to question their having been Men. That those Figures had their peculiar Mineral Veins, that the inward Head, and all the Bones were of pure Gold, and that was the Reason why those Figures had been destroy'd.

Palissi, in his Treatise of Metals, tells us of such another *Another.* Phænomenon. He affirms he saw *a Stone of Lapis Calaminaris, in which there was a Fish of that same Substance;* he adds, that *in the Country of Mansfeld, abundance of Fishes are found converted into Metal.*

Silver grows. It is also an undoubted Matter of Fact, that much Silver has been found in the Mines of *Lipes*, which had been wrought long before. I know they answer to this, that formerly they were so rich, that the smaller Quantities were not regarded; but I much question whether Men would voluntariy lose what they had, when it was to cost but very little Labour: If to these Facts we add, what has been said of the Washing-Places of *Adacol*, and of the Mountain of S. *Joseph*, where the Copper is form'd, there will be no longer Occasion to doubt, that Silver and other Metals are daily form'd in certain Places. Experience daily shews it in relation to Quick-silver. if it be true that
it

it breeds in the Earth, or in a Cellar, by putting in a Mixture of Sulphur and Saltpeter, as Monsieur *Chambon* affirms.

Besides, there want not Natural Philosophers, who place *Metals,* Metals among Vegetables, and pretend that they proceed *Vegetables.* from an Egg; an Opinion which nevertheless does not please all Men, and to maintain which, they alledge Facts that are too wonderful to be easily believ'd.

Theophrastus affirms, that in the Island of *Cyprus*, there grows a sort of Copper very like Gold, which being sow'd in Bits, shoots like a Plant. *Palissi* says, that in *Hungary* a very fine sort of Gold has been seen, which winding about a certain Plant like Fibres, increas'd from time to time. See *John Webster's Metallographia, London.*

The Ancient Philosophers, and some of the Modern, *Metals not* have ascribed to the Sun the Forming of Metals; but besides *form'd by the* that it is incomprehensible that his Heat can penetrate to *Sun.* an infinite Depth, a Man may undeceive himself in regard to this Opinion, by reflecting on an indisputable matter of Fact, which follows.

About 30 Years ago, a Flash of Lightning fell on the *Prov'd by a* Mountain of *Ilimanni*, which is above *La Paz*, otherwise *good Instance.* call'd *Chuquiago*, a Town in *Peru*, 80 Leagues from *Arica*; it beat down a Part of it, the Pieces or Shivers whereof, found scatter'd about the Town and Country adjoining, were full of Gold, and yet the Mountain has been Time out of Mind cover'd with Snow. Therefore the Heat of the Sun, which has not been strong enough to thaw the Snow, could not have the Power to form the Gold that was under it, and which it has cover'd without any Intermission.

This Fact farther proves, that we are here misinform'd as to the Country of the Mines; for *Vallemon*, in his occult Philosophy, says, ' That Mines are known or dis-
' cover'd, when there is a white Frost on the Ground
' and there is none on the Veins of Metals, because they
' exhale dry and hot Vapours, which hinder it from freez-
' ing

'ing there; and that for the same Reason the Snow does 'not lie long there. If that be true in some Places, it is not so in *Peru*, nor at the Silver Mines of S. *John* in *Chili*, which are cover'd with Snow eight Months in the Year.

How Metals are form'd. I, who cannot admit of any Conjectures but such as are grounded on Experience, should be more inclinable to ascribe the Formation of Metals to subterraneous Fires; and without troubling myself about the Central Fire of certain Philosophers, I should not want Proofs to make it appear, that all that Part of *America* is full of them, as appears by the burning Mountains, which from time to time are there seen to break out and flame, such are those of *Arequipa*, *Quito*, and *Chili*, which are in the Mine Country. Nor is it impossible that those of *Mexico* should have some share in it, tho' to Appearance somewhat remote; for there is no Reason why the Earth may not be compared to a Charcoal Kiln, where one Hole is sufficient to give Air and preserve the Fire in the opposite Side.

This Heat being well establish'd, it must give Motion to the Salts, the Sulphurs, and the other Principles the Earth contains, and which may be Ingredients in the Composition of Metals, and being exagitated and rarify'd like a Vapour, insinuate themselves into the Pores of the Stone, and particularly those of the Piles of Rock, like a Plate or strange Body, enclosed in Heterogeneous Masses. There that Exhalation fixes itself, and condenses like Wax, by the Disposition of the Pores it is forced into. We have a sensible Experience hereof in Mercury, which becomes Volatile in Smoak, as has been observ'd before, and condenses again when it returns to the Water. If that Metal can be reduced to the Consistence of the others, as Chymists pretend, the Conjecture appears to be well grounded.

Pretences of Chymists. " 1. *Paracelsus* says, that Gold is Mercury coagulated, " or congeal'd.

" 2. *Christian* I. Elector of *Saxony*, converted Mer- " cury, Copper, and other Metals, into real Gold and " Silver; and Prince *Augustus*, about the Year 1590, with " some

" some of a certain Tincture, converted 1604 times as
" much Mercury into Gold, which went through all Tryals,
" *Joan. Kunkeli Obfervationes, Lond.*

" 3. *Zweifer*, in his Book entitled, *Pharmacopœia Regia*,
" Part 1. Cap. 1. says, that the Emperor *Ferdinand* III.
" having with his own Hands made two Pounds and a
" half of good Gold of three Pounds of ordinary Mercury,
" by Means of a certain Philosophical Tincture, caus'd a
" Medal to be made of it; on the one Side of which was
" an *Apollo*, with an Inscription certifying that Transmu-
" tation; and on the Reverse he prais'd God, for having
" communicated to Men some Part of his Divine Know-
" ledge, which may be better seen in the Original *Latin*
" Words, which I have here inserted.

About the Apollo.	*On the Reverse.*
DIVINA METAMORPHOSIS.	RARIS HÆC VT HOMINIBVS NOTA EST ARS ITA RARO IN LVCEM PRODIT LAVDETVR DEVS IN ÆTERNVM QVI PARTEM INFINITÆ SVÆ SCIENTIÆ ABIEC TISSIMIS SVIS CREATV RIS COMMVNI CAT
Then follow'd, EXIBITA PRAGÆ XV JAN. A°O MDCXLVIII. IN. PRÆSENTIA SAC. CÆS. MAIESTAT FERDINANDI TERTII	

" In *English* thus: The Divine Metamorphosis, or Trans-
" mutation, perform'd at *Prague*, on the 15th of *Janu-
" ary*, in the Year 1648, in the Presence of the sacred Im-
" perial Majesty of *Ferdinand* III. *Then on the Reverse:*
" As this Art is known to few Men, so it seldom appears
" abroad. God be prais'd for ever, who has communi-
" cated Part of his Divine Knowledge to his most abject
" Creatures.

" The same *Zweifer* takes care to observe that the said
" Gold was very good, *not at all Sophistical*, and that the
" Emperor was too sharp a Man to suffer himself to be im

"posed upon by any artful Substituting of Natural Gold, "instead of that he made.

I will not here fall into the Dreams of those Searchers after the Philosophers-Stone; nay, I will believe, notwithstanding all the most plausible Stories they tell us, as above, in the Words of *Zweifer*, upon the Experiments that have been seen made, that they are fraudulent Sleights of Hand, which have gain'd Reputation to that vain Employment; but tho' they have not attain'd the Degree of the Perfection of Gold, it is still certain that they have imitated it very well with Mercury. This is sufficient to establish my Opinion about the Formation of Metals. May it not be thence inferr'd, that the Mechanism of Nature in those Productions differs from this only, in that it is more perfect? I am beholden for this Thought only to the Observation I have made of the several Sorts of Ore that have fallen into my Hands, tho', in the main, it be something agreeable to that of Messieurs *Vossius* and *Vallemont*, who look upon the subterraneous Fires as the first Principle for the Formation of Metals.

Exhalations of the Mines. Be that as it will, it is certain that there are continually strong Exhalations coming from the Mines. The *Spaniards*, who live over them, are obliged frequently to drink of the Herb of *Paraguay*, or *Mate*, to moisten their Breasts, without which they are liable to a Sort of Suffocation. The very Mules that pass along those Places, tho' much less steep and mountanous than others, where they trip it away, are forced to stand almost every Minute to recover their Wind. But those Exhalations are much more sensible within; they have such an Effect on Bodies that are not used to them, that a Man who goes in for a Moment, comes out as it were benumb'd, or blasted with such a Pain in all his Limbs, that he is not able to stir, which often lasts above a Day; and then the Remedy is to carry the Diseas'd Person back into the Mine. The *Spaniards* call that Distemper *Quebrantahuessos*, that is, *Bone-Breaker*. Even the

Indians,

the South-Sea.   167

Indians, who are used to it, are obliged to relieve one another alternatively, almost every Day.

It has also happened sometimes, that in working in certain Parts of the Mines, pestilential Exhalations have broke out, which have kill'd the Workmen upon the Spot; so that they have been forced to abandon them. For the same Reason in those *Hungarian* Silver and Gold Mines, which are clayish and so glutinous, that they are obliged to make good Fires to dry them; the Workmen are oblig'd to get out immediately. Those Sorts of clayish Mines are in all Likelihood very rare in *Peru*; for I have never heard of them. *Clayish Mines.*

The *Indians*, to preserve themselves against the ill Air they breathe in the Mines, are there continually chewing *Coca*, a Sort of *Betele*, and they pretend that without it they could not work there. *Coca Preservative.*

The Mines which at present yield most Silver, are those of *Oruro*, a little Town eighty Leagues from *Arica*. In the Year 1712, one so rich was found at *Ollachea*, near *Cusco*, that it yielded 2500 Marks, of 8 Ounces each, out of every Chest; that is, almost one fifth Part of the Ore; but it has declined much, and is now reckon'd but among the ordinary Sort. Next to these are those of *Lipes*, which have had the same Fate. Lastly, those of *Potosi* yield little, and cause a great Expence, by reason of their great Depth. *Rich Mines.*

As for Gold Mines, they are very rare in the South Part of *Peru*; there are none but in the Province of *Guanuco* towards *Lima*; in that of the *Chichas*, where the Town of *Tarija* is, and at *Chuquiaguillo*, two Leagues from *La Paz*, and other Places there-about, which for that Reason are in the *Indian* Tongue call'd *Chuquiago*, signifying a House, or Farm of Gold. There are there in short, very plentiful Washing-places, where Grains of Virgin or Pure Gold have been found of a prodigious Magnitude; two among the rest, one of which, weighing 64 Marks and some odd Ounces, (the Mark, as has been often said, being eight Ounces) was *Gold Mines rare in Peru.* *Large Grains of Gold.*

bought

bought by the Count *de la Moncloa*, Viceroy of *Peru*, to present it to the King of *Spain*; the other fell into the Hands of *Don John de Mur* in 1710, whilst he was *Corregidor*, or chief Magistrate of *Arica*. This is shaped like an Ox's Heart in little, and weighs 45 Marks, that is 360 Ounces, of three different Degrees of Fineness; to the best of my Remembrance of 11, 18, and 21 Carats, which is very remarkable in the same natural Mass.

Land of Mines cold and barren.
All the Places above-mention'd where there are Mines, are so cold and barren, that the Inhabitants of them are obliged to seek their Provisions from the Coast. The Reason of that Barrenness is plain, if we consider the bad Exhalations which continually issue from the Mines, as has been observ'd before, they certainly containing Salts and Sulphurs contrary to the Vegetation of Plants.

Others in temperate Places.
If those Places are inhabited, it is only in regard to their great Wealth, which draw thither all the Necessaries of Life; however, there is no Want of Mines towards the Coast, in more temperate Places, as appears by that newly discover'd at *Iquique*: It is even pretended, that there are Mines in all the Mountains about *Arica*, but that they are not rich enough to be at the Expence of working them.

Salt Mines, &c.
In the same Mountains there is an infinite Number of Mines of Salt, and some of the fine Lime-stone for making of Plaister of *Paris*; as also certain Spungey Stones, serving to filtrate or strain Water, and a Sort of transparent Alabaster, used in some Places instead of Glass for Windows.

Plants.
In other respects they are all barren; no Green is to be seen there but what is down in the Vales. In that of *Arica* there is Jalop, the Root whereof is of great Use in Physick; there is also *China* Root and *Mechoacan*, which the Inhabitants, if I mistake not, call *Jonqui*. There is also the *Molle* Tree, spoken of in the Article of *Valparaiso*; the *Tara* Tree, somewhat resembling the *Acacia*; the Fruit of it, which is a Cod like the *French* Beans, serves to make Writing-Ink, as has been said of the *Algarroba*, or Carob. On the Mountains near *La Paz*, there is a Sort of Moss, call'd

call'd *Hiareta*, which being put into the Fire, makes a Smoak which immediately blinds those whose Eyes it reaches; it also yields a Gum, which is of good Use in some Distempers.

Removal to another Ship.

AFTER having waited above a Month at *Arica*, for an Opportunity to prosecute my Voyage, I embarqued on the 8th of *August* on a little Ship of 150 Tons, commanded by Monsieur *de Russy*, who was bound for *Hilo*, and thence for *Callao*, to join its Commandant the Great Holy Ghost.

The same Day a Suspension of Arms for four Months, between the *European* Crowns was proclaim'd, and an Order to the *Corregidores*, or chief Magistrates, to seize and confiscate the Effects of the *French* that were in *Peru* and *Chili*, and to oblige them to embarque, in order to return to *France*. *Suspension of Arms.*

The same Express also inform'd us, that an *English* Privateer had taken a *Spanish* Ship laden with Sugar, near *Guayaquil*, and that he had put half his Men into the Prize, which was said to be of 24 Guns: The Viceroy sent Captain *S. Juan*, Commander of the *S. Rose* in quest of him; but the Ship being cast away on the Coast, he found only two or three Men.

Departure from Arica.

THE 10th of *August* in the Morning, we sail'd with a small Gale at N. E. the Land Breeze, which is generally expected in order to get out of the Creek of *Arica*, where the Tides often drive down and detain Ships in calm Weather, for several Days, towards the Inlet of *Quiaca*, for they always set that Way. Most Ships are made sensible of the Difficulty of getting out, because the Land Breeze which holds from Midnight till Day, is succeeded *Difficulty of getting clear of Arica.*

by that from S. W. being too soon to turn the Head-land of *Sama*, lying W. N. W. from that of *Arica*, and the more for that the Tides sensibly come from above; and for this Difficulty in turning of it, on our Chart it is call'd the *Devil's Head-land*. By good Fortune the Land Breeze carry'd us far enough out to Sea, not to apprehend any thing during a Calm that lasted five Days, because the Tides were not then very strong: In case of being too much forced back towards the Land, and no possibility of working up again, there is the Remedy of being able to come to an Anchor a League to the Southward of *Quiaca*, in 30 or 40 Foot Water; the Bottom greenish Owze, like an Olive Colour, in some Places mix'd with Sand.

Marks to know Hilo by. At length, after eight Days spent in sailing thirty Leagues, we arriv'd at *Hilo*, on the 18th of *August*: That Road is to be known to the Windward, by a plain Point of Land, low in Comparison of the high Mountains. From five or six Leagues distance to the Sea-ward, it looks almost like an Island; that is it which they call the Point *de Coles*, at the End whereof is a very low Rock, which seems to rise higher as you draw nearer to it.

Description of the Road of Hilo.

Plate XXIII. THE Road being scarce any other than a strait Coast, the Ships that are at Anchor there, are seen at a Distance; and for the same Reason, there must be a great Sea upon all Winds. In short, there is but one Place to land at, among the Rocks, which appear at the Entrance of the Vale E. and by N. or E. N. E. from the Anchoring-place; when you have 15 or 12 Fathom Water, the Bottom fine Sand, somewhat Owzy, and to the Northward of the Little Island, which is at the Point of *Coles*.

Landing-Place.

The Ridge of Rocks, which covers the Creek where they land out of Boats, is divided into two: The second Cut makes a little Creek on the Starboard-Side, where,

not-

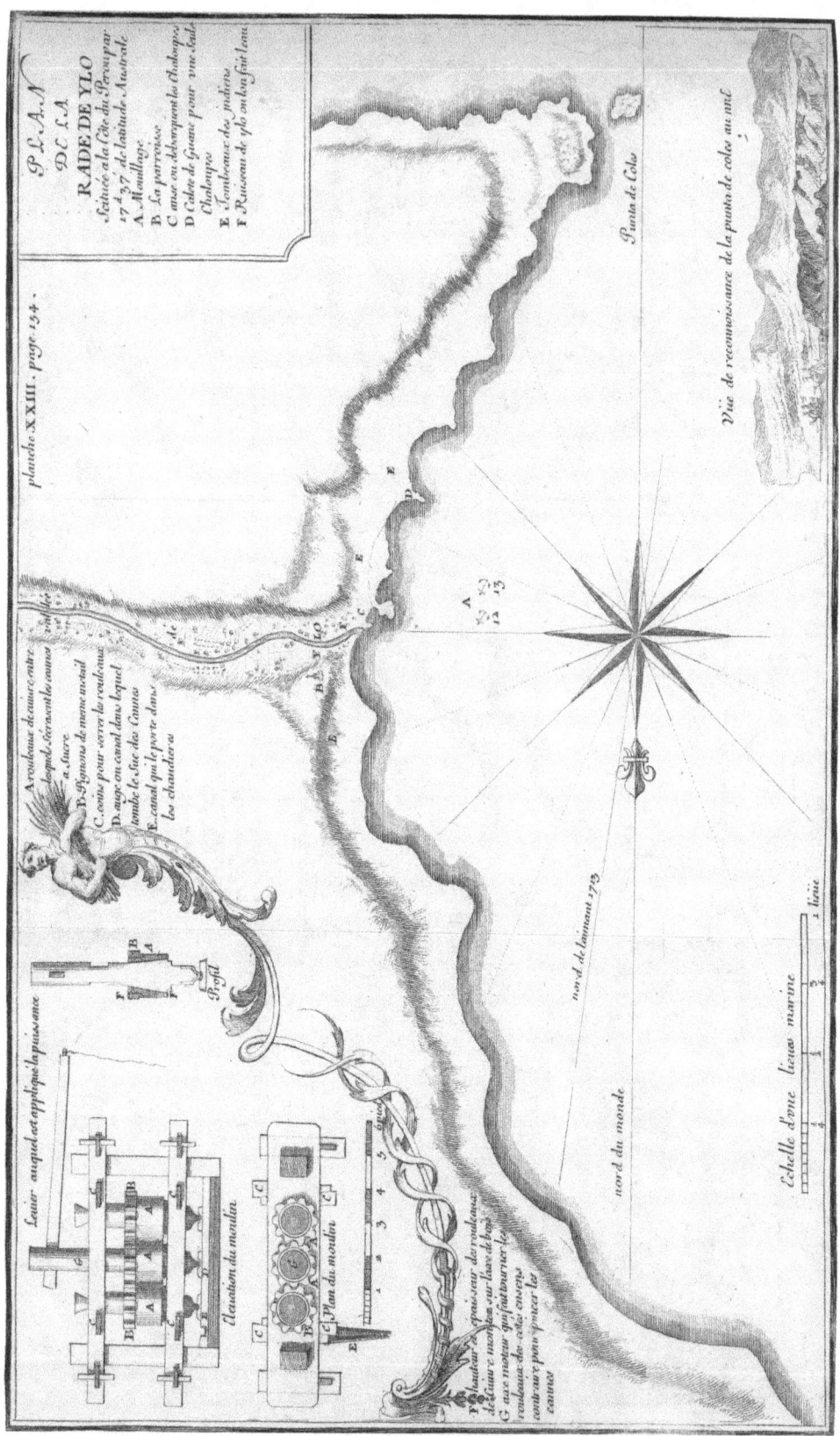

The material originally positioned here is too large for reproduction in this reissue. A PDF can be downloaded from the web address given on page iv of this book, by clicking on 'Resources Available'.

notwithstanding the Shelter of the Rocks, the Sea generally runs high, and is impracticable, when there is a little Swelling in the Road. It is to be observ'd, that in coasting along the first Rocks, there is a Shoal which does not appear, and lies to the N. W. of another that is in Sight, and always visible: The Way to avoid it, is by keeping the Rock that advances farthest out on a red Ground there is on the Coast, half a League South of that Passage. There also is a Landing-Place, where they set ashore the *Guana*, or Dung above spoken of; but it is so small, that there is only Room for one single Canoe, or Boat.

Plate XXIII. *Page* 171. *explain'd in* English.

The Plan of the Road of *HILO*, on the Coast of *Peru, in* 17 Degrees, 37 Minutes of South Latitude.

A. *The Anchoring Place.*
B. *The Parish.*
C. *The Creek, or Landing-place for Boats.*
D. *The Creek of* Guana, *for only one Boat.*
E. *Indian Tombs.*
F. *The Rivulet of* Hilo, *where they water.*

References to the Compartment.

A. *Copper Rollers, between which the Sugar Canes are crush'd.*
B. *The Nuts of the same Metal.*
C. *Wedges to close the Rollers.*
D. *The Trough into which the Juice of the Canes runs.*
E. *The Spout through which it is convey'd into the Boilers.*
Levier au quel on applique la Puissance, *The Leaver for turning the Rollers.*
Elevation du Moulin, *The Elevation of the Mill.*
Profil, *The Profile.*
Plan du Moulin, *The Plan of the Mill.*
Pied, *Feet.*
F. *The Height and Thickness of the Copper Rollers, standing on the Wooden Axle-tree.*
G. *The moving Axle-tree, which causes the Rollers to turn the contrary Way to one another, to crush the Canes.*
Nord de l'aimant, *The North Point of the Compass.*
Nord du Monde, *the true North Point.*
Punta de Coles, *Point Coles.*
Echelle d'une lieüe Marine, *A Scale of a Sea League.*
Lieüe, *A League.*
Vuë de reconnoissance de la punta de Coles au N. N. E. *Thus Point Coles appears to the* N. N. E.

Hilo Village.   The Vale of *Hilo*, upon coming into the Road, looks only like a narrow Gut, which appears opening by Degrees, as you draw near, till the Church appears, and about fifty Cottages made of the Branches of Trees, scatter'd up and down near the Rivulet, which runs winding along the Middle of the Vale: That is all the Village of *Hilo*; most of it is built and inhabited by *French*. It is certainly too great an Honour to call it a little Town, as *Dampier* does.

Watering-Place.   That Rivulet, where Ships water, is sometimes subject to be dried up, during the six Months that the Sun is to the Southward, when the Winter has not prov'd rainy on the high Mountains. They were sensible of that Drought in the Year 1713, when they were fain to bury Casks in the Sand, to receive what drain'd from the Land, whence a Water flows, which is naught and unwholsome. The great Diseases, which that Year carry'd off the one half of the Crews of the *French* Ships that happen'd to be there, were ascribed to it; but it was a Sort of Plague, which was felt 18 Leagues from thence, at *Moquegua*, and even as far as *Arequipa*, which is 40 Leagues distant.

Wooding.   The Conveniency of Wooding is better there than the Watering, because the Vale is cover'd with Trees; but the great Quantity the *French* have fell'd within 14 Years past, has remov'd it a League from the Sea. Besides the Wood for Fewel, that Vale is in several Places planted with fine Rows of Olive-trees, which afford the best Oil in *Peru*; *Fruit-trees.* as also abundance of Fruit-trees, as Orange, Lemon, Fig, Guayava, Banana and Lucumo-trees, of which Mention has been made before. There is also of that Sort of Fruit call'd *Paltas* in *Peru*, and *Avocats* in the *French Caribbee* Islands; they are like a large Pear, and contain a round Kernel, somewhat pointed, of the Consistence and Bulk of a Chesnut, but of no other Use than a Musk Colour Dye: The Substance that incloses it is greenish, and almost as soft as Butter, and has something in it of that

Taste,

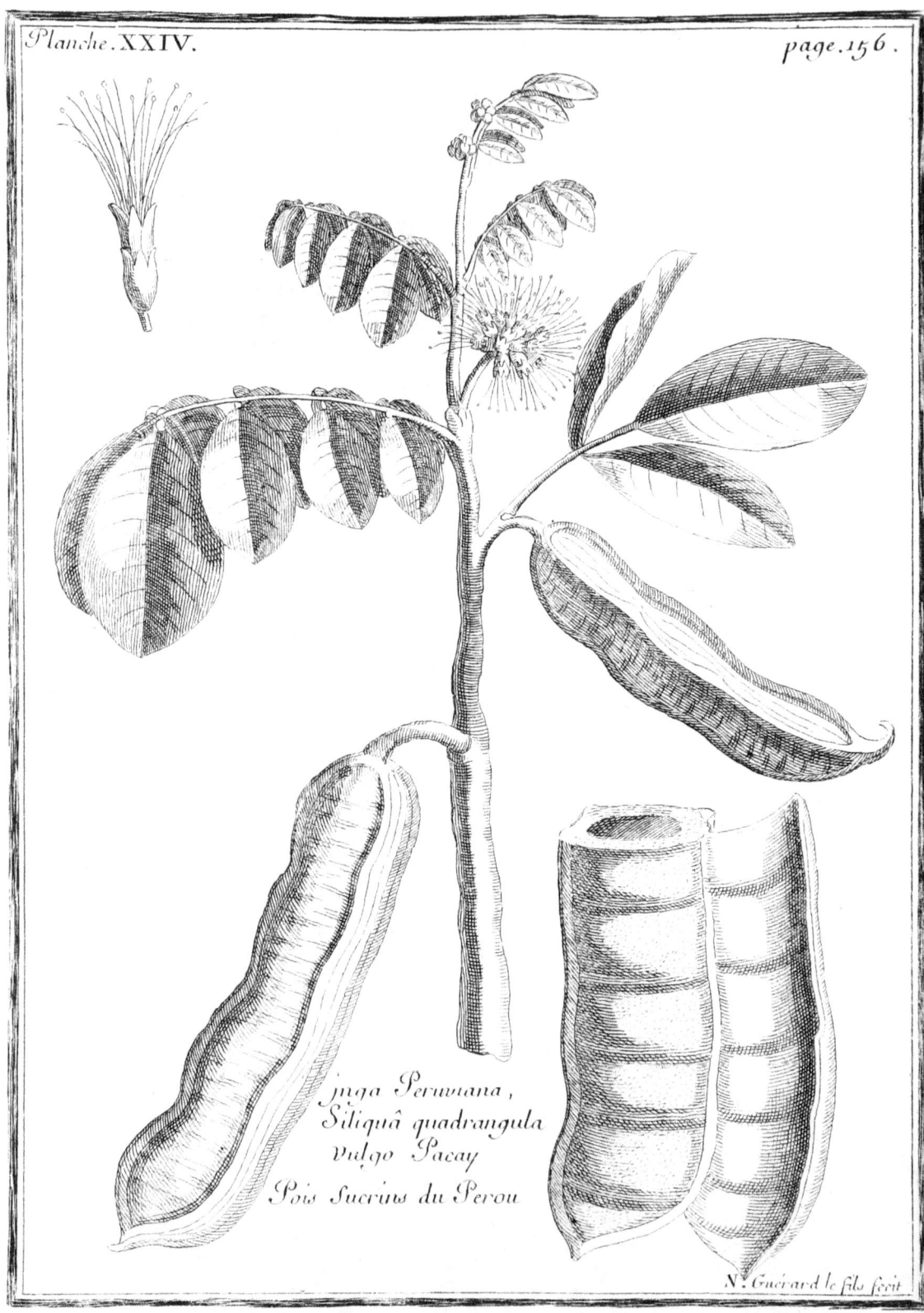

Taste, with a Mixture of that of a Hazle-Nut, eaten with Salt.

The best way of Eating it, is to pound it with Sugar and the Juice of a Lemon: That Fruit is very wholsome, and good for the Stomach; they say it is a Provocative to Love.

I saw a Tree call'd *Pacay*, whose Leaves are like those of the Walnut-tree, but of several Sizes. They are disposed by Pairs along the same Side; so that they increase as they remove farther from the Stem. Its Blossoms are almost the same as those of the *Inga*, mention'd by *Pison* and Father *Plumier*; but the Fruit is different. The Cod, whose Figure that Father has given us, is Octogon; and that of the *Pacay* has only four Faces, or Sides, of which the two largest are about 16, or 18 Parts of an Inch broad, and the small seven or eight: As for the Length, it is very uncertain; some Cods are four Inches long, and others above a Foot. They are divided within into several little Cells, each containing a Grain like a flat Bean, inclosed in a white Substance, all Filamens or Threads, which a Man would take for Cotton; but, in Reality, it is only a congeal'd Oil, which is eaten to refresh the Body, and leaves in the Mouth a little Taste of Musk, very agreeable, which has given it the Name of *Pois Sucrin*, or Sugar-Pea, among the *French*. *Plate* XXIV. Pacay Tree.

In the same Vale, there are also some of those Trees that bear the *Cassia*, which the *Spaniards* call *Canna Fistola*. That Fruit so famous in Physick for a gentle Purge, is a round Cod, 12 or 15 Inches long, growing on a great Tree; the Leaf whereof is like that of the fine Laurel. It is full of a yellowish Substance, which contains the Grains of the Seed, which grows black, and becomes viscous as it ripens. Cassia Fistula.

In

Plate XXIV. Page 173. explain'd in *English*.

The *Pacay* Plant, call'd by *European* Botanists *Inga* of *Peru*, bearing a Square Cod.

Sugar-Peas of Peru.

Sugar Canes, and how made. In the same Place where the Tree was, I also saw a Sugar Cane Garden: The Canes from which they press the Juice to extract that agreeable Salt, are sufficiently known by all Men, as is the Manner of making it; but the Form of the Mill they use to bruize them, being in a Manner new to me, and the Knowledge of Machines belonging to my Profession, I thought fit to take the Proportions. This Mill is composed of three Rollers of Brass, the Middlemost of which turns the two others, by means of the cast Nuts of the same Piece, that hitch one within another. Those Rollers, which turn contrary Ways, pinch the Canes put between them, and draw them in at the same time, crushing them, so that all the Juice runs out into a Trough, which conveys it into the Cauldrons. There it is three times boil'd, taking great Care to skim it, and to put Juice of Lemon and other Ingredients to it; and when it is sufficiently boil'd, they put it into Pots of a Conical Figure cut short, where it congeals into very brown Clods. To refine and whiten it, they only cover it with Earth temper'd with Water, 4 or 5 Inches thick, and kept fresh by watering it every Day. That Moisture makes the finest Juice run, which drops by Degrees, and the rest congeals into a white Loaf. They refine and whiten it in the same manner in *Brasil*, with Clay steep'd, the whitest of which is the best; but they must first scrape off a hard Film, that grows over the Pot, and would hinder the Water from penetrating through it. Lastly, the Refiners in *France* make it white and hard by the help of Lime and Alom.

Other Product. They also in the Vale of *Hilo* sow some little Corn and Herbs, but much more Trefoil, whereof there is a great Consumption, when any Ships are in the Road, because the Merchants, who come from several remote Parts, are forced to bring thither a great Number of Mules, to change those that are loaden, for fear lest tiring in Desart Places they should die by the way, when they are not able to keep up with the others. They divide the Gangs of Mules, which

which they call *Requas*, into several *Piaras*, or small Parcels of 10 Mules each, which are committed to the Care of two Men; and there being sometimes 30 or 40 Leagues to travel over high and steep Mountains, without either Water or Pasture, the Mules carry'd to change and relieve the others, are sometimes double the Number of the *Piaras*, or small Parcels loaded; notwithstanding all this Precaution, such great Numbers of them die, that the Roads in Peru are not better known by the Tract of their Feet, than by the Skeletons of those that tire out of the Vales, where they can have nothing to subsist on, for there is scarce ever any Grass or Water; for which Reason they are obliged every Year to bring 80 or 100000 Mules from *Tucuman* and *Chili*, to make good that continual Loss. *Destruction of Mules.*

However, notwithstanding the Trouble of traveling thro' those desart Places, the Inhabitants are not afraid of a Journey of two or three hundred Leagues. The Merchants come to *Hilo*, from *Cusco*, *Puno*, *Chucuito*, *Arequipa*, and from *Moquegua*, as to the nearest Sea-Port; and if there are no Ships at *Arica*, they also come from *La Paz*, *Oruro*, *La Plata*, *Potosi* and *Lipes*; so that in short, this is the best Port in all the Coast for *European* Commodities. *Resort to Hilo.*

The City of *Cusco* is one of the chiefest for the Consumption of those Commodities, next to *Potosi*; there are reckon'd in it above 30000 Communicants, whereof near three Quarters are *Indians*. Its Manufactures of Bays and Cotton Cloth, are some small Prejudice to the Trade of *Europe*. They there also make all Sorts of Work in Leather, as well for the Use of Men, as for the Furniture of Horses and Mules. That City is also famous for the vast Number of Pictures the *Indians* there make, and wherewith they fill all the Kingdom, as wretched as they are. It is 130 Leagues from *Hilo*, in a cold Country, where the Weather is so uncertain, that they have all Sorts of it in one and the same Day. *Cusco City.*

Puno

Puno Town. *Puno* is a little Town of about 150 Families, 70 Leagues from *Cusco*, and 76 from *Hilo*, on the same Road: It is considerable for the many Silver Mines there are about it. In the Year 1713, they supply'd three Grindstone-Mills, and three of those that pound with Hammers: The Climate is bad.

Arequipa Town. *Arequipa* is a Town containing about 600 *Spanish* Families, who trade in Wine and Brandy: It is only 24 Leagues from the Sea; but the Port of *Quilca* being little resorted to, because it is bad, the Merchants repair to *Hilo* to drive on their Trade. The Town is seated at the Foot of a burning Mountain, which does not smoak now, but did formerly vomit such great Quantities, that the Ashes were carried 30 Leagues about.

Moquegua Town. *Moquegua* is a small Town of 150 Families, within the Dependences whereof there may be 4000 Men fit to bear Arms. They, there drive a great Trade of Wine and Brandy, which is transported to *La Puna*, that is, to the Mountains. It is incredible, that in so small a Territory as that is said to be, they should make 100000 Jars, which amount to above 3200000 *Paris* Pints; and at 20 Royals the Jar is worth 400000 Pieces of Eight, that is now 1600000 Livres *French* Money. A Nation of friendly free **Chunco's Indians.** Indians, call'd *Chunco's*, who inhabit the East-side of the Ridge of Mountains call'd *La Cordillera*, come every Year to trade at *Moquegua* for their own Country. In their Way through *Potosi* they sell Works made of Ostrich Feathers, as *Umbrellas*, Fans to drive the Flies away, &c. They also carry the Fruit call'd *Quinaquina*, which is like an Almond, and of use in several Distempers, and some other Things of the Country; with the Silver they receive for them, they buy Wine and some *European* Commodities fit for their Use.

Mines of S. Anthony rich. Forty Leagues from *Moquegua*, and five from *Cailloma*, have been lately discover'd the Mines of *S. Anthony*, which promise much Wealth, and the Silver of them is the finest

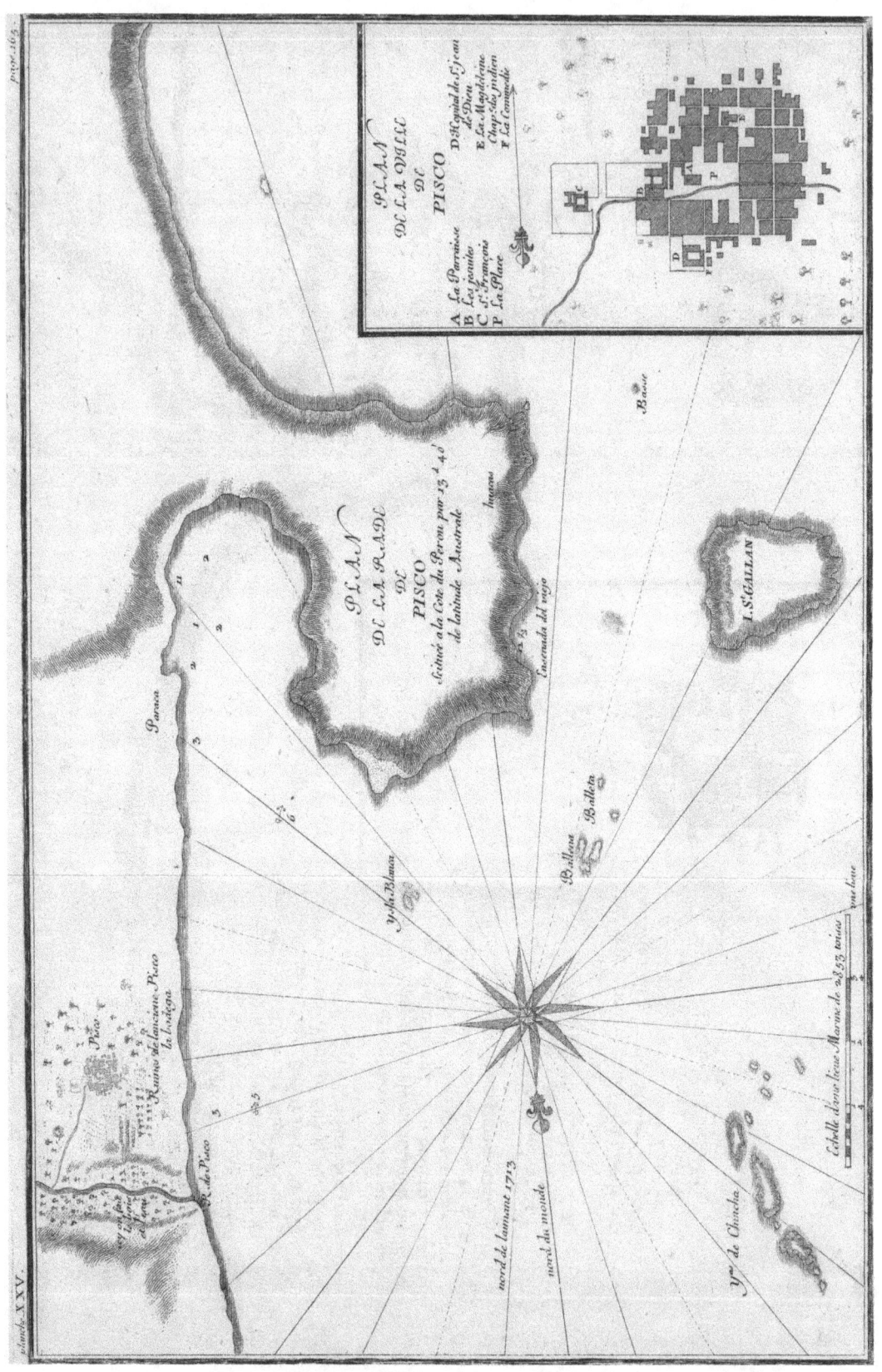

in *Peru*. In the Year 1713, they were erecting Mills there, which will be still more advantageous to the Port of *Hilo*.

Tho' the Neighbourhood of many Mines, by their Concurrence, make that a good Mart, it is in other respects bad enough for the Conveniencies of Life. Water, as has been said, is apt to fall short there, because very much is consumed in watering the Vineyards of *Moquegna*. Beeves are there scarce, and their Fish naught, except in Winter, because the Mists which are then frequent refresh and moisten the Top of the Mountain, which causes some little Pasture to grow: In short, other Provisions sometimes fall short for the Inhabitants. There is scarce any kind of Game, except a Sort of small Fallow Deer, found in the Breaks of the Mountains. There is no Want of Fish in the Road; but the Sea runs so high near the Shore, that there is no drawing of a Net any where. *[margin: Inconveniencies of Hilo.]*

The Vale of *Hilo*, in which there are not at present above three or four Farms, formerly maintain'd an *Indian* Town, the Remains of which are still to be seen 2 Leagues from the Sea. The Houses which were made of Canes, are there to be seen razed even with the Ground; a dismal Effect of the Ravages the *Spaniards* have made among the *Indians*.

There are still more moving Marks of the Misfortune of that poor Nation, near *Arica*, above the Church of *Hilo*, and all along the Shore, as far as the Point of *Coles*, being an infinite Number of Tombs, where they bury'd themselves alive with their Families and Goods; which is the Reason that when they happen to dig at this very Time, they find Bodies almost entire with their Cloaths, and very often Gold and Silver Vessels. Those I have seen are dug in the Sand the depth of a Man, and inclosed with a Wall of dry Stone: They are cover'd with Wattles of Canes, on which there is a Bed or Layer of Earth, and Sand laid over, to the end the Place where they were, might not be observ'd. *[margin: Tombs of Indians.]*

A a
The

Tho' the *Spaniards* freely acknowledge the Cruelties they exercis'd on the *Indians* at the Time of the Conquest, there are some who do not ascribe the Invention of those Tombs to the Dread of the *Indians*; but tell us, that they worshipping the Sun, follow'd him in his Course, fancying they might draw nearer to him; and that at length being stopp'd by the Sea, which was their Boundary to the Westward, they bury'd themselves on the Shore that they might before they died have Sight of him till the Moment when he seems to hide himself in the Water. The Custom of the great Men, who when dying, order'd themselves to be carry'd to the Brink of the Sea, is a Proof of this Opinion; but the most receiv'd Notion is, that they were in such a Fright, that they thought they must all die, when they were inform'd that the Conquerors had not spared even their King *Atahualpa*, who among them was look'd upon as the Offspring of the Sun. To escape out of the Hands of the *Spaniards*, they fled as far as they could Westward, but being stopp'd by the Sea, they hid themselves on the Edge of it, to implore Mercy of the Sun, whom they thought they had greatly offended, since he brought upon them such cruel and powerful Enemies, who also said they were descended from him.

We are here to observe, that there is much Difference between these Voluntary Tombs, and those they erected for Men of Note; the latter are above the Ground, built with unburnt Bricks and round, like little Pigeon Houses, 5 or 6 Foot Diameter, and 12 or 14 in Height, arch'd like the Top of an Oven, in which the Dead were placed sitting, and then they were wall'd up. In traveling through the Country, there are still many to be seen, even of those before the Conquest by the *Spaniards*.

Re-

Removal to another Ship.

THERE were two *French* Ships at *Hilo*, come from *China* six Months before; one of them of 44 Guns, commanded by Monsieur *De Ragucine Mareuil*, a Sea Lieutenant, who had purchas'd Silks at *Canton*; the other of 16 Guns, commanded by the Sieur *du Bocage* of *Havre*, who had laden with the same Commodities at *Emoi*. The first of them was in a bad Condition, as having suffer'd by Storms, and wanted to careen; but because the Port of *Hilo* is not proper for that Work, and that the Prohibition of the Trade of *China* is very severe at *Callao*, which is the best Harbour for careening, he thought fit to purchase the *S. Charles*, and to lade it with his Goods, to the end he might be in a Condition to stand the Search. That Purchase made me take the Advantage of Monsieur *de Ragueine*'s Courtesy, he giving me my Passage for *Callao*.

Departure from Hilo.

ON the 5th of *September* we sail'd from the Road of *Hilo*, in Company with a *Spanish* Ship, which had desired to be convoy'd by us, being apprehensive of the *English* Privateer. We had the good Fortune of a fresh Gale at E. S. E. which in four Days carry'd us as far as *Morro Quemado*, or the burnt Head-land. Before we reach'd that, we had sight of *La Mesa de Donna Maria*, or *Donna Maria*'s Table, being a Mountain flat on the Top, like a Table, whence it has the Name.

Eight Leagues to the Northward of it is the Island of *Lobos*, or Wolves, being a League and half N. W. from *Morro Quemado*, or burnt Head-land; it is indifferent high, about three Quarters of a League long, in the greatest Extent N. W. and S. E. Between this Island and the Head-land, there are flat and very low Rocks, which stretch

Diff'rent Marks for knowing of Morro Quemado from Pisco.

out towards the Continent half way the Channel, leaving a Passage through which many Ships have gone, mistaking it for that between the Island of St. *Gallan*, and the Continent of *Paraca*; but it is easy to know them asunder, because in the latter there are no Low Rocks, as there are at the Foot of that of *Lobos*, and a Sugar-Loaf Breaker. Besides, the Land of *Paraca* is of an equal Height that of *Morro quemado* comes down in a Descent on the Northside to a little Creek, where there is Anchorage on the Starboard side. In case a Ship happens to advance into that Passage, Care is to be taken, that in coming out to the Northward of the Island of *Lobos*, there is a Shoal about the third Part of the Channel over from the Continent. I have also been told, by those who have gone into that Channel, through a Mistake, that to the Northward of the Island there is a smooth flat Bank of Sand, which forms a Creek, where the Sea is so still, that a Ship may anchor there in 8 Fathom Water, and even, if Occasion were, careen there in Safety.

Being assured by the Sight of the Island *Lobos*, of the Distance we were at from that of S. *Gallan*, we lay by that Night; and the next Day we pass'd between that Island and the Continent of *Paraca*, coasting along it within a Quarter of a League, that is, within one third of the Channel from the Land, for fear of a Shoal, which is within half a League S. S. E. from the Island.

The Road of *Pisco*.

Plate XXV. WE sailed along within the Length of two Cables of a little Creek, call'd *Ensenada del Viejo*, or the old Man's Bay, where some *French* Ships have anchor'd, in 10 or 12 Fathom Water, to unlade their Goods privately. Being becalm'd, when we were within a Cable's Length of the North Point of that Creek, we found 15 Fathom Water, the Bottom Sand and Shells, and thence proceeded to anchor in the Bay of *Paraca*, in 15 Fathom Water, the

Bottom

Bottom a sandy Owze, N. W. from *La Bodega*; being six or seven Houses, for the Conveniency of unlading of Ships, that choose to anchor there, tho' two Leagues distant from *Pisco*, rather than go up before the Town, because the Sea runs so high at the Shore, that it is almost impossible to land there in the Day-time; however, sometimes in the Morning it is possible to land there with a good Hawser, or small Cable, and a good Anchor, but it is always with much Trouble and Danger. The Ships that anchor before the Town, wood and water half a League farther to the Northward, in the Hollow, through which the River of *Pisco* runs, and those that anchor at *Paraca*, do it on the Strand, half a League to the S. E. of the Houses, as is done at *Arica*. *Anchorage at Paraca.*

The Road of *Pisco* is large enough to contain a whole Navy Royal. It is open to the Northward, whence no dangerous Wind blows in that Latitude, and Ships are shelter'd from the usual Winds, which blow from S. S. W. to S. E. If they would careen, they may go up to the Bottom of the Bay of *Paraca*, where there is no rough Sea, and *Pisco Road.*

Plate XXV *Page* 181. *explain'd in* English.

The Plan of the Road of P I S C O, on the Coast of *Peru*, in 13 Degrees 40 Minutes of South Latitude.

Icy on fait le bois & l'eau, *Here Ships wood and water.*
Ruines de l'ancienne Pisco, *The Ruins of the ancient* Pisco.
Isla Blanca, *white Island.*
Nord de l'aimant, *The North Point of the Compass.*
Nord du monde, *The true North Point.*
Ensenada del Viejo, *The old Man's Bay.*
Echelle d'une lieüe marine de 2853 Toises, *A Scale of a Sea League, containing* 2853 *Fathoms.*
Une Lieüe, *A League.*

In the Compartiment.

The Plan of the Town of P I S C O.

A. *The Parish Church.*
B. *The Jesuites.*
C. *S. Francis.*
P. *The Square.*
D. *The Hospital of* S. John of God.
E. *The Magdalen, a Chappel of the Indians.*
F. *The Play-House.*

and there is Anchorage every where, from 5 to 11 Fathom Water. On the West-side there are several little Islands, all of them clear, and between which Ships may pass without Fear; but generally it is more convenient to pass within that of *St. Gallan*, and to coast along the Continent of *Paraca*, to gain upon the Wind. Then they come up to anchor towards the Houses, in 4 or 5 Fathom Water. Among those little Islands there is one cut quite through in two Places, so that it looks like a Bridge from the Anchoring-Place.

From the Houses of *Paraca* to the Town, the Distance is two Leagues, all a sandy barren Plain.

The Description of the Town of Pisco.

THIS Town, which was formerly on the Edge of the Sea, is now a quarter of a League from it. That Removal was made on the 19th of *October* 1682, by so violent an Earthquake, that the Sea drew back half a League, and then return'd with such Fury, that it overflow'd almost as much Land beyond its Bounds; so that it destroy'd the Town of *Pisco*, the Ruins whereof are still to be seen, extending from the Shore to the New Town. Several Curious Persons having follow'd the Sea, as it withdrew, were swallow'd up by it, at its Return. Since that Time the Town has been built on the Place which the Overflowing did not reach.

Plate XXV. Churches and Hospital. It is divided into regular Quarters, as may be seen in the Plan I here present. The Parish Church of *S. Clement* is in the middle of the Town, in a Square as large as one of the Quarters. Behind this Church is that of the *Jesuites*; to the Eastward that of *S. Francis*, small but very neat. On the North-side is the Hospital of *S. John of God*, and on the South-side is the *Magdalen*, a Chappel belonging to the *Indians*, before which is a little Square.

Inhabitants and Government. The whole Town consists of 300 Families, most of them *Mestizo's*, *Mulatto's* and *Blacks*; the Whites being the

smallest

smallest Number. There is a *Corregidor*, or chief Magistrate, and a *Cabildo*, or Council for the Administration of Justice, and very often a Judge to hinder the Commerce with the *French*, and the Fraud of the Masses of Silver, which they bring from the Mines.

When the *French* were not permitted to go to trade at *Callao*, that was one of the best Ports for Trade; because it is naturally the Mart for the Towns of *Ica*, *Guancavelica*, *Guamanga* and *Andagaylas*, and for all those that lie to the Northward of *Lima*.

Ica is a Town three times as populous as *Pisco*; they drive a Trade there of Glass made with Saltpeter; it is green, foul, and ill wrought; there is also store of Wine and Brandy.

Ica Town.

Guancavelica is a small Town of about 100 Families, 60 Leagues from *Pisco*, rich and famous for the vast Quantity of Quicksilver taken there from a Mine, which is 40 *Varas*, or *Spanish* Yards in Front, and which alone furnishes all the Gold and Silver Mills in that Kingdom. Private Persons work there at their own Expence, and are obliged to deliver up to the King all they get, under Pain of Forfeiture of their Estates, Banishment, and perpetual Servitude at *Baldivia*. His Majesty pays a set rate for the same, which at present is 60 Pieces of Eight the Quintal, or Hundred Weight, upon the Spot; and he sells it for 80, at the remote Mines. When a sufficient Quantity has been taken out, the King causes the Mouth of the Mine to be stopp'd up, and no Man can have any but what comes from his Stores.

Guancavelica Town.

Quick-silver Mine.

The Earth or Mineral, which contains the Quick-silver, is of a whitish Red, like ill-burnt Brick; they pound and put it into an Earthen Furnace, the Head or Top whereof is a Vault like the top of an Oven, a little Spheroid. They lay it on an Iron Grate cover'd with Earth, under which they keep a small Fire made of the Shrub they call *Icho* which is properer for that purpose than any other combustible Matter; for which Reason there is a Prohibition

tion to cut it in 20 Leagues round. The Heat paſſes to it through that Earth, and ſo fires the pounded Mineral, that the Quick-ſilver flies out Volatile in Smoak, but the Cap or Covering being cloſe ſtopp'd, it finds no way out, but only through a little Hole which leads to a Succeſſion of Earthen Veſſels, like Gourds, round and join'd by the Necks, one within another; there that Smoak circulates and condenſes by means of a little Water there is at the bottom of each Gourd, into which the Quick-ſilver falls condens'd, and in well form'd Liquor. It is leſs form'd in the firſt Gourds than the laſt; and becauſe they grow ſo hot that they break, Care is taken to cool the Outſides of them with Water.

Water that petrifies.

In that Town there is another thing peculiar, which is a Spring, whoſe Water petrifies ſo eaſily and ſo quick, that moſt of the Houſes in the Town are built with it. I ſaw ſome Stones at *Lima*, which they had carry'd thither, and they are white, with a yellowiſh Caſt, light and hard enough.

Guamanga City.

Guamanga is a Biſhop's See, 80 Leagues from *Piſco*, ſaid to contain about 10000 Communicants. It's principal Trade conſiſts in Leather, and Boxes of Confectionary, Paſtes, Marmelade, Jellies, preſerv'd Quinces, and others the moſt valuable in the Kingdom, where there is a conſiderable Conſumption. They alſo there make Pavillions, or Field Beds, whereof there is a notable Manufacture, as there is of ſeveral ſorts of printed and gilt Leather. The Town is ſeated at the Foot of a high Mountain, in a plain Country, very wholſome, and fruitful of all ſorts of Proviſions.

Avancay and Andaguailas.

I do not here take Notice of the Boroughs of *Avancay* and *Andeguailas*, which are ſmall Places of 60 or 80 Families each; however, tho' they are not remarkable for the Number of Inhabitants, they are ſo for the great Quantity of Sugar made there, which is the beſt in all *Peru*.

Apurima wonderful Bridge.

Near to *Andaguailas* is the famous Bridge of *Apurima*, which has been repreſented to me as a wonderful Thing.

They

They say, there is a Cleft or Opening in a Mountain, about 120 Fathoms in Length, and the Depth under it dreadful, which Nature has cut perpendicular down in the Rock, to make Way for a River; and whereas the Waters of that River run with such Violence, that they carry away very large Stones, there is no fording of it under 25 or 30 Leagues from that Place. The Width and Depth of that Breach, and the Necessity of passing that way, have occasion'd the Invention of a Bridge of Ropes, made of the Barks of Trees, being about 6 Foot broad, interwoven with cross Pieces of Wood, on which they pass over, even with loaded Mules, tho' not without Dread; for about the Middle of it is felt a Shaking, which may occasion the Head to swim; but in regard they must go 6 or 7 Days Journey about, to take another Way, all the Provisions and Commodities that circulate between *Lima* and *Cusco*, and the *Upper Peru*, passes over that Bridge. Towards the keeping of it in Repair, they pay a Toll of four Royals for each Mule's Load, which brings an immense Sum in to the King, besides what it costs in Repairs.

The Trade for *European* Commodities is not the only Thing that brings Ships to *Pisco*; they also resort thither for their Stores of Wine and Brandy, which is there cheaper and more plentiful than in any other Port; because besides what the Territory produces, it is brought thither, as I have said before, from *Ica*, from *Chinca*, which is six Leagues North of *Pisco*, where the Temple of the Sun was, before the Conquest by the *Spaniards*; and lastly it is brought from *Lanasque*, 20 Leagues distant towards the S. E. being look'd upon as the best Wines in *Peru*; but all those Wines are extraordinary strong, and not very wholsome; which is the Reason why the *Spaniards* scarce drink any of them; the Sale being almost entirely among the Blacks, the *Indians*, the *Mulattoes*, and such-like People. Instead of Wine, many *Spaniards*, out of an extravagant Prejudice, drink Brandy.

Trade of Pisco.

Vineyards and Wine. The Vineyards of the Country about *Pisco*, which cannot conveniently be water'd by Trenches, are planted in such a Manner as not to need it, tho' it never rains there. Every Stock is in a Hole four or five Foot deep, where there is a general Moisture, which Nature has spread through the Earth to supply the Want of River and Rain-Water; for the Country is desart, and so dry, that there are no Places habitable, but a few Plains and Vales, where that Relief is to be had; besides, the Bottom is almost pure Salt, whence proceeds that brackish Taste which is found in most of the Wines of that Country Growth.

Fruit. There are also about *Pisco* all Sorts of Fruit, Apples, Pears, Oranges, Lemons, Guayavas, Bananas, Dates, &c. Many have fancy'd they have observ'd, that when a Date Tree is alone, it produces no Fruit, unless it be near another, which is call'd the Female: But all Men do not agree in this Particular; some of the Inhabitants represented that Observation to me as a Mistake. There is a Sort of Cucumber which Father *Feüillée* calls *Melongena lauri folia fructu turbinato variegato*, the Inhabitants *Pepo*, or *Pepino*, that is Cucumber. It is very refreshing, and has some Taste of a Melon, but fady. The *Camotes*, or *Patatas*, are not so good there as in *Brasil*; there are red, yellow, and white.

Many Fruit. They have also a Sort of Fruit there, which grows in a Cod that does not rise out of the Earth, in which are some Grains, or Seeds, like round Lupins; which being toasted in the Oven in their Cod, have a pleasant Taste like a toasted Hazle-nut. They eat Abundance of them, tho' they are very hot, and provoking to Love: It is in all likelihood the *Araquidna* of some Botanists; the Inhabitants call it *Many*.

The Plenty of Provisions the Country affords, together with a good Trade, makes the Inhabitants easy; so that they often divert themselves with publick Shows, such as Bull-Feasts, Plays, and Masquerades.

I was

I was there, at the time when the Mulattoes kept a Fe- *Feast of the Scapular.*
stival in Honour of *Our Lady of Mount Carmel*: Those
poor People, like all the other *Creolian Spaniards*, that is, the
mix'd Races, are so much infatuated with a thousand Apparitions, either true or false, that they make them the
principal Object of their Devotion. This Abuse is occasion'd by the Ignorance of the Friers, who having neither
Literature nor Criticism, to discern between Truth and
Falshood, give themselves up to a Tradition, and Customs
establish'd before their Time, by those of their Order, for
their private Interest. There being no *Carmelites* throughout all *Peru* and *Chili*, the *Mercenarian* Friers have taken to
themselves the Direction of the Brotherhood of the *Scapular*; and because they have no Monastery at *Pisco*, one of
them comes from *Lima* to be present at that Festival.

On *Thursday* the 14th of *September*; the *Mulatto*'s began *Scandalous Play.*
the Solemnity with a Play call'd *El Principe Poderoso*, or,
The Powerful Prince; written by a *Spanish European* Poet.
The depraved Taste of that Nation leading them to mix in
their Shows, Things Sacred with Prophane; I observ'd,
that in this they had indulged their Natural Genius, beyond
the Bounds of good Sense and Decency: In short, nothing
could be seen more ridiculous than the Decoration of the
farther Part of the Stage, the Point of Perspective thereof
terminating in an Altar, on which was the Image of our
Lady of Mount Carmel, with lighted Candles about it; and
all the Actors began their Prologue kneeling, with a Dedication

---

* See Monsieur de Lannoy's Treatise, De Visione *Simonis Stokii* & Ori-
gine Scapularii, *where he makes it appear, that very long after the Death of*
Simon Stock, *two* Carmelites, *whose Names were* Gregory of S. Pasil, *and*
Mark Anthony de Cazamate, *contrived to set up the Scapular upon an Appa-
rition of the Blessed Virgin to* Simon, *and upon two Bulls, the one of Pope* John
the XXII. *quoted in their Writings after so different a Manner, not only as to
the Expressions, but also as to the Inequality of the Length of the Discourse, that
it plainly appears to be Counterfeit; not to mention other Reasons which make it
plain, the second of Pope* Urban V. *dated at* Rome, *where that Pope who died
at* Florence *had never been since his Coronation.*

dication of the Play to the Blessed Virgin. One would have judg'd by this pious Invocation, that the Play would be to the Edification of the Spectators; but I was sufficiently undeceiv'd of that Notion, when I beheld on the Stage the disagreeing Medley of *Sigismund*'s Piety embracing a Crucifix, to which he made his Application under an Adversity, and the Licentiousness of Buffoons in the Play; and of Interludes, or little Farces between the Acts, which consisted of gross Obscenities, but a little wrapp'd up, or disguised.

Bull-Feast. The next Day there was the Show of the Bull-Feast, which was no better than that at *Valparaiso*, before spoken of; a Spectacle as unfit to honour the Blessed Virgin as such Comedies, since it is forbid by the Ecclesiastical Laws, by reason of the Danger of Death Men expose themselves to, without any Necessity, as frequently happens, and at this Time it was very near happening to a Black, the Bull leaving him on the Ground so much hurt, that it was questioned whether he could recover.

Masquerade. On *Saturday* Night there was a Masquerade of People running about the Streets by Candle-light, as they do in *France* at the Carnaval or Shrovetide: The Prime Actors were in a Cart, preceded by others on Horse-back. On that Cart I took Notice of a Man clad in the Habit of the Friers of S. *John of God*, who I was assured was really a Frier; but I could not persuade myself that it was any other than a Mask, for on the Cart he stood up and danc'd with Women such a Posture Dance as the Blacks of the Islands dance at their *Bangala*, or Instrument, which is all that can be said with Modesty. Be that as it will, the Name of *Our Lady of Mount Carmel* often resounded in the extravagant Cries, amidst the Reproaches and the most infamous Absurdities with which they accosted such as pass'd by at the very same time, when on the other hand they were making the Procession of the Rosary. As ridiculous as this Custom appear'd, it may be said as great Extravagancies have been seen in *France* on the Feast of Fools.

The

" The Priests and Clerks went mask'd to the Church, and
" at their Return from thence went about the Streets in
" Carts, and mounted on Stages, performing all the most
" impudent Postures and Buffoonries with which Water-
" men are wont to divert the foolish Mobb." That Festival
continued in *France* above 150 Years, from the Twelfth to
the Fifteenth Century. *Mez. Phil.* II.

Sunday Night they acted the Comedy of the Life of S. A- <small>*Another Play.*</small>
lexius, written by the *Spanish* Poet *Moreto*, which I have
since found in the Tenth Volume of the Collection of *Spanish* Plays, printed at *Madrid* with Licence, in the Year 1658,
by the Name of, *Nuevo Teatro de Comedias varias de diferentes
Autores*, or the New Theatre of Variety of Plays by sun-
dry Authors. I thought it very strange in the first Act, to
see S. *Alexius*'s Guardian Angel, and the Devil, disputing a-
bout persuading him to leave or stay with his Wife : In the
second, the Devil appears in the Shape of a poor Man, or
Beggar, and in the third in that of a Sailor; and about the
End of the second, a Choir of Angels shut up in an Hermitage, twice sings the first Part of the *Te Deum*, to the
Musick of the Bells. The Extravagancy of those Conceits,
and of the Persons the Poet brings upon the Stage, was to
us *Frenchmen*, who happen'd to be present at that Spectacle, a Subject the more ridiculous, in regard that we were
used to correct Pieces, and wherein the Respect that is paid
to Things sacred, admits of no Mixture of what is prophane,
as was in this I am speaking of, where the Licentiousness
of Farce intermix'd added to the Preposterousness. I do
not give this Relation as if it were a Thing extraordinary
or new in *Europe* ; there is no Man that has travel'd in *Spain*
but is acquainted with the Taste of their Dramatick Poems,
in which the Subject of Devotion has always some Part ; so
that we still find among them what was used at the first
Rise of our *French* Stage, as is related by one of our Poets.

Chez nos devots Ayeux le Theatre abhorré
Fut long-temps dans la France un plaisir ignoré.

De Pelerins, dit on, une troupe grossiere
En public à Paris y monta la premiere,
Et sotement zelée en sa simplicité,
Joüa les Saints, la Vierge, & Dieu par pieté.
Le savoir à la fin dissipant l'ignorance,
Fit voir de ce projet la devote imprudence.
Despreaux Art. Poet. Chant III.

Our pious Fathers, in their godly Age,
As impious and prophane, abhorr'd the Stage.
A Troop of silly Pilgrims, as 'tis said,
Foolishly Zealous, scandalously play'd
The Angels, God, the Virgin and the Saints,
Instead of Heroes and of Love Complaints;
At last, right Reason did her Laws reveal,
And shew'd the Folly of their ill-plac'd Zeal.

As for the particular Faults in that Piece, the Distance of Time and Place therein is shocking. S. *Alexius* in the first and last Act is at *Rome*, and during the second he is several Years visiting the Holy Land; however, that Variety is not look'd upon as a Fault among the *Spaniards*, as *Despreaux* has observ'd in his Art of Poetry, in these Words,

Un Rimeur, sans péril, de là les Pyrennées,
Sur la Scene, en un jour, renferme des années.
Là souvent le Heros d'un Spectacle grossier,
Enfant au premier Acte, est barbon au dernier.
Mais nous, que la raison à ses regles engage,
Nous voulons qu'avec art l'action se ménage :
Qu'en un lieu, qu'en un jour, un seul fait accompli,
Tienne jusqu'à la fin le Spectacle rempli.

A *Spanish* Poet may, with good Event,
In one Day's Space whole Ages represent.
There, oft the Heroe of a wandring Stage
Begins a Child, and ends the Play at Age;

But we, who are by Reason's Rules confin'd,
Will, that with Art the Poem be design'd,
That Unity of Action, Time and Place
Keep the Stage full, and all your Labours grace.

But that which ought to be blamable in all Countries is, that S. *Alexius* is represented as not over-scrupulous, as to Lying; for the Author makes him use some mental Reservations which are much to the same Effect, when he endeavours to conceal himself from a Man sent by his Father to look after him. He says of himself, that he knows S. *Alexius*, but that he is gone very far before. The *Spanish* Words are these:

Conosco esse Cavallèro
Porque he venido con el,
Y me conto su sucesso,
Mas ya va muy adelante.

That is, I know that Gentleman, because I came along with him, and he told me his Story; but he is now far before, or, according to the double Meaning of the Word, much advanced.

In other respects, in such a little Town, nothing better could be expected as to the Decorations of the Theatre, which was contracted into a small Compass, after our Manner; and it may be said, that the Actors, being of the meanest of the People, for they were all *Mulatto's*, and who did not make Acting their Profession, play'd their Parts well enough, according to the *Spanish* Taste. I observ'd in their Interludes, or little Farces between the Acts, an Affectation of introducing Doctors in their Robes, representing Extravagancies. I do not understand how the Church-men, who are almost the only Persons entitled Doctors, have the Complaisance to admit of those Sports; for if there be any impertinent Part, the Man in the Cap is sure to have a Share in it.

After the Play of S. *Alxius*, they acted *Sigifmund*, and ran about in Mafquerade to make up the Octave, which I could not fee concluded, becaufe the Weather was proper to fail.

We left the *Princefs* in the Road, under the Command of *Martin*, which came from *Emoi* in *China*, and the *Margaret* of S. *Malo* from *France*.

Departure from Pifco. Thurfday September 21, we fet Sail for *Callao* with a frefh Gale at S. E. The next Day we had Sight of the Ifland of *Afia*: *Saturday* the Calm kept us in Sight of *Morro Solar*, and the Ifland of S. *Laurence*, which appear'd to us thus to the Northward.

Plate XXVI. *Callao how known.* That Ifland is eafily known, becaufe it is indifferent high, feparated from the little Ifland of *Callao*; and in the Opening between them there are two fmall Ifles, or rather Rocks: There is alfo a third very low, half a League out at Sea S. S. E. from the N. W. Point of the Ifland of S. *Laurence*. We heav'd the Lead at about two Cables Diftance from that Point, and found 60 Fathom Water, an owzy Bottom. At length we anchor'd a League Weft of *Callao*, in 14 Fathom Water, the Bottom an Olive Colour Owze.

Monfieur *de Ragueine* ftay'd thus without at the Opening of the Road, till he had Leave from the Viceroy to anchor under the Cannon of the Town to careen, which was granted him without any Difficulty. Then he fail'd in, and faluted the Town with nine Guns, and receiv'd no Anfwer, tho' they knew that he was the King's Officer. Two *French* Ships of S. *Malo*, and the *Mary-Anne* of *Marfeilles*, which were in the Road, paid him the Refpect due to his Poft, each of them faluting him with nine Guns, and Monfieur *de Ragueine* anfwer'd each of them apart. Befides thofe three Ships, there were 18 *Spaniards*; and among them the *Incarnation*, a *Portugueze* Three-Deck Prize, which the Sieur *Brignon* of S. *Malo* had juft then fold to the Viceroy for 10000 Pieces of Eight, for the King's Service. His Excellency came to take Poffeffion of it in Perfon on the 30th of *September*. Upon his Arrival at *Callao*, he was

faluted

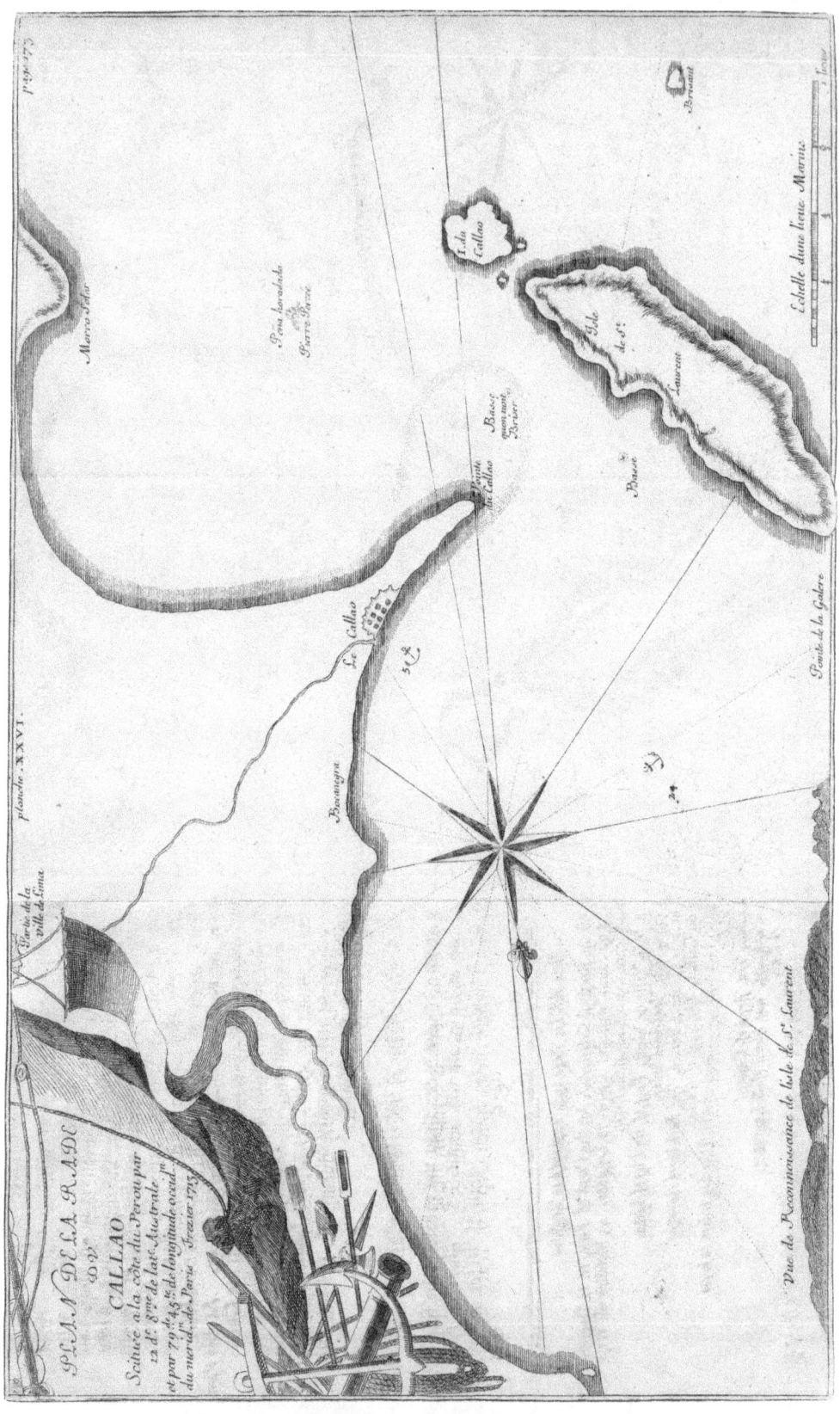

The material originally positioned here is too large for reproduction in this reissue. A PDF can be downloaded from the web address given on page iv of this book, by clicking on 'Resources Available'.

saluted by all the Artillery on the Ramparts of the Town; and when he went out of the Road, he was saluted with 13 Guns by each *French* Ship. It will seem amazing, that a Ship of that Magnitude, or Rate, should be sold at so low a Price in a Country where those of 400 Tons are worth four times as much: It was a Contrivance of the Viceroy, who renew'd the Prohibition to the *Spaniards* to buy any *French* Ship, to the end he might have it at his own rate.

In short, he return'd to *Lima* the same Day. At his Departure from *Callao* he was again saluted with ten Guns: His Retinue consisted of some Horse-Guards, but his Attendance had nothing resembling the Viceroyship. The Truth is, it was the Bishop of *Quito*, Don *Pedro Ladron de Guevara*, who enjoy'd that Post only during the Interim, till the Court of *Spain* sent another.

Viceroy

The Description of the Road of Callao.

THE Road of *Callao* is certainly the greatest, the finest, and the safest in all the South-Sea. There is Anchorage every where in as much Depth of Water as any one

Plate XXVI.

Plate XXVI. Page 193. explain'd in English.

The Plan of the Road of CALLAO, on the Coast of *Peru*, in 12 Degrees 8 Minutes of South Latitude, and in 79 Degrees, 45 Minutes of West Longitude from the Meridian of *Paris*.

Partie de la Ville de Lima, *Part of the City of* Lima.
Morro Solar, *The Head-land* Solar.
Penna horadada, Pierre Percée, *The Rock bored through.*
Pointe du Callao, *The Point of* Callao.
Basse qu on voit brisser, *A Shoal on which the Sea is seen to break.*
Basse, *A Shoal.*
I. de Callao, *The Island of* Callao.
Isle de S. Laurent, *The Island of S.* Laurent.
Brisant, *A Rock.*
Vue de Reconnoissance de l' Isle de S. Laurent, *Thus appears the Island of* S. Laurence.
Pointe de la Galere, *Point* Galera, *or of the Galley.*
Echelle d'une lieüe marine, *A Scale of a Sea League.*

one likes, on an Olive-Colour Owze, without Danger of any Rocks or Shoals, excepting one which is three Cables Length from the Shore, about the Middle of the Island of S. *Laurence,* opposite to *La Galera.* The Sea is there always so still, that Ships careen at all Seasons, without fearing to be surpriz'd by any sudden Gusts: However, it is open from the North to the N. N. W. but those Winds hardly ever blow above a small easy Gale, which does not cause the Sea to swell to any Danger. The Island of S. *Laurence* breaks the Surges that come from the S. W. to the S. E. That Island is defenceless: In the Year 1624, it was a Receptacle to *James l' Hermite,* who fortify'd himself there, in order to take *Callao;* but being disappointed therein, he burnt above 30 Ships that were in the Road. It is also a Place of Banishment for the Blacks and Mulatto's, who are condemn'd for any Crimes, to dig Stone for the publick Structures, and indirectly for the private. This Punishment being equivalent to that of the Galleys in *Spain,* the Name of *La Galera,* or the Galley, is given to the West Point of the Island. We have said elsewhere, that *Baldivia* is instead of the Galleys for the Whites.

S. Laurence Island.

The general Anchoring-Place in the Road is E. and by N. of the Point *Galera,* two or three Cables Length from the Town. There Ships are also shelter'd from the South Wind by the Point of *Callao,* which is a low Strip of Land, between which and the Island of *Callao* there is a narrow Channel, and somewhat dangerous; however, Ships pass through it, coasting close along the Island in four or five Fathom Water. Next the Continent is a Bank of Sand stretching out from the Point to a Shoal, where the Sea is seen to break from far off.

Anchorage.

In the Port of *Callao* are to be found all Conveniences and Necessaries for Navigation. The Watering is easy at the little River of *Lima,* which falls into the Sea under Walls of *Callao.* Wooding, however, costs more Trouble, being half a League to the Northward, at *Bocanegra;* they cut the Wood half a League up the Country, and pay the

Jesuites

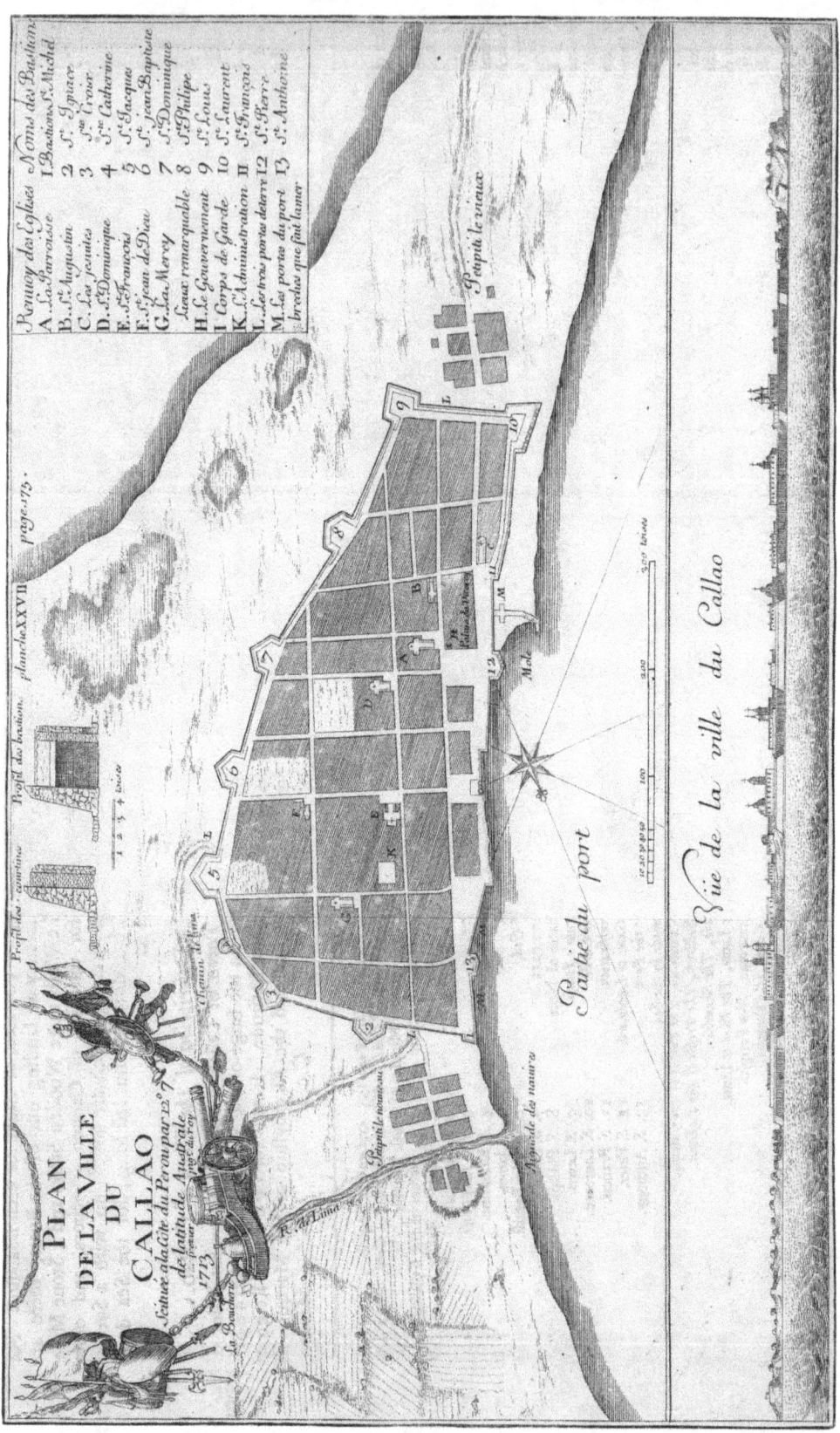

The material originally positioned here is too large for reproduction in this reissue. A PDF can be downloaded from the web address given on page iv of this book, by clicking on 'Resources Available'.

Jesuites 25 or 30 Pieces of Eight for each Boat-full. For the Conveniency of landing out of the Boats, there are close by the Walls three Wooden Stairs and a Stone Mole, design'd for unlading of Cannon, Anchors, and other Things of Weight, which are hoisted up with a Sort of Crane. That Mole will not last long; for the Sea daily demolishes it.

The Description of the Town of Callao.

THE Town of *Callao* is built on a low flat Point of Land, on the Edge of the Sea, in 12 Degrees 10 Minutes of South Latitude It was fortify'd in the Reign of King *Philip* IV. and the Viceroyship of the Marquis de Mancera, Plate XXVII.

Plate XXVII. Page 195. explain'd in English.
The Plan of the Town of *CALLAO*, on the Coast of *Peru*, in 12 Degrees 7 Minutes of South Latitude.

References of Churches.
A. *The Parish Church.*
B. *S. Augustin.*
C. *The Jesuites.*
D. *S. Dominick.*
E. *S. Francis.*
F. *S. John of God.*
G. *The Mercenarians.*

Places of Note.
H. *The Governor's House.*
I. *The Corps de Garde.*
K. *The Administration.*
L. *The three Gates to Landward.*
M. *Gates next the Port.*

Names of the Bastions.
1. *S. Michael's Bastion.*
2. *S. Ignatius.*
3. *The Holy Cross.*
4. *S. Katharine.*
5. *S. James.*
6. *S. John Baptist.*
7. *S. Dominick.*
8. *S. Philip.*
9. *S. Lewis.*
10. *S. Laurence.*
11. *S. Francis.*
12. *S. Peter.*
13. *S. Anthony.*

Breaches made by the Sea.
Profil des Courtines, *The Profile of the Curtins.*
Profil des Bastions, *The Profile of the Bastions.*
La Boucherie, *The Shambles.*
Chemin de Lima, *The Road to Lima.*
Petipiti le nouveau, *New* Petipiti.
Petipiti le vieux, *Old* Petipiti.
Aiguade des navires, *The Watering-Place for Ships.*
Mole, *The Mole.*
Partie du Port, *Part of the Port.*
Toises, *Fathoms.*
Vuë de la Ville de Callao, *A Prospect of the Town of* Callao.

Mancera, with an Enclosure flank'd by 10 Bastions on the Land-side, and by some Redans and plain Bastions on the Edge of the Sea, where there are four Batteries of Cannon to command the Port and Road. This Port was in a bad Condition in the Year 1713; there were five Breaches in it, and the Sea daily ruins the Wall, since there has been a Stone Key built, the Situation whereof stops the S. W. Surf, and occasions a Return of the Water, which saps the Walls of the Town.

Fortifications. See the Top of Plate XXVII.

The Breadth of the Rampart is of two different Extents; the Curtins are at the Top but eight Foot thick, two and a half of Earth, as much Banquette, and three of Stone, with Mortar made of Sand and Lime; the rest of the Thickness is of unburnt Bricks, with a little Stone Wall within: The Rampart of the Bastions has five Fathoms of Earth, laid with unequal Planks, to serve for a Platform for the Cannon, the whole of unsolid Masonry, because ill built.

Artillery.

Every Bastion is vaulted, and has its Magazine of Powder, Balls, and other Necessaries, for the Service of the Artillery that is mounted on it. There are generally two, three, or four Pieces of Brass Cannon always mounted on each of them; in the whole Compass there were in my Time 41, and there are to be 70 of several Sizes, from 12 to 24 Pounders, *Spanish* Weight, which with us makes Bastard Bores. Among those Pieces there are 10 Culverins from 17 to 18 Foot long, and 24 Pounders, whereof there are eight mounted, to fire upon the Road, which are said to carry as far as the Point *de la Galera*, of the Island of *S. Laurence*, which is almost two Leagues.

Besides the Artillery on the Rampart, there are nine Field-Pieces mounted, and ready for Service. There are also above 120 Brass Guns of several Sizes, design'd for the King's Ships, call'd *La Almiranta, La Capitana,* and *El Govierno*, which serv'd when the Galeons came to *Portobelo* to convoy the *Armadilla*, or little Fleet of *Panama*, and to transport to *Peru* the Commodities that came from *Europe*,

rope, and the King's Allowance to *Chili*, and the Recruits of Men they had Occasion for, before the Peace concluded with the *Indians*. At present those Ships are so much neglected, that they are unfit to put to Sea without much Refitting; however, the King still maintains the Marine Troops, of which here follows a Particular, after those of the Land Service.

A Particular of the Land Forces paid by the King of Spain, at Callao, *in* 1713.

	Pieces of Eight.
THE Governor General	7000

A Colonel of the Place, appointed by the King, his yearly Allowance, 3217 Pieces of Eight, and 4 Royals.

A Town Major, appointed also by the King	1200
A Town Adjutant yearly	600
Seven Companies of *Spanish* Foot, 100 Men each	
Every Captain yearly	1800
Seven Ensigns, each	672
Seven Serjeants, each	348
Fourteen Drums, each	240
Seven Ensign-Carriers	240
Seven Fiefs, each	240
An Adjutant	396
Six hundred Foot which compose the Garrison, each	240

Each Company has 4 Heads of Brigades, or Corporals, being generally the oldest Soldiers, two of whom march before the Colours, and two behind them, each of them has *per* Month 20

A Drum Major of the Place, yearly 240

All the above Officers, are appointed by the Viceroy, with the King's Approbation, excepting the 3 first, whom the King appoints.

Artillery

Artillery for the Land Service.

	Pieces of Eight.
A Lieutenant General, yearly	1944
A Master Gunner	486
A Captain of the Artillery	606
Ten Master Gunners, each	400
Two Aids-Majors, each	396
Seventy Gunners, each	396

Marine Troops in Pay.

The General of the Sea, or Admiral, yearly	2200

He has the same Honours and Privileges as the General of the Galeons.

Two Chief Pilots, each	1200
Four Masters of Ships, each	540
Four Masters Mates, each	396
Four Master Gunners, each	444
Five Chaplains, one of whom serves the Chappel in the Island of *Callao*, each	396
Four Pursers, each	600
Four Clerks, each	396
Four Stewards, each	396
Four Master Carpenters, each	396
Four Master Calkers, each	396
Four Divers, each	396
Twenty four Gunners, each	396
A Major of the Marine	600
Two Aids-Majors, or Adjutants, each	396
Twenty four Officers Mariners, that is Quarter-Masters, each	240
Forty Sailors, each	180
Sixteen Grummets, each	180

Marine Troops to serve in two small Fregates.

Two Captains, each of them to command a Fregate, each — 600
Four Officers Mariners, or Quarter-Masters, each — 244
Eight Sailors, each — 180

All the Officers and Sailors, besides their Pay, have their Allowances, each according to his Degree.

Militia.

In the Town of *Callao*, there are three Companies, which receive no Pay.

The first is composed of Seamen.

The second of Inhabitants and Traders in the Town.

The third of the Masters Carpenters, Calkers, and other Workmen belonging to those Trades, to whom are added the Mulattoes and free Blacks, who work in the King's Yards.

Moreover four Companies of *Indians*, with their Officers of the same Nation; whereof one is of those in the Town, another of those in the Suburbs of *Petipiti*, and two of those of the *Magdalen*, *Miraflores*, and *Churillos*, and other neighbouring Farms. These are obliged to repair to the Town upon the Signal of a Gun, and are appointed for transporting of Ammunition and Provisions. These Companies have a Major of their own. Thus much as to the Strength of Men; let us now see that of the Situation of the Place.

Situation of Callao

The Level of the Town is not above 9 or 10 Foot above the High-water Mark, which does not rise and fall above 4 or 5 Foot. However, it sometimes exceeds, so that it floods the Out-Skirts of the Town, as happen'd in September 1713, so that it is to be fear'd it may some time or other destroy the same.

Tho

Tho' the Inside is not divided into Quarters of the usual Dimensions of the *Quadra,* or common Square used in other Towns, the Streets are all in a Line; but so troublesome for Dust, as is not tolerable but in a Village.

Streets.

Square.

On the Edge of the Sea, is the Governor's House, and the Viceroy's Palace, which take up two Sides of a Square, the Parish Church making the third, and a Battery of three Pieces of Cannon the fourth. The Corps de Garde, and the Hall for the Arms are also by the Viceroy's Lodgings. In the same Street, on the North-side, are the Ware-houses for the Commodities the *Spanish* Ships bring from *Chili, Peru* and *Mexico.*

Trade to Callao.
Commodities of Chili.

From *Chili,* they bring Cordage, Leather, Tallow, dry'd Flesh, and Corn; from *Chiloe,* Cedar Planks, a very light Wood, before spoken of, Woollen Manufactures, and particularly Carpets, like those of *Turky,* to spread on the *Estrados,* or Places where the Women sit on Cushions.

Of Peru.

From *Peru,* Sugars of *Andaguaylas, Guayaquil* and other Places; Wines and Brandy from *Lanasco* and *Pisco;* Masts, Cordage, Timber for Shipping, Cacao of *Guayaquil* and the Country about, Tabacco, and some little Honey of Sugar. The Cacao is afterwards transported to *Mexico.*

Of Mexico.

From *Mexico,* as from *Sonsonate, Realejo* and *Guatemala,* Pitch and Tar, which is only fit for Wood, because it burns the Cordage, Woods for dying, Sulphur, and Balsam, which bears the Name of Balsam of *Peru;* but which in reality comes most from *Guatemala.* There are two sorts of it, White and Brown; the latter is most valued, and they put it into Coco Shells, when it is of the Consistence of Tar; but generally it comes in Earthen Pots liquid, and then it is liable to be falsify'd and mix'd with Oil to increase the Quantity. From the same Places they bring fine Works, which they call of *Caray,* and Commodities of *China,* by the way of *Acapulco,* tho' contraband.

Besides these Warehouses, there is another for laying up of the *European* Commodities, which they call *la Administra-*
cion

cion. The *French* Ships that have had leave to trade to *Callao*, have been obliged to put into it all they had aboard. They exact upon the felling Price 13 *per Cent.* of such as come with their whole Lading, and sometimes even 16, of those who have already sold much in other Ports along the Coast, and three in the Thousand for other Royal Duties and Consulship, without reckoning the Presents that are to be privately made to the Viceroy and the King's Officers, who will not transgress the Laws of the Kingdom for nothing, in a Place where they have the Power in their own Hands. It is not to be wonder'd that the hungry Officers should be corrupted, they buying their Places only to enrich themselves, and consequently are little concern'd for the Publick Good, provided they find their own Account therein. It is true, there seems to be some Reason for permitting the *French* to trade, during these late Wars, considering the Scarcity of Merchandizes there was in the Country, by reason of the Stoppage of the Trade of the Galeons; but it must also be own'd, that the *Spaniards* have permitted it without any Discretion, with so much Ease, that it has been prejudicial to both; because the *French* resorting thither without Measure, have carry'd many more Goods than the Country could use; that Plenty has obliged them to sell the said Goods at very low Rates, and has ruin'd the *Spanish* Merchants, and consequently the *French* for several Years. Three Ships, with each of them Goods to the Value of a Million of Pieces of Eight, would have been sufficient for *Peru* yearly; for *Chili* cannot take off for above the Value of 400000 Pieces of Eight; the Merchants would have bought to a more certain Profit, and one *French* Ship would have made more Profit than three or four: But enough of this Reflexion, which can be of no Advantage.

<small>*French* Trade.</small>

Besides the publick Structures already mention'd, there are none of Note, except the Churches, which, considering they are built with Canes interwoven, and cover'd with Clay or Timber painted white, are nevertheless very neat.

<small>Churches, Monasteries, and Inhabitants.</small>

There are five Monasteries of Religious Men, *Dominicans*, *Franciscans*, *Augustins*, *Mercenarians*, and *Jesuites*; besides the Hospital of S. *John of God*. The Number of the Inhabitants does not exceed 400 Families, tho' they reckon 600.

Garrison. Tho' the King of *Spain* has settled a Fund of 292171 Pieces of Eight a Year, for maintaining of the Garrison of *Callao*; there are scarce Soldiers enow to mount the Guard at the Place of Arms.

Governor and Ingineer. The Governor is generally a considerable *European*, who is reliev'd by the Court of *Spain* every five Years. His Catholick Majesty also keeps an Engineer there, who serves for all the Places in *South America*; which are *Baldivia*, *Valparaiso*, *Callao*, *Lima*, and *Truxillo*.

Since the Death of Monsieur *Rossemin*, the *French* Engineer, the Charge of the Fortifications has been committed to Signior *Peralto*, a *Creollo*, or Mongrel *Spaniard* of *Lima*, Astrologer and Astronomer of the City; but tho' the King allows 30000 Pieces of Eight assign'd upon the Excise on Flesh, for repairing the Walls of *Calao*, they let them run to ruin next the Sea; so that they will be obliged to rebuild near one Half of them.

Without the Walls of *Callao* there are two *Indian* Suburbs call'd *Pitipiti*, and distinguish'd by the Names of the Old and New; the first of them is on the South, and the other on the North Side, into which runs the River of *Rimac*, or of *Lima*.

Road to Lima. On that Side is the Road that leads to *Lima*, which is only two Leagues distant, the Way good and pleasant, along a fine Plain. At the Mid-way is a Chappel of S. *John of God* call'd *La Legua*, or the League: A Quarter of a League beyond it, the Road parts into two Branches, of which that on the Left Hand leads to the Royal Gate of *Lima*, and the other to that call'd *Juan Simon*, which answers to the Middle of the City, and is consequently more frequented than the other.

That

That Way I enter'd on the 2d of *October* 1713, in Order to stay at *Lima* till a Ship sail'd for *France*. Two Days after my Arrival there, they celebrated the Feast of S. *Francis* of *Assisium*, which is none of the least in the Year; for the *Spaniards* being possess'd and infatuated by the Friers, especially the *Franciscans* and the *Dominicans*, look upon the Founders of those two Orders as the greatest Saints in Heaven. The Veneration they pay them extends even to the Habits of their Orders, much beyond other Monastical Habits.

Arrival at Lima.

They chiefly believe they gain great Indulgences by kissing that of S. *Francis*: The *Franciscans* to keep up that Notion, send some of their Friers into the most frequented Churches, to give their Sleeve to kiss to those who are hearing Mass: Even the questing Brothers presume to interrupt People at their Prayers to have that Honour done them. But in order to heighten the general Respect paid to their Order, and render its Grandeur the more observable to the Publick, they on the Festival of their Founder make magnificent Fire-works and Processions, and embellish their Cloisters within and without with the richest Things they can come at. Thus they cast Dust into the Eyes of the Carnal People, who are taken with fine Appearances, and in some Measure ease them of the truly Religious Life.

The Festival began at the Evensong of the Eve, by a Procession of the *Dominicans*, in which ten Men carry'd the Figure of S. *Dominick*, going to visit his Friend S. *Francis*. He was clad in rich Gold Stuffs, and glittering with small Stars of Silver, strew'd upon him, that he might be seen at a Distance.

S. *Francis* being inform'd of the Honour his Friend was coming to do him, came to meet him as far as the Square, which is about half Way: Before the Palace Gate they complimented one another, by means of the Organs of their Children, for tho' they made Gestures, they had not the Advantage of speaking. The latter being more Modest than the former, came in his *Franciscan* Frier's Cloth;

Procession.

Cloth; but amidst that Poverty, he was encompass'd by an Arch of Silver Rays, and had at his Feet such a Quantity of Gold and Silver Vessels, that 18 Men bow'd under that Wealth.

They were both receiv'd at S. *Francis*'s Church Door by four Giants of several Colours, a white, a black, a Mulatto, and an *Indian*, which came to the Square to dance before the Procession. They were made of Basket-work, cover'd with painted Paper, and real Scarecrows for their Figure, Masks, Hats and Perukes. In the midst of the Giants was the *Tarasca*, a chimerical Monster, known in some Provinces of *France*, bearing on its Back a Basket, from which issu'd a Puppet, or Maulkin, that danced and skipp'd to divert the People. At length they enter'd the Church amidst a great Number of Tapers and little Angels two or three Foot high, set on Tables, like Puppets, among great Candlesticks six or seven Foot high.

Fire-works. At the Close of the Evening there were Fire-works in the Square before the Church: They consisted of three Castles, each of them eight or nine Foot wide, and 15 or 16 in height. On the Top of one of them was a Bull, and on another a Lion. The Steeples of the Church were adorn'd with Ensigns and Streamers of all Colours, and illuminated with Lanthorns. They began the Entertainment by throwing up Sky-Rockets, small and ill made; then they play'd some running Fires, one of which separated into three long Squibs, which rested on the Middle and the two Ends of the Line, leaving two little Globes of bright Fire at the two Intervals.* This was the only Fire-work that deserv'd to be taken Notice of. At last, a Man on Horseback came down from a Steeple by a Rope, and came to attack in the Air one of those Castles; they set fire to it, and successively burnt the Giants, and the *Tarasca*, or Monster; and so all was reduced to Ashes.

The

---

* How that is done, may be seen in my Treatise of Artificial Fire-works.

The next Day there was a long Sermon, and Musick, where they sung *Spanish* Motetts. The Monastery was open'd to the Women, and at Night another Procession carry'd S. *Dominick* home: Then, tho' it was Day, there was another Fire-work, and a Giant came down by a Rope to attack a Castle, and fight a Serpent with three Heads.

This Solemnity, tho' very expensive, was, as they say, much inferiour to the former, which were sometimes so magnificent, that they were obliged to limit them; whence may be inferr'd in how great Esteem those Friers are, since by means of their Wallets they get enough not only to maintain above 1500 Persons, as well Friers as Servants, in four Monasteries, and to erect sumptuous Structures for that Country, for the Monastery of S. *Francis* is the finest and largest in *Lima*; but have enough left for Expences of meer Ostentation, which have sometimes amounted to 50000 Pieces of Eight, of what is the Right of the Poor, of whom there is no Want there, any more than elsewhere. In short, if what is superfluo C in the Laity belongs to them, with much more Reason does that which those Friers have to spare, they themselves professing such rigorous Poverty, that they do not pretend to have a Right to the very Bread they are actually eating, as we are inform'd by that pleasant Piece of History so well known by a Bull of Pope *John* XXII.

We need not be surprized at these Expences, if we consider the extraordinary Produce of the Quest, since the great Monastery alone has 24 Questors at *Lima*, one of whom, who died in 1708, had in 20 Years gather'd 350000 Pieces of Eight: Besides, it is very common among the *Spaniards* to wrong their nearest Relations of considerable Sums of Money, and even of their lawful Inheritance, in Favour of the Church and the Monasteries, which they there call making their Soul their Heir.

In the second place, it may be observ'd how little Taste and Genius there is among them; for in their Shows there is no Fancy, Design, nor Subject: But I have dwelt too long

long upon a Festival, which does not deserve so much. It is time to speak of what I saw worth taking notice of at *Lima*, during my Stay there.

The Description of the City of Lima.

Situation. THE City of *Lima*, Capital of *Peru*, is seated two Leagues from the Port of *Callao*, in 12 Degrees, 6 Minutes and 28 Seconds of South Latitude, and 79 Degrees 45 Minutes of Western Longitude, or Difference from the Meridian of *Paris: Peralta* and Father *Feüillée* say 12 Degrees, 1 Minute and 15 Seconds Latitude, and 79 Degrees, 9 Minutes and 30 Seconds Longitude. It is built in a fine Plain, at the Bottom of a Vale, formerly call'd *Rimac*, of the Name of a noted Idol of the *Indians*, which was famous for Oracles; whence, by Corruption, and through the Difficulty those People found in pronouncing the Letter *R* as harshly as the *Spaniards*, came the Name of *Lima*, which is quite different from that its first Founder gave it: For *Francis Pizarro*, who began it in the Reign of the Emperor *Charles* V. and first King of *Spain* of that Name, and of Queen *Joanna*, his Mother, both of them reigning jointly in *Castile*, call'd it, *La Ciudad de los Reyes*, that is, the City of the Kings; meaning the three Wise Men that came out of the East to worship

---

Plate XXVIII. *Page* 206. *explain'd in* English.
The Plan of the City of *LIMA*, the Capital of *Peru*, in 12 Degrees 6 Minutes 28 Seconds of South Latitude, 2 Leagues from the Port of *Callao*.

a. *S.* Rose, *A House of devout Women.*
b. *The House of Divorce.*
c. *The House of poor Women.*
d. *S.* Ildephonsus.
e. *The Hospital for Priests.*
f. *The College of Maidens.*
g. *The Recollection of the Society.*
h. *S.* Peter *of* Alcantara.
i. *The Congregation of Priests.*
k. *Devotes of the Mother of God.*
l. *The Seminary of S.* Toribius.
m. *Our Lady of* Cocharcas.
n. *S.* Philip *the Royal.*
o. *The College.*
p. *A Chappel.*

Places

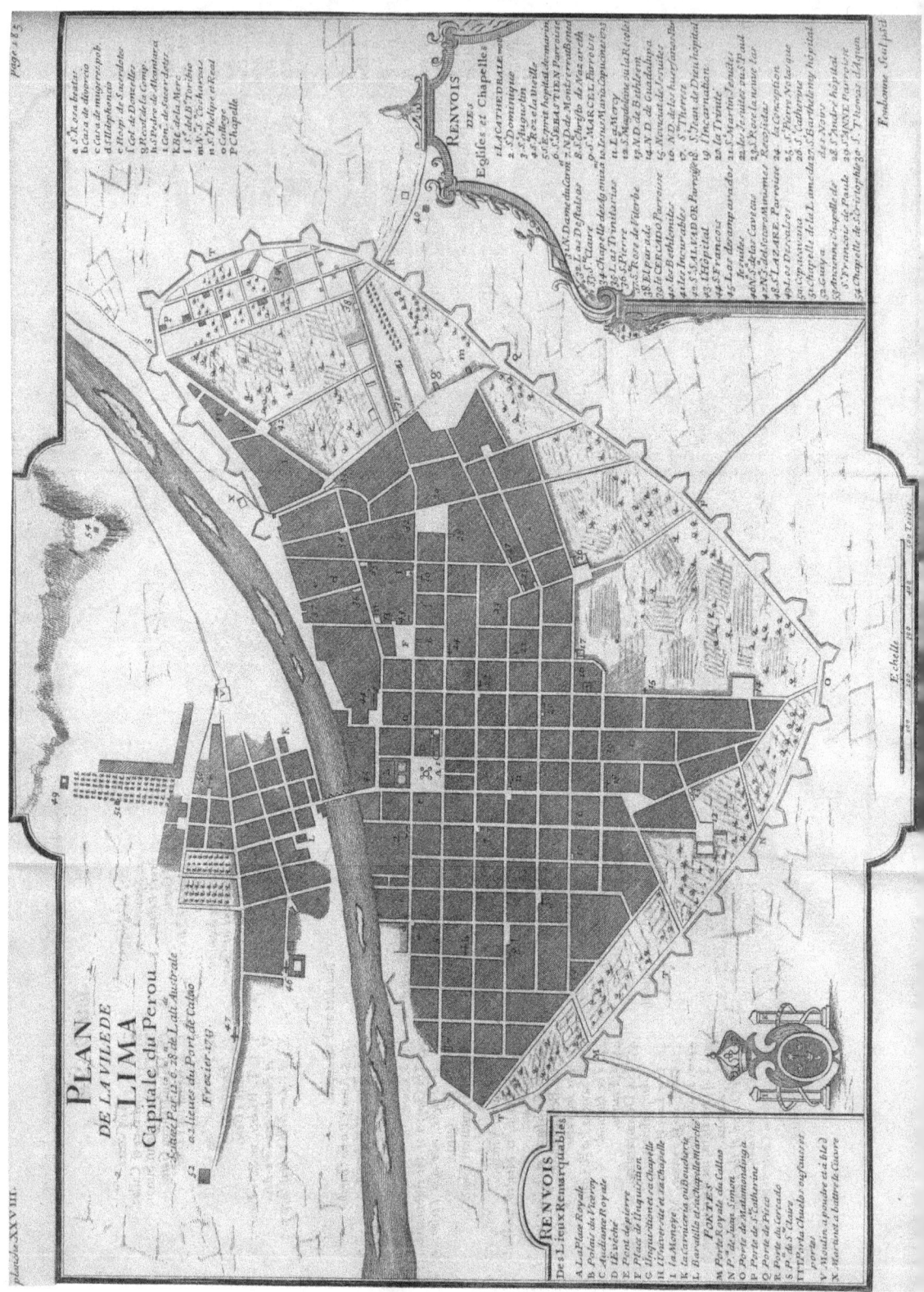

The material originally positioned here is too large for reproduction in this reissue. A PDF can be downloaded from the web address given on page iv of this book, by clicking on 'Resources Available'.

Places of Note.
A. *The Royal Square.*
B. *The Viceroy's Palace.*
C. *The Royal Court.*
D. *The Archbishop's Palace.*
E. *The Stone Bridge.*
F. *The Square of the Inquisition.*
G. *The Inquisition and its Chappel.*
H. *The University and its Chappel.*
I. *The Mint.*
K. *The Flesh Market.*
L. *The Market for small Wares, and its Chappel.*

The Gates.
M. *The Royal Gate of* Callao.
N. *The Gate of* John Simon.
O. Matamendinga *Gate.*
P. *S.* Katharine's *Gate.*
Q. Pisco *Gate.*
R. *The Gate of the* Cercado, *or the Enclosure.*
S. *S.* Clare's *Gate.*
T. T. T. *Wickets, or Sally Ports.*
V. *A Powder and Corn-Mill.*
X. *A Water-Mill to beat Copper.*

Churches and Chappels.
1. *The Cathedral.*
2. *S.* Dominick.
3. *S.* Augustin.
4. *Old S.* Rose.
5. *The Holy Ghost, an Hospital for Sailors.*
6. *S.* Sebastian, *a Parish.*
7. *Our Lady of* Monserrat, *Benedictins.*
8. *The Holy* CHRIST *of* Nazareth.
9. *S.* Marcellus *Parish Church.*
10. JESUS Mary, *Capucines.*
11. *The Mercenarians.*
12. *S.* Mary Magdalen, *or the Recollection.*
13. *Our Lady of* Bethlehem.
14. *Our Lady of* Guadalupe.
15. *The Noviciate of the* Jesuites.
16. *Our Lady of the Orphans.*
17. *S.* Teresa.
18. *S.* John of God, *an Hospital.*
19. *The Incarnation.*
20. *The Trinity.*
21. *S.* Martin, Jesuites.
22. *S.* Paul, *Jesuites.*
23. *New S.* Rose, *Retired Women.*
24. *The Conception.*
25. *S.* Peter Nolascus.
26. *S.* Katharine.
27. *S.* Bartholomew's *Hospital for Blacks.*
28. *S.* Andrew's *Hospital.*
29. *S.* Anne's *Parish Church.*
30. *S.* Thomas of Aquin.
31. *Our Lady of* Mount Carmel.
32. *The Barefoot Nuns.*
33. *S.* Clare.
34. *The Chappel of the* Agonizantes, *or Priests, who assist Persons in the last Agony.*
35. *The Trinitarian Nuns.*
36. *S.* Peter.
37. *S.* Rose of Viterbo.
38. *The* Prado, *or Meadow, or Walling-Place.*
39. *The Enclosure Parish Church.*
40. *The Bethlehemites.*
41. *The Incurable.*
42. *S.* Saviour *Parish Church.*
43. *The Hospital.*
44. *S.* Francis.
45. Los Desamparados, *or the Forsaken,* Jesuites.
46. *Our Lady of* Cavecas.
47. *Our Lady of* Succour, Minimes.
48. *S.* Lazarus *Parish Church.*
49. Los Descalços, *the Barefoot Friers.*
50. Copacavana.
51. *The Chappel of the Poplar Grove.*
52. Guia, *the Guide.*
53. *The ancient Chappel of S.* Francis of Paula.
54. *S.* Christopher's *Chappel.*

CHRIST

CHRIST new born; perhaps because the *Spaniards* conquer'd that Vale on the Day of the Epiphany, as many pretend. The Arms of the City seem to favour both Opinions, the Escutcheon is charged with three Crowns *Or*, two and one, in a Field *Azure*, in chief a Star darting Beams, some add, in the Escutcheon, *Hercules*'s Pillars, but in several Places they only stand without as Supporters, with these two Words, *Plus ultra*, and the two Letters *J* and *K*, to denote the Names of *Joanna* and *Charles*, being their Initials. Be that as it will, it is certain that Name was not given it on Account of its having been founded on the Day of the Epiphany, as Father *Feüillée* says, after *Garcilasso de la Vega*, and in the Year 1534; but on the 18th of *Janudry* 1535, the Festival of S. *Peter*'s Chair, as *Francisco Antonio de Montalvo* relates, in the Life of the Blessed *Toribio*, Bishop of *Lima*, printed by the Title of *El Sol del Nuevo Mundo*, or the Sun of the New World, by the Procurement of *D. J. Fr. de Valladolid*, School Master of the Metropolitan Church of that City, and Procurator General at *Rome*, for the Canonization of that Prelate. This Circumstance, and the Particular of the Names of the Commissioners appointed to choose a Place for the Situation of the City, and of the first Inhabitants, are strong Presumptions against *Garcilasso*. It is true, that *Herrera* concurrs with him as to the Day of the Foundation; but he agrees with *Montalvo* as to the Year 1535.

This Epocha is also determin'd by the Reasons *Pizarro* had for building a City in the Place where *Lima* now stands; for the same *Herrera* tells us, that the *Adelantado*, or Lord Lieutenant *Don Pedro de Alvarado*, coming from *Guatemala* to *Peru*, with an Army, with a Design to make himself Master there, *Pizarro* came to make a Settlement in the Vale of *Lima*, near the Port of *Callao*, which is the best on the Coast, to obstruct his coming by Sea, whilst *Don Diego de Almagro* march'd to oppose him in the Province of *Quito*.

The

The *Spaniards*, who out of a commendable Emulation, are always attentive to the exteriour Duties of Religion, before they erected any Structure, laid the Foundations of the Church, much about the midst of the City; then *Pizarro* laid down the Streets, distributed the Spaces for the Houses, by Quarters of 150 *Varas* or *Spanish* Yards, that is, 64 Fathoms square, as has been said of *Santiago*. Twelve *Spaniards*, who were the first Citizens under his Direction, began to build for themselves there; afterwards 30 Men from *San Galian*, and some others that were at *Xauxa*, came and join'd them, and made up, in all, the Number of 70 Inhabitants, who are considerably increas'd, for it is now the largest City in all *South America*.

The Distribution of the Plan is very beautiful, the Streets are in a direct Line, and of a convenient Breadth. In the midst of the City is the *Plaça Real*, or Royal Square, in which are to be found together all Things for the Publick Service. The East-side is taken up by the Cathedral, and the Archbishop's Palace; the North-side by the Viceroy's Palace; the West by the Council House, the Court of Justice, the Prison, and the Guard Chamber, with a Row of uniform Portico's: Lastly, the South-side is like the latter, adorn'd with Portico's and Shops. *Plan of the City. Great Square.*

In the midst of the Square is a Brass Fountain, adorn'd with a Statue of Fame, and eight Lions of the same Metal, which are to spout Water all about. This Fountain is also encompass'd by four other little Basons at the Angles, very rich in Metal. *Fountains.*

One Quarter from the Royal Square, on the North-side, runs the River of *Lima*, which is almost always fordable, except in Summer, when the Rains fall on the Mountains, and the Snow thaws. There are Trenches drawn from it in several Places, to water the Fields, and the Streets and Gardens in the City, where they convey it much in the same manner as is done at *Santiago*, but in cover'd Passages. *River and Trenches.*

E e The

Bridge.   The Part of this-River, which is cut off on the North-side, has a Communication with the main Body of the City, by means of a Stone-Bridge compofed of five Arches, well enough built, in the Viceroyfhip of *Montefclaros*. The Street it runs through leads directly to the Church of S. *Lazarus*, the Parifh-Church of a Suburb call'd *Malambo*, *Fine Walk.* and terminates near the *Alameda*, being a Walk of five Rows of Orange Trees, about 200 Fathoms long, the broadeft of the Walks between them being adorn'd with three Stone Bafons for Fountains. The Beauty of thofe Trees always green, the fweet Odor of the Flowers lafting almoft all the Year, and the Concourfe of the Calefhes daily reforting thither at the time of taking the Air, make that Walk a moft delicious Place about Five in the Evening.

Chappel.   About the middle of it is a Chappel, of the Invocation of S. *Liberata*, built in the Year 1711, in a Place where the Hofts of the Holy *Ciborium* of the Cathedral, which had been ftolen and bury'd under a Tree, were found. That little Walk terminates at the Foot of the Mountain, where *Monaftery.* is a Monaftery of the Obfervants reform'd by S. *Francis Solano*, a Native of *Paraguay*. Farther to the Eaftward is another Mountain, contiguous with the former, on which is the Hermitage of S. *Chriftopher*, whofe Name it bears, at the Foot whereof runs a Branch of the River, whofe Pool drives feveral Corn-Mills, and one Powder-Mill, and is the common Bathing Place.

Earthquakes.   The Earthquakes, which are very frequent in *Peru*, have much damaged this City, and daily make the Inhabitants uneafy. There was one in the Year 1678, on the 17th of *June*, which ruin'd a great Part of it, and particularly the Churches dedicated to the Bleffed Virgin. *Montalvo*, who has made this Remark, in the Life of S. *Toribio*, fays, it was as if God the Son had rifen for his Mother: But that in the Year 1682, was fo violent, that it almoft entirely demolifh'd the Place, infomuch that it was debated, whether they fhould not remove it to fome better Situation. The Memory of that dreadful Earthquake is

yearly

yearly revived there, on the 19th of *October*, by publick Prayers. If we may believe the publick Report, it was foretold by a Religious Man of the Order of the *Mercenarians*, who several Days before it, ran along the Streets like another *Jonas*, crying, *Do Penance*. In short, the Day came when it quaked after so extraordinary a manner, that every half Quarter of an Hour, it gave horrid Shocks, so that they reckoned above 200 in less than 24 Hours.

As dreadful as that Earthquake appears, there happen'd *Another.* one still more unparallell'd in the Year 1692, in the Province of *Quito*, at the Towns of *Ambata, Latacunga* and *Riobamba*. This shook the Earth in such manner, that it tore off great Pieces of it, which were seen to run entire three or four Leagues from the Place where they had been before, and thus to remove whole Fields, with the Trees and Houses standing; which occasion'd the most extraordinary Law-Suits that were ever heard of, brought to *Lima*, to decide to whom those Estates belong'd; he on one side alledging, they are within my Jurisdiction or Lordship; and the other pleading, I am upon my own Land.

The like had happen'd in the Year 1581, near *Chuquiago, Again.* or *La Paz*, as *Acosta* l. 3. c. 27. reports. The Borough called *Angoango*, inhabited by *Indians*, on a sudden fell to Ruin, and the Earth ran and spread over the Country, for the Space of a League and a half, as if it had been Water, or melted Wax, in such manner that it stopp'd and fill'd up a Lake, and so continued spread over that Country, *Psalm* 97. *The Hills melted like Wax at the Presence of the Lord*.

A much more amazing Earthquake happen'd in *Canada Another.* which began on the 5th of *February* 1663, and continued till *July* the same Year, occasioning incredible Alterations on the Surface of the Earth for above 400 Leagues through the Country. See the *Life of the Venerable Mother* Mary *of the* Incarnation, *an* Ursuline *Nun in* New France, *printed at* Paris 1677.

Conjectures concerning Earthquakes.

There is no reflecting upon such extraordinary Phænomenons, without being led by natural Curiosity to enquire into the Cause of them. That which Philosophers generally assign for Earthquakes, does not always appear satisfactory. They are ascribed to subterraneous Winds and Fires; but it is likely they ought rather to be look'd upon as an Effect of the Waters the Earth is inwardly moisten'd with, as living Bodies are by the Veins. There needs only digging, and the Truth of this Supposition almost every where appears; now the Waters may occasion Earthquakes after several Manners, either by dissolving the Salts scatter'd through the Earth, or by penetrating through porous Lands, mix'd with Stones, which they insensibly loosen, the Fall or Removal whereof must cause a Stroke or Shock, such as is felt in Earthquakes. Lastly, the Water penetrating some Sulphureous Bodies, must there cause a Fermentation, and then the Heat produces Winds and foul Exhalations, which infect the Air when they open the Earth, whence it is, that after great Earthquakes abundance of People die, as has been related at *Santiago* and *Lima*. The Facility of this Fermentation is proved by the Example of Lime, and by a curious Experiment of Monsieur *Lemery*, particulariz'd in the Memoirs of the Academy of Sciences, for the Year 1700.

Philosophical Experiment.

If after having temper'd equal Parts of Filings of Iron, and of Sulphur to a certain Quantity, as of 30 or 40 Pounds, with Water; that Amalgama, or Paste, be bury'd in the Ground a Foot deep, it will open and cast forth hot Vapours, and then Flames.

Why more Earthquakes near the Coast than up the Inland.

Now in *Peru* and *Chili* the Earth is all full of Mines of Salt, of Sulphur and of Metals; add to this, that there are burning Mountains, which calcine the Stones, and dilate the Sulphurs; Earthquakes must therefore be there very frequent, and particularly along the Sea Coasts, which are more water'd than towards the Top of the Ridge of Mountains call'd *la Cordillera*, which is very agreeable to Experience, for there are some Places where the said Earthquakes are very rare,

Conjectures concerning Earthquakes.

rare, as at *Cuſco, Guamanga*, and elſewhere; for the ſame Reaſon that they are more frequent in *Italy* than about the *Alps*. In fine, it cannot but be own'd that the Water has a great Share in Earthquakes, when we ſee Fields run like melted Wax, and Lakes form'd on a ſudden in Places that ſink, becauſe the Earth ſubſiding in the Water, obliges it to riſe above it, if the Quantity be conſiderable, or elſe to glide like Sand, when the Baſe is diſſolv'd and on an inclining Plan. *How Earth may run.*

The Dread of Earthquakes has not obſtructed their building many fine Churches, and high Steeples at *Lima*. It is true, that moſt of the Arches are only of Timber, whitiſh, or elſe of Cane Work, but ſo well order'd, that unleſs told it, no Man can diſcern it. The Walls of the great Structures are of burnt Bricks, and thoſe of the leſſer of unburnt Bricks. The Houſes have only a Ground Floor, in which there is ſometimes one upper Story made of Canes, that it may be light; and laſtly, they are all without Roofs, becauſe it never rains there. *Churches and Houſes.*

A Phænomenon ſo contrary to what we ſee in our Climates, immediately occaſions two Queſtions. *Two Queſtions.*

The firſt, how the Earth can produce, without Rain?

The ſecond, how comes it, that it never rains along the Coaſt, tho' it rains 15 or 20 Leagues from the Sea, up the Country

To anſwer the firſt, I muſt declare, that this Want of Rain renders almoſt all the Country fruitleſs in the Highlands; there are only ſome Vales, through which Rivulets glide, coming down from the Mountains, where it rains and ſnows, which afford any Product, and which can conſequently be inhabited; but in theſe Places the Earth is ſo fruitful, and on the other hand the Country is ſo thin peopled, that thoſe Vales are ſufficient, and ſupply all Things plentifully for the Subſiſtence of the Inhabitants The ancient *Indians* were extraordinary induſtrious in conveying the Water of the Rivers to their Dwellings, there are ſtill to be ſeen in many Places Aqueducts of Earth, *Fertility and Barrenneſs.*

and

Indian Aqueducts. and of dry Stones carry'd on and turn'd off very ingeniously along the Sides of Hills, with an infinite Number of Windings; which shews that those People, as unpolish'd as they were, very well understood the Art of leveling. As for what relates to the Hills along the Coast, there is Grafs to be found on them in some Places, which are least expos'd to the Heat of the Sun, because the Clouds stoop down to their Tops in Winter, and sufficiently moisten them to furnish the necessary Juice for Plants.

Why it never rains there. As to the second Question, *Zarate*, in his Conquest of *Peru*, has endeavour'd to give a Reason for the Perpetual Drought that is observ'd on that Coast: " Those, *says he*, " who have carefully examin'd the Thing, pretend that the " natural Cause of that Effect is a South-West Wind which " prevails thoughout the Year along that Coast, and in the " Plain, and which blows so violently, that it carries a- " way the Vapors which rise from the Earth, or from the " Sea, before they can rise high enough in the Air to unite " and form Drops of Water, which fall again in Rain. In " short, *adds he*, it often happens, that looking from the " Tops of the High Mountains, these Vapours are seen " much below those that are on the said Tops, and make " the Air in the Plain look thick and cloudy, tho it be " very clear and serene on the Mountains.

This way of Reasoning is nothing likely, for it is not true that the S. W. Winds obstruct the Rising of the Vapors, since there are Clouds agitated by that Wind seen at a very great Height. And tho' that should be granted, those Winds would not nevertheless hinder thse Vapors forming themselves into Rain, since Experience manifestly shews us, in the *Alps*, that the low Clouds afford Rain, as well as the highest; the Sky often appears serene on the Top of the Mountain, when it rains most violently at the Foot thereof. So far from it, that they ought more naturally to yield it, because being lower they are heavier, and consequently compos'd of more bulky Drops of Rain than the highest Clouds.

I

I fancy I discern a better Reason, grounded on the different Degrees of Heat on the Coast, and in the Inland. It is known by Experience, that the Heat the Sun imparts to the Earth, dissolves into Rain, and attracts the Clouds the more, by how much it is more violently heated. I will explain how that Attraction is made: It is observ'd in *France*, that it rains as much, that is, that there falls as much Water, and even more, during the Months of *July* and *August*, as during the other Months of the Year, tho' it rains but very seldom, because the Drops of Water are then much larger than in Winter. This Observation is supported by the great Store of Rain that falls in the Torrid Zone, during some Months in the Year, after the Earth has been heated by the less oblique Rays. Now, it is known that the inner Part of *Peru*, which is almost all of it in that Zone, is very hot in the Valleys, which receive during the whole Day almost perpendicular Rays, whose Force is still increas'd by the many dry Rocks which encompass them, and reflect those Rays every way; and lastly, that the said Heat is not temper'd by the Winds. It is farther known, that the high Mountains call'd *La Cordillera* and *Los Andes*, which are almost continually cover'd with Snow, make the Country extremely cold in some Places, so that in a very small Distance the two contrary Extremes are to be found.

The Sun therefore, by his Presence, causes a violent Dilatation and a scorching Heat in the Valleys, during the Day, that is, one half of the Time; and during the Night, or the other Half, the neighbouring Snows suddenly cool the Air, which condenses a new. To this Vicissitude of Condensation and Rarefaction is certainly to be assign'd, as to the first Principle, the Inequality of Weather that is observ'd at *Cusco*, at *Puna*, *La Paz*, and other Places, where they almost daily are sensible of the Changeableness of the Weather, of Thunder, Rain, Lightning; of Fair and Cloudy Weather; of Heat and Cold; but in other Places it is hot for a long
Time,

Time, without any Interruption, and then the Rains take their Turn.

It is not so along the Coast, where the S. W. and S. S. W. Winds blow regularly, which coming from the cold Climates of the South Pole, continually refresh the Air, and constantly keep it almost in the same Degree of Condensation. Much more must they bring thither Salt Particles, which they gather from the Sea Fogs, wherewith the Air must be fill'd and thicken'd much, as we conceive Brine is by the Salt it contains. That Air therefore has more Strength to support the Clouds, and is not hot enough, nor in sufficient Motion to agitate the Particles, and consequently to gather the little Drops of Water, and form some greater than the Bulk of the Air to which they answer; and tho' those Clouds draw very near the Earth during the Season when they are least attracted by the Sun, yet they do not dissolve into Rain; thus at *Lima* the Weather is almost continually close, and it never rains.

If it were now requisite to shew why the hottest Countries attract the Rain, I could make use of the Conjectures of some modern Philosophers, * who are of Opinion, that the Clouds are frozen Vapours, or a Sort of very loose Ice, like Snow. According to that Notion, it is evident, that when the Heat of the Earth sufficiently heats the Air, to rise to the Height of the Clouds, they must then thaw and fall in Rain; but that way of Reasoning, which I often think very true, is not so always, as I can affirm upon my own Experience, having been upon high Mountains, where at the same time that I saw Clouds flying both above and below me, I was myself encompass'd with others between them, which in Truth I thought very cold, but in other respects to differ in nothing from the Fogs we see sweep along the Earth. It is therefore upon no solid Ground that they distinguish those Clouds from the Fogs.

Be that as it will, Heat may also attract Rain, by giving the Particles of the Air a Spiral Motion, which may gather many little Drops of Water into one larger Drop. This

Regis.

Motion is easy to conceive, by that which is obferv'd in the Current of Rivers, or, if you pleafe, by that of a Mathematical Spindle; if the Sun attracts Vapours after that Manner, it is not to be admired that the Earth heated fhould attract the Clouds.

In fine, I could farther ground this Attraction on a Piece of Experience, which fhews us, that Fire to fubfift requires a Flux of Air. If a burning Coal be put into a Bottle, and it be clofe ftopp'd, it is immediately quench'd. Thus reafoning from the greater to the leffer, a Body much heated may be compared to a Coal, and it may be concluded that the faid Heat cannot fubfift without a Flux, or Paffage of the Air about it, which being more condens'd, pufhes on and draws towards the Fire, as we fee the outward Air enter into a Chamber through little Holes, with more Rapidity when it is heated, than when there is no Fire in it.

I leave it to Philofophers to give more convincing Reafons for that Drought; it is enough for a Traveler, in declaring of Facts, flightly to explain them, to credit what he relates, and prepare the Reader for what he fays that is extraordinary. Thus becaufe it never rains at *Lima*, the Houfes are only cover'd with a fingle Mat laid flat, with the Thicknefs of a Finger of Afhes on it, to fuck up the Moifture of the Fogs; and the beautifulleft are built only with unburnt Bricks, that are made of Clay, work'd up with a little Grafs, and dry'd in the Sun, which neverthelefs lafts Ages, becaufe the Rain never wafhes it away. *Houfes cover'd with Mats.*

The Walls of the City, which ought to be an everlafting Work, are no otherwife built; they are between 18 and 25 Foot high, and nine in Thicknefs at the Gordon; fo that, in all the Compafs of the Town, there is no one Place broad enough to mount a Cannon, which makes me believe, that they were built only to oppofe any Attempts of the *Indians*. The Wall is flank'd with Baftions, whofe Flank is of about 15 Fathoms perpendicular with the Curtin, and the Face of about 30 Fathoms, which make the Angle of the Epaule of 130 Degrees, which *Fortifications.*

occasions such a fichant Defence, that two Thirds of the Curtin are upon a second Flank; and the flank'd Angles are often too acute. Those Curtins being about 80 Fathoms in Length, the great Line of Defence is of about 110: Besides this, there is neither Ditch nor Outworks. These Fortifications were made about the Year 1685, in the Vice-royship of the Duke *de la Palata*, by a *Flemish* Priest, whose Name was *Don John Ramond*.

The Number of *Spanish* Families in *Lima* may make up about 8 or 9000 Whites; the rest are only Mestizo's, Mulatto's Blacks, and some *Indians*; tho', in the whole, there are about 25, or 30000 Souls, including the Friers and Nuns, who take up at least a Quarter of the City.

Immense Wealth.

As in the Cities of *Europe* we reckon the Coaches to denote their Magnificence, so at *Lima* they reckon 4000 Calashes, the common Carriage for Gentry in that Country, drawn by Mules. But to give some Idea of the Wealth of that City, it will suffice to relate what Treasure the Merchants there exposed about the Year 1682, when the Duke *de la Palata* made his Entry: Coming to take Possession of the Place, they caus'd the Streets, call'd *de la Merced*, or of the *Mercendrians*, and *de los Mercaderes*, or of the Merchants, extending through two of the Quarters, and through which he was to pass to the Royal Square, where the Palace is, to be paved with Ingots of Silver, that had paid the Fifth to the King, and generally weigh about 200 Marks, of eight Ounces each, between 12 and 15 Inches long, four or five in Breadth, and two or three in Thickness, which might amount to the Sum of 80 Millions of Crowns, and 320 Millions of Livres *French* Money, as it was in the Year 1715. It is true, that *Lima* is in some Sort the Repository of the Treasures of *Peru*, whose Capital it is. It was computed some Years ago, that above six Millions of Crowns were expended there. Much must be abated at present, since the *French* Trade has carry'd thither the Commodities of *Europe* at an easy rate, and since the Trade they have drove at *Arica*, *Hilo* and *Pisco*,
has

has diverted the Plate that came formerly to *Lima*: which is the Reason that the City is now poor, to what it formerly was.

Both Men and Women are equally inclined to be costly *Costly Habits.* in their Dress; the Women not satisfy'd with the Expence of the richest Silks, adorn them, after their Manner, with a prodigious Quantity of Lace, and are insatiable as to Pearls and Jewels, for Bracelets, Pendants and other Ornaments; the Fashion whereof, which amounts to very much, ruins the Husbands and the Gallants. We saw Ladies, who had about them above the Value of 60000 Pieces of Eight in Jewels: They are generally beautiful enough, of a sprightly Mien, and more engaging than in other Places; and perhaps one part of their Beauty is owing to the Toils of the *Mulattas, Blacks, Indians,* and other hideous Faces, which are the most numerous throughout the Country.

The City of *Lima* is the usual Residence of the Viceroy *Viceroy.* of *Peru*, who is as absolute as the King himself in the Courts of *Lima, Chuquisaca, Quito, Panama, Chili,* and *Tierra Firme,* as Governor * and Captain-General of all the Kingdoms and Provinces of that Part of the new World, as is express'd in his Titles. His Allowance is 40000 Pieces of Eight yearly, without taking Notice of his extraordinary Perquisites; as when he goes a Progress into any Provinces, he is allow'd 10000 Pieces of Eight, and 3000 for going only to *Callao,* which is but two Leagues from *Lima.* He has the Nomination of above a hundred *Corregidores,* or supreme Magistrates of considerable Places; and, in short, he has the Disposal of all Triennial Employments, both Civil and Military.

It is to be observ'd, that most Employments are given, or sold only for a limited Time.

---

* *The same Person has those two Titles, which are distinguish'd in the pretended Manuscript of* Oexmelin. *See the History of the* Buccaniers.

Politicks.

The Viceroys and Presidents generally hold theirs seven Years; some *Corregidores* and Governors have theirs for five, and the greater Number but for three. It is easy to see into the Design of that Regulation, which is, doubtless, to prevent their having Time to gain Creatures, and form Parties against a King, who is so remote from them, that it requires Years to receive his Orders; but it must also be granted, that this Policy is attended with many inevitable Inconveniences, which, in my Opinion, are the main Cause of the ill Government of the Colony, and of the little Profit it affords the King of *Spain*; for the Officers look upon the Time their Employments last as a Jubilee, which is to come but once in their Lives; at the End whereof they will be laugh'd at, if they have not made their Fortune: And as it is hard not to be overcome by the Temptation of privately conniving for Money at certain Abuses, which by long Use are become Customs, the honestest Persons follow the Steps of their Predecessors, being possess'd of the Opinion, that howsoever they behave themselves, they shall not perhaps miss of being charged with Mal-Administration; the only Means to clear themselves of which, is to appease their Judges with Presents, giving them Part of what they have wrong'd the King and the Subjects of. I bring this Reflexion from its Original, and do not lay it down here as a Conjecture. *Munera, crede mihi, placant hominesque Deosque.* Believe me, Gifts appease both Men and Gods.

Bribery.

Hence it is that so many Masses of Silver are convey'd from the Mines cross long Countries, and are at last convey'd aboard the Ships trading along the Coast, without paying the Fifth to the King, because the Merchants pay the Governor so much *per Cent.* the *Corregidor*, or supreme Magistrate, pays the *Juez de Descamino*, or Judge of Concealments or Confiscations, and he perhaps the Viceroy's Officers.

For this Reason scarce any one of them takes to Heart the publick Good, being convinced, that he shall soon be out of Place, and out of Power to continue the good Order

der he shall establish, and which his Successor will perhaps overthrow as soon as he is in the Post.

In short, this is the Cause why the Orders from the Court of *Spain* are not at all, or very ill put in Execution: They are satisfy'd with only publishing them for Formality; * the Fear of losing an Employment for Life is no Motive to them; they are sure to lose it in a short Time; and besides, they come off at an easy rate with the Viceroy, who reasons exactly as they do, tho' he has a Sovereign Authority and Power in his Hands.

* Se obedece la orden, y no se cumple. The Order is obey'd, but not executed.

His usual Guard is composed of three Parcels; being a Company of 100 Halbardiers, a Troop of 100 Horse, and a Company of 100 Foot; the two last are paid by the King, and the Halbardiers are maintain'd out of a Fund left by a Lady of *Lima*, who was extraordinary rich. There is another Company of 50 select Persons, all Men of Distinction, who walk by his Side when he makes his Entry.

There is a Royal Chappel in his Palace, serv'd by six Chaplains, a Sacristan, and a Choir of Musick, pay'd by the King. *Chappel.*

The Garrison of *Lima* consists only of the Militia of the Inhabitants, who have no Pay from the King, except the General Officers, and the Sergeants of the Foot-Companies: Whereof these are the Particulars. *Garrison.*

Fourteen Companies of *Spanish* Infantry of the Inhabitants. *Foot.*

Seven Companies of the Corporation of the Commerce, who have more than the former; a Major, and two Aids de Camp.

Eight-Companies of *Indians*, Natives of *Lima*, who, besides the usual Officers, have a Colonel, a Major, and an Adjutant.

Six Companies of *Mulatto's* and free Blacks, who have a Major, two Adjutants, and a Lieutenant-General.

Each of the above-mention'd Companies consists of 100 Men, and has no other Officers, but a Captain, an Ensign, and a Sergeant.

Ten

Horse.   Ten Troops of *Spanish* Horse, of 50 Men each; six whereof are of the City, and four of the Neighbouring Country-Houses, and adjacent Farms.

Each Troop has a Captain, a Lieutenant, and a Cornet.

General Officers in the King's Pay.

The Captain-General and Viceroy, Pieces of Eight *per Annum*.	40000
The Governor General	7000
The Lieutenant General of the Horse	1500
The Commissary General of the Horse	1500
The Lieutenant to the Lieutenant General	1200
The Lieutenant to the Captain General	1200

Other Officers appointed by the Viceroy.

The Captain of the Guard Chamber	1200
A Lieutenant of the Artillery	1200
Two Adjutants of the Artillery, each	300
Four Master Gunners, each	540
A chief Armorer	1500
Four Armorers, each	600
A Master Carpenter	1000

It is reported, that in case of need, the Viceroy can raise 100000 Foot and 20000 Horse, throughout the whole Extent of the Kingdom; but it is certain he could not arm the 5th Part of them, as I have been inform'd by Men who have travelled some of the Inland Parts of *Peru*.

Under the Viceroy's Authority, the Government of the Kingdom depends on that of the Royal Court, where he presides for matters of Moment. That Court, which may in some Measure be compared to a *French* Parliament, is composed of 16 *Oidores*, that is, Judges or Assessors, four *Alcaldes de Corte*, or Justices of the King's Houshold, two *Fiscales*, or Attorneys General, an *Alquazil Major*, or chief Serjeant, and a General Protector of the *Indians*. Each of those

those Persons in the said Employments has 3000 Pieces of Eight, and 13 Royals Salary; but the *Oidores*, or Judges, have moreover other Allowances belonging to the peculiar Courts where they are employ'd. That Body has also titular Officers, as Advocates, Solicitors, Notaries, Serjeants, &c.

The Royal Court is subdivided into a Court of Justice, a Criminal Court, a Court of Accounts, and two Courts of the Treasury, or Exchequer, one of which is entrusted with the Revenues which rich *Indians* have left at their Death to relieve the Wants of the Poor of their Nation. Lastly, it includes the Chancery, which is composed of only one Oidor, and one Chancellor, who has that Title given him with a very small Salary, because the Great Chancellor is always in *Spain*. *Several Courts.*

The *Cabildo*, or Council of the City, is next to the Royal Court. There are more Regidores, or Aldermen, belonging to it, than in other Towns. *City Council.*

There is also an *Alguazil Mayor*, or chief Sergeant of the City, for Military Affairs, and a great Provost, call'd *Alcalde de la Hermandad*, who has Power of Life and Death in the open Country.

The Court of the Royal Treasury is establish'd for the King's Revenues, as the Fifth of the Silver taken out of the Mines; the Duty of *Alcavala*, being 4 *per Cent.* on all Sorts of Commodities and Grain, and other Impositions, which are but few in that Colony. It has Judges, Tellers, Secretaries, &c. *Treasury:*

There is also a Court of the Mint, which has its Treasurers, Comptrollers, Directors, Keepers, Clerks, &c. as also an *Oidor*, or Judge, who has a Salary independent of that of the Royal Court. *Mint.*

The Court of the Commerce is the Consulship, where a Prior and two Consuls preside, who are chosen from among the Merchants, who best understand Trade. *Consulship.*

And, to the end that nothing may be wanting to that City, which may contribute towards preserving of good *Spiritual Courts.*

Order,

Order, and making it flourish, several Courts of Ecclesiastical Jurisdiction have been erected in it.

The Archbishop's. The first is the Archbishop's Court, composed of the Chapter of the Cathedral, and the Officiality; its Officers are, a Fiscal, or Attorney, a Solicitor, a Sergeant, and Notaries.

Inquisition. The second, and most dreadful of all Courts, is that of the Inquisition, whose Name alone gives a Terror every where, because, 1*st*, The Informer is reckon'd as a Witness: 2*dly*, The Accused have no Knowledge given them of their Accusers: 3*dly*, There is no Confronting of Witnesses; so that innocent Persons are daily taken up, whose only Crime is, that there are Persons, whose Interest it is to ruin them. However, they say at *Lima*, that there is no Cause to complain of the Inquisition, perhaps because the Viceroy and the Archbishops are at the Head of that Body.

The Inquisition was settled at *Lima* in the Year 1569, with all the Ministers, Counsellors, Qualificators, *Familiares*, Secretaries, and chief Sergeants, as it is in *Spain*. It has three superiour Judges, who have each 3000 Pieces of Eight Salary: Their Jurisdiction extends throughout all the *Spanish South America*.

Croisade. The third Spiritual Court is that of the Croisade, which is in some Manner a Part of the Royal Court, because there belongs to it an *Oidor*, or Judge of the Court of Justice. It was erected at *Lima*, in the Year 1603, under the Direction of a Commissary-General, who keeps his Court in his own House, where he judges, with the Assistance of a Judge Conservator, a Secretary, a Comptroller, a Treasurer, and other Officers, requisite for the Distribution of the Bulls, and Examination of the Jubilee and Indulgences. His Salary is only 1000 Pieces of Eight, which is too much for so useless an Employment.

Court for Wills. Lastly, There is a fourth Court for the last Wills and Testaments of the Dead, which calls to account Executors and Administrators, and takes Care of Chappelanies and their Foundations, for which it has several Officers.

In order to furnish so many Courts with proper Persons, the Emperor *Charles* V. in the Year 1545, founded an University at *Lima*, under the Title of S. *Mark*, and granted it several Privileges, which were confirm'd by Pope *Paul* III. and *Pius* V. who in 1572 incorporated it into that of *Salamanca*, that it might enjoy the same Privileges and Immunities: It is govern'd by a Rector, who is chosen yearly; they reckon in it about 180 Doctors of Divinity, Civil and Canon Law, Physick and Philosophy, and generally near 2000 Scholars. Some proceed thence able enough in the Scholastick and Tricking Part, but very few in the Positive. *{University.}*

There are in the University three Royal Colleges, with 20 Professorships, which have good Revenues. The first was founded by *Don Francisco de Toledo*, Viceroy of *Peru*, under the Invocation of S. *Philip* and S. *Mark*. The second by the Viceroy *Don Martin Henriquez*, for the Entertainment of 80 Collegians, or Students in Humanity, Civil Law and Divinity, the *Jesuites* are Rectors and Professors in it; and it is call'd S. *Martin*. The third by the Archbishop *Don Toribio Alphonso Mongrovejo*, under the Title of S. *Toribio*, Bishop, for the Maintenance of 80 Collegians, who serve in the Choir of the Cathedral. Their Habit is gray, with a Purple Welt double behind; they study Ecclesiastical Literature under a Priest, who is their Rector. The College also maintains six Boys for the Choir, under the Direction of the Master of the Chappel, and of the Vicar or SubDeacon, who resides there. The College has a Revenue of above 14000 Pieces of Eight. *{Colleges.}*

The Chapter of the Cathedral is composed of a Dean, an Archdeacon, a Chanter, a School-master, a Treasurer, and 10 Canons; one of which Number has been retrench'd, to give his Revenue to the Inquisition. Each of those Dignitaries has 7000, the Canons 5000, the six *Racionero's*, or Prebendaries, 3000; and the 30 Chaplains each 600 Pieces *{Chapter.}*

of Eight a Year, without reckoning the Musicians and Singing-Boys.

Cathedral. This Church, which was the first Structure in *Lima*, was by *Francis Pizarro* put under the Invocation of the *Assumption*; but Pope *Paul* III. having made it a Cathedral in the Year 1541, alter'd it to that of S. *John the Evangelist*, to distinguish it from that of *Cuzco*, which had that Name before. It was Suffragan to *Sevil* till the Year 1546, when the same Pope made it Metropolitan; and the Suffragans to it are the Bishopricks of *Panama, Quito, Truxillo, Guamanga, Arequipa, Cusco, Santiago,* and *La Conception* of *Chili.*

Archbishops. The first Archbishop was *Don Fray Jeronimo de Loaysa,* a Dominican. He assembled two Provincial Synods; the first on the 4th of *October* 1551, at which never a Suffragan was present, but only the Deputies of the Bishops of *Panama, Quito,* and *Cusco*: The second was open'd the 2d of *March* 1567; the Bishops of *La Plata, Quito,* and *La Imperial,* were present at it, with the Deputies of the other Chapters. He rebuilt the Church then ruin'd, and cover'd it with Mangrove Timber.

The 3d Archbishop, *Don Toribio,* is reckon'd a Saint.

The 9th, *Don Melchor de Linnan y Cisneros,* upon the Death of the Marquis *de Malagon,* was appointed Viceroy, Governor, and Captain General of the Provinces of *Peru*: He was the first in whom those two Dignities were united, which indeed do not seem compatible in the same Person.

Eight Parishes. The City of *Lima* contains eight Parishes. The first is the Cathedral, which has four Curates and two Vicars, which is contrary to the Canon Law, whereby only one Curate is assign'd to a Church, because one Body is to have but one Head. The Church is handsome enough, well built, and has three equal Isles. In it is preserv'd a Piece of the Cross of *CHRIST.*

The second is that of S. *Anne,* which has two Curates and one Vicar.

The third S. *Sebastian*, which has also two.

The fourth S. *Marcellus*, one Curate.

The fifth S. *Lazarus*, one Curate, Vicar of the Cathedral.

The sixth *Our Lady of Atocha*, annex'd to, and dependent on the Cathedral; they call it *Los Huerfanos*, or the Orphans.

The seventh is *El Cercado*, or the Inclosure; which was the Parish Church to an *Indian* Suburb that has been brought into the City since it was wall'd in; the *Jesuites* are its Curates.

The eighth has been added of late Years, and is call'd *San Salvador*, or S. *Saviour*.

There are several Hospitals for the Sick and Poor of the City. The first, call'd S. *Andrew*, is a Royal Foundation for the *Spaniards*, that is, the Whites: It is serv'd by the Merchants and four Priests. *Twelve Hospitals.*

That of *San Diego*, or S. *James*, is founded for those who are Convalescents, or upon Recovery, after having been in that of S. *Andrew*; they are serv'd by the Brothers of S. *John of God*.

That of S. *Peter* was founded only for Priests by the Archbishop *Toribio* above-mention'd.

That of the Holy Ghost, for Seafaring Men, is maintain'd by the Alms and Contributions collected of Trading Vessels.

That of S. *Bartholomew* was founded for the Blacks by Father *Bartholomew de Vadillo*.

In that of S. *Lazarus* they take Care of Lepers, and such as have the Venereal Distemper. It is a Royal Foundation, and serves also for the Falling Sickness and Mad Folks.

There is a House for Foundlings, adjoining to *Our Lady of Atocha*, call'd *Los Huerfanos*, or the Orphans.

The Hospital of S. *Cosmas* and S. *Damianus*, was founded by the Inhabitants of *Lima*, for *Spanish* Women.

That of *S. Anne* was founded by *Don Ieronymo de Loaysa*, the first Archbishop for the *Indians*; the King now defrays the Charge of it.

There is one for the *Incurable*, serv'd by the *Bethlehemites*.

Another for the Convalescent, or recovering *Indians*, without the City, where those who come from *S. Anne* and other Hospitals are receiv'd.

There are also Officers to dispose of the Foundations made by the richest *Indians*, for the Poor of their Nation, as has been said.

Lastly, there is one founded by a Priest, for convalescent, or recovering Priests.

Charity. Besides the Hospitals for the Sick, there is a House of Charity, in the Square of the Inquisition, for poor Women. There young Maids are marry'd or made Nuns.

Portions for Maids. In the College of *Santa Cruz de las Ninas*, or the Holy Cross of the Girls, they bring up a Number of Foundling Girls, to whom the Inquisitors give Portions, when they marry.

A Priest has also left a Foundation of above 600000 Pieces of Eight, under the Direction of the Dean of the Cathedral, and the Prior of *S. Dominick*, to marry 20 Maids, and give them 500 Pieces of Eight each.

The Brotherhood of *Conception* marries 40, after the Rate of 450 Pieces of Eight each.

There is a Foundation under the Title of *Our Lady of Cocharcas*, for the Poor Daughters of *Caciques*, and a College for breeding their Sons, where they have all sorts of Masters.

Monasteries. The Monastical State, which has overspread all *Europe*, has also extended beyond the vast Seas into the remotest Colonies, where it fills the farthest Corners inhabited by Christians; but at *Lima* particularly there are Legions of Friers, whose Monasteries have taken up the finest and greatest Part of the City.

The *Dominicans* have four Monasteries there; the chief- **Dominicans.**
est is that of the *Rosary*; next the *Recollection of the Magdalen*; *S. Thomas* of *Aquin*, where their Schools are, and
S. *Rose* of *Lima*.

The *Franciscans* have four, *viz.* that of *JESUS*, or **Franciscans.**
the Great Monastery, call'd also S. *Francis*, contains 700
Men, as well Friers, as Servants, and takes up the
Space of four Quarters, being the finest in the City. The
second is the *Recollection of S. Mary of the Angels*, or
Guadalupe; the third is the College of S. *Bonaventure*;
and the fourth the Barefoot Friers of S. *James*.

The *Augustins* have also four, which contain above 500 **Augustins.**
Friers, and are, S. *Augustin*, *Our Lady of Capacavana*, the
College of S. *Ildefonsus*, and the *Noviciate*, which is
without the City, or the Reform of *Our Lady of Guidance*.

The Order of the *Mercenarians* has three, *viz.* the *Mer-* **Mercenarians.**
cenarians; the *Recollection of our Lady of Bethlehem*; and
the College of S. *Peter Nolascus*.

The *Jesuites* have five, *viz.* S. *Paul*, S. *Martin*, the *No-* **Jesuites.**
viciate, or S. *Anthony*; the *Cercado*, or Inclosure, by the
Name of S. *James*, where they are Curates; and *Los Desamparados*, that is, the Forsaken, or *Our Lady of Sorrow*,
which is their profess'd House.

The *Benedictines* have that of *Our Lady of Mont-* **Benedictines.**
serrat.

The *Minims* have lately been in Possession of the Church **Minims.**
of *Our Lady of Succour*, which also bears the Name of
S. *Francis* of *Paula*, and a Chappel of *Our Lady of Victory*,
where the great Monastery was, which is call'd by the
Name of their *Patriarch*.

The *Brothers* of S. *John of God*, have the Direction of **S. John of**
the Hospital of S. *James*. **God.**

The *Bethlehemites* have two, that of the *Incurable*, and **Bethlehe-**
Our Lady of Mountcarmel, which is without the City. **mites.**
These Friers came lately from the Town of *Guatemala*, in
the Kingdom of *Mexico*, where the Venerable Brother
Peter

Peter *Joseph, de Betancourt* * founded them to serve the Poor. Pope *Innocent* XI. approved of the Institution, in the Year 1697. They have already Nine Monasteries in *Peru*. Those Friers, tho' to outward Appearance very simple, are reckoned refined Politicians, as may be judg'd by the Name of the Quintessence of *Carmelites* and *Jesuites*, given them by the People. They are Brothers. They choose for their Chaplain a Secular Priest, whom they keep in their House at a certain Allowance; but he has no Vote among them. They are clad like the *Capucins*, excepting that under their Beard they have a Bib, a quarter of a Yard long, ending in a Point. Their Founder, as those good Friers give out, had, during Eleven Years, the Company of our Saviour visibly carrying his Cross. The other Apparitions and Revelations they place to his Account, and which they publish by Word of Mouth, and by Pictures, are of the same Reputation.

Nuns. There are somewhat fewer Nuns at *Lima*, than Friers; there are only twelve Monasteries of them. 1. That of the *Incarnation* of Regular Canonesses of S. *Augustin*. 2. The *Conception* of the same Order. 3. The *Trinity* of the Order of S. *Bernard*. 4. S. *Joseph* of the Conception, more austere than the other, contains the Barefoot Nuns of the Order of S. *Augustin*. 5. S. *Clare*, founded by the Archbishop *Toribio*, preserves the Heart of its Founder, and contains above 300 *Franciscan* Nuns. 6. S. *Katharine* of *Siena*, of the Order of S. *Dominick*. 7. S. *Rose* of S. *Mary*, of the same Order. 8. That they call *del Prado*, or of the Meadow, of Recolet *Augustins*. 9. S. *Teresa*, of *Carmelites*. 10. S. *Rose* of *Viterbo*. 11. The *Trinitarians*. 12. The *JESUS-Mary* of Capuchins, erected in 1713, by four Nuns that came from *Spain*, by the way of *Buenos Ayres*, whom

---

* *Perhaps he was a Descendent of a French Gentleman named* Betancourt, *who having stole a young Woman, fled to the Island of* Madera, *where he first planted a Christian Colony.* F. du Tertre, *p.* 59. *says, He in the Year* 1642, *saw a* Franciscan *in that Island, who said he was of that Family.*

whom we mention'd before. In short, they reckon there are above 4000 Nuns, among which there are four or five Monasteries of very regular Religious Women.

We might here add a House founded by the Archbishop *Toribio*, for Women divorced. It is incredible to what an Excess that Abuse has been carry'd; there are People daily unmarry'd, with as much Ease as if Matrimony were nothing but a civil Contract, upon bare Complaints of Mis-understanding, Want of Health or Satisfaction, and what is still more amazing, they afterwards marry others. *This is all a gross Mistake for such Houses, in Spain and the Indies, are only to separate from Bed and Board, such as cannot live together in Peace.*

This Abuse was brought them from *Spain*, at the very Time of the Settling of this Colony. The Intercourse they had long had with the *Moors* had made it so common, that Cardinal *Ximenes* thought himself obliged to apply some Remedy to it; and because the Pretence of Spiritual Affinity very often authorized Divorces, the Council of *Toledo*, which he assembled in the Year 1497, ordain'd, that at Christenings Care should be taken to write down the Names of the Godfathers and Godmothers, that the Truth might be known.

The Penitent Women have also a Place of Retreat, which I do not think is very full, because of the little Scruple they make in that Country of Libertinism, and the little Care that is taken to curb it. They call them *las Amparadas de la Conception*, or the Protected of the Conception. *Penitent Women.*

It may seem that by the great Number of Monasteries and Religious Houses of both Sexes, we may imagine *Lima* to be a Place much addicted to Devotion; but that Outside is far from being made good by those who live in them; for most of the Friers lead such a licentious Life there, that even the Superiors and Provincials draw from the Monasteries considerable Sums of Money to defray the Expences of a worldly Life, and sometimes of such open Lewdness, that they make no Difficulty to own the Children that are got, and to keep about them those undeniable Proofs of their disorderly Life, to whom they often leave as an Inheritance the Habit they are clad in, which sometimes extends beyond one Generation: If I may believe what has been told me on the Spot.

The Nuns, except three or four Monasteries, have also but an Appearance of Regularity, which they only owe to the Inclosure; for instead of living in Community and Poverty according to their Vow, they live each apart at their own Cost, with a great Retinue of Black and Mulatta Women Slaves and Servants, whom they make subservient to the Gallantries they have at the Grates.

We cannot speak of the Lives of both Sexes without applying to them the Words of S. *Paul*, 1 *Cor.* vi. 15. *Shall I then take the Members of Christ, and make them the Members of an Harlot?*

By the Example of those People, who by their Example ought to edify the Laity, it is easy to guess at the prevailing Passion of that Country. Its Fruitfulness, the Plenty of all Things, and the sedate Tranquillity they perpetually enjoy there, do not a little contribute to the amorous Temper which reigns there. They are never sensible of any intemperate Air, which always preserves a just Mean, between the Cold of the Night and the Heat of the Day. The Clouds there generally cover the Sky to preserve that happy Climate from the Rays the Sun would dart down perpendicularly; and those Clouds never dissolve into Rain to obstruct taking the Air, or the Pleasures of Life; they only sometimes stoop down in Fogs, to cool the Surface of the Earth, so that they are always there sure what Weather it will be the next Day; and if the Pleasure of living continually in an Air of an equal Temper, were not interrupted by the frequent Earthquakes, I do not think there is a fitter Place to give us an Idea of the Terrestrial Paradise; for the Soil is also Fertile in all sorts of Fruits.

Various Fruits. Besides those which have been transported thither from *Europe*, as Pears, Apples, Figs, Grapes, Olives, &c. there are those of the *Caribbee* Islands, as *Ananas, Guayavas, Patatas,*

tatas, Bananas, Melons and Watermelons, besides others peculiar to *Peru*. The most valu'd of the last Sort are the *Chirimoyas*, resembling in small the *Ananas* and Pine Apples, being full of a white solid Substance, mix'd with Seeds as big as Kidney Beans; the Leaf is somewhat like that of the Mulberry Tree, and the Wood resembles that of the Hazle.

The *Granadillas* are a Sort of Pomgranates, full of black-Granadillas. ish Kernels, swimming in a Viscous Substance, of the Colour of the White of an Egg, very cooling, and of an agreeable Taste. The Leaves are somewhat like those of the Lime Tree, and the Imagination of the *Spaniards* forms in the Flowers all the Instruments of the Passion. Father *Feuillée*, who has drawn this Fruit, calls it *Granadilla Pomifera Tiliæ folio*.

Those they call *Higas de Tuna*, or *Tuna* Figs, are the Higas de Fruit of the Raquette, or Euphorbium, as big as a green Tuna. Walnut, cover'd with Points, almost as sharp as those of the outward Rind of the Chestnut; they are good and wholsome. The *Lucumas, Pacayas, Pepinos, Ciruelas*, Plums like *Jujubs*, are there very plentiful.

There is this Conveniency at *Lima*, that there is Fruit Odd Seasons. all the Year long, because as soon as they begin to fail in the Plain, they are ripe on the neighbouring Hills. This is also to be observ'd, that the Seasons should be so different in the same Latitude, that those which agree to the Southern Latitudes, should be there at the time of those of the Northern Latitude.

Several Persons have ask'd me, how that could come to pass, and why that Torrid Zone, which ancient Philosophers, and even such great Men as S. *Augustin* and S. *Thomas*, thought to be uninhabitable by reason of the excessive Heat, should be so in several Places, thro' intolerable Cold, tho' directly under the Sun.

It is not to be required of a Traveler to shew Reasons for Reason for the Phænonemons he speaks of; and I would have referr'd the same. the Readers who are not vers'd in Natural Philosophy, to Fa-

H h ther

ther *du Tertre*'s History of the *Caribbee* Islands; if the three Reasons he assigns for the Temperature of that Zone, could be apply'd to the Country I am speaking of; but there are two of them which do not suit it; for the Regular or Trade Winds do not prevail throughout all the Zone, and the Inlands of South *America* are not cool'd by the Neighbourhood of the Sea.

There is therefore no general Reason, but what is grounded on the Equality of Time, the Presence and the Absence of the Sun, and the Obliquity of his Rays for some Hours, at his Rising and Setting; but tho' it may prove much, it will not hold for *Lima*, if we compare the little Heat there is there, with that which is felt at *Bahia de todos os Santos*, which is almost under the same Parallel, and on the Sea Shore. It must therefore be added, that the Neighbourhood of the Mountains which cross *Peru*, contributes much towards tempering of the Air that is there breath'd.

But it is farther urged, why those Mountains are as cold as these in our Climates. To that I answer, that besides the general Reasons which may be assign'd, the Situation of the Mountains call'd *La Cordillera*, or the *Andes*, is another Cause; for they generally run North and South, whence it follows:

See Plate XX. 1. That if there are Rocks R, standing perpendicular like a Wall, it is evident that their Faces exposed to the East, or West, would not receive the Sun for above six Hours, even tho' they were in the Middle of a Plain; and if any Mountain happens to stand before them, they will receive much less, that is, less than half the Rays the Plain receives, and about only the fourth Part of the natural Day.

2. But to make a Supposition on which to ground a general Argument, we will allow the Inclination, or Bent of our Mountains an Angle of 45 Degrees, which may be look'd upon as an exact Mean between those which are steeper and those that have an easier Ascent. It will then appear, that those which are not blinded by other Mountains,

tains, as A C may be, muſt be lighted three Quarters of the Day; but we know, that from Sun-riſing till Nine of the Clock, the Obliquity of his Rays on the general Face, and the Oppoſition of an Air condens'd by the Cold of fifteen Hours Abſence, on which they muſt have an Effect to put it into Motion, render his Action but little ſenſible till he is got up to a certain Height; for according to ſome able Philoſophers, Cold conſiſts in a ceaſing from Motion.

3. If one Mountain is contiguous to another, it is evident that the ſame will be cover'd till the Sun has attain'd the Height of the Angle T D C, which the Horizon forms with the Line drawn from the Foot of one Mountain to the Top of the other; then the Sun will not operate on all the Face E D above ſix Hours; and tho' he operates a long time on the Top, it will be never the more heated, becauſe the Rays reflect upwards, as S A to N, where their Operation is interrupted by the continual Flux of the Air, whoſe violent Agitation in a ſtrait Line is oppoſite to the Heat, as Experience ſhews by the Wind, or if you pleaſe by a ſtrong Blaſt, cloſing the Lips, which cools the Hand that receives it.

In fine, when the Sun, being in the Zenith, violently heats the Plain, it only half heats the Mountains, as is plain to thoſe who underſtand a little of Geometry; for ſuppoſing the Rays of the Sun Parallel, the Surface E D receives no more than the Perpendicular E Y, equal to X D, which may be look'd upon as in the Plain, tho the Line E Y be much longer, but the Triangle being rectangular, and *Iſoſceles*, the Squares of thoſe Lines which expreſs like Surfaces, being to one another as 25 to 49, that is, almoſt as 1 is to 2, it will appear, that the Mountain receives half the Rays leſs than the Plain, which anſwers to a Quarter of the natural Day, as in the firſt Caſe; the Sun there will require half as much more Time to render the Earth capable of producing on the Mountain, than it will need on the Plain; therefore the Harveſt will be long after, and it is not to be wonder'd that this Difference ſhould extend to ſix Months.

I shall not regard the Objections that may be made, nor go about to apply this Discourse to Valleys and Mountains that lie East and West; it is not proper for me to say any more: I will proceed to another Remark, concerning the Vale of *Lima*.

Since the Earthquake in 1678, the Earth has not produced Corn as it did before, for which Reason they find it cheaper to have it brought from *Chili*, from whence enough is every Year exported to maintain 50 or 60000 Men, as I have elsewhere computed. The Mountain and the rest of the Country is sufficient to maintain the Inhabitants.

Flowers. As for Garden Flowers, I have not seen any peculiar to that Country, except the *Niorbos*, which somewhat resemble the Orange Flower; their Scent is not so strong, but more pleasant.

Carapullo Plant. I must not here omit the Singularities of some Plants I have heard Persons of Credit speak of. There is an Herb call'd *Carapullo*, which grows like a Tuft of Grass, and yields an Ear, the Decoction of which makes such as drink it delirious for some Days: The *Indians* make use of it to discover the natural Disposition of their Children. At the Time when it has its Operation, they place by them the Tools of all such Trades as they may follow; as by a Maiden a Spindle, Wool, Scissors, Cloth, Kitchen Furniture, &c. And by a Youth Accoutrements for a Horse, Awls, Hammers, &c. and that Tool they take most Fancy to in their Delirium, is a certain Indication of the Trade they are fittest for, as I was assured by a *French* Surgeon, who was an Eye Witness of this Rarity.

Paradise Flower. In the Plains of *Truxillo* there is a Sort of Tree, which bears 20 or 30 Flowers, all of them different, and of divers Colours, hanging together like a Bunch of Grapes; it is call'd *Flor del Paraiso*, or the Flower of Paradise.

About *Caxatambo* and *San Matheo*, a Village in the Territory of *Lima*, at the Foot of the Mountains, there are certain Shrubs bearing blue Blossoms, each of which as it changes

changes into Fruit, produces a Cross so exactly form'd, Cross Flowers. that it could not be better done by Art.

In the Province *de los Charcas*, on the Banks of the great River *Misque*, there grow large Trees, whose Leaf is like that of the Myrtle, and the Fruit is a Cluster of green Hearts, somewhat less than the Palm of the Hand, which being open'd there appear several little white Films, like the Leaves of a Book, and on each Leaf is a Heart, in the midst of which is a Cross, with three Nails at the Foot of it. I do not question, but that the *Spanish* Imagination forms some Part of these Representations.

In the same Province is the Plant call'd *Pito real*, which Pito Real being reduc'd to Powder, dissolves Iron and Steel: It is Plant. so call'd from the Name of a Bird, that uses it as a Purge, and is green and small like a Parrot, excepting that it has a Copple Crown and a long Beak. They say, that in the Kingdom of *Mexico*, to get some of this Herb, they stop the Entrance into the Nests of those Birds on the Trees with Iron Wire; and that the Bird breaks those Wires by means of the said Herb, whose Leaves it brings, which are found there. It is farther added, that Prisoners have made their Escape, getting off their Fetters with it. This looks somewhat suspicious.

There is also *Maguey*, from which they get Honey, Vi-Maguey. negar and Drink. The Stalks and Leaves are good to eat: They may also be wrought like Hemp; and from them they draw the Thread call'd *Pita*. The Wood of it serves to cover Houses; its Prickles, or Thorns, for Needles; and the *Indians* use the Fruit instead of Soap.

Salsaparilla, Quinquina, whose Tree is like the Almond-Tree; *Quesnoa* or *Quiuna*, a little white Seed, like that of Mustard, but not smooth, which is good against Falls, and a Distemper they call *Pasmos*, whose Fits are Convulsions: Dragons Blood, some Rhubarb, Tamarind, Camina Oil, and *Alamaaca*, are also to be found in *Peru*. The Balsam, which bears the Name, comes thither but in a small

Quantity;

Quantity; it is brought from *Mexico*, as I have said before.

Pico Infect. It remains to say something of a very troublesome little Insect, call'd *Pico*. It gets insensibly into the Feet, betwixt the Flesh and the Skin, where it feeds and grows as big as a Pea, and then gnaws the Part, if Care be not taken to get it out; and being full of little Eggs, like Nits, if it be broken in taking out, those Nits which scatter about the Sore, produce as many new Insects; but, to kill them, they apply Tobacco, or Tallow.

Customs and Manners of the Spaniards *of* Peru.

BEfore we leave *Peru*, it will be proper, in this Place, to say something of what I could observe of the Manners of the *Creolian Spaniards*, that is, those born in that Country. To begin with Religion, I must observe, that, like those in *Europe*, they value themselves upon being the best Christians of all Nations; they even pretend to distinguish betwixt themselves and us by that Qualification; so that among them it is a very usual Way of speaking, to say a Christian and a *French* Man to signify a *Spaniard* and a *French* Man: But, without diving into the Interior of either, they have nothing of the outward Practice of the Church Discipline, by which they may merit that Preeminence. The Abstinence from Flesh is among them much changed by the Use of that they call *Grossura*, that is, Offal Meat, which consists in Heads, Tongues, Entrails, Feet, and the extreme Parts of Beasts, which they eat on Fish-Days, not to mention the Use of what they call *Manteca*, being Hogs-Lard and Beef-Suet, which they use instead of Butter: (*Note,* (*tho the Author takes no Notice of it*) *that these Things are only permitted on* Saturdays, *but not in* Lent, *or on* Fridays, *or other Fasting Days.*) Excepting the Mass, it is not usual to assist at any other Divine Service. Those who are above three Leagues from the Parish Church and the Christian *Indians*, who are but a League distant, are

exempted

exempted from hearing of Mass on Days of Obligation. At *Lima* they dispense with themselves for going to the Parish Church, because there are few good Houses but what have Oratories, that is Chappels, where Mass is said, for the Conveniency of the Inhabitants, which cherishes their Sloth, and keeps them from the Parish Duty.

In short, if their particular Devotion be strictly exa-*Rosary Devo-*min'd, it seems to be all reduced to that of the Rosary. It *tion.* is said in all Towns and Villages twice or thrice a Week, at the Processions which are made in the Night, in private Families, or else every Person apart, at least every Evening, at the falling of the Night. Religious Men wear their Beads about their Necks, and the Laity under their Cloaths. The Confidence they repose in that pious Invention of S. *Dominick Guzman*, which they believe was brought down from Heaven, is so great, that they ground their Salvation upon it, and expect nothing less than Miracles from it, being amused with the fabulous Accounts daily given them, and by the Notion of the good Success every one applies to that Devotion in the Course of his Affairs. But, what will hardly be believ'd, I have often observ'd, that they also depend upon it for the Success of their amorous Intrigues.

Next to the Rosary follows the Devotion of Mount *Car-* Mount Car-*mel*, which is no less beneficial to the *Mercenarians*, than mel. the former is to the *Dominicans*.

That of the immaculate Conception is next; the *Fran-* Conception. *ciscans* and the *Jesuites* have gain'd it such Reputation, that they mention it at commencing all Actions, even the most indifferent. Praised be, say they, when a Sermon begins, at Grace, and at Candle-lighting, in every House, praised be the most Holy Sacrament of the Altar, and the Virgin *Mary*, our Lady, conceiv'd without Blemish or original Sin, from the first Instant of her natural Being. They add to the Litanies, *Absque labe concepta*, *Thou who art conceiv'd without Blemish*. In short, this Sentence is foisted in at all Times, when it can neither serve for the Instruction, nor

the

the Edification of the Faithful; and the Expressions in the Hymns they sing, in Honour of that Opinion, are so singular, that it will not be ungrateful to see some Staves of them here with the Notes.

In them may be observ'd an Application of the 6th Verse of the 18th *Psalm*, according to the Vulgate, *In sole posuit tabernaculum suum*, He placed his Tabernacle in the Sun; by which it appears, that the Author of that Hymn was not well vers'd in the Language of Holy Writ, which the *Spaniards* seldom learn; for if he had consulted the *Hebrew*, he would certainly have perceiv'd, that the Meaning of that Passage is, that God has placed the Throne of the Sun in the Heavens, *Soli posuit solium suum in eis*, He placed the Throne for the Sun in them, that is, in the Heavens, which does not suit with their Subject.

Ma-ri-a, todo es Ma-ri—a,   *Mary, all is Mary,*

Ma-ri-a, to-do es à vos: *Mary, all is yours:*

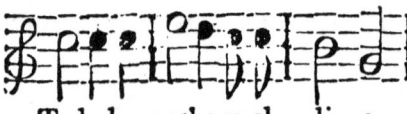

Toda la noche y el di—a   *All the Day and Night*

Se me vai en pensar en vos.   *I think on nothing but you.*

2.
Toda vos resplandeceis
Con soberano arrebol,
Y vuestra casa en el Sol
Dice David que teneis.

2.
You are all glittering
With Sovereign Light,
And David says
Your House is in the Sun.

3. Vuestro

3.	3.
Vueſtro calçado es la Luna,	*The Moon is your Footſtool,*
Vueſtra veſtidura el Sol,	*The Sun your Garment,*
Manto bordado de Eſtrellas,	*Your Veil embroider'd with Stars*
Por corona el miſmo Dios.	*God himſelf your Crown.*
4.	4.
Aunque le peſe al Demonio,	*Tho it fret the Devil,*
Y reviente Satanas,	*And Satan burſt for Rage,*
Alabemos à Maria	*Let us praiſe Mary*
Sin pecado original.	*Conceiv'd without original Sin.*
5.	5.
El Demonio eſta muy mal,	*The Devil is very ill,*
Y no tiene mejoria,	*And not likely to mend,*
Porque no puede eſtorbar	*Becauſe he cannot obſtruct*
La devocion de Maria.	*The Devotion to Mary.*

This Fragment of Poetry may alſo ſerve to ſhew the Taſte of the *Spaniſh* Nation, which is only fond of Metaphors and extravagant Compariſons, taken from the Sun, the Moon and the Stars, or from precious Stones, which often carries them into a Sort of Ridicule, and an out-of-the-way Flight, which they take for Sublime. Thus, in this Hymn, the Poet aſſigns the Virgin the Moon for her Footſtool, the Stars for the Embroidery of her Veil, at the ſame time that he places her Houſe in the Sun; which, of Conſequence, muſt include them all: But if he has wanted Judgment in his Poetical Enthuſiaſm, it may be ſaid he is much miſtaken, when he ſays that the Devil is burſting with Rage to ſee the Devotion to the Virgin in Repute in *Peru.* That Devotion is certainly too much intermix'd with Vices and Senſuality, to make us believe it can be very meritorious to them. I know they are very careful to ſay the Roſary often daily; but it may be ſaid they are therein true *Phariſees,* and think that Prayer conſiſts in much Talking, tho' meerly with the Lips, and with ſo little Attention,

tention, that they often mutter over their Beads, whilst they are talking of Things that are no way compatible with pious Exercises. Besides, they all live in a State of Presumption of their Salvation, grounded on the Protection of the Virgin and the Saints, which they believe they merit by some Brotherhood Exercises, in which the Friers have associated them, without making them sensible that the prime Devotion consists in the Reformation of the Heart, and the Practice of good Manners. It rather looks as if, by means of Revelations, and the ill-grounded Miracles they affect continually to tell them in the Pulpit at their Sermons, they would impose upon the amazing Facility with which those People believe Things most ridiculous and contrary to good Morality, which is certainly most pernicious to the Purity of Religion, and strictly prohibited by a Constitution of Pope *Leo* X. dated 1516. I could quote some Examples, if the Grosness of those Fictions would not render the Credit suspected. Thence it proceeds, that those People scarce know what it is to pray to God; but they only address themselves to the Virgin and the Saints. Thus the Accessory of Religion almost extinguishes the Principal.

Those People are not only credulous to excess, but also superstitious. They add to the Beads they wear about their Necks some *Habillas*, being a Sort of Sea Chesnuts, and another Sort of Fruit of the like Nature, resembling the Shape of a Pear, call'd *Chonta*, with Nutmegs, and other such Things, to preserve themselves against Witchcraft and infectious Air. The Ladies wear Amulets about their Necks, being Medals without any Impression, and a little Jeat Hand, a Quarter of an Inch long, or else made of Fig-tree Wood, and call'd *Higa*, the Fingers closed, but the Thumb standing out. The Notion they have of the Vertue of those Amulets, or Counter-Charms, is to preserve themselves from the Harm that might be done by such as admire their Beauty, which they call, as in *English*, an evil Eye. These Preservatives are made larger for Children.

dren. This Superstition is common among the Ladies and the meaner People; but there is another which is almost general, and of great Moment for avoiding the Pains of the other World, which is, to take care in this to provide a religious Habit, which they buy, to die and be bury'd in; being perfuaded, that when clad in a Livery so much respected here below, they shall, without any Difficulty, be admitted into Heaven, and cannot be drove into the utter Darkness, as the Friers give them to understand. This is not to be wonder'd at: It is known, that this Devotion, which began in *France*, in the 12th Century, being advantageous to the Communities, made the *Franciscans* advance, that *S. Francis once a Year regularly came down into Purgatory, and took out all those who had died in the Holy Habit of his Order*, with some other Follies which were condemn'd by the Council of *Basil* in the 15th Century, which those Friers in *Peru* have little regarded, as also in the *Portugueze* Colonies I have seen; for their Churches are still full of Pictures, representing this yearly Descent of *S. Francis* into Purgatory; the other Orders say no less of their Patriarch.

They have also form'd another Method, by abusing the Credulity of the Rich, to draw to themselves some Part of their Wealth; which is, to persuade them, that the nearer the Altar they are bury'd, the more they partake of the Benefit of the Prayers of the Faithful; and there are some Cullies foolish enough to believe them, and tacitly to flatter themselves, that God will make Exception of Persons. Of this Sort were two Persons some Days before I came away from *Lima*, who had each of them given 6000 Pieces of Eight, to be bury'd in the Charnel House of the *Augustins* of this City.

Non enim est acceptatio personarum apud Deum. *Rom.* 2.

Experience making it appear, that these Honours and Advantages are at an End with the Solemnity of the Funeral; notwithstanding the great Sums they have cost, Recourse is had to pious Legacies, under the Denomination of Foundations for Masses or other Prayers. There is no dying

Perſon to whom the Neceſſity of making ſome ſuch Foundation to avoid the Pains of the other Life, is not inculcated; the Merit of theſe Donations is ſo highly extoll'd, that all Men are for redeeming their Sins, to the Prejudice of what Charity and natural Inclination require, with reſpect to the neareſt Relations, Creditors and the Poor, through whoſe Hands we are to redeem them, according to the Scripture Rule; but in regard that the Good which is done to either, is ſoon. bury'd in Oblivion, Self-love, which ſtill leaves in the Heart a Deſire of Eternizing one's ſelf, when going to be cut off from the Number of Men, makes us preferr Foundations above other good Works, becauſe they are more proper for that End, and perhaps becauſe they are thought more Efficacious. In a word, whether it be through the Fear of Pains, which touches us moſt to the Quick, or for the Love of God and one's ſelf, the Cuſtom is become ſo univerſal, and has ſo much enrich'd the Monaſteries of *Lima*, and of ſome other Cities, within a Hundred Years, that the Laity have ſcarce any real Eſtates left; their Wealth is reduced to Moveables, and there are few that do not pay Rent to the Church, either for their Houſes or Farms. It would be for the Good of thoſe Colonies, to make ſuch a Regulation as the *Venetians* made in the Year 1605, which prohibits the Alienation of real Eſtates in Favour of the Church, or in Mortmain, without the Conſent of the Republick, in Imitation of thoſe of the Emperors *Valentinian, Charlemagne*, and *Charles* V. and of ſeveral Kings of *France* from S. *Lewis* down to *Henry* III. But the Court of *Rome* taking the Alarm, caus'd that Decree to be for ſome time ſuſpended, in a Country where it has leſs Power than in *Spain*; thus this Abuſe, in all Likelihood, will continue there; and in a ſhort Time the Laity will find themſelves under a greater Dependency on Communities for Temporals, than they are for Spirituals.

I will ſay nothing here of the Honour they pay to Images; conſidering the Care they take to adorn them in their Houses, and to burn Frankincense before them, I know not whether they might not be suspected of carrying that Worship very near to Idolatry. The Questers, a sort of People who never fail to make their Advantage of the Prepossession of the People, in order to draw Alms from them, carry Pictures along the Streets, on Foot and on Horseback, in great Frames, and with Glasses over them, which they give to be kiss'd for what they receive. It is true, that we see the best Things frequently misused in *Europe*, as well as in *America*, which obliged the Bishops of *France* to desire of the Council of *Trent* some Reformation as to that Article.

Either through Interest or Ignorance, the Clergy and the Friers take little Care to undeceive them, and to teach them to adore God in Spirit and Truth, to fear his Judgments, and not to lay any more Stress on the Protection of the Virgin and the Saints, than as they imitate their Vertues. On the contrary, if they make their Panegyricks, they extoll them without Discretion, never intermixing Points of Morality; so that those Sermons, which are the most frequent throughout the Year, become of no Use to them, and feed them in their usual Presumptions.

To conclude, tho' such Persons should with their Mouths preach up Christian Vertues, what Fruit could they produce whilst they give such ill Example? If it were upon Modesty and Meekness, they are impudent in the highest Degree; may I presume to say it, most of them are generally arm'd with a Dagger it is not to be thought that is to murder, but at least to oppose any that should oppose their Pleasures, or offend them. Should the Subject be Poverty, and the Contempt of Riches; the most Regular of them trade and have their Slaves of both Sexes; and several Churchmen appear in colour'd Cloaths adorn'd with Gold, under their usual Habit. Should it be Humility; they are insufferably Proud, a true Copy of the Pharisees, who would take Place every where, and be saluted in publick Places In short, not satisfy'd with the

low

low Bows made them, they offer their Sleeves to be kifs'd in the open Streets and in the Churches, whither they go on Purpose to disturb the Faithful, who are attentive to the Sacrifice, to have Homage done to their pretended Dignity; differing very much therein from the Sentiments of the first of the Western Monks, S. *Benedict*, who chose for his Religious Men the Habit of the Poor in his Time, and S. *Francis*, a ridiculous Habit, to render himself contemptible in the Eyes of Men. In short, it is well known that to prevent their meddling with worldly Affairs the King of *Spain* has been formerly obliged to make use of his Authority, and yet he has not prevail'd. Herrera, Anno 1551, writes thus: *The King charged* Don Lewis de Velasco, *the Viceroy, to take Care that the Prelates and Religious Men should keep within the Bounds of their own Employments, without interfering with those of others, as they had sometimes done, because that belong'd to the King and his Lieutenants.* To conclude, shall they preach up the Example of Continence? this is the general Vice, which scarce allows of any Exception among those whom Age has not disabled. Neither are they very reserv'd as to this Point, but excuse themselves with the Necessity of having a She-Friend to take Care of them, because the Monasteries allow them nothing but Diet; so that they are obliged to intrigue to keep in with them, dealing in Merchandize, and sometimes in Slight of Hand, which have often warn'd the *French* trading along the Coast to mistrust them as Sharpers. The Captain of the *Mary Anne*, in which I went thither, had severe Experience of it, one of them taking a Bag of 800 Pieces of Eight out of his Round-house.

This Dissipation is also the Reason why they scarce apply themselves to Study; out of the great Towns there are some, who can scarce read *Latin*, to say Mass. Nay, I knew a Professor of Divinity in a Monastery, who perform'd it very imperfectly. In short, it is manifest, that most of them only make themselves Friers in order to lead a more easy and more honourable Life. It is said, that
the

the King of *Spain* is sensible of this Evil, and will regulate the Number of Communities.

I owe this Testimony to Truth, that these Remarks do not concern the *Jesuites*, who Study, Preach, Catechize, even in Publick Places, with much Zeal; and I believe, that were it not for them, the Faithful would scarce be instructed in the Principal Articles of Faith.

I must also here honour the Probity and good Behaviour of the Bishops, who are not altogether to be charged with the Disorders of their Flock, who by ancient Custom are in a manner entituled to live a little more Licentious, especially the Friers, who are Masters, and own no other Ecclesiastical Jurisdiction, but that of their Superiors, pretending they only depend on them, and on the Pope, as Supreme. A Monstrous Independence, according to the ingenious Opinion of S. *Bernard*, as if a Finger were taken from the Hand, to affix it directly to the Head.

I have happen'd to compare the Friers to the *Pharisees*, whereas according to their Institute of Life, I should have set them in the same Rank with the *Essenians*; but instead of shewing that their Righteousness abounded more than that of those *Jews*, I should have exposed Vertues that would confound the pretended Perfection of some Christian Communities. *Eusebius, lib.* 8. *Præp. Evang.* speaking of the *Essenians*, says, *There are no Boys or raw Youths among them, because of the Unsettledness of that Age. They do not live in Cities, believing that as an infectious Air is hurtful to the Body, so the Conversation of the Multitude is to the Mind. No one of them makes Instruments of War; nor do they follow those Professions, which cause Men easily to fall into Wickedness. There is no Merchandizing, no Victualling, no Navigation known among them; there is no Slave among them, but being all Free, they serve one another; for Nature like a Mother, say they, brought forth all; wherefore, tho' not call'd so, we are all really Brothers.*

In short, I do not, by what I have said, pretend to exclude the worthy and learned People of *Peru* and *Chili*. I know

know there are such among all Conditions; there have been some of eminent Piety, whom the Church has admitted into the Catalogue of Saints. *Lima* has produced within its Territory S. *Rose* of *S. Mary* of the third Order of S. *Dominick*. The Bishop of that City *Toribius*, an *European*, sanctify'd himself there; and they there honour the Blessed *Francis Solano*, a Native of *Paraguay*. But after all, I differ very much from the Opinion of the Anthor of the Life of the Holy *Toribius*, who says, that *in all Likelihood* Peru *will afford Heaven more Saints, than it has given Silver to the Earth*. Vertue seems to me to be more common among the Laity, than among the Friers and the Clergy; I make no scruple to say so, it would be a false Nicety to spare Men who dishonour their Profession without Controul, under Pretence that they are consecrated to God by solemn Vows.

All Vices, says *Juvenal*, are the more criminal, by as much as he is the greater who is guilty of them.

This is what I have to object, as a Traveler, who observe what is done in the Countries where I happen to be, and who deduce as a Consequence from the Behaviour of such People, that they have little Religion in their Hearts, notwithstanding their Gravity and outward Affectation.

Creolians or Spaniards born in Peru.

If we next examine the Character and Inclinations of the Secular *Creolians*, we shall find among them, as among other Nations, a Mixture of Good and Evil. It is said, that the Inhabitants of *la Puna*, that is, the Mountain Country of *Peru*, are well enough to deal with, and that there are very worthy People among them, generous and ready to do a good Turn, especially if it can feed their Vanity, and shew the Greatness of their Souls, which they there call *Punto*, that is, Point of Honour, which most of them value themselves upon, as a Qualification that raises them above other Nations, and is a Proof of the Purity of the *Spanish* Blood, and of the Nobility all the Whites boast of. The most beggarly and meanest of the *Europeans* become Gentlemen as soon as they find themselves transplanted

among

among the *Indians*, Blacks, Mulattoes, *Meſtizo's*, and others of mixt Blood. That imaginary Nobility cauſes them to perform moſt of their good Actions. I found in *Chili*, that they practiſed much Hoſpitality, eſpecially abroad in the Country, where they entertain Strangers very generouſly, and keep them long enough in their Houſes without any Intereſt. Thus the little Merchants of *Biſcay*, and other *European Spaniards*, travel much, with ſmall Expence.

In the great Towns, and along the Coaſt, we now find that the *Creolians* are fallen off from thoſe good Qualities our firſt *French* Men had found among them, and which all Men applauded; perhaps the Natural Antipathy they have for our Nation, is increaſ'd by the ill Succeſs of the Trade they have drove with us. This Antipathy extends ſo far as to leſſen the Affection they ought to have for their King, becauſe he is a *Frenchman*. *Lima* was at firſt divided into two Parties; and ſo on the Mountains; and the Clergy and Friers impudently pray'd for his Competitor; but the *Biſcainers* ſcatter'd about the Country, and moſt of the *European Spaniards*, being inform'd of the Valour and Vertue of *Philip* V. always exerted their Fidelity to him; ſo that the *Creolians* being convinced of their ill-grounded Prejudice, began to have an Affection for the *Holy King*, for ſo they call him; and tho' there ſhould ſtill remain any obſtinate Spirits, they will become more cautious, ſeeing his Crown fix'd by the unanimous Conſent of all Nations. They are timorous and eaſy to be govern'd, tho' diſperſed and remote from their Superiors, and have a Thouſand Retreats of Deſarts and Plains to eſcape Puniſhment; and beſides, there is no Country where Juſtice is leſs ſevere; for ſcarce any Body is puniſh'd with Death. Nevertheleſs, they ſtand in awe of the King's Officers; four Troopers, who are no better than Meſſengers, coming from the Viceroy, make all Men quake at the Diſtance of 400 Leagues from him.

As for Wit in general, the *Creolians* of *Lima* do not want it, they have a Vivacity and Diſpoſition to Sciences; thoſe of the Mountains somewhat less; but both Sorts of them fancy they much exceed the *European Spaniards*, whom among themselves they call *Cavallos*, that is Horses, or Brutes; perhaps this is an Effect of the Antipathy there is between them, tho they are Subjects of the same Monarch. I believe one of the principal Reasons of that Aversion is, because they always see those Strangers in Possession of the Prime Places in the State, and driving the best of their Trade, which is the only Employment of the Whites, who scorn to apply themselves to Arts, for which they have no Relish.

In other Points, they are little addicted to War; the easy Tranquillity they live in, makes them apprehensive of disturbing their Repose; however they undergo the Fatigue of long Journeys by Land, with much Satisfaction; 4 or 500 Leagues traveling through Desarts, and over uncouth Mountains, does not fright them any more than the ill Fare they meet with by the Way; whence may be concluded, that they are good for the Country they live in.

In relation to Commerce, they are as Sharp and Understanding as the *Europeans*; but being dainty and slothful, and not vouchsafing to deal without there be considerable Profit, the *Biscainers*, and other *European Spaniards*, who are more Laborious, grow Rich sooner. The very Workmen, who live barely on the Labour of their Hands, are so indulgent to themselves, as not to spare taking the *Siesta*, that is, a Nap after Dinner; whence it follows, that losing the best Part of the Day, they do not half the Work they might, and by that Means make all Workmanship excessively dear.

Delicacy and Slothfulness seem to be peculiar to the Country, perhaps because it is too good; for it is observ'd, that those who have been bred to Labour in *Spain*, grow idle there in a short Time, like the *Creolians*. In short, Men are more Robust and Laborious in a poor Country than in a Fruitful. For this Reason *Cyrus* would never suffer the *Persians* to quit the uncouth Mountains and Barren Country they inhabited, to seek a better; alledging,

that

that the Manners of Men are relax'd and corrupted by the Goodness of the Place they live in. In short, the Strength is kept up by the Exercise of the Body; whereas Ease softens it, through too much Want of Action, and enervates it with Pleasures.

The *Creolians* are generally outwardly composed, and do not depart from that Gravity which is natural to them. They are sober as to Wine; but they eat greedily, and after an indecent Manner, sometimes all in the same Dish, commonly a Portion, like the Friers. At any considerable Entertainment, they set before the Guests several Plates of different Sorts of Food successively; and then each of them gives the same to his Servants, and to those that stand by, and are not at the Table, to the end, say they, that all may partake of the good Chear. When the *Creolians* came to eat Aboard our Ships, where they were serv'd after the *French* Fashion in great Dishes, placed according to Art and Symmetry, they boldly took them off to give to their Slaves, sometimes before they had been touch'd; but when the Captains durst not make them sensible of that Indecency, our Cooks, who were jealous of their own Labour, did not spare to let them understand that they discomposed the Beauty of the Entertainment. Not having the Use of Forks, they are obliged to wash after eating, which they all do in the same Bason, and with that general and disagreeable Washing-Water they do not stick to wash their Lips. The Meat they eat is season'd with *Axi*, or *Pimiento*, that sort of Spice we have before spoken of, which is so hot, that Strangers cannot possibly endure it; but that which makes it still worse, is a greasy Taste the Lard gives to all their Cookery. Besides, they have not the Art of roasting great Joints, because they do not turn them continually, as we do, which they admired the most of all our Dishes. They make two Meals, one at 10 in the Morning, the other at four in the Evening, which is instead of a Dinner at *Lima*, and a Collation at Midnight In other Places they eat as we do in *France*.

Herb of Paraguay.

See Plate XXIX.

During the Day, they make much Use of the Herb of *Paraguay*, which some call S. *Bartholomew*'s Herb, who they pretend came into those Provinces, where he made it wholsome and beneficial, whereas before it was venomous: Being only brought dry, and almost in Powder, I cannot describe it. Instead of drinking the Tincture, or Infusion, apart, as we drink Tea, they put the Herb into a Cup, or Bowl, made of a Calabash, or Gourd, tipp'd with Silver, which they call *Mate*; they add Sugar, and pour on it the hot Water, which they drink immediately, without giving it Time to infuse, because it turns as black as Ink. To avoid drinking the Herb which swims at the Top, they make use of a Silver Pipe, at the End whereof is a Bowl, full of little Holes; so that the Liquor suck'd in at the other End is clear from the Herb. They drink round with the same Pipe, pouring hot Water on the same Herb, as it is drank off. Instead of a Pipe, which they call *Bombilla*, some part the Herb with a Silver Separation, call'd *Apartador*, full of little Holes. The Reluctancy the *French* have shewn to drink after all Sorts of People, in a Country where many are pox'd, has occasion'd the inventing of the Use of little Glass-Pipes, which they begin to use at *Lima*. That Liquor, in my Opinion, is better than Tea; it has a Flavour of the Herb, which is agreeable enough; the People of the Country are so used to it, that even the Poorest use it once a Day, when they rise in the Morning.

Trade of Paraguay Herb.

The Trade for the Herb of *Paraguay* is carry'd on at *Santa Fe*, whither it is brought up the River of *Plate*, and in Carts. There are two Sorts of it; the one call'd *Yerba de Palos*; the other, which is finer, and of more Vertue, *Yerba de Camini*: This last is brought from the Lands belonging to the *Jesuites*. The great Consumption of it is between *La Paz* and *Cuzco*, where it is worth half as much more as the other, which is spent from *Potosi* to *La Paz*. There comes yearly from *Paraguay* into *Peru* above 50000 *Arrovas*, being 12000 Hundred Weight of both Sorts; whereof

whereof, at least, one Third is of the *Camini*, without reckoning 25000 *Arrovas*, of that of *Palos* for *Chili*. They pay for each Parcel, containing six or seven *Arrovas*, four Royals for the Duty call'd *Alcavala*, being a Rate upon all Goods sold; which, with the Charge of Carriage, being above 600 Leagues, double the first Price, which is about two Pieces of Eight; so that at *Potosi* it comes to about five Pieces of Eight the *Arrova*. The Carriage is commonly by Carts, which carry 150 *Arrovas* from *Santa Fe* to *Jujuy*, the last Town of the Province of *Tucuman*; and from thence to *Potosi*, which is 100 Leagues farther, it is carry'd on Mules.

I have elsewhere observ'd, that the Use of this Herb is necessary where there are Mines, and on the Mountains of *Peru*, where the Whites think the Use of Wine pernicious; they rather choose to drink Brandy, and leave the Wine to the *Indians* and Blacks, which they like very well.

If the *Spaniards* are sober as to Wine, they are not very reserv'd as to Continency. In Matters of Love they yield to no Nation: They freely sacrifice most of what they have to that Passion; and tho' covetous enough upon all other Occasions, they are generous beyond Measure to Women. To add the Pleasure of Liberty to the rest, they seldom marry in the Face of the Church; but, to use their own Way of Expression, they all generally marry behind the Church, that is, they are all engaged in a decent Sort of Concubinage, which among them is nothing scandalous; so far from it, that it is a Disgrace not to keep a Mistris, upon Condition she be true to them; but they are as apt to observe that Fidelity, as Wives do to their Husbands in *Europe*. It is even frequent enough to see marry'd Men forsake their Wives to adhere to *Mulatta's* and Blacks, which often occasions Disorders in Families. Thus the two ancient Ways of Marrying still subsist in that Country; that of keeping a Mistris is very answerable to that which was call'd by Use, and there is some Remainder of the other in the Ceremony of Marriage. The Bridegroom puts into the Bride's Hand 13 Pieces of Money, which she
then

then drops into the Curate's Hand; so in the Marriage *per Coemptionem*, the Bride and Bridegroom gave one another a Piece of Money, which is call'd *Convenire in manum*.

The Priests and Friers, as I have said before, make no Scruple of it; and the Publick is no farther scandalized, than as Jealousy concurrs, because they often keep their Mistrisses finer than others, by which the *Mulatta* Women are often known. Several Bishops, to put a Stop to that Abuse, every Year, at *Easter*, excommunicate all that are engaged to Concubines; but as the Evil is universal, and the Confessors are Parties concern'd, they are not severe in that Particular; whence it follows, that those People, who are otherwise easily frighted by the Church Thunderbolts, do not much fear these. The Friers evade those Strokes, on account that they, not being free, are not look'd upon as Concubinaries in the utmost Forms; and that, besides, they have not the Intention to be so. A pleasant Solution, the Invention whereof must doubtless be assign'd to some cunning Casuist, grounded on *Justinian's Code*, which declares Conventions invalid which are made among Persons that are not free, and on the wise Maxim expounded by those Casuists so much cry'd down in *France*, *That the Intention regulates the Quality of the Action*. In fine, this Custom is so settled, so commodious, and so generally receiv'd, that I question whether it can be ever abolish'd. The Laws of the Kingdom seem to authorize it; for Bastards inherit almost like the lawfully begotten, when they are own'd by the Father; and there is no Disgrace inherent to that Birth, as is among us, where the Crime is wrongfully imputed to the innocent Person, wherein we should perhaps be more favourable, if every Man were well acquainted with his Original.

Women.

Tho' the Women are not shut up like the *Spanish* Women in *Europe*, yet it is not usual for them to go abroad by Day; but about Night Fall they have Liberty to make their Visits, for the most part where it is not expected; for the modestest in open Day are the boldest at Nights, their Faces being then cover'd with their Veils, so that they cannot

A. Espagnole envelopée de Sa mantille ayant le visage a moitié Couuert
B. autre en Revos bordé de dentelles
C. Creole du Perou en habit de Voyage

not be known, they perform the Part which the Men do *Women.*
in *France.*

The Method they use at home, is to sit on Cushions a-
long the Wall, with their Legs a-cross on an *Estrado,* or
Part of the Room raised a Step above the rest, with a Carpet on it, after the *Turkish* Fashion. They spend almost
whole Days in this Manner, without altering their Posture, *See Plate*
even to eat; for they are serv'd apart, on little Chests, *XXIX.*
which they always have before them to put up the Work
they do: This makes them have a heavy Gate, without the
Grace of our *French* Women.

That which they call *Estrado,* as was hinted above, is,
as used in *Spain,* all one End or Side of a Visiting-Room,
rais'd six or seven Inches above the Floor, of the Breadth of
five or six Foot. The Men, on the contrary, sit on Chairs,
and only some very great Familiarity admits them to the
Estrado. In other respects, the Women there have as much
Liberty at home as in *France;* they there receive Company
with a very good Grace, and take Pleasure to entertain
their Guests with playing on the Harp, or the Guitarre, to
which they sing; and if they are desired to dance, they do
it with much Complaisance and Politeness.

Their Manner of Dancing is almost quite different from *Dancing.*
ours, where we value the Motion of the Arms, and sometimes that of the Head. In most of their Dances, their
Arms hang down, or else are wrapp'd up in a Cloak they
wear; so that nothing is seen but the Bending of the Body,
and the Activity of the Feet. They have many Figure
Dances, in which they lay by their Cloaks, or Mantles;
but the Graces they add are rather Actions than Gestures.

The Men dance almost after the same Manner, without
laying aside their long Swords, the Point whereof they
keep before them, that it may not hinder them in rising
or coupeeing, which is sometimes to such a Degree, that it
looks

Plate XXIX. *Page* 255. *Explain'd in* English.
A. *A Spanish Woman wrapp'd up in her Mantle, with her Face half cover'd*
B. *Another with a Veil laced about.*
C. *A Creolian, or Mongrel of* Peru, *in a Traveling Habit.*

256 *A Voyage to*

looks like kneeling. I could wish I had been skill'd in Chorography, to represent some of their Dances. I will, nevertheless, here insert the Tune of one of those that are common with them, as the Minuet is in *France*; they call it *Zapateo*, because, in Dancing, they alternatively strike with the Heel and the Toes, taking some Steps, and coupeeing, without moving far from one Place. By this Piece of Musick may be discern'd what a barren Taste they have in touching the Harp, the Guitarre, and the *Bandola*, which are almost the only Instruments used in that Country. The two last are of the Species of Guitarres, but the *Bandola* has a much sharper and louder Sound. It is to be observ'd, that the Bass is made in *France*, to the Humour of the Harp.

Zapateo, a Dance in Peru and Chili.

These

These agreeable Accomplishments, which *Spanish* Women have from their Education, are the more moving, because they are generally attended with a graceful Air: They are for the most part sprightly enough; their Complexion is good, but not lasting, by reason of their using so much Sublimate, which is contrary to what *Oexmelian* says in his History of the *Buccaniers*; Sublimate, says he, *is also form'd, or metamorphos'd, tho not used in* America, *because the Women there do not paint*: They have sparkling Eyes, their Discourse pleasant, approving of a free Gallantry, to which they answer wittily, and often with such a Turn as has a Taste of Libertinism, according to our Customs. Those Proposals, which a Lover would not dare to make in *France*, without incurring the Indignation of a modest Woman, are so far from scandalizing, that they are pleas'd with them, tho' they be, at the same time, far from consenting; being persuaded that it is the greatest Token of Love that can be shewn them, they return Thanks as for an Honour done them, instead of taking Offence as of an ill Opinion conceiv'd of their Vertue. By these simple and natural Ways we perceive the secret Pleasure and Satisfaction we receive when we find ourselves courted. This Effect of Self-love, which is the Source of reciprocal Affection, is afterwards the Occasion of Disorder, when Decency and Religion do not put a Stop to it; but, without regarding essential Duties, humane Prudence alone ought to suffice to hinder a Man of Sense from being taken in the Snares of the Coquets of that Country; for their obliging Behaviour is generally the Effect of their Avarice, rather than a Token of their Inclination. They are perfectly skill'd in the Art of imposing on the Frailty a Man shews for them, and engaging him in continual Expences, without Discretion; they seem to take a Pride in ruining many Lovers, as a Warrior does in having vanquish'd many Enemies. *And I found more bitter than Death, the Woman whose Heart is Snares and Nets, and her Hands as Bands; whoso pleaseth God, shall escape from her, but the Sinner shall be taken by her*, Eccles. vii. 26. That Misfortune is not the only Punishment of those who suffer themselves to be taken; they there often lose the inestimable Treasure of Health, which they seldom recover, not only because in those temperate Climates they make little Account of the Venereal Diseases, notwithstanding which they attain to the longest old Age, but also because the Scarcity of Physicians, who are only to be found in three or four great Cities, does not afford them the Opportunity of being cured. Some Women only patch up their Distempers with Sarzaparilla, Ptisans of Mallows, and other Herbs of the Country, and especially the Use of Cauteries, which are look'd upon as Specificks, and whereof both Sexes alike make Provision, which the Women so little endeavour to conceal, that, in their serious Visits, they enquire after their Issues, and dress them for one another; so that we may apply to them that Text of Scripture, *James* v. 2, 3. *Your Riches are corrupted, ---- your Gold and Silver is canker'd, and the Rust of them ---- shall eat your Flesh as it were Fire*, for they ruin themselves in debauching with the Women; and they themselves observe, that whether it is that God punishes them for those criminal Expences, or, as others think, that the Estates they have are unjustly usurp'd from the *Indians*, they are scarce ever seen to descend to the third Generation. What the Father rakes together with much Trouble, and often with much Injustice in the Administration of Governments, the Sons do not fail to squander; so that the Grandsons of the greatest Men are often the poorest. They are themselves so far convinced of this Truth, that it is become a Proverb in *Spain*, where they say, *No se logra mas que hazienda de las Indias*: It thrives no better than an *Indian* Estate.

Habit.

The Women, as I have said, are the principal Cause; Vanity and Sensuality render them insatiable as to Ornaments and good Feeding. Tho' the Make of their Habit be of itself plain enough, and not very susceptible of Changes in Fashions, they love to be richly dress'd, whatsoever

soever it costs, even in the most private Places: Even their very Smocks, and Fustian Wastecoats they wear over them, are full of Laces and their Prodigality extends to put it upon Socks and Sheets. The upper Petticoat they commonly wear, call'd *Faldellin*, is open before, and has three Rows of Lace, the Middlemost of Gold and Silver, extraordinary wide, sew'd on Silk Galoons, which terminate at the Edges. The Women, in the Days of K. *Henry* IV. also wore open Petticoats in *France*, which lapp'd over before: Their upper Wastecoat, which they call *Jubon*, is either of rich Cloth of Gold, or, in hot Weather, of fine Linnen, cover d with abundance of Lace, confusedly put on; the Sleeves are large, and have a Pouch hanging down to the Knees, like those of the *Minims*; they are sometimes open like long Engageants, almost like those that were also worn in the Days of King *Henry* IV. But in *Chili* they begin to put down the Pouch, and cut them more even, after the Manner of Boots. If they have a little Apron, it is made of two or three Strips of Silk flower'd with Gold or Silver, sew'd together with Laces. In the cold Countries they are always wrapp'd up in a Mantle, being no other than a mishapen Piece of Bays, one Third longer than it is broad, one Point whereof hangs upon their Heels. The best are of rich Stuffs, cover'd with four or five Rows of broad Lace, and extraordinary fine. In other respects, their formal Dress is the same as that of the *Spanish* Women in *Europe*, *viz.* the Black Taffety Veil, which covers them from the Head to the Feet. They use that they call *Mantilla* for an Undress, to appear the more modest; and it is a Sort of Cloak, or Mantle, round at the Bottom, of a dark Colour, edg'd with Black Taffety. Their Dress in the Black Taffety Veil, a wide upper Petticoat, of a Musk Colour, with little Flowers, under which is another close Coat of colour'd Silk, call'd *Pollera*. In this Dress they go to the Churches, walking gravely, their Faces so veil'd, that generally only one Eye is to be seen. By this Outside a Man would take them for Vestal Virgins, but

See Plate The XXIX.

would be commonly very much deceiv'd, like those Courtisans in *Terence*, Eun. 5. Sc. 4.

Quæ dum foris sunt nihil videtur mundius,
Nec magis compositum quidquam, nec magis elegans, &c.

Who whilst they are Abroad nothing appears more clean, nothing more composed, or more neat. They have no Ornament on the Head, their Hair hangs behind in Tresses; sometimes they tye Ribbons about their Head with Gold or Silver, which in *Peru* they call *Valaca*, in *Chili Hague*; when the Ribbon is broad, adorn'd with Lace, and goes twice about the Forehead, it is call'd *Vincha*. The Breasts and Shoulders are half naked, unless they wear a large Handkerchief, which hangs down behind to the Mid-Leg, and in *Peru* serves instead of a little Cloak, or Mantle call'd *Gregorillo*. They commit not any Offence against Modesty, when they shew their Breasts, which the *Spaniards* look upon with Indifference, but out of a ridiculous Extravagancy they are much in Love with little Feet, of which they take great Notice; and therefore they take extraordinary care to hide them, so that it is a Favour to shew them, which they do with Dexterity.

I do not speak of extraordinary Ornaments of Pearls and Jewels; there must be many Pendants, Bracelets, Necklaces and Rings, to reach the Height of the Fashion, which is much the same as the ancient Mode of *France*.

Mens Habit. As for the Men, they are now clad after the *French* Fashion, but for the most part in Silk Cloaths, with an extravagant Mixture of light Colours. Out of a sort of Vanity peculiar to their Nation, they will not own that they have borrow'd that Mode from us, tho' it has not been used among them any longer than since the Reign of King *Philip* V. They rather choose to call it a Warlike Habit.

Gown-Men. The Gown Men wear the *Golilla*, being a little Band, not hanging, but sticking out forward under the Chin, and

and a Sword as they do in *Spain*, excepting the Judges and Presidents.

The Traveling Habit in *Peru* is a Coat flash'd on both Sides under the Arms, and the Sleeves open above and below, with Button-Holes; it is call'd *Capotillo de dos faldas*.

The Dwellings of the *Spaniards* in *Peru*, are no way answerable to the Magnificence of their Garb. Without *Lima*, in which Place the Buildings are handsome enough, nothing is poorer than the Houses; they consist in only a Ground Floor, 14 or 15 Foot high. The Contrivance of the stateliest of them, is to have a Court at the Entrance, adorn'd with Porticos of Timber Work, the Length of the Building which is always single in *Chili*, because of the Largeness the Top would require; but on the Coast of *Peru*, they make them as deep as they please, because when they cannot have Lights from the Walls, they make them in the Roof, there being no Rain to apprehend. The first Room is a large Hall, about 19 Foot Broad, and between 30 and 40 in Length, which leads into two other Chambers one within another. The first is that where the *Estrado* is to receive Company, and the Bed in a Nook, in the Nature of an Alcove, spacious within, and whose chief Conveniency is, a false Door, to receive or dismiss Company, without being perceiv'd coming in, tho' upon Surprize. There are few of those Beds in the Houses, because the Servants lie on Sheep-Skins upon the Ground. *Houses.*

The Height and Largeness of the Rooms would nevertheless give them some Air of Grandeur, did they know how to make their Lights regularly; but they make so few Windows, that they have always a Dusk and Melancholy Air, and having no Use of Glass, they are letticed with Grates of turn'd Wood, which still lessens the Light. The Houshold Stuff does not make amends for the ill Contrivance of the Building, only the *Estrado* is cover'd with Carpets, and Velvet Cushions for the Women to sit on. The Chairs for the Men are cover'd with Leather, *Furniture.*

printed

printed in Half Relief. There are no Hangings, but abundance of scurvy Pictures made by the *Indians* of *Cuzco*. In fine, there are neither Boarded nor Stone Floors, which makes the Houses damp, especially in *Chili*, where it rains much in Winter.

The common Materials for private Buildings are those they call *Adobes*, that is, large Bricks, about two Foot long, one in breadth, and 4 Inches thick, in *Chili*, and somewhat smaller in *Peru*, because it never rains there; or else the Walls are of Clay ramm'd between two Planks, which they call *Tapias*. That manner of Building was used among the *Romans*, as may be seen in *Vitruvius*; it is not expensive, because the Soil is every where fit for making of those Bricks, and yet it lasts Ages, as appears by the Remains of Structures and Forts, built by the *Indians*, which have stood at least 200 Years. It is true, it is not so in regard to Rain, for they are obliged to cover them in Winter, on the North-side with Thatch, or Planks. Thus they preserve them in *Chili*. The publick Structures are for the most part made of burnt Bricks, and Stone. At *La Conception* they have a greenish sort of a soft Nature; at *Santiago* they have a Stone of a good Grain, dug half a League North-West from the City; at *Coquimbo* they have a white Stone as light as a Pumice Stone; at *Callao* and *Lima* they have a Stone of good Grain brought 12 Leagues by Land, full of Saltpetre, which makes it moulder, tho' otherwise very hard; the Mole of the Port made in 1694, is built with it. There are in the Mountains Quarries of the fine Lime-Stone, whereof *Plaister of Paris* is made; they only use it to make Soap, and to stop Earthen Vessels. All their Lime is made of Shells, whence it is that the same is only fit to whiten the Walls.

Architecture. As for their Taste in Architecture, it must be own'd that the Churches in *Lima* are well built, as to the Case only, which is well proportion'd, lined with Pilasters, adorn'd with Mouldings, and without carv'd Capitals, over which are beautiful Cornishes, and fine Vaults full center'd and contracted; but in the Decoration of the Altars all are confused, crowded and bad, so that a Man cannot but lament the immense Sums they spend on those gilt Disorders.

Of the INDIANS of PERU.

HAving spoken of the *Creolian Spaniards* of *Peru*, it will be proper here to say something of the Natives of the Country, distinguish'd by the Name of *Indians*, whose Customs are very distinct from those of *Chili*, of whom we discours'd before; what they have in common with them, is, that they are no less Drunkards and addicted to Women, and that they are as little covetous of Wealth; but they are quite different from them in relation to Bravery and Boldness; they are Fearful and Heartless, and in other respects Malicious, Dissemblers and Designing. They have a Genius for Arts, and are good at imitating what they see, but very poor at Invention.

The Christian Religion, which they have been oblig'd to embrace, has not yet taken deep Root in the Hearts of most of them, they retain a great Inclination towards their ancient Idolatry; some are often discover'd, who still adore the Deity of their Forefathers; I mean the Sun. However they are naturally docible and capable of receiving good Impressions as to Manners and Religion, if they had good Examples before their Eyes; but being ill instructed, and on the other hand seeing that those who teach them, by their Actions give the Lye to what their Mouths utter, they know not what to believe. In short, when they are forbid having to do with Women, and see the Curate has two or three, they must deduce this natural Consequence, that either he does not believe what he says, or that it is a matter of small Consequence to transgress the Law.

Besides, the Curate is to them, not a Pastor to take Care of, and endeavour to ease them; but a Tyrant, who goes Hand in Hand with the *Spanish* Governors, to squeeze and draw from them all he is able; who makes them work for him, without any Reward for their Pains; but instead of it, upon the least Disgust cudgels them severely. There are certain Days in the Week, on which the *Indians*, pursuant to an Ordinance of the King of *Spain*, are obliged to come to be catechized; if they happen to come somewhat late, the Curate's brotherly Correction is a good Thrashing bestow'd without Ceremony, even in the Church; so that to gain the Curate's Favour, every one of them brings his Present, either of *Maiz*, that is *Indian* Wheat, for his Mules, or of Fruit, Grain or Wood for his House.

If they are to bury the Dead, or administer the Sacraments, they have several Methods to enhance their Dues, as making of Stations, or certain Ceremonies, to which they affix a certain Price. They have even preserv'd the Remains of the ancient Idolatry; such is their Custom of carrying Meat and Drink to the Graves of the Dead; so that their Superstition has only changed its Aspect, by becoming a Ceremony advantageous to the Curates.

If the Friers go into the Country, a questing for their Monastery, they do it like the Strollers of an Army; they first take Possession of what is for their turn, and if the *Indian* Owner will not freely part with that extorted Alms, they change their Form of Intreaty into Reproaches, attended with Blows, to oblige the *Indian* to part with it.

The *Jesuites* in their Missions behave themselves more discreetly and dexterously; they have found the Art of gaining the Ascendant over the *Indians*, and by their obliging Behaviour, have the Method of Subjecting them so entirely, that they do what they will with them; and as they give a good Example, those People are fond of the Yoak, and many of them become Christians. Those Missioners would be really praise-worthy, were they not accused of labouring only for their own Advantage, as they have done near *La Paz*, among the *Yongos*, and the *Moxos*, among whom they convert some to the Faith, and make many Subjects to the Society; so that they permit no other *Spaniard* to be among them, as they have done in *Paraguay*; but their Reasons may be seen in the 8th Volume of the *Lettres edifiantes & curieuses*.

‘ As

'As it has been found by long Experience, that the Commerce of the *Spaniards* is very prejudicial to the *Indians*, either in regard that they treat them very severely, putting them to hard Labour, or that they scandalize them by their licentious and disorderly Life; a Decree has been obtain'd from his Catholick Majesty, forbidding all *Spaniards* to enter that Mission of the *Moxos*, or to have any Communication with the *Indians* it is composed of; so that, if through Necessity, or by Accident, any *Spaniard* comes into that Country, the Father Missioners, after having charitably received him, and exercised the Rights of Christian Hospitality, send him afterwards into the Countries belonging to the *Spaniards*. This is a specious Pretence; but the Example of *Paraguay* seems to discover another End; for it is known that the said Society have made themselves Masters of a great Kingdom, lying between *Brazil* and the River of *Plate*, where they have settled so good a Government, that the *Spaniards* have never been able to penetrate into it, tho' the Governors of *Buenos Ayres* have made several Attempts, by Order of the Court of *Spain*. In short, besides their good Discipline, they have got among them *Europeans* to make Arms, and all other Trades necessary in a Commonwealth, who have taught others of the Natives. They breed up the Youth as is done in *Europe*, teaching them Latin, Musick, Dancing, and other proper Exercises, as I have been told from good Hands. I do not descend to the Particulars of that Government, of which I can only speak by Hear-say, and must avoid deviating from my Subject.

The Curates are but one half of the Misfortune of the *Indians* of *Peru*, the Corregidores or Governors treat them in the harshest manner, as they have always done, notwithstanding the Prohibitions of the King of *Spain*. *Herrera*, An. 1551, says, *The King commanded, that no Viceroy, or other Minister should make use of the Service of Indians, without paying them their Wages.* The same Author again,

again, *Dec.* 4. *lib.* 4. *And that no Man passing through* Indian *Dwellings, or Towns, should receive Provisions from them, unless freely given, or paying the Value thereof.* Nevertheless they oblige the *Indians* to work for them, and serve them in the Trade they drive, without giving them any thing, not even a Subsistence; thus they cause prodigious Numbers of Mules to be brought from *Tucuman* and *Chili*, which they do so arrogate to themselves the Right of selling, that no Man dares procure them any other way, tho' they sell them at an excessive Rate to the *Indians* of their Precinct, whom they force to buy their own Labour. The Authority the King allows them, that they only may sell such *European* Commodities as the *Indians* have occasion for, within their own Jurisdiction, supplies them with another Means of being Vexatious; thus, when they have not ready Money, they get Goods of their Friends upon Trust, which are sold to them at three times their real Value; for this Reason, that in Case of Death, they run a Hazard of losing the Debt, as happens almost Daily in that Country. It is easy to judge how much they afterwards raise them upon the *Indians*; and because they are by Way of Lots, or Species, the poor *Indian* must take a Piece of Cloth, or such other Commodity as he has no Occasion for; for by fair or foul Means he must buy what is allotted him.

The Governors are not the only Persons that take upon them to pillage the *Indians*; the Merchants and other *Spaniards* who travel, boldly take from them, and generally without paying for it, whatsoever they have Occasion for, without the Owners daring to speak one Word, unless he will run the Hazard of being pay'd in Blows; this is an ancient Custom, which is never the less used for having been prohibited, as has been said above; so that in many Places, those People being worn out with so many Vexations, keep nothing in their Houses, not even to eat; they sow no more *Maiz*, or *Indian* Corn, than is requisite for their Family, and hide in some Caves the Quantity they know by Experience

perience they have occasion for throughout the Year. They divide it into 52 Parts, for every Week in the Year, and the Father and Mother, who alone know the Secret, go every Week to bring out a Week's Allowance. There is no doubt but these People, being drove to despair by the Hardness of the *Spanish* Domination, only wish for an Opportunity to shake it off *Do not imagine,* said the *Scythians* to *Alexander* the Great, *that those you conquer can love you; there is never any Affection between the Master and the Slave, the Right of making War ever continues in the midst of Peace.* Nay, from Time to Time they make some Attempts at *Cusco,* where they are the main Part of the City, but it being expresly forbidden them to carry Arms, without a particular Licence, and being besides nothing courageous, the *Spaniards* know how to appease them with Threats, and to amuse them with fair Promises. *Herrera,* to this Purpose, *Ann.* 1551. says thus, *It was ordain'd that no Indian should wear Arms, and that if any prime Man wore them, it should be with Leave; and this was understood of Sword and Dagger; because being much addicted to Drunkenness, many were kill'd and wounded, without any Check, to their own great Detriment.*

Besides, the *Spanish* Party is somewhat reinforced, by the great Number of Black Slaves they yearly have brought them from *Guinea* and *Angola,* by the way of *Portobelo* and *Panama,* where are the Factories of the Contractors. The Reason is, that not being permitted to keep the *Indians* as Slaves, they have less Regard for them than for the Blacks, who cost them much Money, and whose Number is the greatest Part of their Wealth and Grandeur. Those Blacks being sensible of the Affection of their Masters, imitate their Behaviour in respect of the *Indians,* and take upon them an Ascendant over them, which occasions an implacable Hatred betwixt the two Nations. The Laws of the Kingdom have also provided, that there should be no Alliances between them, for the Black Men and Women are expresly forbid having any Carnal Communication with the *Indian* Men and Women, upon Penalty to the Black Males to have their Genitals cut off, and the Females to be severely bastinado'd; thus the Black Slaves, who in other Colonies are Enemies to the Whites, here take Part with their Masters: However, they are not permitted to wear any Weapons; because they might make an ill Use thereof, as has been sometimes seen.

The implacable Hatred this barbarous Behaviour has drawn upon the *Spaniards* from the *Indians*, is the Reason why the hidden Treasures and the rich Mines, the Knowledge whereof they communicate to one another, remain unknown and useless to both of them; for the *Indians* use them not for themselves, being satisfy'd to live poorly by their Labour, and in extreme Misery. The *Spaniards* fancy they enchant them, and tell several Tales of surprizing Deaths befallen those who would have discover'd some of them; as that they had been on a sudden found dead and strangled, to of e been lost in Fogs, and taken away in Thunder and Lightning; but no great Account is to be made of the Wonders they tell, for in Point of Credulity they are meer Children. It is certain, that the *Indians* know several rich Mines which they will not discover, for fear of being made to work in them, and to the end the *Spaniards* may not make their Advantage of them. This has appear'd several times, but more particularly in the famous Mine of *Salcedo*, a quarter of a League from *Puno*, on the Mountain of *Hijacota*, where they cut the Massy Silver in a Body, with Chisels; for it was discover'd to him by an *Indian* Mistris, who was desperately in love with him. The Malice and the Avarice of the *Spaniards* have produced Accusations against *Salcedo*, which caus'd him to be condemn'd to Death, upon a false Suspicion of revolting, because he grew too great, which occasion'd Civil Wars, about 50 Years since, about inheriting his immense Treasures; but during those Debates, the Mine was so fill'd with Water, that it could never since be drain'd, which the *Spaniards* look upon as a Judgment

from

from Heaven. The King of *Spain* having been convinced of *Salcedo*'s Innocence, restored the Mine to his Son, with some Employments.

It is not to be thought strange, that the *Indians* should be so exact in keeping the Secret as to the Mines they know, since they are at the Trouble of fetching out the Ore, and have no Advantage by it. It must be own'd, that they alone are fit for that Work, where the Blacks cannot be employ'd, because they all die.

These are robust, and infinitely more hardy for Labour, than the *Spaniards*, who look upon Bodily Labour as scandalous to a White Man. To be a Man of a white Face, is a Dignity which exempts *Europeans* from working; but, on the other hand, they may, without any Disgrace, be Pedlars, and carry Packs in the Streets. The Author of *Bleau*'s Geography was mistaken, when he said, Vol. X. that the *Spaniards* in the Mines must make use of *African* Blacks, or other Slaves, from the *East-Indies*, which they carry thither. Nothing is more remote from Truth, than this Trade of Slaves from the *East-Indies*.

It is pretended, that the Use of the *Coca*, that Herb so famous in the Histories of *Peru*, adds much to the Strength of the *Indians*. Others affirm, that they use Charms; when, for Instance, the Mine of Ore is too hard, they throw upon it a Handful of that Herb chew'd, and immediately get out the said Ore with more Ease, and in a greater Quantity. Fishermen also put some of that Herb chew'd to their Hook when they can take no Fish, and they are said to have better Success thereupon. In short, they apply it to so many several Uses, most of them bad, that the *Spaniards* generally believe it has none of those Effects, but by vertue of a Compact the *Indians* have with the Devil. For this Reason, the Use of it is prohibited in the Northern Part of *Peru*; and in the South it is allow'd in regard to those who work in the Mines, and cannot subsist without it. Those pretended Charms, or perhaps, with more Reason, the Vertue of that Leaf, are the Cause why the

Coca Herb.

Inquisition punishes those who transgress against the Prohibition.

This Leaf is a little smoother, and less nervous, than that of the Pear-Tree; but in other respects very like it. Others compare it to that of the Strawberry, but much thinner; the Shrub that bears it, does not grow above four or five Foot high: The greatest Quantity of it grows 30 Leagues from *Cicacica*, among the *Yunnas*, on the Frontiers of the *Yunghos*: The Taste of it is so harsh, that it fleas the Tongues of such as are not used to it, occasions the spitting of a loathsome Froth, and makes the *Indians*, who chew it continually, stink abominably. It is said to supply the Want of Food, and that by the Help of it a Man may live several Days without eating, and not be sensibly weakned. Nevertheless, they are slothful and lazy at their Work, perhaps because that Herb, taking away their Stomach, they do not receive other Nourishment sufficient: It is thought to fasten the Teeth, and to ease their Distempers. Others say it is good for Sores. Be that as it will, it serves the *Indians* no otherwise than Tobacco does such as are used to chew it without swallowing.

Habit of Peru.

The Habit of the Natives of *Peru* differs little from that of the *Chilinians*, bating that the Women wear more than the others, a Piece of the Country Cloth of several lively Colours, which they sometimes fold on their Heads, and sometimes on their Shoulders, like an Amice; but along the Coast generally on their Arms, as the Canons carry their Aumusses. The Men, instead of the *Poncho* before described, have a Surtout, made like a Sack, the Sleeves whereof come not down to the Elbow: Those have been added but of late. Formerly there were only Holes to put the Arms through, as may be seen in a Figure of the ancient *Ingas*, which I drew after a Picture painted by the *Indians* of *Cusco*. This was the first of a Succession of 12 others as big as the Life, representing the 12 Emperors they had since *Manco Capac* reduced into one Kingdom all *Taguantin Suyu*, so *Peru* was call'd before the Conquest

See Plate XXXI.

planche. XXXI.   page. 247.

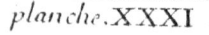

A. Incas, ou Roy du Perou. B. Coïa ou Reine. ces deux figures ont été dessinées
d'après un tableau fait par les indiens du Cusco.
C. indien du Perou D. indienne portant la mantilla E. leurs maisons —
F. moitié du plan de la Bicharra ou fourneau a bruler de l'herbe Icho G. profil de la Bicharra
H. differentes formes de vases trouvés dans les tombeaux des anciens indiens

by the *Spaniards*, and gave them Laws, establishing among them the Adoration of the Sun, whom he made his Father. Whereupon I will here make a Remark, which is, that the Tradition of the *Indians* does not agree with what *Garcilasso de la Vega* has writ. According to his History, and that of *Montalvo*, only eight *Ingas* ought to be reckon'd; and, according to the Tradition of the Pictures, they reckon twelve; whose Names I here subjoin, with those of their Wives.

Names of the Ingas.	Names of their Wives.
1. Manco Capac.	Mama Oella Vaco.
2. Sinchi Roca.	Cora.
3. Llogue Yupangui.	Anavarqui.
4. Maita Capac.	Yachi.
5. Capac Yupangui.	Clava.
6. Inga Roca.	Micay.
7. Yavarvac.	Chicia.
8. Viracocha Inga.	Runtu.
9. Pachacuti.	Anavarqui.
10. Inga Yupangui.	Chinipa Oello.
11. Tupac Inga Yupangui.	Mama Oello.
12. Guaina Capac.	Coia Pilico Vaco.

The Names of the *Ingas* according to the *Historians*.

1. Mango Capac.
2. Inga Roca.
3. Yaguarguaque.
4. Vira Cocha.
5. Pachacuti Inga Yupangui.
6. Topa Inga Yupangui.
7. Guaina Capac.
8. Guascar y Atahualpa.

The

Plate XXXI. Page 271. explain'd in *English*.
A. *An* Inga, *or Sovereign of* Peru.
B. *The* Coia, *or Queen: These two Figures were taken from a Picture drawn by the* Indians *of* Cusco.
C. *A Native of* Peru.
D. *An* Indian *Woman wearing a Mantle.*
E. *Their Houses.*
F. *Half the Plan of the* Bicharra, *or Furnace for burning the Plant call'd* Icho.
G. *The Profile of the same.*
H. *Several Sorts of Vessels found in the Tombs of the ancient* Indians.

See Plate XXXI.

The Ensign of Royalty was a Tossel, or Piece of Fringe, of red Wool, hanging on the Middle of their Forehead. On the Day of putting that on, there was great Rejoicing among them, as it is with us in *Europe* at the Coronation of Kings, and many Sacrifices were offer'd, an infinite Number of Vessels of Gold and Silver being then expos'd to publick View, with little Figures of Flowers, and several Creatures, especially of those Sheep of the Country before spoken of There are still some found in the *Huacas*, or Tombs, which now and then are accidentally discover'd.

Race of Ingas. Notwithstanding the Wars and the Destruction of the *Indians*, there is still a Family of the Race of the *Ingas* living at *Lima*, whose Chief, call'd *Ampuero*, is acknowledg'd by the King of *Spain* as a Descendent of the Emperors of *Peru:* As such, his Catholick Majesty gives him the Title of Cousin, and orders the Viceroy, at his entring into *Lima*, to pay him a Sort of publick Homage. *Ampuero* sits in a Balcony, under a Canopy, with his Wife; and the Viceroy, mounted on a Horse managed for that Ceremony, causes him to bow his Knees three times, as paying him Obeysance so often. Thus, at every Change of a Viceroy, they still, in Show, honour the Memory of the Sovereignty of that Emperor, whom they have unjustly deprived of his Dominions; and that of the Memory of the Death of *Atahualpa*, whom *Francis Pizarro* caused to be cruelly murder'd, as is well known. The *Indians* have not forgot him: The Love they bore their native Kings makes them still sigh for those Times, of which they know nothing, but what they have been told by their Ancestors. In most of the great Towns up the Country, they revive the Memory of that Death by a Sort of Tragedy they act in the Streets on the Day of the Nativity of the Virgin. They cloathe themselves after the ancient Manner, and still carry the Images of the Sun their Deity, of the Moon, and of the other Symbols of their Idolatry; as for instance, Caps in the Shape of the Heads of Eagles, or the Birds

they

they call *Condors*, or Garments of Feathers with Wings, so well fitted, that at a Distance they look like Birds. On those Days they drink much, and have in a manner all Sorts of Liberty. Being very dextrous at throwing Stones, either with their Hands, or Slings, Wo be to them that light of their Strokes on those Festivals, and during their Drunkenness; the *Spaniards*, so much dreaded among them, are not then safe: The Discreetest of them shut themselves up in their Houses, because the Conclusion of those Festivals is always fatal to some of them. Endeavours are constantly used to suppress those Festivals; and they have of late Years debarr'd them the Use of the Stage, on which they represented the Death of the *Inga*.

The Manner of the *Indians* Dwellings in the Mountain Country is singular. They build their Houses round, like a Cone, or rather like our Glass-Houses, with such a low Door, that there is no going in at it, without bowing quite down, for the more Warmth. Wood being very scarce there, they burn nothing but the Dung of Mules, Guanacos and Llamas, when their Flocks are sufficient to furnish them: It is easily gather'd, because those Creatures, by natural Instinct, go all to empty themselves in one Place, near that where they graze. For want of this Dung, they burn *Icho*, above spoken of; but that Plant not being lasting, they have Earthen Furnaces, call'd *Bicharras*, so contrived, that putting in some Handfuls now and then, they make several Pots boil at once, as may be seen by the Plans and Profile I here give, after the Manner of the Province of *Tarama*; where it appears, that when they would have only the third boil, they must fill the first and second with Water, to the end that the Flame, finding the nearest Passages stopp'd, may be forced to extend to the third Pot. *Indian Houses.*

See Fig. G. E. *in Plate* XXXI.

They generally use Earthen Ware, according to their ancient Custom, as appears by that which is found in the Tombs of the Ancients. I lighted on several of their Vessels, which may be seen in Plate XXXI. and among them one that is in the Collection of Rarities of Monsieur *de la Falaise*, *Earthen Ware.*

Falaise, Chaplain of *S. Malo*, who has gather'd all the Earthen and Silver Vessels, *Indian* Pictures, and other Curiosities he could, of that Country, where he has been. That Vessel consists of two Bottles join'd together, each about six Inches high, having a Hole of Communication at the Bottom: The one of them is open, and the other has on its Orifice a little Animal, like a Monkey, eating a Cod of some Sort; under which is a Hole, which makes a whistling when Water is pour'd out at the Mouth of the other Bottle, or when that within it is but shaken, because the Air, being press'd along the Surface of both Bottles, is forced out at that little Hole in a violent Manner; whence I have concluded, that it might be one of their Instruments, since the Smalness and Shape of that Vessel did not make it commodious, or large enough to contain Liquors to drink. That Animal may be a Sort of Monkey they call *Corachupa*, whose Tail is naked, the Teeth all of a Piece, without any Division, and two Skins covering its Stomach and Belly, like a Vest, into which they put their young when they run away. There are none of them at the Coast; they are common along the River *Mississipi*, where they are call'd Wild Rats.

Inhabitants. The Number of the Inhabitants of that great Empire of *Peru*, which Historians represent by Millions, is considerably diminish'd since the Conquest by the *Spaniards*: The Work at the Mines has contributed much towards it, especially those of *Guancavelica*, because, when they have been there a while, the Quicksilver does so penetrate into them, that most of them have a Quaking, and die stupid.

The Cruelties of the *Corregidores* and Curates have also obliged many to go and join the Neighbouring *Indian* Nations that are not conquer'd, not being any longer able to endure the Tyrannical Dominion of the *Spaniards*.

Removal

Removal to another Ship.

IT being my Duty to endeavour to return to *France* as soon as possible, because the Time of my Leave drew near to an End, I contrived to get aboard the Ship that was to sail first, which was the *Mary Anne* of *Marseilles*, before spoken of, commanded by Monsieur *Pisson*, of the State of *Savoy*, who was willing to take me aboard, and of whom I receiv'd so many Civilities, during the Voyage, that I can never sufficiently commend that gallant Man, as well as Monsieur *Roux*, the Merchant of the same Ship.

Departure from Callao.

I Embarqued on *Monday* the 9th of *October*, and the next Day, being the 10th, about Noon we sail'd for *La Conception*, to take in the necessary Provisions and Stores for our Voyage, because they are there better and cheaper than at *Callao*.

The 14th of the same Month one of our Sailors died of an Impostume in his Stomach, which choak'd him. The 15th, after having sail'd four Days without an Observation, we found ourselves One, and according to some, Two Degrees farther to the Southward, than our Reckoning, in about 17; whence we concluded, that it was the Effect of the Currents. The three Ships which came out after us, found much about the same Error.

The Reason of these Currents is easily conceiv'd, when a Man is inform'd, that along the Coast of *Peru* the Sea always sets to the Northward; that continual Flux the same Way cannot be supported but by an Eddy Motion; the Waters therefore out at Sea must needs flow to the South, to succeed those that run along the Coast to the North. *Zarate*, in his History of the Conquest of *Peru*, ascribes that Current Northward to the S. W. Winds, which prevail along the Coast all the Year; and he adds, *Why Currents out at Sea are contrary to those on the Coast.*

that the Waters of the North Sea paffing through the Streights of *Magellan* in a violent Manner, drive thofe of the Coaft of *Peru* to the Northward, following the Bearing of the fame. This laft Argument, form'd at a Time when it had not been yet difcover'd that there was a larger Paffage beyond *Tierra del Fuego*, might have had fome Refemblance of Truth, if the fame Current had been obferv'd along the South Part of *Chili*; but Time, which difcovers all Things, has fhewn, that inftead of the North Sea's running into the South Sea, there is Reafon to believe that the South Sea runs into the North Sea, fince at Cape *Horn* the Currents generally fet Eaft, which feveral Ships have evidently perceiv'd, not only by their Reck'ning and by the Charts, on which there is no relying, but upon Sight of Land, according to the beft Journals.

Tokens of being near Land.

The common Winds, which prevail from E.S.E. to S.E. attended us to 37 Degrees of Latitude, blowing frefh, and obliged us to run upon a Stretch 200 Leagues out to Sea, and then they fell to South, S.S.W. and W.S.W. Making towards the Land in that Latitude, we perceiv'd an Alteration in the Waters, being ftill above 60 Leagues out at Sea. The Obfervation is generally made in thofe Parts, even at 80 Leagues Diftance from the Land.

The Regularity of the Winds at E.S.E. and S.E. and the Breezes at S.W. along the Coaft of *Peru*, made the Navigation fo tedious, before the Method was found of running out to Sea, that Ships were fix or feven Months failing from *Lima* to *La Conception*, becaufe they only advanced by the Help of fome fmall Northern Blafts and the Land-Breezes, during the Night, and fome Part of the Morning. This fhews, that the Want of underftanding Natural Philofophy among Sailors, is a greater Evil than is imagined; for, in fhort, I fancy that this Difcovery, which is owing only to Chance, may be made by downright Reafoning.

Why the Winds are oppofite beyond the Torrid Zone.

The continual Flux of Air being from the Eaft in the Torrid Zone at Sea, and not on the Land, where thofe Winds are not regular, muft be made good by another Air coming

coming also from the Sea; consequently, beyond the Torrid Zone, the Flux of the Air must be quite contrary: Therefore, about the Tropicks the Winds must be much upon the West and South, as we draw near the Land, which lies almost North and South from the Streights of *Magellan* to *Arica*, in about 18 Degrees of South Latitude.

The Winds blowing always from the East in the great Ocean, along the Torrid Zone, is a Consequence of the daily Motion of the Earth from West to East, because that Zone containing the greatest Circles of the Sphere, is hurry'd away with more Rapidity, than the others which are nearer the Poles; and the Land having a grosser Bulk, it is also swifter than the Atmosphere of the Air which encompasses it: We must therefore consider the Resistance, as if the Air flow'd on an immoveable Body; and this Resistance the Wind makes on the Sea, and not on the Land, because the Inequality of the Surface, mix'd with Cavities shut up between Mountains, carries off the lower Part which we breathe. *Why the Wind is always the same in the Torrid Zone.*

Why those Winds are regular at Sea, and not on the Land.

Experience proves all the Circumstances of this Argument, because, as the *South-Sea* is the vastest, so there those Winds are most regular. In running from the Coast of *Peru* to *China*, the Winds are always East. In the *Indian* Sea they are the same, having on each Side opposite Winds, that is West Winds inclining more or less to the North or South, according as the Disposition of the Lands drives them back, and according to the Season; a Particularity, which it is needless to relate in this Place.

In short, it is also evident, that between the opposite Winds there must be Calms and Irregularities, occasion'd by the Eddies of the Air, which jostle one another, which we also had Experience of in 30 Degrees of South Latitude.

After a short Calm, we made Land at the Point of *Lavapie* precisely, and exactly according to my Reck'ning, making use of the Manuscript Chart I have spoken of without regarding its Longitude, but only the Difference of the Meridian of *Lima*, transporting in like manner all the Coast to the Westward, according to the Observation of *Don Pedro Peralta*, one Degree 45 Minutes more to the West, than it was laid down in *la Connoissance des Temps*, at *Paris*, in 1712. The Sieur *Alexander*, a *Frenchman*, living at *Lima*, who has taken Observations apart and with *Peralta*, by the Eclipses of *Jupiter*'s Satellites, placed it still 30 Minutes more to the Westward, that is, it is 80 Degrees 15 Minutes, or 5 Hours 21 Minutes Difference from the Meridian of *Paris*, according to Monsieur *Cassini*'s Tables; but Father *Feüillee*, upon an Observation taken by the Sieur *Alexander Durand*, places it in 79 Degrees, 9 Minutes, and 30 Seconds.

Errors of Charts.

Those who had made use of the printed Charts of *Peter Goos*, *Van Keulen*, and *Edmund Halley*, counted themselves 70, 80, and even above 110 Leagues within the Land, * according to the last, which are the worst of them for the *South Sea*, tho' the newest and corrected on the Coast of *Brasil* by Astronomical Observations. All the *French* Ships which return from *Callao* to *La Conception*, find the same Errors; whence it must be concluded, that it is about five Degrees more to the Eastward than *Lima*, and consequently I judged that it must within a very small matter be 75 Degrees 15 Minutes, or 5 Hours 1 Minute of Western Difference from the Meridian of *Paris*, which amounts to the 303 Degrees 51 Minutes from *Teneriff*. This Computation is also confirm'd by the Position of the Coast, very well known in many Places, which would be needless and very tedious to particularize; but in short, I found it rectify'd by the Obser-

---

* *This Author, for Reasons unknown, seeks all Occasions to cavil at the Performance of Mr.* Halley, *in his Chart of the Variations. He might know that that Chart pretends to describe the* South Sea *no otherwise than by borrowing from former Maps, he having no Experience there, as himself acknowledges. But if M.* Frezier's *Sailors could be mistaken a Degree or two in Latitude, in five Days Sailing, as he owns, p. 275, what hinders but in this five Weeks Voyage, they might err three times as much in Longitude. A farther Answer to this, and some other such like Exceptions, shall follow at the End of the Book.*

Observation of Father *Feuillée*, who places *La Conception* in 75 Degrees 32 Minutes.

The Day after we had made Land, being the 13th of November, 1713, we anchor'd at *Irequin*, in the Bay of *La Conception*, where we found 3 *French* Ships, the *S. John Baptist*, the *Francis*, and the *Peter*, laden with Goods, and commanded by *S. Malo* Men. Fifteen Days after our Arrival, we careen'd at *Talcaguana*, upon a *Spanish* Ship. Monday the 25th of *November*, the *S. Michael*, a *Spanish* Ship, which came from *Callao* to load Corn, brought us the News of the Peace concluded between all the crown'd Heads in *Europe*, except the Emperor, which was like to be in a few Days. That Advice was confirm'd by *le Beger*, who arrived some Days after from the same Port. *Arrival at La Conception.*

The 8th of *December*, being the Feast of the *Conception*, we saw it solemnized, as being the Patronage of the City, by an Assembly of Horsemen, composing 4 Troops of Pikemen a Horseback, and one of Foot, who by the ill Condition of their old Muskets with Rests, and some Firelocks they had, shew'd the Scarcity of Arms there is in the Country. *Feast of the Conception.*

I will not here speak of the Ceremony of the Reception of a new Ensign; there was nothing in it remarkable, besides the manner how the Horsemen made their Horses trip it gently along, and the pleasant Trappings of his Horse, that cover'd him down to the Ground with Ribbons of all Sorts of Colours; to complete that State, he was preceded by two Pair of Wooden Kettle-Drums, and two Kettle-Drummers in Liveries, with naked Legs.

The next Day the President set forth an Order for all the *French* to depart the Kingdom, and be obliged to embarque within two Days, with a Prohibition to allow them Provisions or Lodgings in the Town, or hire them Horses, under the Penalty of 500 Pieces of Eight; but those Prohibitions were still more strict, in regard of 7 Ships which had been fitted out at *Marseilles* by the *Genoeze*, and were *Order to dismiss all the French.*

to come thither to trade, as was mention'd in the King's Order.

Nevertheless, after this Publication, there arrived in *December* and *January*, 7 *French* Ships, almost all of them commanded by Men of *S. Malo*. The first was the *Martial* of 50 Guns; the *Chancelor*, the *Mary Anne*, the *Flyboat* under the Direction of the *Chancelor*, the *Well-beloved*, which had been detain'd at *Buenos Ayres*, with the Captain and the Supercargo; but the former having found Means to make his Escape, came by Land to his Ship at *La Conception*. The *Flying-Fish*, after having stay'd 8 Days in the Road, went away to *Valparaiso*, where he was refused the Port, so that he was obliged to proceed to *Quintero*, to join the *Assumption*, which was under the same Circumstances.

Besides those Ships arrived from *Europe*, several others of those that were upon the Coast came together; the *Holy Ghost*, and the *Prince of Asturias* arrived from *Callao*; the *Margaret* from *Pisco*; the *S. Barbara* Tartane, from *Valparaiso*; and the *Concord* from the same Place, bringing their Plate to be sent to *France*. So that there assembled at *La Conception* 15 Sail of *French*, great and small, and about 2600 Men.

Tho' the *Corregidor*, or Governor, a mortal Enemy to the Nation, sought all means to do Harm to the *French*, yet he could not have the Orders publish'd against the *French* put in Execution, either because he was hindred by his own Interest, endeavouring to extort some Contributions from them, or because that Multitude imposed a little on him; or lastly, because the Inhabitants privately dissuaded him, that they might make the better Market of their Provisions. He was satisfy'd with offering all the Affronts he could to the Officers and Ships Crews, as hamstringing their Horses, when they went out of Town to take the Air; imprisoning them upon the least Pretence of Misbehaviour, and talking to them in publick in the vilest Language, and most provoking Expressions. That wicked

Man,

Man, who was a small Merchant disguized, was always boasting, that he had hang'd up a *Frenchman* by the Heels, when he was only Lieutenant-General, and impudently added in the Street, that he should not die with Satisfaction till he had hang'd up another by those Parts which Modesty does not allow to name. Chance, which had furnish'd his wicked Inclination with an Opportunity to put to that Shame, upon the slight Pretence of an Insult, the Nephew of a Captain of a Ship belonging to the *East-India* Company, who happen'd to be in the Road, in the Year 1712, presented him another to execute his base Design in Part.

The Armourer of the Ship call'd the *Holy Ghost*, quarreling with a *Spaniard*, ran him through, and kill'd him; he immediately clapp'd him in Gaol, and condemn'd him to Death; whatsoever Offers were made, he would not be mollify'd, nor brought to abate of that extraordinary Severity, in a Country where the most heinous of Crimes are not punish'd after that Manner; but we being upon the Point of Sailing, *Grout*, the Captain of the Ship, left that Man exposed to the Malice of the *Corregidor*, either through Caution or Timorousness, whereas he might have demanded him to have him punish'd in *France*. Be that as it will, we were afterwards inform'd, that he had been rescued by disguized Friers, who for Money forced the Guards.

The same Day, being the 17th of *February*, the *Cæsar* of *Marseilles* arriv'd from *France*, to trade along the Coast.

In fine, after having lain there 3 Months, we sail'd on the 19th of *February* on our Return for *France*, in Company with the *Shepherd*, the *Prince of Asturias*, and the *Holy Ghost*, which was admitted as Commadore, designing to put in together into *Bahia de todos os Santos*, in *Brasil*.

PART

Part III.

Containing the Return from the South-Sea *into* France.

Departure from La Conception.

E sail'd four Ships together, on the 19th of *February*, with a fresh Gale at S. W. and S. S. W. which carry'd us into 39 Degrees Latitude, and 80 Leagues out to Sea, where we found the Wind at W. and N. W. blowing fresh, and the Weather foggy, after which much Wind. We not being so good Sailors as our Comrades, crowding Sail to keep up with them, split our Main-yard in the middle.

The 9th of *March*, in 57 Degrees Latitude, and 74 Degrees 30 Minutes Longitude, we made a Signal of Distress, and they lay by for us. We immediately hoisted up a small Top-sail, instead of the Main-sail, to make the others lose as little time as possible. The next Day the Yard was mended and hoisted up in its Place.

The same crowding Sail to keep up with them, made us the next Day lose a great Stay-sail.

Our Comrades seeing us out of order on account of our Main-sail, conspired to leave us; little regarding the Parole of Honour they had given to convoy us to *France*, tho' before satisfy'd that we were not so good Sailors as they, and knowing that on that account we had waited for them above a Month. In short, we were apprehensive

of

of meeting with Pirates, who were said to be on the Coast of *Brasil*, where Ships in their Return generally put in, and among the rest one of 300 Men, that had been fitted out at *Jamaica* for the *South Sea*; not to take Notice here of some Obligations the chief Men among them ow'd Monsieur *Pisson*; all these Considerations did not prevail with them, whose original Unworthiness got the upper Hand. On the 12th of *March* they made the best of their way, and got clear of us, by help of the Fog, so that by Five in the Evening we had lost Sight of them. It avail'd us little to hang out Lights at Night; they answer'd us not, and to as little Purpose we fired some Cannon the next Morning at Break of Day.

We were not much concern'd to lose the Company of Ships of S. *Malo*, on which there is so little relying, that it is become a Proverb as such, even among the People of the same Province; but we had reason to be concern'd for having follow'd them in the most foolish Navigation imaginable, which had brought us into 58 Degrees 40 Minutes Latitude, when we might pass with all Safety at least 40 Leagues more Northward, and have shortned our Voyage by six Days, without running so far into those hard Climates, where much must be endured, and Dangers unforeseen may be met with.

In short, whilst we were taken up, looking out for them in the Fog, we discover'd, about 3 Quarters of a League West from us, a Shoal of Ice, which might be at least 200 Foot high above the Water, and above 3 Cables long. It was at first Sight taken for an unknown Island, but the Weather clearing up a little, it perfectly appear'd to be Ice, whose blewish Colour in some Parts look'd like Smoak; the small Pieces of Ice we immediately saw floating on both sides of the Ship, left us no farther room to doubt. *Unexpected Ice on March 13, 1714. in 58 Degrees 30 Minutes Latitude, and 68 Degrees 22 Minutes Longitude W.*

We were becalm'd in a very rolling Sea, and scarce had a small Gale at S. W. made us advance 2 Leagues N. E. that is, E. N. E. as to the Globe, before we spy'd at E. and by N. about a League and a Quarter from us, another Float *Another Float of Ice.*

of Ice, much higher than the former, which look'd like a Coaſt four or five Leagues long; the End whereof we could not well ſee, by reaſon of the Fog. Then frighted, with good Reaſon, at ſo unexpected a Danger, we lamented the fair N. W. Winds we had loſt, to follow the ridiculous Navigation of the Faithleſs S. *Malo* Men. The Wind luckily freſhning at Weſt, permitted us to ſtand to the Northward, and in leſs than an Hour we ſaw no more Pieces of Ice.

Tho' thoſe Parts have been frequented for 14 Years paſt, at all Times of the Year, very few Ships have met with Ice, ſo that it was not apprehended. Only the *Aſſumption*, commanded by *Poree*, in 1708, ſaw a vaſt Float, like a Coaſt. Our Comrade, who, lying near the Wind, had got to E. N. E. had no View of thoſe we ſaw, but they affirm'd they had met with a large Piece in 54 Degrees and 3-qrs. This Accident may be a Warning to ſuch as attempt to paſs Cape *Horn* in Winter, as we did in the S. *Joſeph*, becauſe the Length of the Nights, and the Darkneſs of the Days, do not afford Opportunity of avoiding them eaſily. Perhaps the *Autumn* is the moſt dangerous Seaſon, becauſe then the Ice breaks and ſeparates by means of the little Heat there has been in the Summer; however, being extremely thick, it does not thaw till the next Summer, for that Height which appears above the Water, is only the third part of the true Thickneſs, the reſt being below.

Terra Auſtralis Chimerical. If it be true, as many pretend, that the Ice in the Sea is only form'd of the freſh Water, which runs down from the Land, it muſt be concluded that there is Land towards the South Pole; but it is not true that there are any more to the Northward than 63 Degrees of Latitude for the Extent of above 200 Leagues, from 55 of Longitude to 80; for that Space has been run over by ſeveral Ships, which the S. W. and S. S. W. Winds have obliged to ſtand far to the Southward, to double the End of the Lands. Thus thoſe Southern Lands, or *Terra Auſtralis* generally laid down in the old Charts, are meer Chimeras, which have been juſtly left out of the new Charts.

But tho' thofe falfe Lands have been put out, *Brouvers* Streight has been again put in, which is no lefs imaginary than *Terra Auftralis*; for all the Ships which have pafs'd to the Eaftward of *Staten Landt*, have found no other Land to the Eaftward, either in fight of Land, or out at Sea, which is the way that almoft all the Ships returning from the *South-Sea* pafs. We ourfelves doubtlefs pafs'd through thofe Parts. *De Fer's America* 1700.

In fine, they have not yet corrected the Errors in the Lands that are known, which are very ill laid down, both as to Longitude and Latitude. There we fee Cape *Horn* in 57 Degrees and half and 58 Degrees Latitude, and above 20 Leagues, and even 140 Leagues diftant from Streight *le Maire*, tho' in Reality it is only in 55 Degrees 45 Minutes, and 40 or 50 Leagues at moft from Streight *le Maire*. I fay nothing here of the Longitude, which is not pofitively known, but which may be pretty near afcertain'd by that of *La Conception*, whereof we have fpoken, according to the greateft Conformity between the Computations, at 310, or 311 Degrees from the Meridian of *Teneriff*, inftead of 303, or 304, as laid down in the Charts, which is at leaft 6 Degrees Difference. Thence alfo proceeds the Falfity of the laying down of the Coaft, from that Cape to Cape *Pillars*, which lie S. E. by E. and N. W. by Weft, inftead of S. E. by S. and N. W. by N. as they are laid down; and near Cape *Horn* it has a little more of the Weft, as has been obferv'd by thofe who have feen a great Part of the Coaft, which moft Charts mark as unknown, with Points; but at prefent, tho' we are not perfectly acquainted as to the Particulars, we at leaft know the main bearing. *Error in Sea Charts.* *Longitude of Cape Horn.*

All thefe Confiderations have mov'd me to gather Memoirs for drawing of the Chart I here infert, in which may be feen two new Difcoveries. The one is a Paffage into *Tierra del Fuego*, through which Chance carry'd the Tartane *S. Barbara*, commanded by *Marcanil*, out of the Streights of *Magallon* into the *South-Sea*, on the 15th of *May*, 1713. *See Plate XXXII.*

About

A new Channel in Terra del Fuego, discovered, Ann. 1713.

About Six in the Morning they sail'd from *Elizabeth* Bay, steering S. W. and S. W. by S. they took the common Channel for that of the River *Massacre*, and were standing to S. W. on an Island, which they took for the *Dauphin's*, assisted by the Currents which favour'd them, and a good Gale at N. E. they ran along that Island, and an Hour after they had pass'd it, they found themselves in a large Channel, where on the South-side they saw no other Land, but a Number of small Islands among Breakers. Then perceiving they had miss'd their Way, they sought for Anchorage, to gain time to send the Boat to discover where they were. They found a little Bay, where they anchor'd in 14 Fathom Water, the Bottom gray Sand, and white Gravel.

The next Day, being the 26th of *May*, they made ready at 7 in the Morning, and after making some Trips to get out of the Bay, which is open to the E. S. E. they stood South,

e

Plate XXXII. Page 286. explain'd in English.

A contracted Chart of the extreme Part of SOUTH AMERICA, *in which are contain'd the new Islands discover'd by the Ships of S.* Malo, *since* 1700, *the Western Part whereof is still unknown. The Passage here call'd by the Name of S.* Barbara, *was lately found out by a Tartane of the same Name, on the 25th of* May, 1713.

A. *The Island of S.* Elizabeth.
B. *The Island of S.* Bartholomew.
C. *The Island of Sea Wolves or Seals.*
D. *The Island of* Louis le Grand.
E. *The* Dauphin's *Bay.*
F. *Port* Philipeau.
G. *Cape S.* Lewis.
I. *The Company's Channel.*
K. Mort au Pain.
L. *Cape* Garde, *or* Quad.
M. *Cape S.* Jerome.
N. *Anchoring Place newly discovered.*
The Roman *Numbers shew the Variation of the Compass.*

a a. *The way of the Ship call'd* le Maurepas, *in* 1706.
b b. *The Way of the Ship call'd the S.* John Baptist, *in* 1712.
c c. *The Way of the Ship call'd the S.* Lewis, *in* 1706.
d d. *The Way of the Ship call'd the* Assumption, *in* 1708. *which ran twice along this Coast, taking it for a new Island, which is thought to be more to the Eastward in regard of the Continent.*
q q. *The way of the Tartane S.* Barbara, *in May* 1713.
F. *The Port where the Tartan anchor'd.*

Echelle de Longitude du Meridien de Paris, *a Scale of Longitude from the Meridian of* Paris.

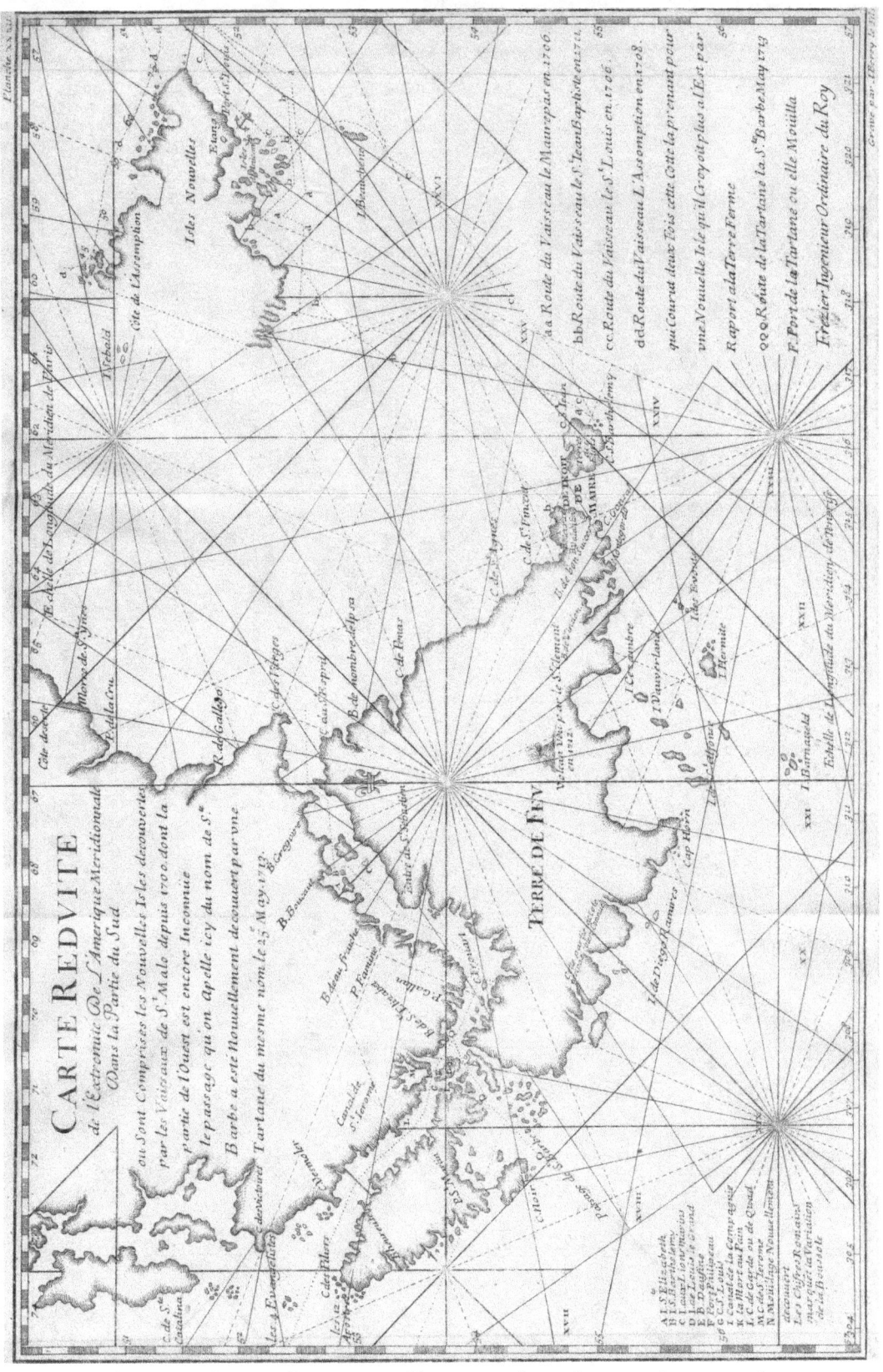

South S. and by W. and S. S. W. and at Noon were got out from between the Lands. They took an Obfervation with very fair Weather, and found 54 Degrees 34 Minutes Latitude. This Obfervation was confirm'd by that they took the next Day, in Sight of a fmall Ifland, which bore Eaft from them according to the Globe; they found 54 Degrees 29 Minutes.

That little Ifland was to the Southward of a great one, the S. E. Point whereof was call'd *Black Cape*, becaufe it is of that Colour. The little Ifland here fpoken of, is a Rock fhaped like a Tower, of an extraordinary Height; clofe by which there is a fmaller much of the fame Shape, by which it appears, that it would be impoffible to mifs that Channel, if it were fought after by its Latitude, upon fuch fingular Land-Marks. The Ship's Crew fay, that there is a good Bottom, and that great Ships may pafs there without any Danger, the fame being about two Leagues broad. *Tokens to know the new Channel.*

This Streight is perhaps the fame as that of *Jelouchte*, which Monfieur *de Lifle* has laid down in his laft Map of *Chili*; but as the *Englifh* Memoirs, which he has been pleas'd to fhew me, feem to place it South of Cape *Frouvart*, it may be fuppos'd that they are two different Streights.

Perhaps alfo it is the fame through which the Squadron of Monfieur *de Gennes* pafs'd out in the Year 1696.

If I have in this Chart fupprefs'd imaginary Lands, I have alfo added fome real, in 51 Degrees Latitude, which I have call'd new Iflands, becaufe difcover'd fince the Year 1700, moft of them by Ships of *S. Malo*. I have laid them down according to the Memoirs or Obfervations of the *Manrepas* and the *S. Lewis*, Ships belonging to the *India* Company, which faw them near at hand; and even the latter was water'd there in a Pool, which I have fet down, near Port *S. Lewis*. The Water was fomewhat ruddy and unfavory; in other refpects good for the Sea. Both of them ran along feveral Parts of them, but none coafted along fo clofe as the *S. John Baptift*, commanded by *Doublet* *New Iflands.*

blet of *Havre*, who endeavour'd to pafs into an Opening he faw about the Middle; but having fpy'd fome low Iflands, almoft level with the Water, he thought fit to tack about. This Range of Iflands is the fame that Monfieur *Fouquet* of S. *Malo* difcover'd, and to which he gave the Name of *Anican*, the Perfon that had fet him out. The Tracks I have traced will fhew the Bearing of thofe Lands in regard to Streight *le Maire*, which the S. *John Baptift* was come out of, when he faw them, and with refpect to *Staten Landt*, which the other two had feen before they found them.

Anican Iflands.

The North Part of thofe Lands, which is here under the Name of the Coaft of the *Affumption*, was difcover'd on the 16th of *July* 1708, by *Porez* of S. *Malo*, who gave it the Name of the Ship he commanded. It was look'd upon as a new Land, about 100 Leagues Eaft of the new Ifles I fpeak of; but I have made no Difficulty to join it to the others, having convincing Reafons for fo doing.

Coaft of the Affumption.

The firft is, that the Latitudes obferv'd to the Northward and to the Southward of thofe Iflands, and the Bearing of the Parts known, anfwer exactly to the fame Point of Reunion on the Eaft-fide, without leaving any Space between them.

The fecond is, that there is no Reafon to judge that Coaft of the *Affumption* to be Eaft of the Ifles of *Anican*; for Monfieur *le Gobien de Saint Jean*, who has been pleas'd to fhew me an Extract of his Journal, judges it to lie South from the Mouth of the River of *Plate*, which being taken ftrictly, could not remove it above two or three Degrees to the Eaftward, that is, about 25 or 30 Leagues; but the Diverfity of Judgments is always a Token of Uncertainty. The firft Time they faw that Coaft, as they came from the Ifland of S. *Katharine*, they judg'd it to be in 329 Degrees; and the fecond, coming from the River of *Plate*, whither the contrary Winds had obliged him to go and anchor, after having attempted to pafs Cape *Horn*, they judg'd it to be in 322 Degrees, and, according to fome, in 324, on *Peter Goos* his Charts, the Errors whereof we have

have taken Notice of at Page 30; so that little Regard is to be had to them. However, they reposing Confidence in them, thought themselves very far from the Continent; and reckoning they were too much to the Eastward, ran also 300 Leagues too far West in the *South-Sea*; so that they thought they had been running upon *Guinea*, when they made Land at *Hilo*; but the third and most convincing is, that we and our Comrades must have run over that new Land, according to the Longitude in which it was laid down in the Manuscript Chart; and it is morally impossible that a Ship should have had no Sight of it, being about 50 Leagues in Length E. S. E. and W. N. W. Thus there is no Room to doubt, but that it was the North Part of the new Islands, whose Western Part, which is yet unknown, Time will discover.

These Islands are certainly the same which Sir *Richard Hawkins* discover'd in 1593. Being to the Eastward of the Desart Coast, in about 50 Degrees, he was drove by a Storm upon an unknown Land; he ran along that Island about 60 Leagues, and saw Fires, which made him conclude that it was inhabited.

Hitherto those Lands have been call'd *Sibald*'s Islands, because it was believ'd, that the three which bear that Name on the Charts were so laid down at Will, for want of better Knowledge; but the Ship the *Incarnation*, commanded by the Sieur *Brignon* of S. *Malo*, had a near View of them in fair Weather, in 1711, coming out of *Rio de Janeiro*. They are, in short, three little Islands, about half a League in Length, lying in a Triangle, as they are laid down in the Charts. They pass'd by at three or four Leagues Distance, and they had no Sight of Land, tho' in very open Weather, which proves, that they are at least seven or eight Leagues from the new Islands.

In fine, I have set down in *Roman* Numbers the Variations of the Needle observ'd in those Parts, where its Declination is very considerable to the N. E. for we have observ'd it to 27 Degrees, being to the Eaftward of the new Iflands.

After having got clear of the Ice, we were favour'd with a ftiff Gale at S. W. and S. S. W. as far as 35 Degrees Latitude, and 39 of Longitude, where we had fome Calms; and then the Eaft Winds, which carry'd us as far as the Tropick of *Capricorn.* There we had four Days of Calm, and pouring Rain, fo heavy, that the Cataracts of Heaven feem'd to be open'd.

After that, a little Wind came up; and on *Sunday,* the 8th of *April,* we had Sight of the Ifland of the *Afcenfion,* when, according to my Reckoning, we were to fee it exactly on the Manufcript Chart corrected, as I have faid; having taken our Departure from *La Conception* at 75 Degrees 15 Minutes, which anfwer to the 303 Degrees 5 Minutes from the Meridian of *Teneriff,* inftead of 298, which is that of the *Dutch* Charts. Thus I found that Ifland in 32 Degrees 5 Minutes, which anfwer to the 346 Degrees 15 Minutes, that is, three more to the Weftward than it is laid down. Thofe who had taken their Departure from *La Conception* on the Charts, found it 150 Leagues more to the Weft. This Error in Longitude is not the only one; it is alfo wrong laid down as to Latitude in 20 Degrees; for it is in 20 Degrees 25 Minutes, as I obferv'd at Anchor near the Land.

This Ifland, call'd, according to the *Portugueze* Name, *Afcenzao,* to diftinguifh it from another *Afcenfion* Ifland, which is in about fix Degrees towards the Coaft of *Guinea,* is properly no other than a Rock, about a League and a half long, very eafily to be known on the South and Weft Sides, by a round Body of Stone like a Tower, fomewhat conical, and almoft as high as the Ifland. On the Eaft it forms as it were two Heads, which terminate the Cape. It is ftill better to be known by three fmall Iflands, one of which is about half a League long, lying E. and by N. according to the Compafs, from the great Ifland of the *Afcenfion.* Thofe three fmall Iflands have caufed fome to believe,

lieve, that this Island and that of *Trinidad* were the same, grounding their Opinion on this, that some Ships have sought for the other in its Latitude, without finding it: But I * also know, that Ships have seen it at their Return from the *East-Indies*, and have also water'd there in a Pool. It is therefore without Reason, that *Edmund Halley* has in his great Chart suppress'd the Island of the *Trinity*, and given that Name to the Island of the *Ascension*, which he lays down very well in its Latitude of 20 Degrees 25 Minutes.

See the Postscript.

We were glad to have met with this Island, because we hoped to find Water there, and by that Means pursue our Voyage without losing Time, by putting in any where.

We therefore came to an Anchor at West, five Degrees North, or W. and by N. according to the Globe, from that Peek, about four Cables Length from the Shore, in 30 Fathom Water, the Bottom Sand and Owze. The Boat was immediately sent to find shoaler Water, and found it in 25 Fathom, large black Sand, N. N. W. of a small Cleft Island, more to the Northward than we.

Anchoring.

The next Day the Boat was sent to look out for Water, and found a curious Fall, which would have supply'd a whole Squadron; but the Shore is so set with great Stones, and the Sea was so rough, that there was no going a Shore without Danger. Thus, during the whole Morning, we could get but two Casks of Water, which stunk in 3 or 4 Days, for which Reason, doubt may be made, whether it comes from a Spring. Thus our fine Project miscarry'd, and we were obliged to resolve to put into *Bahia de todos os santos*, where the appointed Rendezvous was.

Monday the 9th of *April* we made ready, and perceiv'd that there was near the Island a Current setting to the N. W. and N. N. W. for the Calms kept us there some Days.

At length, the 20th of the same Month, in 12 Degrees 50 Minutes Latitude, we had Sight of the Coast of *Brasil*, which we found more remote from the Island of the *Ascension* than is laid down in the Charts of *Peter Goos, Robin, Vankeulen,* and *Loots,* almost the one half in some of them,

Coast of Brasil.

P p 2
and

and a Third in others; for there are about nine Degrees of Longitude between the Island and the nearest Land.

From what I have said, it is easy to conclude what an Error they must be in, who had taken their Measures by the Charts; for having taken their Departure from *Le Conception*, 5 or 6 Degrees too far to the West, and the Coast of *Brasil* being advanced too far East by as many Degrees, they found an Error of at least 200 Leagues, according to which they must have penetrated into the Land, as happen'd to the Ships of our Squadron, by their own Confession. These Errors have always been much the same with all Ships that have put into *Brasil*, or the Island of *Fernando de Noronha*, in their Return from the *South-Sea*.

The Ignorance of the Theory, which prevails among our Navigators, made them ascribe this Difference in Judgment, and the Charts, to the Currents, which they said did set East, without being undeceiv'd by a sort of uniform Error, not only in their making the Land of *Brasil*, but even that of *France*, after a Navigation of 14 Years, tho' they saw they found the Lands of *Brasil* too far to the West; and that correcting their Point on the Charts, they found the Land of *Europe* too far to the East, much about the same Quantity or Distance, as they had made their Reck'ning. In this they at least discover their want of Curiosity in not seeking to be better inform'd; but they are still more excusable than their principal Hydrographers, who ought to make their Advantage of the Observations which the Gentlemen of the Academy of Sciences publish in their *Connoiffance des Temps*. But those things being too far above their Reach, to understand and reduce them to the common Calculation of the *Dutch* Maps, which are commonly made use of, they are guilty of so much Folly, as to despise them, as the Productions of Learned Men who want Experience. Thus in a Manuscript Instruction D. G. of S. *Malo* affirms, that the Coast of *Brasil* is right laid down on those same Charts, wherein, nevertheless,

according

according to the Observations taken at *Olinda* and *Cayenne*, there must be six Degrees Error to the East.

The next Day after we had made Land, being *Sunday* in the Morning, we saw a small Vessel of two Masts, which seem'd to stand as we did S. W. After having lain by a little, he stood about directly upon us, bearing up close to the Wind, with only the Main Course. This extraordinary working, made us take him for a Pyrate; and the rather, because he seem'd to be *English* built; we put up our Fights, and expected him with our Arms in our Hands. When he was within Cannon Shot, we put up *French* Colours, and he immediately answer'd with *Portugueze*, still lying as close upon the Wind as he could. We could never know what to think of it; for when we came to *Bahia de todos os Santos*, they assured us, that no Ship had sail'd from thence in a long time.

We held our Course towards the Land, on which many white Spots appear'd; then stood off at Night, and yet when it was Day found ourselves within a League of the Coast, the Sea running high, the Wind in Gusts, and the Rain pouring, which made us fear, because the Coast is foul.

That foul Weather obliged us to stand out to Sea, to expect some more favourable to make the Bay, and to the Southward against the Currents, which set us to the N. E. as is observ'd in the *Grand Flambeau de Mer*, at this Season of the Year; that is, from *March* till *September*, during which time the S. E. and S. S. E. Winds also prevail; so that Ships must keep to the Southward as is there discreetly advised.

At length, on the 26th of *April,* we discovered *Praya de Zumba*, a Place very easy to be known by an infinite Number of white Spots, which look like Linnen hung out to dry, as far as within 2 or 3 Leagues of Cape S. *Anthony*. The Interval *Bahia de todos os Santos* makes between that Cape, and the Isle of *Taporica*, makes it look discontinued,

Praya de Zumba.

when

Plate XXXIII.

Marks to know the Bay of all Saints.

when seen to the N. W. and the Island, or the Larboard Coast very confusedly.

Drawing near the Land, Fort S. *Anthony* appears at the End of the Cape, in the midst whereof is a Tower, ending at the Top in a Point, which looks like a Pavillion.

Before that Cape is a flat Rock, on which there are 4 or 5 Fathoms Water at low Ebb. It runs out about a Quarter of a League S. W.

Taporica Island.

The Island of *Taporica*, which forms the Mouth on the Larboard-side, is still fouler, having before it a Shoal, which stretches out above a League S. E. and is seen to break very high upon the Ebb; so that Ships must bear up due North along the middle of the Channel to get in safe, and take heed of the Tides, which are of 3 Hours and 3 Quarters.

Mouth of the Bay.

The Mouth being two Leagues and a half wide, Ships may pass out of the Point Blank reach of the Cannon of the Forts of S. *Anthony* and S. *Mary*; so that they are less to be apprehended in passing, than they are fit to obstruct a Descent in the Sandy Creeks on the Starboard-side.

As we come in by Degrees, we discover on the same side, on an Eminence, one part of the City, which affords a pleasant Prospect enough, extending to the most Northern Cape, on which is the Fort of *Our Lady of Monserrat*.

In that Bay, at the Foot of the City, is the Port where the *Portugueze* Ships come to an Anchor, closed on the South and West-side by the Bank call'd *Alberto*, on which the Water Castle stands, which might be call'd a *Pate*, or Horse-shooe, by reason of its Roundness. In 1624, when the

---

Plate XXXIII. Page 294. *explain'd in* English.

Vue de Reconnoissance du Cap Saint Antoine, *Thus the Land appears for knowing of Cape S. Anthony.*

The Plan of the Bay of all Saints, *on the Coast of* Brasil, *in* 13 *Degrees of South Latitude.*

Baye de tous les Saints, *The Bay of all Saints.*

Vue de Reconnoissance du cap: Saint Antoine

no 2 li

PLAN de la Baye de tous les Saints Située a la Côte du Bresil par 13.d de lat. australe

Monsarate

S.t Philipe

Baye de tous les Saints

isle Taporica

S.t Maria

S.t Antoine

Pequa de Zumbi

Echelle estimée

During that Time, I employ'd myself in seeing the City, and the Parts about it, as far as was in my Power, notwithstanding the almost continual Rains, intermix'd at Intervals with scorching Heats. Those Inconveniences, together with our short stay, would not permit me to take so exact a Plan as I could have wish'd. However, I can give it as a very good Idea, differing but little from the Truth in what is essential. Besides, it would have been no Advantage to me, if we had stay'd long there; some indiscreet Persons of our Squadron having made me known to the *Portugueze* Officers for an Engineer, it was not proper for me to expose myself to some Affront in a Place, where the Memory of the Expedition to *Rio de Janeiro*, still fresh, render'd our Nation suspected. In short, they had doubled the Guards every where, and even erected new Corps de Garde, because there were already five *French* Ships in the Road, among which were two of Force, the one of 50, and the other of 70 Guns.

The Description of the City of S. Salvador, *or* S. Saviour, *the Capital of* Brasil.

Plate XXXIV.

THE Town which our Charts call S. *Salvador*, or S. *Saviour*, is in the Language of the Country plainly call'd *Cidade da Bahia*, the City of the Bay. It is in about 12 Degrees 45 Minutes of South Latitude, on an Eminence of about 100 Fathoms, form'd by the East-side of the Bay of all Saints. The Access to it is so difficult, by reason of its great Steepness, that they have been forced to have recourse to Machines for carrying up, and letting down of Goods from the Town to the Port.

The Plan of the Upper Town is as regularly drawn, as the Unevenness of the Mountainous Soil would permit; but tho' the Streets there are Straight, and of a good Breadth, most of them have so steep a Descent, that they would

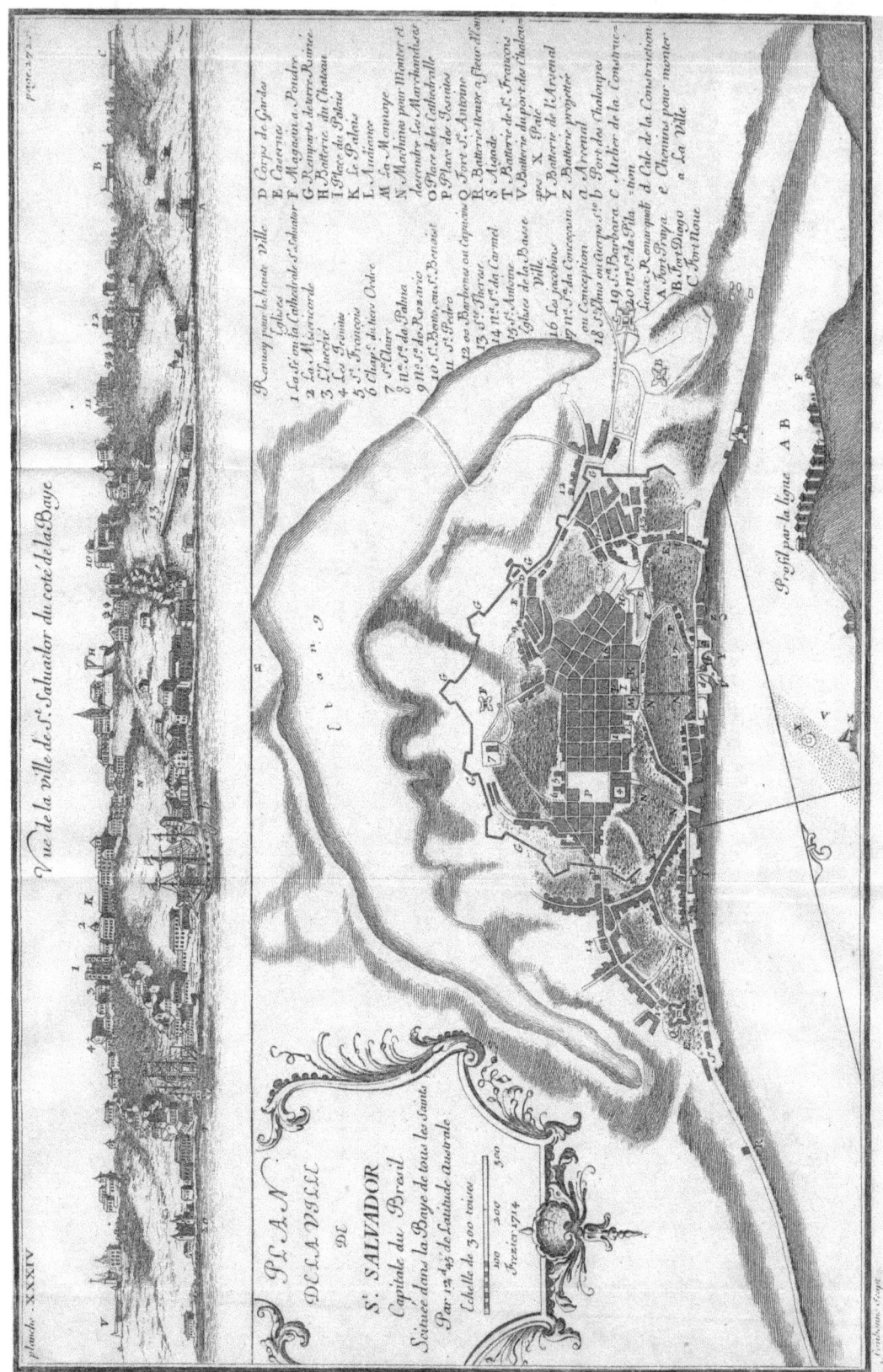

would be impracticable for our Coaches, and even for our Chairs.

The rich People, notwithstanding that Inconveniency, do not go a Foot; being always industrious, as well in *America*, as in *Europe*, to find Means to distinguish themselves from the rest of Mankind, they would be ashamed to make use of the Legs which Nature has given us to walk. They lazily

---

Plate XXXIV. *Page* 297. *Explain'd in* English.

A Prospect of the City of San Salvador *next the Bay.*

The Plan of the City of San Salvador, the Capital of Brasil, in the Bay of All Saints, and in 12 Degrees 45 Minutes of South Latitude.
A Scale of 300 *Fathoms.*

References in the Upper Town.

Churches.
1. *The Cathedral, or S. Saviour.*
2. *The Misericordia, or House of Mercy.*
3. *The Bishop's Palace.*
4. *The Jesuites.*
5. *S. Francis.*
6. *The Chappel of the 3d Order.*
7. *S. Clare.*
8. *Our Lady of Palma.*
9. *Our Lady of the Rosary.*
10. *S. Benedict.*
11. *S. Peter.*
12. *The Capucins.*
13. *S. Teresa.*
14. *The Carmelites.*
15. *S. Anthony.*

Churches in the Lower Town.
16. *The Dominicans.*
17. *Our Lady of the Conception.*
18. *S. Elmo.*
19. *S. Barbara.*
20. *Our Lady de* Pila.

Places of Note.
A. *The Fort on the Strand.*
B. *Fort* James.
C. *New Fort.*

D. *Corps du Garde.*
E. *Cascones.*
F. *The Powder Magazine.*
G. *A ruin'd Rampart of Earth.*
H. *The Battery of the Castle.*
I. *The Palace-yard.*
K. *The Palace.*
L. *The Court of Justice.*
M. *The Mint.*
N. *Cranes to draw up and let down Goods.*
O. *The Square before the Cathedral.*
P. *The* Jesuites *Square.*
Q. *Fort S. Anthony.*
R. *A new Battery level with the Water.*
S. *The Watering Place.*
T. *S. Francis's Battery.*
V. *The Battery for the Port where the Boats lie.*
X. *A Paté, or Platform.*
Y. *The Battery of the* Arsenal.
Z. *A projected Battery.*
a. *The Arsenal.*
b. *The Port for the Boats.*
c. *The Docks and Yards.*
d. *The Creek for building.*
e. *Ways to go up to the Town.*

Profil par la Ligne A. B. *The Profile by the Line* A. B.

Plate XXXV. lazily cause themselves to be carry'd in Beds of fine Cotton, hanging by the Ends to a Pole, which two Blacks carry on their Heads or Shoulders; and to be there conceal'd, and that neither the Rain, nor the Heat of the Sun may offend them, that Bed is cover'd with a Tester, to which they hang Curtains to be drawn when they please. Thus lying along there at their Ease, with the Head on a rich Pillow, they are carry'd about more gently than in Coaches or Chairs. Those Cotton Hammocks are call'd *Serpentins*, and not *Palankins*, as some Travelers say.

If this great Unevenness of the Ground is inconvenient to the Inhabitants, it is on the other hand very advantageous to the Fortifications. With a small Expence this might be made a Town morally impregnable; Nature has See Plate there made Ditches and Outworks flanking one another, XXXIV. where the Ground might be disputed Inch by Inch. The East-side is almost inaccessible, as may be seen in the Profile, by the Line A. B. being almost cover'd by a deep Pool, having 15 or 20 Fathom Water in some Places, which lies down in a Vale between two Hills, the Ascent whereof is very steep.

From that Pool, which comes very near the Sea, on the North-side, they have drawn a little Stream, that serves for Ships to Water.

In short, to approach the Town on the South-side, the Landing must be near the Forts I have mention'd, or farther in among the Batteries, which are on the Coast; which would certainly be very difficult, tho' the Opposition were never so small.

The *Dutch*, in 1624, having taken this Place, when under the Dominion of the *Spaniards*, fortify'd it on the Landside with a Rampart, or rather a great Entrenchment of Earth, which enclosed the Body of the Upper Town, the 3d Part of a League in Length; which did not prevent the *Spaniards* retaking of it the next Year 1625. That Enclosure is now quite ruin'd; it has been neglected to endeavour

The material originally positioned here is too large for reproduction in this reissue. A PDF can be downloaded from the web address given on page iv of this book, by clicking on 'Resources Available'.

vour to fortify the Approaches by a Number of Forts made in several Places.

The first, on the South-side is the *New*, or *S. Peter's* Fort, made of Earth, faced with Stone-work, which they were working upon when we were there. It is a regular Square, with 4 Bastions, of 20 Foot in the Face, as much Curtin, and 4 Fathoms Flank; furnish'd with Cannon, which on the one side plays upon the Road, but much under Metal; about it is a little Ditch, five or six Fathoms wide. S. Peter's Fort

The second, on the same side nearer the Town, is Fort *Diego*, or *James*. It is also a Square of Stone-work, without a Ditch, with 4 Bastions of 8 Fathoms in the Face. It is a Battery of Bombs for the Road, and serves now for a Magazine. Fort James.

The third, is the great Powder Magazine, call'd *Casa da Polvora*, or the Powder-House. It is also a Square of Stone-work, without a Ditch; the Bastions of 6 Fathoms Face, the Curtins of 14, and the Flanks of 2. It contains 8 distinct Magazines, vaulted and cover'd Pyramid-wise, with as many Globes on the Tops; said to contain 2 or 3000 Barrels of Powder; but there are often under 100. Casa da Polvora.

The fourth, is Fort *S. Anthony*, on the North, which is directly over the Watering-Place, of Stone-Work, square like the others, but somewhat larger and better contriv'd. The Bastions have about 16 Fathoms Face, the Flanks 4 or 5, and the Curtin 25, with a good Ditch. One side of it plays upon the Road, but it does not well defend a Depth, by which Men may come under Covert to the Counterscarp, and by the same way go to the Town. Half a Cannon Shot from this, towards the N. E. is Fort *Nossa Senhora da Victoria*, the Fort of our Lady of Victory, made of Earth, to which I could not go, nor to the others that are farther off, as that of *S. Bartholomew*, which defends a little Harbour, where Ships may careen; that of *Montserate*, nor to those at the Entrance, before mention'd. S. Anthony's Fort. Nossa Senhora da Victoria Fort.

Troops.   To secure these Forts and the Town, the King of *Portugal* maintains six Companies of Regular Forces, uniformly cloath'd, and not in brown Linnen, as *Dampier* says; that is alter'd; they are well disciplin'd and pay'd; those I saw were in a very good Condition, well arm'd, and full of fine Men; they want nothing but the Reputation of being good Soldiers.

The City of *Bahia*, as is well known, is the Capital and Metropolis of *Brasil*, and the usual Seat of a Viceroy; however, the Governor has not always that Title, Witness he that was in our Time.

Manners.   The Inhabitants have an Out-side good enough as to Politeness, Neatness, and the manner of giving themselves a good Air, much like the *French*. I mean the Men only, for there are so few Women to be seen, that but a very imperfect Account can be given of them. The *Portugueze* are so jealous, that they scarce allow them to go to Mass on *Sundays* and Holidays; nevertheless, in Spight of all their Precautions, they are almost all of them Libertines, and find Means to impose upon the Watchfulness of their Fathers and Husbands, exposing themselves to the Cruelty of the latter, who kill them without Fear of Punishment, when they discover their Intrigues. Instances hereof are so frequent, that they reck'ned above 30 Women murder'd by their Husbands within a Year. Fathers shew more Humanity towards their Daughters; when they cannot hide their Shame by marrying them off, they turn them out of Doors, and then they are at Liberty to be common. A fine Expedient!

Quod licet ingratum est, quod non licet acrius urit, *Ovid.* Matres omnes filiis in peccato adjutrices, auxilio in paterna injuria solent esse. *Ter. Heaut.*
    Whether it be the Effect of the Climate, or of our natural Bent after that which others endeavour to keep from us by Force, there is no need of any extraordinary Efforts to be admitted to the last Familiarity. The Mothers help the Daughters to keep out of the sight of their Fathers, either through Compassion, or out of a Principle of the Law of Nature, which enjoins us to do by another as we would

be

be done by; but in short, tho' they did not themselves meet Men half way, the Scarcity of white Women would draw the Crowd after them; for 19 in 20 of the People we see there, are Blacks, Men and Women, all naked, except those Parts which Modesty obliges to cover; so that the City looks like a new *Guinea*. In short, the Streets are full of none but hideous Figures of Black Men and Women Slaves, whom Delicacy and Avarice, rather than Necessity, have transplanted from the Coast of *Africa*, to make up the State of the Rich, and contribute towards the Sloth of the Poor, who ease themselves of their Labour on them, so that there are always above 20 Blacks to one White. Who would believe it? there are Shops full of those poor Wretches, who are exposed there stark naked, and bought like Cattle, over whom the Buyers have the same Power; so that upon slight Disgusts, they may kill them almost without Fear of Punishment, or at least treat them as cruelly as they please. I know not how such Barbarity can be reconciled to the Maxims of Religion, which makes them Members of the same Body with the Whites, when they have been baptized, and raises them to the Dignity of Sons of God, *All Sons of the most High*; doubtless they will not suffer themselves to be convinced of that Truth; for those poor Slaves are too much abused by their Brethren, who scorn that Relation.

I here make this Comparison, because the *Portugueze* are Christians who make a great outward Shew of Religion, even more than the *Spaniards*; for most of them walk along the Streets with their Beads in their Hands, a Figure of S. *Anthony* on their Breasts, or hanging about their Necks, and with an extravagant Furniture of a long *Spanish* Sword on their Left, and a Dagger almost as long as a short *French* Sword on their Right; to the end that when Occasion shall offer, neither Arm may be useless towards destroying of their Enemies. In reality, those outward Tokens of Religion are very deceitful among them, not only in regard to true Probity, but even to Christian

Sen-

Sentiments; they often serve to conceal from the Eyes of the World a great Number of *Jews*; an amazing Instance has been seen in that Town. A Curate, after having for several Years behaved himself outwardly to Edification, at last made his Escape with the Sacred Ornaments into *Holland*, to live there as a *Jew*; for which Reason, to be admitted to the Clergy, a Man must prove himself an old Christian, as they call it, that is, of ancient Christian Descent.

Cathedral. The Upper Town is adorn'd with several Churches, the most remarkable of which is the Cathedral, which having the Title of S. *Saviour*, has communicated its Name to all the Town. Before it, is a small open Place, like a Platform, whence is a Prospect of all the Bay, and several Islands, forming an agreeable Landskip. Adjoining to that Place is the Hospital under the Name of *Nossa Senhora da Misericordia*, or our Lady of Mercy. On the Cathedral depend the two Parishes of S. *Anthony* and S. *Peter*, and if I mistake not, S. *Barbara*. To the North of the Cathedral is the Monastery of the *Jesuites*, whose Church is all built with Marble carry'd from *Europe*. The Sacristy is very beautiful, as well on account of the neat Work the Buffets, or Places for vesting, the curious Wood, inlaying and Ivory they are made of, as for a Series of little Pictures that adorns them. But we must not with *Froger* call the Painting on the Cieling fine, being unworthy to be taken notice of by a Man of Skill. The other Churches and Monasteries have nothing remarkable. There are *Benedictins, Franciscans, Carmelites, Dominicans, Barefoot Augustins*, and a Monastery of *Capucins*, which formerly consisted of all *French*, but they were turn'd out during the last Wars, to put in *Italians*; they are there call'd, *os Barbudos*, or the Bearded Friers. I know of but one Monastery of Nuns, call'd as *Freiras da Incarnaçao*, or the Nuns of the Incarnation. In the Lower Town there are other Chappels of Brotherhoods, S. *Barbara*, our Lady of

Jesuites Church.

the *Rosary*, and *de Pila*; this last for the Soldiers, *Corpo Santo* for poor People, and the *Conception* for Sailors.

The great Trade that is drove at the Bay, for the Country Commodities, makes the Inhabitants easy. Every Year about *March*, there arrives a Fleet of about 20 Ships from *Lisbon*, laden with Linnen and Woollen Cloths and Stuffs, especially Serges, Perpetuanas, Bays, and Says, which the Women use for their Veils, instead of black Taffety, as the Women wear in *Spain*; which Fashion they follow pretty near: The Use of that Stuff is a Piece of Modesty forced upon them by the King's Order, who prohibits the wearing of Silk. The other saleable Commodities, are Stockings, Hats, Iron, Kitchen Furniture; but above all, Bisket, Meal, Wine, Oil, Butter, Cheese, &c. The same Ships, in Exchange, carry back Gold, Sugar, Tobacco, Wood for Dying, call'd *Brasil* Wood, Balsam, Oil of *Copayva*, *Hypecacuana*, some raw Hides, &c. *Trade in Europe.*

The Town standing on a steep Eminence, they have erected three Machines for carrying up, and letting down of Goods to and from the Upper Town. Of those three, one is at the *Jesuites*, not only for the Publick, who pay for the Use of it, but also for the Use of that Community, which is certainly no Enemy to Trade. Those Machines consist of two great Wheels, like Drums, which have one common Axle-Tree, over which is wound a Cable, made fast to a Sledge or Cart, which is drawn up by Blacks, who going in the Wheels, wind the Cable up the Spindle, and to the end that the Sledge may meet with no Opposition, but come up easily, it slides along a boarded Way, reaching from the Top of the Hill to the Bottom, being about 140 Fathoms in Length, and not 250, as is said in *Le Flambeau de la Mer*. *Machines.*

Besides the Trade of *European* Commodities, the *Portugueze* have another considerable in *Guinea*. They carry thither Linnen Cloth, made in the Islands of *Cape Verde*, Glass Beads, and other Trifles, and bring back Gold, Ivory and Blacks to sell at *Brasil*. *Trade to Guinea.*

Wealth, &c.

The Correspondence with *Rio de Janeiro*, near which are the Gold Mines of the *Paulistas*, which afford great Plenty, still adds to the Wealth of the Bay. The Houses there are well built, the Inhabitants handsomely lodg'd and furnish'd; the Men and Women are modest in their Habit, because they are wisely forbid wearing of Gold or Silver Lace; but they shew their Wealth in certain Ornaments of Massive Gold, even on their black Women Slaves, who are adorn'd with rich Chains several times about their Necks, great Rings and Pendants in their Ears, Crosses, Plates they wear on their Foreheads, and other very weighty Ornaments of Gold.

Strangers not to trade thither.

Contrary to the usual Policy of other Crowns, the King of *Portugal* does not permit Strangers to resort thither, to carry away the Product of the Country, tho' they buy with Specie, much less to carry Goods to sell or exchange, wherein he is more faithfully serv'd than the King of *Spain* in *Peru*. This Regulation is grounded on two good Reasons; the first, to oblige his Subjects to take Pains, and by that means procure them all the Profit of the Commerce. The second and the chiefest, to prevent the Duties he has upon all Commodities being sunk by the Viceroys and Governors, for all Ships being obliged to come and unlade in his Sight at *Lisbon*, nothing can escape him.

Tho' this Bay of *All Saints* be a very populous Place, where they reckon there are about 2000 Houses, it is not nevertheless a good Place for Ships to put in, especially in Winter, not only because of the great Rains it is subject to at that time, but also because Provisions are not good there; the Meal and Wine carry'd thither from *Europe*, are always the worse for that Passage; the Beef there is worth nothing; there is no Mutton, and Fowls are scarce and dear. The Fruits of that Season, as the *Bananas*, and the Oranges, will not keep long at Sea, and Garden Stuff is there almost unknown, either through the Supineness of the *Portugueze*, or because it is a difficult Matter to cultivate the same, by reason of the great Multitude of Pismires which destroy the Plants and the Fruit almost every where, so that they are the Bane of Agriculture in *Brasil*.

Departure from the Bay.

AFTER having refitted and victual'd, we fail'd in Company with our former Comrades, on *Monday*, the 7th of *May*. Being at Noon two Leagues and a half to the Southward of Cape S. *Anthony*, I found by Obfer- vation 13 Degrees of Latitude, whence I concluded, that it lies in 12 Degrees 50 Minutes, and the City in 12 Degrees 45 Minutes, and according to the Obfervation of *Olinda*, set down in *La Connoissance des Temps*, of 1712, it should be in 41 Degrees 30 Minutes of West Longitude, or Difference of the Meridian from *Paris*, which differs from the Position, the *Dutch* Charts affign it 6 Degrees more Westward; for instead of 336 Degrees 50 Minutes, it is 343 Degrees from the Meridian of *Teneriff*. *Error in Charts.*

On the 18th, *Beauvais Grant* came to ask our Point, perhaps not so much to ascertain his own, as to make a Signal to the others for them to crowd more Sail the next Day, and leave us. In short, they did not fail of so doing; they bore up to make the more way, knowing that it concern'd us more than them to gain Ground to the Eastward. They succeeded, and we lost Sight of them before Night, without endeavouring to bear up with them, and keep such Company as the Advice of the Peace had render'd useless, and their Infidelity odious.

From the time of our putting into the Bay till we came to the Line, we had almost continual cloudy Weather, with Gusts of Wind and Rain, Calms, and little Wind, the Winds blowing from S.S.E. to E.S.E. and tho' the Current sets to the Northward near the Coast, out at Sea we found it rather set us a little to the Southward; but when we were once come into 4 Degrees of North Latitude, we found a very great Difference in our Reck'ning on that side; we attributed it to the General Current, setting N.W. which prevails in that Latitude along the Coast of *Brasil* and *Guiana*. *Currents.*

In that Latitude we began to feel the Trade Winds from East to N. N. E. fresh enough, which carry'd on us to 26 Degrees, and turn'd back to the Longitude of Cape S. *Augustin.* Then we began to be becalm'd, which kept us near a Month, making little Way.

From thence forward we began to be sensible of many Currents, and Runs of Tides, and to see a sort of Drift in small Grains like Gooseberries, said to come from the Channel of *Bahama*, which was nevertheless about 600 Leagues to the Westward of us. The Reason for that Conjecture is, that none of that sort is found either about the *Azores*, or *Canary* Islands, which are the nearest Lands; and that on the other hand, sailing to the Westward, there are great Quantities of them found. If it be so, they must be brought by the Currents, which set to the Eastward. The Currents observ'd about the Coast of *Guiana*, serve to make good the Waters that run out at that Channel, which is also the Reason that the Ships coming from *Brasil*, gain as much to the Eastward, under the Tropick of *Cancer*, as they lose to the Westward, under the Line.

On the 15th of *June*, in about 21 Degrees of North Latitude, a Sailor died of the Bloody Flux.

Whiteness in the Sea. *Wednesday* the 4th of *July*, in 36 Degrees 50 Minutes Latitude, and 36 Degrees 16 Minutes Longitude, the Sea being still, we saw within Cannon Shot a Whiteness on the Water, as if it had broke a little, we immediately judg'd there might be a Shoal. The Captain had a mind to be satisfy'd, but the Boat being too much dry'd up by the great Heats for two Months past, was not fit to put to Sea. However, most Men thought that might be Foam, or something floating on the Water.

The next day we had sight of a small Vessel, which seem'd to stand to the Eastward, as we did. The Calm held us in sight of one another three Days. We put up our Fights, and made a Signal by firing a Gun and lowering our Topsails, to persuade him to make towards us, that we might hear some News from *Europe*; but a Gale coming up at West,

West, he stood away to the North. We chas'd him for some Hours, till considering we lost so much Way, we stood our own Course without having been able to come up with him.

Tuesday the 10th, we spy'd another, towards the Evening, and the next Morning about Break of Day he was within Cannon-shot of us. We again made ready, and lay by for him, but he stood away S. W. and left us.

That same Evening we had sight of the Peeke of one of the Islands of *Azores*, to which that Mountain has given its Name. It is like a Sugar-loaf, and so high, that it can be seen at 30 Leagues Distance, like that of *Teneriff*. *Peek of the Azores.*

We were then about 25 Leagues from it, S. and by E. according to the Globe, and saw it distinctly.

This Sight of Land was very pleasing to us; for the Tokens of Currents which we had observ'd, made us very uncertain as to our Reck'nings; and it was a double Satisfaction to find them answer within a very small Matter. I do not pretend to talk of any but those of the Officers, who having not made slight of what I had observ'd to them concerning the Position of *Olinda*, had taken their Departure 6 Degrees more to the Westward than the Longitude of the Bay on the *Dutch* Charts. The Currents we had observ'd for some Days, could not obstruct the Exactness, because they sometimes did set to the North, and sometimes to the South; and within Sight of Land, we observ'd that they were N. W. and S. E.

For this Reason, and perhaps partly through the Error of the Charts, we, within three Days after seeing the Peek, discover'd the Island of S. *Michael*, 20 Leagues sooner than we expected. In short, I am of Opinion, that *Peter Goos* places those two Islands too near together, and the *Flambeau de la Mer* at too great a Distance from each other. *Island of S. Michael.*

We also observ'd the same Error, as we drew near the Island *Tercera*, where we thought fit to put in, for fear lest the Calms continuing, we might want Provisions.

Tercera Island.

That Island is indifferent high, and to be known on the S. E. Side by a Point of low Land that runs out East, and by a Cape cut on the West-side, form'd by a Point of Land, on which there are two Risings; lastly, by two small Isles cut Perpendicular, which are a League to the Eastward of the said Cape, call'd *Ilheos*. Half a League S. S. E. from these, there are three Breakers, even with the Surface of the Water; all of them ill placed in the *Flambeau de la Mer*.

Saturday, July the 14th, about Night falling, we came to an Anchor in the Road of the City of *Angra*, in 20 Fathom Water, the Bottom a gray Sand, broken Shells, and small white Coral, Cape S. *Anthony* bearing from us S. W. and by W. the Cathedral N. W. and by N. the *Ilheos*, or little Islands above mention'd E. S. E. and Fort S. *Sebastian* N. N. W. This Position is to be observ'd, in order to avoid it upon Occasion, because the Bottom is there mix'd with great Stones. We saluted the Town with 9 Guns, which it return'd the next Morning Gun for Gun.

A Pilot of the Town coming aboard to advise us to change our Station, when we were about weighing, the Anchor was found engaged among Stones, so that it was requisite to put such Stress to get it loose that the Yard broke; but that Pilot, either through Malice or Ignorance, instead of carrying us somewhat farther out into 30 Fathom of Water, in the midst between the little Islands and the Hillocks, where the Men of War anchor, having brought us into 66 Fathom Water, we thought fit to remove to the usual Place, in 13 Fathom, the Bottom blackish Sand

---

Plate XXXVI. Page 259. explain'd in English.

A. *A* Spanish Woman of Peru, *in her Stays and wide Petticoat.*
B. *Another with a Cap and Mantle.*
C. *Another sitting holding a silver Pipe to suck through it the Tincture or Decoction of the Herb of* Paraguay.
D. *A Bowl made of a Gourd adorn'd with Silver.*
E. *A Silver Pot to heat the Water, in the midst of which is the Fire, in a Place made for it* G.

Planche XXXVI. page 236.

A Espagnole du perou en Chupon et faldellin. B. autre en Montera et greaorillo. C. autre assise tenant un Chalumeau d'argent pour sucer la teinture de l'herbe du paraguay. D. Maté ou Coupe de Calebasse armée d'argent. E. pot d'argent pour Chauffer l'eau au milieu de la quelle est le feu dans un reservoir G.

Sand and Owze, mix'd with some few Shells, and about a good Cable's Length from the Land. Then Fort S. *Sebastian* bore from us S. W. and by W. that of S. *Anthony* N. and by E. we rode there only by a small Stream Anchor, because there the Tide is very small. They say the Ebb begins at the Rising of the Moon, and sets S. E. and the Flood N. W. There a Ship is near the City Gate, where the Key and the Watering-Place are.

The Description of the City of ANGRA.

THE City of *Angra* is seated on the Edge of the Sea, about the middle of the South-side of the Island *Tercera*, at the Bottom of a small Bay, form'd by a very high Point of Land, call'd *Monto de Brasil*, or the Mount of *Brasil*. *Plate* XXXVII

I call that little and bad Port a Bay, being open from the East to the S. W. not above 4 Cables long in Breadth, and perhaps not two of good Bottom, where Ships cannot ride in Safety any longer than in the fair Summer Weather, because then only gentle Winds prevail, from the West to the N. N. W. but as soon as the Winter begins, there are such violent Storms, that the shortest way for Men to save their Lives, is to sail as soon as ever they see the least ill Tokens in the Air. The Inhabitants, by long Experience, are seldom mistaken; for then the high Mountain is cover'd and grows dark, and the Birds for some Days before come and cry about the City, as it were to give them Notice.

Those Mariners, who are obliged to stay in the Road, being detain'd on Account of Trade, forsake their Ships, or else bring small Vessels ashore, at the Foot of Fort S. *Sebastian*, and all of them stay in the Town, till the Storm is over. A fatal Experience has shewn that they were in the Right. In *September* 1713, seven Sail perish'd there, being drove ashore; and not one Man of all their Crews was saved. *Shipwreck.*

As

S. Anthony's Fort.

As small and bad as that Port is, the *Portugueze* have fortify'd it very well. They have raised a triple Battery, almost upon the Level of the Water, upon the most advanced Cape on the Starboard side, going in, being that of S. *Anthony*, a Name which is never wanting in Places belonging to the *Portugueze*. It is then continued in good Stone-work all

---

Plate 36. Page 310. *explain'd in* English.

The Plan of the Town, Citadel and Forts of *ANGRA*, on the Southside of the Island *Tercera*, one of the *Azores*, in 39 Degrees of South Latitude.

Churches.
1. *The Cathedral.*
2. *Our Lady of Hope, Nuns.*
3. *Our Lady of Grace.*
4. *S. Peter.*
5. *S. Katharine's Chappel.*
6. *S. Gonzalo.*
7. *A Chappel.*
8. *The* Misericordia, *or* Mercy.
9. Corpo Santo, *or the Chappel of the Holy Body.*
10. *The Chappel of the Incarnation.*
11. *Our Lady of the Incarnation, a Priory.*
12. *The Nuns of the* Conception.
13. *The Chappel of S.* Benedict.
14. *S.* Anthony, *Recolets.*
15. *A Chappel.*
16. *S. John's Chappel.*
17. *S. Lucy's Chappel.*
18. *The Jesuite's College.*
19. *S.* Francis, *Friers.*
20. *The Capucin Nuns.*
21. *The Chappel of the Chiefs.*

Quartier de S. Pedro, *S. Peter's Quarter.*
Castello de San Joao, *S. John's Castle.*
Ouest du Monde, *the due West Point.*
Ouest de l'aimant, declinant de 8 Degrez, *the West Point of the Compass, varying 8 Degrees.*
Montagne du Bresil, *the Mountain of* Brasil.
Tours des Sentinels, *the Sentinel's Towers.*
Echelle de 500 Toises, *a Scale of 500 Fathoms.*

Places of Note.
A. *The Square of the Castle.*
B. *The Gate and* Corps du Garde.
C. *A Chappel not finish'd.*
D. Cazerns.
E. *Square Wells dug in the Ditch.*
F. *The Horse-shooe.*
G. *The Rampart carry'd down to the Sea.*
H. *Redoubts and Chappel of S. Anthony.*
I. *Intrenchments and Batteries on the Edge of the Sea.*
K. *A* Moineau, *or Plat Bastion.*
L. *S. Anthony's Battery.*
M. *The Upper Brasil Gate.*
N. *The Key at the landing Place.*
O. *The Sea Gate.*
P. *The Square and Fountain in it.*
Q. *The Town-House.*
R. *The Goal.*
S. *Fort S. Sebastian.*
T. *A low Battery.*
V. *The old Creek.*

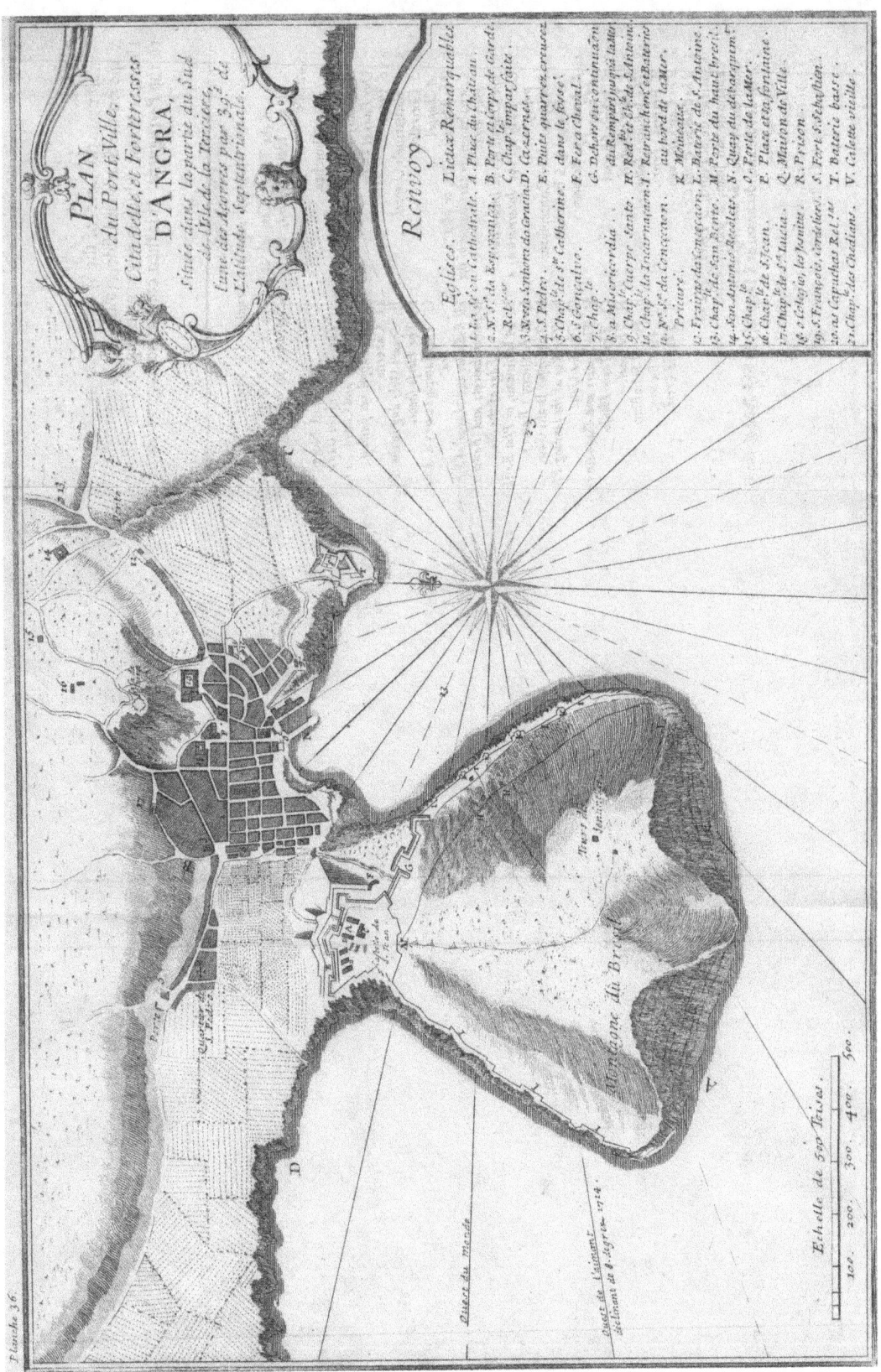

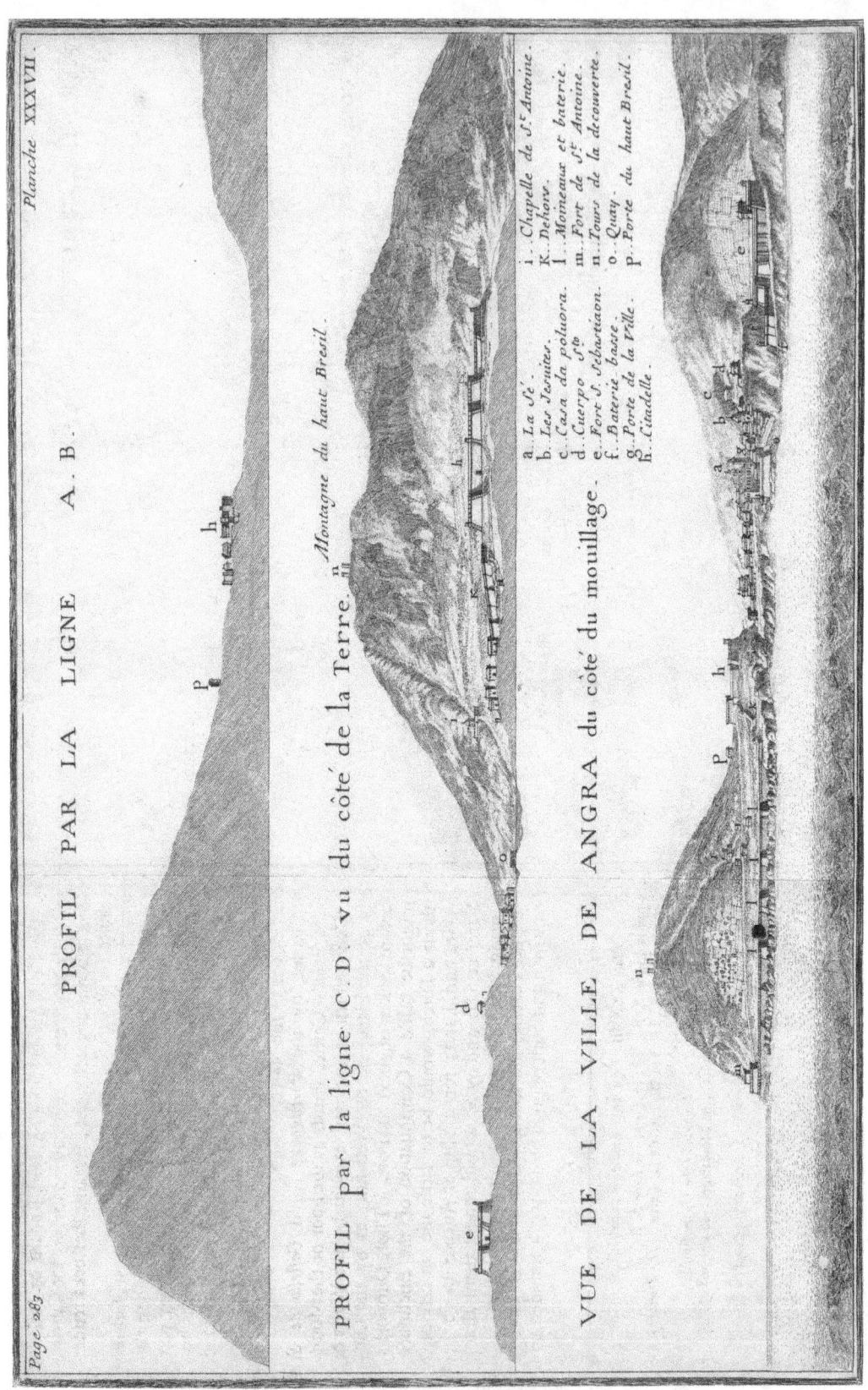

all along the Coast to the Citadel, with Redans or Indentures, and little Moineaus, or Plat Bastions before the Curtin, which flank it, without much need; because the Rocks render it inaccessible for Boats.

To secure a Communication between Fort S. *Anthony* and the Citadel, they have thrown up a Trench along the Mountain, cross'd by a little Gully, over which they pass on a Bridge, defended by two Redoubts, in the midst between which is a Chappel of S. *Anthony*, and a good Spring. *His Chappel.*

The Batteries of the Coast join without the Citadel, and come down to the Shore. *Batteries.*

The Citadel, by the *Portugueze* call'd *Castello de S. Joao*, or S. *John*'s Castle, stands at the Foot of the Mountain of *Brasil*, which it incloses, as well by the Walls of the Body of the Place, on the West-side, as by the Outworks before spoken of, next the Port. Those Outworks, which might be call'd a Continuation of the Enclosure, tho' without a Ditch, would be of little use, in case of a Siege by Sea and Land; for a Ship at Anchor in 50 Fathom Water at S. E. and by S. would render them almost useless, firing into them on Reverse and by Enfilade. *Citadel.*

The Upper Fort has not that Defect; it is well enough seated, contriv'd and built of good Stone-work, founded on a Rock

---

Plate XXXVII. Page 311. explain'd in English.

Profil par la Ligne A. B. *The Profile by the Line* A. B.
Profil par la Ligne C. D. Vuë du coté de la Terre. *The Profile by the Line* C. D. *seen from the Land-side.*
Montagne du haut Bresil. *The Mountain of the Upper* Brasil.
Vuë de la Ville de Angra du Coté du Mouillage. *A Prospect of the Town of* Angra *next the Anchoring place.*

a. *The Cathedral.*
b. *The Jesuites.*
c. *The Powder-house.*
d. *Corpo Santo.*
f. *A low Battery.*
g. *The City Gate.*
h. *The Citadel.*
i. *S. Anthony's Chappel.*
k. *Out-Parts.*
l. *A Plat Bastion and Battery.*
m. *S. Anthony's Fort.*
n. *Tower to look out.*
o. *The Key.*
p. *The Port of the upper* Brasil.

Rock, in which is dug a Ditch, between 4 and 5 Fathoms deep, and 10 or 12 in Breadth. At the Bottom of the Ditch, all along the Escarpe, there is a Row of Wells or Pits, 2 or 3 Fathoms square, and 10 or 12 Foot deep, which are so near one another, that they are only parted by a Traverse of the same Rock, 2 or 3 Foot thick. Before the Curtin, where the Gate is, those Rows of Wells or Pits are triple, and advanced within 4 or 5 Fathoms of the Counterscarp.

The Depth of the Ditch, the Reinforcement of those Pits, the Height of the Walls, and the Solidity of the Stonework, make the *Portugueze* fancy, that their Castle is impregnable; and the rather, because the *Spaniards* stood a Siege of three Years in it, till at last a Supply of 6000 *French* obliged them to abandon the Place, and get away by Sea, where they were taken.

By this may be judg'd what the Strength of the *Portugueze* was, and the manner of their Attacks; for in the first place, that Fortress has no other Outworks, besides a Horse-shooe next the Port, and a little Cover'd-way, now without Palisades; the Glacis whereof, at the Salliant Angle of the Bastion next the Town, is so steep, that it might well serve for a *Rideau*, or Covert, to take the Ditch by Sappe; and the more, for that it is mostly of Earth thrown up together, and the Rock under it seems to be very easy to cut.

Then the Ditch is only defended by three Pieces of Cannon; for the Flanks of the Bastion are so small, that they can hold no more; that is, one in the lower Flank, or Cazematte, one on the Back Flank above, and one in the Epaulment.

At the Entrance into the Fort, under the Rampart, is a good handsome Corps de Garde, vaulted, but not Bomb Proof, in my Opinion. I did not hear there was any thing else under Ground, besides the Powder Magazine.

In the Castle there are two fine Cisterns; and, in case of Necessity, they can also have Water from S. *Anthony*'s Spring,
which

which is on the Mountain of *Brafil*, which cannot be come at without paffing by the Fort, becaufe the Weft Coaft is lined with Batteries, almoft like that on the Eaft, and the South Side is fteep, with inacceffible Banks; for which Reafon the Fort has no other Enclofure, but a plain Wall on that Side. On the Top of the Eaft Hill there are two Towers call'd *Facha*, in which there is a Sentinel continually, to difcover what Ships come near the Ifland, the Number whereof he denotes by that of the Colours he puts out, as far as five; and for a Fleet they have another Signal.

As for the Building of the Body of the Place, it is faced with good Stone-Work of the Sort of the Millftones, on which is a Parapet fix or feven Foot thick, of the fame Subftance. The Rampart behind it is generally upon the Level with Earth-work, and the Jettees on the Weft-fide.

The Defence of the Baftions is Razant, the Faces are of about 28 Fathoms, the Flanks of 8, and the Curtins of 35 or 40. There are about Twenty Pieces of Cannon; and they fay there is a Magazine of 4000 Arms.

The Caftle of S. *John* having been formerly built by *Fort S. Sebaftian.* the *Spaniards*, on the Weft-fide of the Port, rather to command the Land than the Sea; the *Portugueze* have fince built a fmall Fort on the Eaft-fide, call'd Fort S. *Sebaftian*, to command the Road. It is a fquare Piece of Stone-Work, of about 60 Fathoms on the Out-fide, with the Entrance on the Land-fide with a little Ditch; and next the Sea, a Battery of a Salliant Angle before the Curtin, defended by the Faces of the little Baftions. Below this, level with the Water, there is another, built following the Turn of the Rock, which carries very well into the Road and the Port.

All the Batteries, and particularly that of S. *Anthony*, are well furnifh'd with Artillery, but in bad Order.

S f There

There are reck'ned above 200 Pieces of Iron Cannon, and about 20 Brass. Of the latter I saw none in the Castle, but a Culverin of 20 Pounds Ball, and 16 or 17 Foot long.

For the Guard of this Place, the King of *Portugal* generally allows 200 Men, but in a very different Manner from those at *Bahia de todos os Santos*; for he allows them so little Pay, that they are all poorly equip'd, and in a very wretched Condition. In short, they are said to have only 7000 Reys a Year, that is, little above Fifty Shillings of our Money, being under Two Pence a Day; but in Case of Need, there are in the Island 6000 Men able to bear Arms, according to the Computation made some Years ago, when they met to oppose Monsieur *du Guay*, who appear'd before that Island, and afterwards took that of S. *George*.

Tho' the City of *Angra* be in the best of the Islands *Terceras*, the Inhabitants thereof are Poor, because they have no other Trade but that of Corn, and some little Wine, which is carry'd to *Lisbon*, which scarce keeps them in Cloaths, so that Money is very scarce there. For this Reason it is perhaps, that they are more Courteous than those of the Bay of *All Saints*; but tho' Poverty humbles Men in outward Appearance, it does not make them the better; and therefore there must be no Confidence reposed in that fine Out-side; for some *European Portugueze* charge these with not having the same always in their Hearts which they utter'd by their Lips.

Churches. The Scarcity of Money has not however obstructed their building a Town that is pretty enough. The Houses there are but one Story high, rarely two, and contrary to ours, handsomer without, than well furnish'd within. The Churches are beautiful enough, built after a manner that has somewhat of Grandeur, by reason of the raised Walks, Platforms, and Galleries, which lead to, and adorn the Entrance, especially the Cathedral of the Invocation

cation of *S. Saviour*. The finest next to it are those of the *Franciscans* and the *Jesuits*, whose House appears fronting the Road, above all the other Buildings in the Town, to be known by that, as in all other Places, *vi* . by the good Choice of the advantageous Situation that Society is always sure to make for itself. There are two other Monasteries of less Note; that of the *Augustins*, call'd *Nossa Senhora da Graça*, or our Lady of Grace; and that of the *Recolets*, by them also call'd *Capucins*, seated on an Eminence without the Town. These, who are commendable for their good Behaviour, live in a fine Place, and an agreeable Poverty, under the Protection of their Patron S. *Anthony*, who among the *Portugueze* answers to S. *Francis* among the *Spaniards* in *Peru*, and S. *Patrick* among the *Irish*.

Answerable to the Four Monasteries of Men, there are Four of Nuns, one of the *Conception*, an Order brought from *Toledo*; one of Poor *Clares*, under the Invocation of *Nossa Senhora da Esperança*, or, our Lady of Hope; one of S. *Gonzalo*, and the fourth of *Capucin* Nuns.

I do not take Notice of many Chappels, which they call *Hermitas*, or Hermitages. They may be seen in the Plan.

Tho' the City is not upon a Level Plain, nor very regularly divided, it is nevertheless very agreeable; they have there the Conveniency of several good Fountains, distributed into every Quarter, and a Brook running through the middle of the City, to drive the necessary Mills for publick Use.

Near those Mills, which are most of them above the City, is an ancient little Fort, call'd by reason of its Neighbourhood *Forte dos Molinhos*, or the Fort of the Mills, and sometimes *Caza da Polvora*, or the Powder-House, because it now serves for a Magazine of Powder. It is a square Pile of Stone-Work of 15 Fathoms on every fide, flank'd after the ancient Manner, with a Half Tower in the middle of each fide. Thence is a Profpect of the whole City, from above; an agreeable Compofition of Land, Sea, Structures and Verdure, making up a pretty Landskip, and a very pleafing Object to the Eye.

In other Refpects, there is not about the Town, next the Country, any Enclofure, or detach'd Fortification; and yet it might be come at by Land, debarking at *Porto Judeo*, or *S. Martin*, which are two or three Leagues from thence, Eaft and Weft, where there is good Anchorage and little Defence: But it is fo little Advantage to the King of *Portugal* to have thofe Iflands, that I do not think any ought to envy him the Poffeffion thereof, for he receives nothing thence that may recommend them, except a little Corn. There are Abundance of thofe call'd *Canary* Birds, which are fmaller than thofe bred in *France*; but on the other hand they exceed them much in ftrength of Voice.

Departure from the Ifland Tercera.

HAving furnifh'd ourfelves with Water, Wood, Meal, Wine, fome Beeves, Fowls, and Greens, we fail'd on *Wednefday* the 15th of *July*.

S. Michael's Ifland.
The 20th we had fight of the Ifland of *S. Michael*, which appear'd to us at S. E. as it were divided into two Iflands, in the midft whereof were feveral little Hills, which might have been taken for little Ifles, had not we known that they were join'd by a low Land, which is loft at four Leagues Diftance, by which that Ifland is particularly to be known on the North-fide.

The 19th at Night, we had the Eaft Point of it, bearing South from us about twelve Leagues diftant, and ftood to the Eaftward during the Night, without apprehending

hending a Shoal laid down in the Charts in our Way, ten or twelve Leagues N. E. of the same Point of the Island of S. *Michael*; so that we must have pass'd over the Place where it is. We should have been very cautious of steering that Course, had not we been assured by the long Experience of a *Portugueze* Captain, that of all the Shoals laid down in the Charts about the *Azores*, there is really none but that of *Formigas*, lying between S. *Mary* and S. *Michael*, the other being barely deep Soundings, on which there is no less than 40 or 50 Fathom Water; but he warn'd us, that in those Places the Sea was much more rough than elsewhere. He did not even except the three or four Shoals laid down about 60 Leagues out at Sea, to the Westward, on which he said Islanders daily go a Fishing, because they there find abundance of Fish. He may be believ'd, yet without relying entirely upon it, or being disturb'd at the Nearness of those Places; for doubtless Mr. *Halley* has not left them out in his new Chart, without good Reasons for so doing, since it is of no less concern than the Loss of such Ships as should confidently make use of the same; wherein in all appearance an Hydrographer should rather err in exceeding than in omitting any thing. The one can only occasion some Loss of Time, or some groundless Fear; but the other may be the Cause of fatal unexpected Shipwrecks, if any thing of that which is doubted should happen to be found. Besides, it is possible that the Sea may fall, and at one Time discover that which was conceal'd at another.

I will here leave the Thread of my Relation, to tell what the said Captain told us concerning the Shoals and the *Abrolhos*, laid down under the Line, to the Northward of Cape S. *Augustin*. He affirms, that several Navigators have convinced him and all other *Portugueze* Captains sailing to *Brasil*, that there are none of those foul Places, except those call'd *Penon de S. Pedro*, which is a

Rock

Rock almoft round, rifing about 50 or 60 Fathoms above the Water, and near about four Cables Length Diameter, fo that it may be feen at four or five Leagues Diftance; and therefore it is not dangerous, and the more becaufe there is no Bottom all about it, which he had the Curiofity to be fatisfy'd in one Day when he was becalm'd very near it, having fent his Boat to found quite round it Mr. *Halley* in his Chart has alfo left out all thofe Shoals, as well as thofe of the *Azores*; but as I have faid elfewhere, he has without Reafon omitted the Ifland of the *Afcenfion*, to confound it with that of the *Trinity*. The fame Captain I am fpeaking of, confirm'd to us, that they were really two diftinct Iflands, and fituated very near as laid down in the *Dutch* Charts, in refpect to one another. Doubtlefs the other Ifland of the *Afcenfion*, which is about fix Degrees, near enough to the firft Meridian, made Mr. *Halley* judge that the other which is diftinguifh'd by the *Portugeze* Name of *Acençaon*, was Suppofititious. Let us return to the Voyage.

We paffed, as has been faid, over an imaginary Shoal, during the Night. The next Day, and the Day after the Winds began to grow boifterous, and the Sea ran high for fome Days, during the which our Mizzen-Sail fplit, and our Main-Top-Maft gave way, fo that we were obliged to change it immediately. During the firft Days that we made from the Iflands, we found fome little Difference with the Reck'ning to the Southward.

As foon as we were about half way over between the *Azores* and the Continent, the Wind became more favourable, and the Sea fmoother; and on the 31ft of *July* we arrived at the Mouth of the *Streights*, without any fenfible Error; whence it may be concluded that thofe Iflands are rightly laid down in the *Grand Flambeau de la Mer*.

Paffing

Paſſing through the Streights of *Gibraltar*, we heard many Cannon-ſhot from the famous Siege of *Ceuta*, which has been beſieged above 30 Years, by the People of *Morocco*; and at the beginning of the Night we ſaw the Fires of their Camp. We then went and anchor'd at Cape *Moulin*, near *Malaga*, to receive our Orders. Laſtly, on the 16th of *Auguſt* we came to an Anchor at the Iſles of *Hieres*, and the next Day at *Marſeilles*.

F I N I S.

POSTSCRIPT.

WE have noted in this Author, *pag.* 278. a Desire to depretiate the Sea-Chart of Mr. *Halley*, made to shew the Variations of the Compass, as not rightly representing the Situation of the Coast of *Peru* and *Chili*. Whether the single Reck'ning of the Ship *Mary-Ann* of *Marseilles* be sufficient to determine this matter, is submitted to the Reader's Judgment: But whatever ground there may be for this Exception, (in a matter wherein *Halley* pretends to no Knowledge of his own, but only to have followed the best Accounts he could at that time procure) yet as to his other Cavil, *p.* 291. he is fully assured that M. *Frezier* is under a gross mistake, when he affirms that the Island of *Ascension* and *Trinidad*, in the Lat. of about 20 Degrees South, are two different Islands; and in that respect gives the Preference to the old *Dutch* Charts. Mr. *Halley* knows, by the Description given of it, that the Island at which M. *Frezier* touched, and which by him is call'd *Ascension*, is the very same he calls *Trinidad*; and he is certain to Demonstration, that to the Eastward of this Island there are no others to be found, except the three Islets, or rather Rocks, which are but about 7 or 8 Leagues to Windward thereof, and which having been seen from the East, have by some been named the Isles of *Martin Vaz*. He affirms that in the Year 1700, he kept the Parallel of 20 Degrees, 20 Minutes South, with a West Course, for above 200 Leagues to the Eastward of this place, and met with no Land, or Sign of Land, by Birds or otherwise, till he first made the said three Rocks, which lie nearly in a Line North and South, and are not above a Mile asunder, the middlemost being the biggest, the other two very small, and the Southermost

very

very much resembling a Bell. Whence 'tis evident, that if our Island were *Ascension*, there can be no such as *Trinidad* East therefrom. And he challenges M. *Frezier* to produce any Authentick Account of Land seen thereabout, that was not in the said Latitude of 20 Degrees 20 Minutes.

Besides, this Latitude has been often examined by Ships which have had the Mischance, for want of an Observation, to miss the Island of *S. Helena*, and have been obliged to look for these Islands, in hopes to find a Watering-place. Particularly Commadore *Warren*, with a Squadron of five Men of War in the Year 1696, being bound to S. *Helena*, and design'd Convoy to the homeward-bound *East-India* Fleet, had the misfortune to fall to Leeward of that Island, and being in great want of Water, he hoped to find relief at some of those Isles which the Charts describe between the Latitudes of 20 and 21 Degrees: And not being sure of their Situation, he spread his Ships so as nothing between those two Parallels could be pass'd by undiscovered: But following a due West Course almost home to the Main of *Brasil*, for near 400 Leagues, he found no other than this single Island which we call *Trinidad*, and the *French Ascension*; which afforded him no sufficient Water-place. Moreover, all the Islands thereabout being by Letters Patents of his late Majesty King *William*, granted to Sir *John Hoskyns*, late of *Harwood* in the County of *Hereford*, Bart. and to his Heirs; the said Honourable Proprietor has caused Possession of the said *Trinidad* to be taken for his Use, in the name of the Crown of *England*, and has put live Stock thereon; having found himself disappointed of all the rest that are laid down in the Charts, which upon due search he was satisfied were not *in rerum natura*.

It must however be owned, as an Obligation from M. *Frezier*, that he does not require the Site of the Islands of *Dos Picos*, *Maria d'Agosta* and *Martin Vaz*, as well as that of *Trinidad*, and that of *Penon de S. Paulo*, which he miscalls *de S. Pedro*, of the Omission whereof he complains in his last Leaf. This latter may, for ought we know to

T t the

the contrary, be an Omiſſion; but then M. *Halley*, when he made his Chart, had no account of its being ever ſeen by the *Engliſh* Pilots, as lying out of the way of their Shipping; much leſs had he any Authority where to place it in reſpect of the adjoining Continent.

Laſtly, M. *Frezier* might have as well obſerved that his new Diſcovery lying N. E. from *Le Maire* Streight, in 51 grad. is found in the aforeſaid Chart of the Variations, by the Name of *Falkland's Iſles*, as to have amuſed his Reader with the Pretences of the Omiſſions of ſuch minute Matters, as are not ordinarily to be expected in a General Chart.

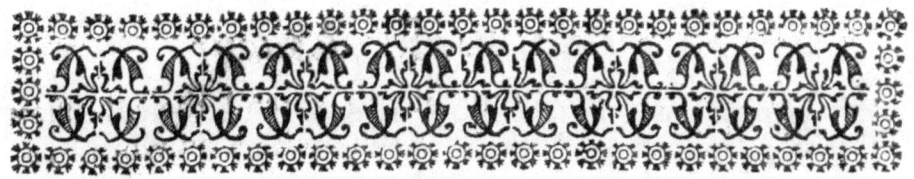

Some * Account of the Settlement of the *JESUITES* in the Spanish Indies.

OF all the Settlements that have been made in the *Indies* since the Conquest of that vast Country by the *Spaniards*, there neither has been, nor ever will be, any so considerable, as that which the Jesuites have form'd there. The first Beginning of this Settlement was only 50 Families of wandring *Indians*, whom the Jesuites were at the pains of collecting together, and fixing upon the Banks of the River *Japsur* in the Heart of the Country; but it has increased in such a manner, that it contains at present above 300000 Families, possess'd of the finest Part of all the Continent, situate 200 Leagues South from the *Portugueze Paulists*, and separated from them by the River of *Loruguay*, which falls into the Great *Parava* and *Japsur*, and these again discharge themselves into the River of *Paraguay*. This last takes it Course, according to the Discoveries of the Jesuites in 1702 and 1703, (which are the best that ever were made) from the foot of the Mountains of *Potosi*. The Air there is temperate, the Land fertile, the *Indian* Inhabitants laborious and tractable; and there must undoubtedly be Plenty of Gold and Silver Mines. Those *Indians* might be brought with ease to submit themselves, could a Method be found to improve and cultivate them.

---

* *This Account is not Monsieur* Frezier's; *neither is it printed in the* Paris *Edition of his Book.*

The Jesuites Settlement

The Jesuites have not been able to extend their Mission that way, for want of Fathers; otherwise they would receive an Augmentation of more than 60000 Families, and 300 Leagues of Ground.

To resume the Thread of our Account, and the Situation of the Jesuites Country, it is, as above observ'd, 200 Leagues South of the *Paulists*, 200 North of the Province of *Buenos Ayres*, 180 from that of *Tucuman*, and 100 from *Paraguay*. These 3 Provinces are separated from the Kingdoms of *Chili* and *Peru* by the Chain of Mountains call'd *La Cordillera*, and were of themselves a Kingdom before the Conquest of the *Indies*.

The Country of the Mission is fruitful, being water'd with a great number of Rivers, which form Islands in many Places. They have Plenty of Timber and Fruit-trees, excellent Pulse, Bread-Corn, Flax, Indigo, Hemp, Cotton, Sugar, *Piemento*, *Hypecacuana*, *Galapa*, *Machecacuana*, a Root they call *Lautrabanda*, and many other Simples of great Use in Pharmacy, particularly the Herb *Paraguay*. Their *Savanna*'s, or Meadow-Lands, are full of Horses, Mules, Cows, Bulls, and Flocks of Sheep: And more than all these, their Gold and Silver Mines are very considerable. 'Tis true, the good Fathers will not own it; but there are too many Proofs of it, to leave any room for Doubt.

The People are good-natured and quiet, handy and laborious; and are brought up to all sorts of Trades. They are at present divided into 42 Parishes, from 1 to 10 Leagues apart, lying along the River of *Paraguay*; and in every Parish there is a Jesuite, who has the Supreme Command, and is obey'd with the exactest Regard and Awe. He punishes the least Fault, if he pleases, with the utmost Severity.

The ordinary Chastisement there, is a certain number of Lashes with a Whip, in proportion to the nature of the Crime. The *Caciques* and others, who are in the best Posts of the Government, whether Civil or Military, are not exempted from it: But which is very particular, he that has been severely whipt, comes and kisses the Father's Sleeve, acknowledges his Fault, and thanks him for the Correction he has received. Thus doth one single Man command 10000 Families, more or less; and 'tis certain, there never was known a more submissive People, or a more perfect Subjection.

The same Method of governing has been introduced into all the Parishes of the Mission. But that is not all: This entire Submission is attended with such a Contentment of Mind, (which the Jesuites have taken care to press upon the *Indians*, in consideration of the Felicities of another Life, whereof they pretend to grant them Shares in this) that the *Indians* are very happy with bare Food and Raiment, and do not repine at the good Fathers reaping all the Benefit of their Labours; for which purpose they have large Ware-houses in every Parish, whither the *Indians* are obliged to carry Provisions, Stuffs, and generally every thing without exception; they not having the liberty so much as to eat a Chick of their own Brood; so that all those Multitudes of *Indians* may justly be reckon'd as so many Slaves to the Jesuites for their Bread; and that Verse of *Virgil* cannot be more properly apply'd, than to them:

Sic vos non vobis fertis aratra, boves.

Let it be consider'd at the same time, what vast Advantages those Sovereign Fathers must needs make of the Labour of so many hands, and what a Trade they drive to all Parts of the *Indies*, with the above-mentioned Commodities, particularly the Herb *Paraguay*, of which they vend an immense Quantity, there being none but what comes from the Jesuites Country, or from the Province of *Paraguay*. That Herb is drank almost like Tea; the *Spaniards* and *Indians*, as well Masters as Slaves, using it Morning and Evening. It is computed, that the Sale of that Herb, at first hand, comes to above a Million of

Crowns

Crowns a Year; and the Jesuites have the best Part of it, which, with the other Commodities they vend to equal Advantage, and with the Gold-Dust, which the *Indians* go and gather up in the Washes where the Waters have been, after their Rivers are sunk below their Banks again, brings in to the Jesuites the Revenue of a Sovereign. For the forming a truer Idea of this matter, be it supposed, that each Family of *Indians* does not produce to the Jesuites above 50 Livres a Year, all Expences borne; why, even at this rate the general Produce of 300000 Families will appear to amount to 5 Millions of Crowns; but this Hint is sufficient to convince any one, that they get a great deal more. However, if you'll believe those good Fathers, their Mission costs them a great deal of Pains, and brings them but little Profit: But this must be taken in the Sense they generally speak, the Interpretation whereof is *Nunquam satis*.

The Gold and Silver, coin'd and uncoin'd, which the Jesuites send by every Opportunity into *Europe*; the Magnificence of their Churches, where massy Gold and Silver are glittering on every side; and their considerable Commerce, which is known to all the *Spaniards*, oblige Men to form a different Judgment.

It may not be amiss to give here a Description of the Church and Apartment of the Father of one of the Parishes, from the Mouths of two *Frenchmen* belonging to the Ship of Monsieur *de la Solliette d'Escaseau* of *Nantes*.

That Ship being in the Port of *Maldonades*, weigh'd Anchor, and set Sail, when the said two *Frenchmen*, one a Captain of Arms on board, and the other a Sergeant, happen'd to be on shoar, and at so great a Distance, that they came too late for the Boat, which was gone off. Not knowing what to do in this case, all the Coast being desart, they resolv'd to advance into the Country, tho' they had no other Sustenance than what their Fusees brought them. Having march'd three Days, they met *Indians* with Beads about their Necks, who received them

very

very kindly, and made a thousand Signs of Friendship to them; for they naturally love the *French*, and distinguish them from all other Nations. They even conducted them to one of the Parishes belonging to the *Mission*, above 200 Leagues from the Place where they first met, and liv'd by the way upon wild Cows, which the *Indians* take at pleasure with incredible Dexterity, by throwing a Noose over their Heads at 4 or 5 Yards distance; after which they hamstring them, and stick them in the Throat. Our two *Frenchmen* being arrived at the *Mission*, were well received by the Jesuite, at whose House they tarry'd four Months, without ever going abroad, and then return'd to *Buenos Ayres* with a Detachment of *Indians* which the Governor demanded. The Account they give, is this: The Parish-Church there is long, and proportionably broad; the principal Entrance into it, is a Portico, and an Ascent of several Steps, at the top of which are 8 Stone Pillars wrought with a good Shew of Art, which help to support the Front of the Portico. Over the Entrance of the Church, is a very spacious Lobby for the Musick in Divine Service, which consists of 60 Persons, Voices and Instruments. There is also a particular Place for the Women, set round with a Balustrade.

The rest of the Church is full of Seats, where the Men place themselves according to their Posts and Ages. The great Altar is shut in by a Balustrade of *India* Wood very curiously wrought. On the Left of the Altar, is a Seat for the *Cacique* and Civil Officers; on the Right, another for the Military: But all in general are placed agreeably to their Rank.

The Facing of the Altar is very sumptuous. In the first place are three large Pictures in Frames of massy Gold and Silver. Above them are carv'd Works and Bass Reliefs in Gold; and higher yet, quite up to the Roof, is a Sculpture of Wood enrich'd with Gold. On the two Sides of the Altar are two Pedestals of Wood cover'd with Plates of Gold engraven, on which stand two Saints of massy
Silver.

Silver. The Tabernacle is of Gold. The Pyx, wherein the Holy Sacrament is kept, is made of Gold, and set round with Emeralds and other precious Stones. The Foot and Sides of the Altar are adorn'd with Cloth of Gold laced. In short, the Candlesticks, and other Vessels of Gold and Silver, with which the Altar is set off at such times as the Service is perform'd with a great number of Wax-Candles, make a Shew almost beyond all Imagination. There are two other Altars on the Right and Left, adorn'd and enrich'd in proportion to the great one; and in the Body of the Church, toward the Balustrade, is a Silver Candlestick of 30 Branches enrich'd with Gold, with a great Silver Chain which reaches quite to the Roof. By this Description one may form some Judgment of the Riches of that Mission, if all the 42 Parishes are upon the same foot, as it is reasonable to believe.

The Presbytery, or Father's House, consists of several spacious Halls adorn'd with a great many Pictures and Images, in which the *Indians* wait till the Father comes out of his Apartment to give Audience. There are moreover large Warehouses, to which the *Indians* bring all the Fruit of their Labour. The rest of the House contains Walks, Gardens, and divers Lodings for the Domestick *Indians*; the whole, with the Church, making a wall'd Inclosure of about 6000 Perches square.

The 42 Jesuites, who have each their Parish to govern, are independent one of another, and are answerable to none but the Principal of the Convent of *Cordoua* in the Province of *Tucuman*, who makes a Progress once a Year to visit the *Missions*, guarded by a great Number of *Indians*. Upon his Arrival, the *Indians* shew all possible Demonstrations of Joy and Respect. The Principal of them do not approach him without Trembling, and Hanging down the Head; and the Common sort are upon their Knees, with their Hands cross'd, as he passes along. During his Stay he makes the Jesuite of every Parish give him an Account of all that hath been brought into the

Store-

Store-Houses, and of the Consumption thereof since his last Visit.

All the Merchandizes mention'd toward the Beginning of this Relation, are carry'd by Water from the *Missions* to *Santa Fe*, which being the Staple for them, the Order hath an Attorney General there; and from *Santa Fe* they are carry'd to *Buenos Ayres* by Land, where they have likewise an Attorney. From those two Places they dibute their Goods into the three Provinces of *Tucuman*, *Paraguay*, and *Buenos Ayres*, and into the Kingdoms of *Chili* and *Peru*; and we may safely affirm, that the *Mission* of the Jesuites alone drives a greater Trade than all the three Provinces together.

The chief Business of the *Caciques*, or Civil Magistrates, is to learn the Number of Families, to make known to all of them the Orders and Intentions of the Father, to visit Houses, to examine every one's Work according to his Abilities, and to promise as a Reward to him who doth the most and the best, that he shall kiss the Father's Sleeve, which is held in great Veneration by those *Indians*, as being the first Step toward attaining to the Beatitude of the next Life. There are other Inspectors for the Country, to whom the *Indians* are obliged to declare every thing they get, even to a single Egg, which they must not dispose of; being to carry all, without Exception, into the Magazines, upon very severe Penalties. There are also Distributors, who give out to every Family, according to its Number, twice a Week, whereon to subsist: And this is done in wonderful Order, in the Jesuite's Presence; to whose Praise it must be said, that their Labours are endless, since they are vigilant, in the last degree, to prevent their *Indians* from running into any Disorder: Not but that they are made ample Amends too, by the vast Profit of the Work of so many Hands.

There were formerly two Jesuites in every Parish; but since their great Accessions, there can be but one, till they get some more over from *Spain*.

The *Indians* do not drink any Wine, or other hot Liquors. Herein the good Fathers copy after the Law of *Mahomet*, who forbad them to his Followers, left being inflamed, they should be apt to raise Commotions, give Disturbance to his Despotick Government, and perhaps shake off the Yoke he had laid upon their Necks.

They marry the *Indians* young, for the sake of Procreation; and the first Catechism they teach their Children, is the Fear of God and of the Jesuite, the Contempt of Temporal Goods, and a plain and humble Life. These, it must be own'd, are pious Dispositions; but then it is no less certain, that the good Fathers find their Account in such political Instructions.

The Military Government is as well establish'd there, as the Civil. Every Parish is obliged to maintain a Number of disciplin'd Troops by Regiments of Horse and Foot, in proportion to its Strength. Each Regiment consists of six Companies of 50 Men, a Colonel, six Captains, six Lieutenants, and a General Officer who exercises them every *Sunday* after Vespers. Those Officers, who are brought up to Arms from Father to Son, are very expert in disciplining their Men, and in leading them when they march in Detachments. It is upon no other Occasion that the Parishes have a Communication, but only to form an Army, which the Senior General Officer commands under the Direction of a Jesuite, who is Generalissimo. The Arms of those *Indians* are Fusees, Swords, Bayonets, and Slings, with which they throw Stones to five Pound Weight, and are very dextrous at that Weapon.

The *Missions* together can assemble 60000 Men in eight Days time. Their Pretence for maintaining so great a Number is, because the *Portugueze Paulists* make Excursions into the Country, to take away their *Indians*: But this doth not go down with the more knowing *Spaniards*, who are convinced that the *Jesuites* keep so many Troops on foot, for no other End than to hinder all the World without

out Exception from having any Communication with their *Miſſion*.

Their Precaution in not teaching the *Indians* the *Spaniſh* Tongue, and in making it a Caſe of Conſcience for them not to converſe with the *Spaniards* when they go to work in the Towns for the King's Service, is declarative enough of the true Deſign of the Father Jeſuites. The Foreigners who are driven by any Accident into their *Miſſions*, as the *Frenchmen* above-mention'd; nay, the *Spaniards* themſelves, who are ſometimes obliged to touch upon them, paſſing to and fro upon the River of *Paraguay*, do not ſtir without the Walls of the Presbytery: But if the *Spaniards* do intreat for Leave to take a Walk in the Town, be ſure the Jeſuite is always at their Side; and the *Indians* being forewarn'd, ſhut their Doors, and are never ſeen in the Streets. Whence 'tis plain, the Jeſuites have very good Reaſons for uſing ſo much Circumſpection with regard even to their own Countrymen. They have moreover the Precaution to make Detachments of 5 or 6000 Men, by Battalions of 4 or 500, to ſcour the Country along the Coaſt, from S. *Gabriel*'s Iſles to the Mountains of *Maldonades*, and the River they call *Rio de los Patos*, to cut off all Communication betwixt thoſe Lands and the *Europeans* or People of the Country, for the ſake of the Gold and Silver Mines, which are there in abundance.

We will here give ſome Inſtances of the Excurſions of thoſe *Indians* along the Coaſt. The Ship *Falmouth* of S. *Malo* being caſt away near the Iſles of *Flores* in the Year 1706, the *Indians* plunder'd a Part of her Cargo, which the Governor of *Buenos Ayres* caus'd them to reſtore, and it is actually in the Fort. The *Atlas*, which periſh'd at the *Caſtiles*, in *December* 1708; whoſe Officers having ſaved ſome of their Goods, and Sails to make Tents, were ſtript of all by the *Indians*, in their March over Land to the *Maldonades*, in order to come back by Sea, and take up their Silver

Silver which they had happily bury'd, to the Value of above 200000 Crowns.

There are considerable Mines at the foot of the Mountains of *Maldonades*, 24 Leagues from the Port, and 14 from *Montevide*, which were discover'd by *Dom Juan Pacheco*, Inhabitant of *Buenos Ayres*, and ancient Miner of *Potosi*. He gave Advice thereof to *Dom Alonso Juan de Valdes Inelau*, Governor of *Buenos Ayres*, who made a Detachment of 15 Men, under the Command of *Dom Joseph de Vermude*, Captain of Foot, and Engineer at *Buenos Ayres*. These embarqued with *Dom Pacheco*, and crossing the River, they march'd to the Head of the Mountains of *Maldonades*, where they search'd the Earth, and return'd with Stones from the Mines containing Gold and Silver: But the Governor, being gain'd by the Jesuites, gave out that he had made a Proof, and found they would not answer the Labour. However, *Dom Pacheco*, who had reserv'd his own, was convinced that this was a meer Fetch of the Jesuites, to prevent a Settlement on the side of their *Mission*.

Some Pieces taken out of those Mines have been brought to *France*, where they may have been try'd, to know their Value: But they were taken from the very Surface of the Earth with Pick-Axes only. The aforesaid *Dom Pacheco*, who is celebrated for the most experienced Miner that hath been in *Peru* these many Years, affirms, that there is no better Earth in the World to search, than that round the Mountains of *Maldonades*, and the Rivers thereabout, in which he doubts not but Gold-Dust might as easily be found, as by the *Portugueze Paulists*, and in as good Quantities. The *Indians* of *S. Dominick de Suvillant* have several times brought such Gold to *Buenos Ayres*, which they found in the Territories of the *Mission*; whence we may conclude, that there is a great deal of it, because this Gold was taken by Stealth by the young *Indians*, who are not so scrupulous as the others.

In the Year 1706, the Sieur *de la Solliette d'Escaseau* of *Nantes*, having cast Anchor in the Port of *Maldonade*, was

accosted

accosted by the *Indians* of a Detachment who came under a Chief upon that Coast, to get Cows together, and drive them to the *Missions*. Monsieur *d'Escaseau* having made them a Present, they proposed to him, in Return, that if he would advance so far into the Country, to a Place they pointed to him, he should find Silver Mines easy to be come at; which proves, that those Mines do not lie deep in the Earth, and also that they are plenty.

The Jesuites have always been apprehensive of the Discovery of those Mines by the *Spaniards*, and will do all that is in their Power to prevent the working them, because the making a Settlement upon that Coast would prejudice the good Fathers, who would be obliged to furnish *Indians* to labour in them. They have even destroy'd all the Horses on that side, to make it the more incommodious for People to settle there.

It remains now to make a just Application of the Conduct of the Jesuites in the Particulars above recited, and to shew that their Ambition of Sovereign Power, and their insatiable Desire of heaping up immense Riches, are the only Objects they pursue. The Method they take in educating and governing their *Indians*, from whom they squeeze all the Fruits of their Labours, leaving them nothing but the Necessaries of a frugal Life; the Care they take to hinder their Communication with the *Spaniards*; their Circumspection when at any time either *Spaniards* or Foreigners are driven by Accident into their *Mission*; the Number of armed Men they continually keep on foot; their perpetual Scouring the Coast by Detachments, to prevent Peoples Settlement on it; all these are plain Proofs, that they aim at making themselves independent, and not only conceal the Advantages of the Country they are possess'd of, but even of what they have not in Possession. Nevertheless, that Country belongs without all Dispute to the King of *Spain*, as Lord and Sovereign of the *Indies:* Nor ought such a Number of People to be reduced under any other Obedience than his
alone

alone. They ought to be free to have Lands, and the Disposal of their Crops and Labour. By this means they would become a Colony in Form; every Man would improve his Talent, with the Gold and Silver Mines of the Country; Money would be coin'd, and all together would cause a Circulation of Trade there as well as in other Colonies; the King's Authority would be acknowledg'd, and his Dominions preserv'd: But nothing of all this; the Jesuites have made themselves Absolute Lords and Masters over all those reduced *Indians*, together with the Country they possess, their Fruits and Labour, and extend themselves farther and farther every Day, without Title or Permission. The *Indians* have nothing of their own; the Jesuites have all; and those poor People, who have a Right to be free, having voluntarily subjected themselves, are treated like true Slaves: And in short, 300000 Families, and more, work for 40 *Jesuites*, and own and obey none but them. One Circumstance which makes good this Assertion, is, that when the Governor of *Buenos Ayres* receiv'd Orders to lay Siege to S. *Gabriel*, in which a Detachment of 4000 *Indian* Horse assisted, with a Jesuite at their Head, the Governor commanded the Sergeant Major to make an Attack at Four o' Clock in the Morning; but the *Indians* refused to obey, because they had not the Jesuite's Order, and were even upon the point of revolting, when the Jesuite (being sent for) arrived, under whom they ranged themselves, and executed the Order from his Mouth. Hence you may judge, how jealous those Fathers are of their Authority with regard to their *Indians*, even to the forbidding them to obey the King's Officers, when 'tis plainly for his Majesty's Service.

The Capitation Tax of a Crown a Head which the Jesuites ought to pay the King yearly for every *Indian*, is not only exhausted by the Payment of the *Indians* employ'd in his Majesty's Works, but there is hardly a Year that the King is not made a Debtor, for three Reasons
equally

equally fallacious. The firſt is, That the Jeſuites do not give in an Account of half their *Indians* for the Capitation. The ſecond, That the Governor of *Buenos Ayres*, who ought once, in the five Years of his Governmet, to viſit the *Miſſions*, and take an Acconnt of the *Indians*, is prevented by the Jeſuites, who making him a Preſent of a round Sum of Money, the End of his Viſit is loſt, and he contents himſelf with the Jeſuites own Liſt of their Families. The third Reaſon is, That when a Detachment of 500 *Indians* is employ'd in the King's Works, they ſet him down 1500, and ſo many his Majeſty pays. Thus is his Catholick Majeſty ſerv'd in the *Indies*, where his Revenues are conſumed in feign'd Employments, Fraud, and Plunder. Theſe Abuſes do however deſerve the moſt ſerious Attention; ſeeing the King's Revenues, which ought to amount at leaſt to 30 Millions of Livres, (were his Majeſty faithfully ſerv'd) are brought to nothing, or to very little, becauſe the Governors and Treaſurers have a good Underſtanding, and only contend who ſhall plunder moſt. What remains therefore, (to anſwer the End of this Relation) but to find Means of reducing the Jeſuites to their Duty, to bridle their Abſolute Power, and to turn ſome Part of the Profits which accrue to them from the Labour of ſo many Hands, to the King's Advantage? Nothing can excuſe the Jeſuites from ſubmitting to it, unleſs they will give Marks of their Diſobedience and wicked Intent: Tho', after all, we are perſuaded, that they'll raiſe Obſtacles enow, and alledge ſeveral ſpecious Pretexts, but eaſy to be anſwered and not ſurrender till the laſt Extremity.

THE INDEX.

A.

Accident unlucky. Page 105
Aconcagua River. 121
Advice for turning of Cape Horn. 42
Agi, *a sort of Guinea Pepper*. 151
  Cultivating of it. 152
Alpaques, *useful Creatures*. 154
Ambergrease. 15
Andaguailas *Borough*. 184
Anican *Islands*. 288
Angra *City described*. 309
  St. Anthony's Fort. 310
  His Chappel, Batteries and Citadel. 311
  Fort S. Sebastian. 313
  Churches. 314
Anil, *a sort of Indigo*. 78
Apurima *wonderful Bridge*. 184
Aqueducts *of* Indians. 214
Architecture *of* Peru. 262
Arequipa *Town*. 176
Arica, *Marks to know it, the Headland, and Description of the Town.* 148
  Landing Places and Fortifications. 149
  Churches and Vale. 151
  Trade there. 152
  Its former Trade. 154
  Difficulty of getting out of it. 169
Ascension *Island*. 290
  Anchoring there. 291

Assumption *Coast*. 288
Avancay *Borough*. 184
Author, *his Inclination, embarques at* S. Malo. 1
  Sails out of that Port. 2
  Puts in again. 3
  Sails again. 4
  Passes the Line, and Ceremonies observ'd there by Sailors. 14
  Repents his going to Sea, and Reflections thereon. 38
  Goes aboard another Ship at Coquimbo. 137
  Removes to another at Arica. 169
  Again to another at Hilo. 179
  Arrives at Lima. 203
  Removes to another Ship at Callao. 275
  Sails for France. 281

B.

Baldivia *City, in* Chili, *with the Cutt of the Port*. 42
  Strength of that Place. 44, 45
Bananas *Fruit*. 25
Bay of all Saints *in* Brasil, *how to know it*. 294
  Mouth of it. ibid.
Beeves, *hunting of them*. 28
Bezoar *Stone*. 142

Bisnaga

The INDEX.

Bisnaga *Plant*.	Page 118
Boldy, *Aromatick Plant*.	78
Brasil *Coast*.	291
Bribery.	220
Bull *Feast*.	188
Butchers Meat in Chili.	122

C.

Calama *Village*.	145
Callao *Port, how known*.	192
Description of its Road.	193
Anchorage there.	194
Description of the Town.	195
Fortifications and Artillery.	196
Forces paid by the King there.	197
Militia and Situation.	199
Streets, Square, Trade.	200
Churches, Monasteries, Inhabitants, Garrison, Governor, Engineer, and Road to Lima.	202
Departure from thence.	275
Calm dead,	15
Camarones *Break*.	148
Corangue *Fish*.	27
Carapucho *Headland*.	146
Carapullo *Plant*.	236
Cassia Fistula.	173
Ceremony us'd by the Chilinians at making Peace.	79
Cerro del Guanaquero.	127
Chacanza *River*.	144
Chanaral *Island*.	138
Channel, a new one discover'd in Tierra del Fuego.	286
Tokens to know it.	287
Charts, Errors in them.	30, 278, 285
Chili, *Towns and Inhabitants there*.	102
Trade there.	115
Why so call'd.	ibid.
No wild Beasts, or venemous Creatures there.	132
Commodities of the Country.	200
Chimists, *Pretences of theirs*.	164
Chiouchiou *Village*.	Page 145
Choros *Island*.	138
Chuncos Indians.	176
Clouds green.	6
Cobija *Port*.	143
Not safe.	144
Cobija *Village*.	ibid.
Coco *Plant, a Preservative*.	167
More of it.	269
Coco Tree.	118
Commodities of Chili, Peru and Mexico.	200
Conception *Festival*.	239
La Conception *Port, Tokens to know it by, with a Cutt of the same*.	47
The Bay describ'd.	50
The best Place to furnish Ships.	51
The Town describ'd, with the Cutt, its Situation.	52
Fortifications and Artillery.	53
Military Government, advanc'd Posts.	54
Civil and Ecclesiastical Government.	55
Trade.	75
Fruit, with the Cutt.	76
Aromatick Herbs.	77
Dying Herbs, and Aromatick Trees.	78
Wild Fowl.	80
Fish.	82
Gold and Copper Mines.	ibid.
Return thither.	179
Departure from thence.	282
Condor Bird.	122
Conjectures concerning Earthquakes.	212
About Currents.	41
Copiapo *Mines, Inhabitants, Product and Trade*.	133
Departure thence.	143
Copper Mines.	82, 134
Coquimbo *Bay, how known*.	128
Describ'd.	ibid.
Caution about anchoring there.	129

The INDEX.

Inconveniences in the Port. Pag. 130
Coquimbo *River.* 130
  Provisions there. 135
  Directions how to get out of the Bay. 137
Corn *Country.* 116
  Its Cheapness. 117
Coral *Port, at* Baldivia. 44
Cotton, how it grows, with the Cutt of it. 25
Countercharms. 242
Crabs. 122
Creolian Spaniards born in Peru. 248
Cruzes *Fort, near* Baldivia. 46
Crucifix Natural. 110
Cuesta de Prado *Hill.* 98
Curoama *Cape.* 88
Currents. 16, 139, 147, 305
Conjectures about them. 41
  Why out at Sea, contrary to those on the Coast. 275
Cusco *City.* 175
Customs and Manners of the Spaniards of Peru. 238

D.

Damiers *Birds.* 29
  Dampier's *Account of Cotton in* Brasil. 26
  His false Account of Arica. 150
Dance call'd Zapateo. 256
Dancing in Peru. 255
Dangerous going to Santiago. 97
Departure from the Island of S. Katharine. 29
  From La Conception. 88
  From Valparaiso. 127
  From Coquimbo. 137
  From Copiapo. 143
  From Arica. 169
  From Hilo. 179
  From Pisco. 192
  From Callao. 275

From La Conception *again.* Pag. 282
From the Bay of all Saints. 305
From the Island Tercera. 316
Desart very great. 142
Devotion of the Rosary. 239
Diego Ramirez *Island.* 87
Directions to sail out of the Bay of Coquimbo. 137
Dorados, or Gilt Backs, Fishes. 6
Ducking of Sailors. 15, 125
Dying Herbs. 78

E.

Earth, *how it may run.* 213
  How it can produce without Rain. 213
Earthen Ware in Peru. 273
Earthquakes in Chili. 101, 123, 210, 211
  Conjectures concerning them. 212
  Why more near the Coast than up the Inlands. ibid.
Engines Royal. 155
Errors of Charts. 278, 285, 305
Essaying of Silver. 156
Exhalations of Mines. 166

F.

FEr's America. 285
  Fertility of Chili. 119
  Of Peru. 152
Festival of the Scapulor 187
  Of the Conception. 273
Fire Works. 204
Fishery. 121
Fishes of several sorts. 27
Flamancos *Birds.* 80
Floats of blown Skins. 120
Floripondio *Plant.* 77
Flowers in Peru. 236
Flying Fishes. 8
Forces paid by the King, at Callao. 197
Fort de la Latte, near S. Malo. 2

Fowl

The INDEX.

Fowl numerous in 21 and 22 Degrees of South Latitude. Page 15
Fraud in Silver. 159
Frenage Road, near S. Malo. 2
French Trade to the South-Sea. 201
   Order to dismiss them all. 279
Frier complimented. 124
Fruit at Pisco. 186
   At Lima. 232
Furniture of Houses in Peru. 261

G.

GAL Island, on the Coast of Peru. 22
Galera Point. 43
Game at S. Katharine's Island. 28
General of the South-Sea. 125
Giacotins Birds. 28
Giants. 84
Gold, how separated from the Dross. 107
   Refining of it, Weight and Fineness, and Product. 108
   Opinion about it. 112
   Disprov'd. 113
   Another reinforced, and more Notions about it. ibid.
   Another more probable. 114
   Plenty of it. 134
   Large Grains of it. 167
Gold Mines. 82
   At Tilsil. 106
   At Lampanqui. 114
   Rare in Peru. 167
Granadillos Fruit. 233
Guaico Mines. 145
Guamanga City. 184
Guana, a sort of Manure. 147
Guanacos Beast of Peru. 142, 154
Guancavelica Town, and Quicksilver Mine. 183
Guarupa, Port of Brasil. 28
Guasco Bay. 138
Guayacum. 25
Guayava. ibid.

H.

Habit of the Inhabitants of the Island of S. Katharine. Page 23
Of the Spaniards of Peru. 258
Of the Natives. 260
Halley, Dr. his Postscript in Vindication of himself. 220 & seqq.
Harillo Plant. 118
Herradura Creek. 128
Hierro Island. 7
Higos de Tuna Fruit. 233
Hilo, Marks to know it by, Description of the Road and Landing Place. 170
   Village, Watering-Place, Wooding, and Plants there. 172
   Other Product. 174
   Resort to it. 175
   Inconveniences there. 177
   Departure from thence. 179
Horn Cape, its Longitude. 285
Houses cover'd with Mats. 217
Houses in Peru. 261, 273

I.

JApsur River. 313
Ica Town. 183
Ice floating in the South-Sea. 283
Jesuites, an Account of their Settlement, &c. in Paraguay. 323 to 335
Indians of Chili. 57
   Their Government. 59
   Servitude of those who are subdued. 60
   Their Assemblies and Sports, with a Cutt. 62
   Their Arms, and Noosing of Horses. 63
   Their Festivals describ'd. 65
   A Tune of theirs. 66
   Their Constitution and Food. 67
   Their Drink and Colour. 68
   Shape and Hair. 69
   Their Habit, with a Cutt. 70
   Their Houses. 71

The INDEX.

Knots in Tossels of Thead us'd by them instead of Writing. Page 73
Their Trade. 74
Stratagem of theirs. 115
Their Tombs. 177
Their Aqueducts. 214
Those of Peru. 263
Their Habit. 270
Their Houses. 273
Ingas *Monarchs of* Peru. 271
One of their Race still honour'd. 272
Inhabitants of Chili, their Number. 102
Of Peru, their Number. 274
Inquisition in Chili. 105
John Fernandes *Island*. 96
Iquique *Island*. 146
Islands of Cape Verde. 7
How to know them. ibid.
Island of Parrots. 29
See it in Plate 3, between 18 and 19

Horse. 222
Courts, Council, Treasury, Mint, Consulship, Spiritual Courts. 223
University, Colleges, Chapter. 225
Cathedral, Archbishops, Parishes. 226
Hospitals. 227
Charity, Portions for Maids, Monasteries. 228, 229
Nuns. 230
Penitent Women. 231
Fruit there. 232
Lions of Peru. 146
Lipes *Mines*. 147
Llamas, *Sheep of* Peru. 152
Loadstone. 83
Lobos *Island*. 179
Log-Line, Remarks on it. 6
Loruguay *River*. 323
Lucumo *Tree*. 136

K.

Knots in Tossels of Thread, used by the Indians instead of Writing. 73

L.

Lagunilla *Creek*. 88
Lampanguy *Gold Mines*. 114
Land unexpectedly discover'd. 39
Lengua de Vaca *Point*. 127
Licti *venomous Tree*. 79
Lictu, or Liusu *Plant*. 79
Light Sea. 7
Lima City described, its Situation. 206
Its Arms and Foundation. 208
Plan, Great Square, Fountains, River, and Trenches. 209
Bridge, Fine Walk, Chappel, Monasteries. 210
Houses cover'd with Mats, Fortifications. 217
Immense Wealth. 218
Costly Habits and Viceroy. 219
Chappel, Garrison, Fort. 221

M.

Machoran *Fish*. 27
Maguey *Plant*. 237
Le Maire's *Streight, with the Cutt*. 31
The Way not to miss it. 32
The Tide there. ibid.
Mangrove *Tree*. 27
Many Fruit. 186
Mowzanilla *Tree*. 27
Marga *Fort at* Baldivia. 45
Masquerade. 188
Maundy Thursday *how celebrated*. 125
Maurice *Port in le* Maire's *Streight*. 32
Men happier with little and Content, than those who thirst after Grandeur. 24
Mercury *how separated from Silver*. 157
Mero *Fish*. 27
Metals Vegetables. 163
How form'd. 164
Meteor not seen before. 37
Another. 39
Mexico, Commodities there. 200
Militia at Callao. 199

Mills

The INDEX.

Mills for Gold Mines.	Page 107
Mines of Gold and Copper in Chili.	82
Of Sulphur and Salt.	83
Of Gold at Tiltil.	106
To whom they belong.	109
Of Gold at Lampanguy.	114
At Copiapo.	133
Of Copper.	134
At Lipes.	145
At Guaico.	ibid.
At Potosi.	ibid.
New ones.	147
Which are richest.	160
Flooded.	161
Two strange Relations of one.	162
Exhalations of them.	166
A clayish sort of them, rich ones, those of Gold rare in Peru.	167
The Land about some cold and barren, others intemperate Places.	168
Of Salt.	ibid.
Of S. Anthony Rich.	176
Of Quicksilver.	183
Molle Tree.	119
Monkeys.	28
Moquequa Town.	176
Morro Bonifacio.	43
Morro de Copiapo.	139
Morrow Gonzales.	43
Morro quemado.	179
Marks to know it by.	180
Mules, Destruction of them.	175

N.

NEW Island.	287
Nuns, Reception of them.	124

O.

Opinion about Gold.	112
Disprov'd.	113
Another reinforc'd, and more Notions about the same.	ibid.
Another more probable.	114
Order to dismiss all French in the West-Indies.	Page 279
Ore, several sorts of it in Silver.	159
Ouaras Birds.	28

P.

PAcay Tree.	173
Palma Island.	6
Palqui Plant.	118
Paraca, Anchorage there.	181
Paradise Flower.	236
Paraguay River.	323
Paraguay Herb.	252
Parava River.	323
Pardelas Birds.	29
Panots.	28
Paste-rose Mallow.	25
Pavellon Island.	146
Paulists Portugueze.	323
Paxaro Nino Rock.	128
Payco Plant.	118
Peek of the Azores.	337
Penguins.	81
Peru, Commodities there.	200
Why it never rains there.	214
Habit us'd there.	258
Of the Men.	260
Houses and Furniture.	261
Architecture there.	262
Of the Indians there.	263
Their Habit.	270
Their Ingas, or Monarchs.	271
Number of Inhabitants.	274
Peumo Tree, good against the Dropsy.	80
Peze gallo Fish.	121
Philosophical Experiment.	212
Pico Insect.	238
Pilosella Plant.	77
Pipelienes Fowl.	80
Piraguera Fish.	27
Pisco Road.	180, 181

De-

The INDEX.

Description of the Town, Churches, Hospital, Inhabitants and Government. Page 182
   Trade there. 185
   Vineyards, Wine and Fruit. 186
   Departure thence. 192
Pito Real *Plant.* 237
Plain Remarkable. 135
Plant poisonous. 136
Plants at the Islands of Cape Verde, *and other Places.* 13, 27, 168, 172, 117, 136
Play scandalous. 187
   Another. 189
Poangue *Vale.* 98
Podaguel *River.* ibid.
Politicks. 220
Poquel, *Herb for Dying.* 78
Potosi *Town and Mines.* 145
Praya de Zumba. 293
Provisions at Coquimbo. 135
Puelches *Indians.* 70
Pulpo, *strange Creature.* 123
Puno *Town.* 176

Q.

Quebrada honda *Break.* 138
   Questions about the Earth's producing. 213
Quiareo *Fish.* 27
Quicksilver Mine. 183
Quillay *Plant.* 118
Quillotay *Vale.* 115
Quinchamali *Plant.* 77
Quiriquina *Island.* 48

R.

Reck'ning at Sea, *Remarks thereon.* 11, 16, 39
Refining of Gold. 108
Reilbon, *Herb for Dying.* 78
Remark very conceited. 146
Revolt at Chiloe. 83

Road from Valparaiso *to* Santiago. Page 98
   From Cobija *to* Potosi. 144
   From Callao *to* Lima. 202
Rosary *Festival.* 96
Rosin. 142

S

S Anthony's *Island, one of those of* Cape Verde. 12
   Fish there. ibid.
S. Katharine's *Island, on the Coast of* Brasil, *describ'd, with a Cutt of the same,* &c. 18
S. James's *Cape* 32
S. Laurence's *Island.* 194
S. Mary *Island.* 46
S. Michael *Island.* 307, 316
S. Salvador, *or* S. Saviour, *Capital of* Brasil. 296
S. Peter's *Fort, Fort* James, *Casa da Polvora,* S. Anthony's *Fort,* Nosta Senhora da Victoria. 299
   Troops, Manners. 300
   Cathedral, Jesuites *Church.* 302
   Trade to Europe, *Machines, Trade to* Guinea. 303
   Wealth, Strangers not to trade thither. 304
S. Vincent, *one of Cape* Verde *Islands, describ'd, with a Cutt of the same.* 10
S. Vincent Cape, *in* America. 32
Saiquidas *Birds.* 28
Salemera *Fish.* 27
Salt Mines. 83, 168
Santiago, *Capital of* Chili *describ'd, its Situation and Cutt.* 98
Foundation. 99
   Plan, Waters, Dyke, Trenches, and Streets. 100
   Royal Square. 101
   Houses and Churches. 102

Military

The INDIX.

Military Power, the Government, the Royal Court. Page 103
City Council, President, Church Government. 104
Inquisition. 105
Sassafras in S. Katharine's Island. 24
Savages naked, in a very cold Country. 34
Sea-Horse. p. 28. See the Cutt of it in Plate 17, at pag. 121.
Seals Fish. 81
Seasons in Peru. 233
La Serena Town descr'b'd. 130
   Plan of it. 132
   Churches there. 133
Sheep with 7 Horns. 122
Sheep of Peru. 152
   Their Burden and Food. 153
Ship cast away. 3, 95
Shoal in the Bay of La Conception. 50
   Marks to avoid it. ibid.
Shrieking Birds. 80
Sibald's Islands. 289
Silver Mines at Lipes, Guaico and Potosi. 145
   New ones. 147
Silver how taken out of the Mines and cleans'd. 155
   Essaying, heating, separating from the Mercury, casting and paying the 5th. 156, 157, 158
Silver Ore, several sorts of it. 159
   Other ways of separating it, and how form'd. 161
   Grows. 162
Simples. 24
Song Spanish. 240
Spiders Monstrous. 123
Spring, a strange one. 135
Stratagems of Indians. 115
Strawberries in Chili. 76
Stream rich. 110
Sugar, its Canes and how made. 174

Sulphur. Page 82, 142
Suspension of Arms. 169
Sweet Basil. 117
Sword Fish. 28

T.

TAlcaguana Anchoring Place. 49
Taporica Island. 294
Taupinambours. 76
Tercera Island. 308
Terra Australis Chimerical. 284
Tetas de Biobio Mountains. 47
Thoupa Plant. 118
Tierra del Fuego. 31
Tiltil Gold Mines and Village. 106
Tokens of being near Land. 276
Tombs of Indians. 177
Tongoy Bay. 127
Tortuga Point. 128
Totoral Creek. 139
Toujouca Creek in Brasil. 29
Towns in Chili. 102
Trade of the Pulches. 74
   At La Conception. 75
   Of Chili. 115
   At Arica. 151
   At Pisco. 185
   At Callao. 200
   Of the French to the South Sea. 201
Travelling bad in Chili. 110

V.

VAle of Arica. 151
Valparaiso Bay describ'd. 90
   The Cutt of the same, between 88, 89
   The Fort describ'd. 91
   Views of the same, between 92, 93
   Cannon in the Fort. 94
   The Town. 95
Variation of the Compass. 289
Venomous Creatures, none in Chili. 132

Vicercy

The INDEX.

Viceroy of Peru. Page 193, 219	
Vicunas wild Beasts, how taken. 153	
Vina de la Mar Vale. 119	
Vineyards at Pisco. 186	
Vitor Break. 148	

W.

Washing Place for Gold. 111
Washing of Silver Ore. 157
Watering after an odd Manner. 149
Water that petrifies. 184
Whiteness in the Sea. 306
Wild Beasts none in Chili. 132
Wild Fowl. Page 122
Winds, why opposite beyond the Torrid Zone. 276
Why always the same in the Torrid Zone, and why regular at Sea, and not at Land. 277
Wine at Pisco. 186
Women of Peru. 254

Z.

Zapata Mountain. 98
Zapateo, a Dance in Peru and Chili. 256

FINIS.

For EU product safety concerns, contact us at Calle de José Abascal, 56–1°, 28003 Madrid, Spain or eugpsr@cambridge.org.

www.ingramcontent.com/pod-product-compliance
Lightning Source LLC
LaVergne TN
LVHW081523060526
838200LV00044B/1980